MUSIC FROM BEHIND THE BRIDGE

MUSIC FROM BEHIND THE BRIDGE

Steelband Spirit and Politics in Trinidad and Tobago

SHANNON DUDLEY

UNIVERSITY PRESS

2008

OXFORD
UNIVERSITY PRESS

Oxford University Press, Inc., publishes works that further
Oxford University's objective of excellence
in research, scholarship, and education.

Oxford   New York
Auckland   Cape Town   Dar es Salaam   Hong Kong   Karachi
Kuala Lumpur   Madrid   Melbourne   Mexico City   Nairobi
New Delhi   Shanghai   Taipei   Toronto

With offices in
Argentina   Austria   Brazil   Chile   Czech Republic   France   Greece
Guatemala   Hungary   Italy   Japan   Poland   Portugal   Singapore
South Korea   Switzerland   Thailand   Turkey   Ukraine   Vietnam

Published by Oxford University Press, Inc.
198 Madison Avenue, New York, New York 10016

www.oup.com

Oxford is a registered trademark of Oxford University Press

Library of Congress Cataloging-in-Publication Data
Dudley, Shannon.
Music from behind the bridge : steelband spirit and politics
in Trinidad and Tobago / Shannon Dudley.
    p.   cm.
Includes bibliographical references, discography, and index.
ISBN 978-0-19-517547-9; 978-0-19-532123-4 (pbk.)
1. Steel band music—Trinidad and Tobago—History and criticism.
2. Steel bands (Music)—Trinidad and Tobago—History. 3. Popular
music—Social aspects—Trinidad and Tobago.   I. Title.
ML3486.T7D84 2007
785'.680972983—dc22   2007007035

Printed in the United States of America
on acid-free paper

To Cliff Alexis,

To Zigilee,

And to my children,
Agueda and Gabriel

ACKNOWLEDGMENTS

My deepest gratitude goes to my wife, Marisol Berríos-Miranda, from whom I have learned so much about music and about what it means to be from the Caribbean, and who is an excellent judge of what is important in scholarship and what is not. The criticism and encouragement I received in the last phase of writing this book from my mother, Anna Carol Dudley, and my brother, David, also helped complete a beautiful circle through which, after exploring far beyond my cultural "roots," I found myself firmly anchored by them again. David also did the wonderful illustrations in appendix I. I am lucky to have such a family.

The other essential contributors to this project are the panmen and pan-women of Trinidad and Tobago who welcomed me, taught me, and shared their music, knowledge, and spirit with me. They are far too many to list here, but I thank them all, collectively, from my heart. Many of them are quoted in this book, or referred to as people with whom I shared memorable experiences, and I would like the reader to remember that what I know about pan is what they have taught me. A few of them I must mention by name, beginning with Cliff Alexis, my teacher for two years (during which I thought I was going to become a tuner) and my friend ever since. Ray Holman, another friend, and colleague for two years as visiting artist at the University of Washington, helped me immeasurably. Patrick Arnold welcomed me to arrange and play with his band, Our Boys, first in San Francisco and then in Tobago; later, as Pan Trinbago president, he opened doors for my research. I am deeply grateful to Godwin Bowen, the late Clive Bradley, Harold and Kenrick Headley, Len "Boogsie" Sharpe, and Jit Samaroo, all of whom taught me their music, encouraged me, and shared their profound understanding of the steelband art form with me. I have also been honored to have the opportunity to speak at length over the years with several of the steelband movement elders, including Neville Jules, Ellie Mannette, and the late Carleton "Zigilee" Constantine, a man whose spirit left an impression on me. Finally I want to thank Michael "Mannish" Robinson and the Mafu twins, three of my first band mates in Trinidad and valued companions in many rehearsals and limes over the years since. Here in the United States I have also played music with some people whose artistry and spirit helped me understand better what I was writing about. First and foremost among these is the great C. K. Ladkekpo, who was both a musical and intellectual mentor during my graduate years at Berkeley. During the past decade in Seattle, I have also had the good fortune to play my pan regularly with Gary Gibson, Jeff Busch, Ganga Clamangou, and (once again) my dear wife, Marisol.

Other good friends helped this project in various ways. Rawle Gibbons, Mike Philips, and my sister Dominique Cyrille read my manuscript and provided wonderful feedback and encouragement. Dr. Anne Osborne, director of music programs at the University of the West Indies, was always quick to help with research questions over e-mail. Kim Johnson and Stephen Stuempfle shared transcripts of their interviews and writings in an exemplary spirit of scholarly collegiality. Alvin Daniell was my "go-to" guy in Trinidad for many kinds of help and information. And George Arnold, Laura and Jimmy Kissoon, and Ray Holman and his son Dale provided me a place to stay in Trinidad.

Trinidadian institutions that aided in my research include the University of the West Indies (especially the Festival Centre for the Arts), the National Archives, and the recording library of the National Broadcasting System. At the University of Washington, I must first thank Eiko Nagahama, whose undergraduate thesis on women in Trinidad steelbands was an important source of information for me, and who helped me with my fieldwork in 2000, and shot some of the Panorama photos in this book. Undergraduate students Brian Bensky and Hillary Funk, as well as librarians Debbie Pierce and John Gibbs, provided invaluable help with research on repertoire. And graduate students in my seminars helped me with the intellectual work of theorizing my research and putting it into a broader scholarly perspective. I am also indebted to the Simpson Center for the Humanities at the University of Washington and to the Royalty Research Fund for financial and intellectual support. My earliest and most extended research in Trinidad was made possible by a Fulbright fellowship. And of course neither this book nor my career would have been possible without my teachers at the University of California at Berkeley, especially Olly Wilson and Bonnie Wade. The contributions of other scholars to my thinking and research will, I hope, be obvious to the reader.

For help with publication I want to thank Cliff Alexis, Patrick Arnold, Dawn Batson, Gerald Charles, Norman Darway, Ron Emritt, Jocelyne Guilbault, Aurélie Helmlinger, Kim Johnson, and Liam Teague for helping me procure photographs. At Oxford University Press, I am especially grateful to Kim Robinson for taking this project on and pitching it successfully to the press, and to the other editors, designers, and staff who shepherded it through to completion, especially Norm Hirschy and Christine Dahlin.

Thank you all, and may you all share in whatever success this book has!

CONTENTS

ILLUSTRATIONS

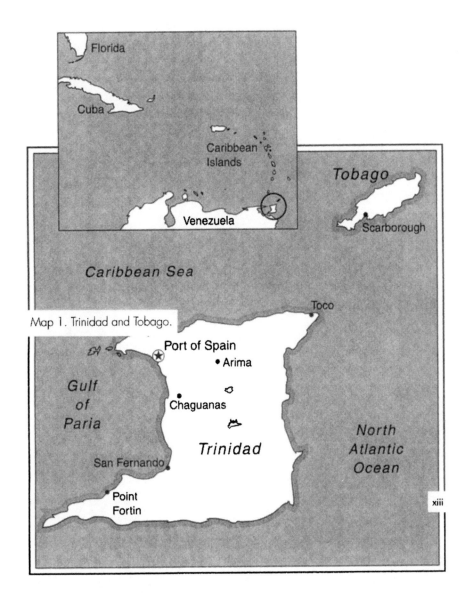

Map 1. Trinidad and Tobago.

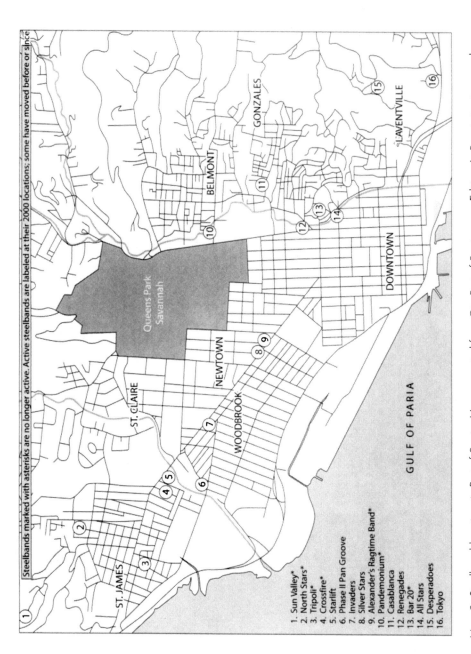

Steelbands marked with asterisks are no longer active. Active steelbands are labeled at their 2000 locations; some have moved before or since.

1. Sun Valley*
2. North Stars*
3. Tripoli*
4. Crossfire*
5. Starlift
6. Phase II Pan Groove
7. Invaders
8. Silver Stars
9. Alexander's Ragtime Band*
10. Pandemonium*
11. Casablanca
12. Renegades
13. Bar 20*
14. All Stars
15. Desperadoes
16. Tokyo

Map 2. Steelband locations in Port of Spain. Map recreated from City Port of Spain map, Edition 6. Permission to reproduce granted by Tyrone D. Leong, Director of Surveys, Lands and Surveys Division, Port of Spain, Trinidad.

MUSIC FROM BEHIND THE BRIDGE

1

Introduction

The reason why I say "false pride" is simply this:
They enjoy the song, they enjoy the music and
yet they so damned prejudice . . .

If your sister talk to a steelband man
The family want to break she han'
Put she out, lick out every teeth in she mouth. Pass
You outcast!

Mighty Sparrow, "Outcast" (1964)

Invoked in many writings and conversations over the years, these lyrics by the Mighty Sparrow affirm a central premise of the steel pan's story, exhorting Trinidadians to remember the hardships endured during the instrument's transformation from junk metal into steel orchestra, from vulgar underclass pastime into national instrument. Tellings like these accentuate the panmen's musical accomplishments by setting them against a historical backdrop of deprivation and prejudice, and chastise the false pride of those who would shun the artists even as they celebrate the art form. Forty years after he first recorded it, Sparrow's song is still invoked to hold middle-class culture lovers responsible to the lower-class communities where most of that culture has its roots.

If there is a single community that can be said to symbolize those roots, it is the one referred to by the term "behind the bridge." As a geographical place, behind the bridge is only one of several neighborhoods where the steelband has important beginnings. The title of this book should not be read as a claim about where pan began, nor does it have any relationship to the rivalry between east steelbands (from neighborhoods such as Laventille or downtown) and west steelbands (from St. James, Woodbrook, and Newtown). In the chapters on origins, tuning, and arranging, it should be evident that key contributions were made by people from all of these neighborhoods. "Behind the bridge" also connotes a condition of social and cultural strife, however, whose role in the steel pan's development is more generally agreed on. Steelband historian Felix Blake expands on this sociocultural concept:

> "Behind the bridge" is, geographically speaking, anywhere East of the Dry River which randomly provides a line of demarcation between the city of Port-of-Spain and its Eastern suburbs nestling jauntily on the hills of Laventille. . . . The other meaning of "behind the bridge" is profoundly sociological, providing clear reference to a person's socio-economic standing as poor, under-privileged and dispossessed—classic profile of the Afro-Trinidadian whose ex-slave forbears [sic] had settled in the hills of Laventille and who, three generations later, was still society's outcast. . . . Today, Laventille can boast of having produced two of the best steel bands in the land (Despers [Desperadoes] and Tokyo),[1] and despite tough economic circumstances, the residents of Laventille remain proud, headstrong, easily aroused and rebellious, sceptical of authority! (1995: 71–72)

Enumerating the African ethnic groups represented in Laventille, Blake goes on to describe the neighborhood as "a bastion of strength against the cultural incursions of the colonial authorities . . . one of the strongholds of the Orisha cult, in open defiance of the ban on drumming which was an integral part of this African religious practice" (73–74).

The association Blake draws here between pan, drumming, and African cultural resistance evokes a narrative of the steelband's origin that often begins with the nineteenth-century carnival disturbances known as the Canboulay riots. At the Port of Spain carnival of 1881, neighborhood stickfighting bands, animated by drumming and singing, joined together to defend themselves against a police attack, and the incident was used by the authorities to push for greater restrictions on carnival performances. Three years later, in 1884, the colonial legislature passed the Peace Preservation Ordinance, which among other things restricted drumming during carnival. The rest is history, as drums were replaced during carnival by an ensemble of

[1] Desperadoes is from Laventille, and Destination Tokyo is from the John John neighborhood at the foot of Laventille Hill.

bamboo stamping tubes called *tamboo bamboo,* and it was out of these bamboo ensembles that the steelband emerged around 1940. Blake's characterization of behind the bridge thus invokes a folk lineage that marks pan's very invention as an act of defiance and as a defeat for colonial authorities who sought to silence and constrain the African people in Trinidad.

This lineage is claimed not just by residents of Laventille, though. Other neighborhoods in Trinidad, such as St. James on the west side of Port of Spain, have also been socially and economically deprived and have been active sites both for the practice of the Orisha religion and the early development of the steelband. Even some of the bands that were located in or near middle-class neighborhoods, such as Invaders in Woodbrook, or Alexander's Ragtime Band in Newtown, were made up of disadvantaged youth, some of whom traveled from other neighborhoods to practice there.[2] I therefore use the term "behind the bridge" not in its geographical sense but in what Blake calls its sociological sense, as a metaphor for the sociocultural conditions in which the steelband first developed. I mean it to refer, that is, to a condition of marginalization and strife. During pan's heady journey to the status of Trinidad and Tobago's national instrument, this sociocultural condition has constituted an enduring touchstone for what Trinidadians call the "steelband movement."

In employing "behind the bridge" as a metaphor, I acknowledge the contentious debates about steelband history it evokes, as well as the contradictory social, cultural, and political meanings attached to the term. Arguments regarding the contributions of other neighborhoods, other social classes, or other ethnic groups to the development of the steelband are often framed in relation to the way behind the bridge is privileged, as both a sociocultural *and* a geographic space, in the political and intellectual discourse about pan. Politicians have traditionally supported Laventille steelbands (Desperadoes in particular) as cultural institutions that can help them garner votes in the area (Lee 1997).

And many Afro-Trinidadian intellectuals have promoted a positive image of Laventille as a cradle of Afro-Trinidadian culture, symbolically identifying themselves with that community and its heritage (Ryan 1997: vii). On the other hand, communities of the East Dry River are also associated in most people's minds with problems like crime, unemployment, and drug abuse that are typical of urban slums everywhere, and these negative connotations of behind the bridge continue to plague the steelband move-

---

[2] Norman Darway told me that many of the youth in Alexander's Ragtime Band, for example, congregated in the Big Yard on Woodford Street in Newtown, but lived farther south toward the waterfront, near Wrightson Road. Ellie Mannette's parents lived next to the Invaders yard on Tragarete Road, but his band (who originally called themselves Oval Boys) consisted of poor boys who were attracted to the Queen's Park Oval sporting grounds across the street.

ment. Thus for Trinidadians, behind the bridge may signify cultural values, social problems, politics (both in the narrow sense related to government, and in the sense that arguments about cultural origins and ownership are political),[3] or all of these things. As a metaphor that evokes both positive and negative reactions, I find "behind the bridge" a useful place to begin thinking about the fulfillments and frustrations of steelband musicians and their communities, which are the main concern of this book.

FIRST IMPRESSIONS

On my first visit to Trinidad in 1989, I spent the carnival season rehearsing with Pandemonium steelband in Belmont and participating in the annual Panorama steelband competition. I knew little then about the politics of party affiliation and government patronage, but the politics of festival competition were quickly obvious. My first lesson came even before Panorama, when my friend Michael "Mannish" Robinson invited me to play in his father's pan-around-the-neck band (a smaller side[4] patterned after early steelbands in which each player walks with a single pan strapped around the neck). I was excited at the opportunity because I had been listening to another pan-around-the-neck side every night near my house in Belmont as it practiced a simple two-chord party song called "Conga Line."[5] In contrast to the meticulous phrase-by-phrase rehearsing I was doing with Pandemonium, this band played a simple arrangement over and over again, with a rhythmic drive and percussive force that drew me out to watch. The players enjoyed themselves and smiled at each other, and people from the neighborhood came by to watch and talk, sometimes to dance a step or two. The easy enjoyment of playing and listening in this small panyard was a nice contrast to Pandemonium's more regulated rehearsals, in which we memorized complex arrangements through exhaustive drilling.

[3] Politics in its narrowest meaning generally refers to the pursuit and exercise of government power, in which Laventille figures importantly. But a broader definition in *Webster's Encyclopedic Unabridged Dictionary of the English Language* is the "use of intrigue or strategy in obtaining any position of power or control." I generally use the term "politics" in this broadest sense to mean power relations, including the accumulation of cultural status, which is an important goal of the steelband movement and a bone of contention among people from different ethnic, class, and regional groups.
[4] The term "side" is used in Trinidad to refer to a sports team and also to a steelband. I don't think it is commonly used for other musical groups, so perhaps it connotes something of the competitive nature of steelbands.
[5] Recorded that year by the Barbadian band Spice on its album *In de Congaline*.

With the pan-around-the-neck competition only two days away, though, our band still had not rehearsed. Finally, on the day before the competition about fifteen of us met with the arranger, who quickly taught us parts to Len "Boogsie" Sharpe's "Fire Down Below," a more harmonically and formally complex song than the Belmont band's "Conga Line." Our arranger also added virtuosic variations on the original melody, in much the same way (though on a smaller scale) that calypsoes are arranged for the large steelbands in Panorama. By the end of the rehearsal, I could barely keep track of the order of things, and we were all struggling too much with our parts to play with verve. The following day we had a quick review in the panyard, and before we could arrange an ending we had to load our pans into a truck and drive down to Woodford Square for the evening competition. As we assembled our band on the street and awaited our turn to play, I asked Mannish how we were going to end, but he didn't know. No one seemed to know. We arranged ourselves in front of the judges' desk anyway, counted off, and began to play. Our performance lacked anything you might call nuance, and with the exception of a few sure-handed "crackshots" who carried the night, it was also relatively spiritless. As we neared the conclusion of what we had arranged, I grew anxious about the ending we didn't have. Then, without any signal that I could see or hear, we turned away from the judges and walked off altogether, playing our last bit of music as we went. I didn't know whether the others had known that would happen, or whether they simply trusted that *something* would happen.

A few hours later, I was surprised to learn that we had scored well above the Belmont band! Apparently the judges preferred our variety and virtuosity over their cohesiveness and energy. I soon found out, in any case, that many of my companions were less concerned with how they had placed than with receiving their share of the band's appearance fee. These young men, who were used to hustling for money, "scrunting" day to day, saw steelband competitions like this as another way to make a little change. Later, I saw some of the better players doing this with as many bands as they could— a quick rehearsal or two, a brief appearance on stage, another day, another dollar. The pan-around-the-neck competition gave me a preview of some tensions—musical spirit versus formal complexity, and community-building versus financial gain—that characterize the Panorama competition as well.

An important difference when it came to Panorama, however, was that my companions in Pandemonium were decidedly *not* indifferent to winning, and their preparation was meticulous. Every night our arranger, Clive Bradley, taught new parts to a small group of section leaders and skilled players, who then took the music back to the full band to drill. After each phase of the competition—preliminaries, zone finals, semifinals, and finals— copies of the judges' evaluations and comments were delivered to the captain, posted on a bulletin board in the yard, and discussed among band members. Bradley proclaimed his disdain for the Panorama judges and his uncompromising commitment to creative music (to his "madness," as he put it). But I did not believe he could ignore the judges' opinions; the people who were paying his fee wanted too badly to impress them. Night by night, Bradley gradually pieced together a spectacular symphonic arrangement of "Somebody" (a calypso sung by Baron that year) for a hundred players. During the month and a half between New Year and carnival we rehearsed every weeknight for four or five hours.

When the day of the preliminary round arrived, we mounted our pans on their large racks with metal canopies and wheeled them out the gates. There we waited to cross the road and enter the Queen's Park Savannah, where the horse racing track in front of the grandstands was converted to a huge outdoor stage for carnival season shows. As we watched other bands (all of which had traveled farther) unload their pans from trucks and assemble them in the field or on the paved track leading to the stage, I was nervous and excited, reluctant to move far from my rack. I knew we were already behind schedule, and I didn't want the band to start without me. My band mates, though, seemed unconcerned as they relaxed and joked in the shade, some of them sipping beers or sweet drinks. Finally, as if by an unspoken signal, they put their shoulders to the racks, pushing and shouting directions to one another, and the whole band suddenly began to move. I was impressed in that moment with everyone's trust and acquiescence in the steelband's collective will—people conserved their energy, not needing to know exactly when the move was going to happen, yet mobilized instantly when it did.

We rolled our pans across the street and onto the track, where we took our place in line behind other bands waiting to perform. The track is a paved road about fifty feet wide that leads from the street almost to the stage, lined on both sides during the carnival season by a wall of stalls where vendors sell drinks and food, and filled with a crowd that swarms around the bands as they make final run-throughs of their arrangements. Some steelband aficionados stay here the whole day, preferring to hear pan in a setting where they can stand close to the band, come and go freely, and avoid buying a ticket for the stands. At the front of our band two attractive young women held long poles with a banner suspended between them, bearing the name of the band and our sponsor, Fertin, a fertilizer company. The banner also included the name of the calypso we had arranged and the calypsonian who sang it ("Somebody," by Baron); our arranger (Clive Bradley); our captain (Barry Nanton); and our tuner (Wallace Austin). Black and yellow jerseys that section leaders passed out to all the players also advertised our band and our sponsor. "Somebody" was written in big letters on the front, and the song's theme of looking for a partner in carnival was illustrated by a picture of a costumed man and woman wining (dancing) together (fig. 1.1). Some players put their jerseys on immediately, while others hung them from a belt or a pan rack, awaiting the ritually appropriate moment.

Pandemonium's pans were now arranged in approximately the configuration we planned to use on stage (fig. 1.2). In the middle was the float, a

Fig. 1.1. The author wearing his 1989 Pandemonium steelband jersey (eighteen years after playing in it).

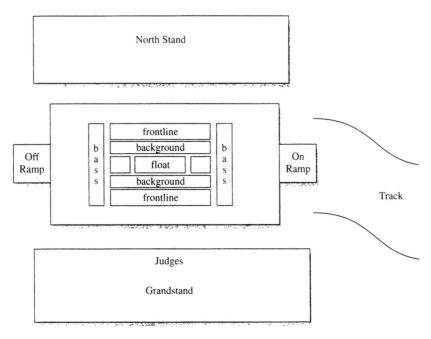

Fig. 1.2. Steelband configuration on Panorama stage. (The boxes in this diagram are a simplified and generic representation of the way frontline, background, and bass pans are distributed on the Panorama stage. They do not represent the individual wheeled racks that are the actual building blocks of the steelband's formation. For a diagram of that kind, see Thomas 1990: 303.)

raised trailer that carried the "engine room" (drum set, congas, irons, and other percussion), lined on its sides with gleaming chromed tenor pans that stood out above the roofs of the surrounding racks. The bass pans (sets of six or nine full-size oil drums each on its own wheeled rack) were positioned to the front and rear (west and east), which would become the right and left flanks of the band when we rolled onto the stage. The "frontline" pans—dozens of tenors, plus double tenors and double seconds—were positioned on the north and south sides of the band so the melody would come across clearly to the audience, the strongest players stationed on the judges' side. "Background" pans—including guitar pans and several other types that mainly strummed harmonies in steady rhythm—were closer to the middle of the band. In all we were one hundred players strong, pared down from a slightly larger rehearsing group to conform to the competition limit.

While we waited we rehearsed our ten-minute arrangement, first at a slow tempo, then at a fast tempo, and then just a bit slower, at the precise tempo we would take on stage. Moving up the track every twenty minutes or so, as one band replaced another on stage, we finally came close enough to the judging area that we had to stop playing. A cloud of dust hung in the air ahead of us where the steelbands had to cross a stretch of the dirt horse-racing track to reach the stage, and we could only faintly see and hear the band performing in front of us. The last few players now pulled their jerseys over their heads, and everyone waited behind his or her pan, resting and getting ready for the big moment. Finally, the band in front of us stopped playing, and even before the crowd's applause had died, their racks were rolling off the far side of the stage. Officials standing at the near side waved us forward.

As my rack approached the ramp, we gained speed to help us climb the slope, then trotted up onto the stage. It was like coming out of the tunnel in a football stadium, entering suddenly into a vast arena surrounded by crowds and noise. Loudspeakers on either side blared Baron's recorded version of "Somebody," and the crowds milled about, especially in the North Stand where the risers were left bare to accommodate boisterous socializing, or "liming," as Trinidadians call it. We hustled to get our racks in position, keeping an eye on the red traffic light at the far end of the stage. Section leaders shouted and waved at the pan pushers, maneuvering the band into as tight a formation as possible. As the traffic light changed from red to yellow, nonmusicians who had come on stage to push the racks (and then stayed to strut in front of the audience) were coaxed and pushed off by officials. The recorded music stopped playing, and I could hear the excited buzz of the crowd. Now everyone had sticks in hand, some fidgeting silently, others jumping, slapping hands and clapping their neighbors on the back, as they waited for the signal to start. The traffic light changed to green and someone rapped loudly on the side of a pan to get our attention. Then, at the sound of a stroke on the iron we bowed in unison. Another stroke brought us back up. Finally the players turned to their pans, and their bodies rocked with the rhythm as a single iron sounded out the starting count (see fig. 1.3).

POW! The explosive sound of a hundred people striking their pans at once almost lifted me off my feet. Even though we had practiced this countless times in the panyard, it felt different here, and it took me a moment to get a grip and settle into my playing. The more experienced players on either side of me appeared unfazed, and they applied themselves ecstatically to the introduction's luscious melody and chords, sweat beading up already on smiling faces. Dozens of heads bobbed in perfect unison, and the waist of the girl in front of me swung back and forth like a pendulum, propelled by (or propelling) the band's pulse, imperturbable in contrast with the agitated and irregular movements of her sticks in the pan. The introduction ended with a stuttering unison break, and when the rhythm resumed and we swung into the melody of the verse, the crowd's cheer penetrated my body and lightened my arms.

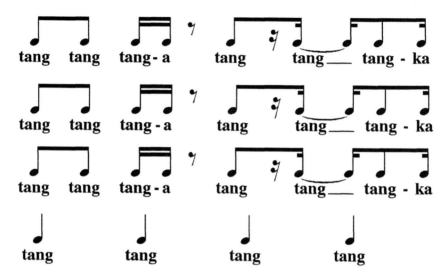

Fig. 1.3. Starting count-off for a Panorama performance.

Bradley had given a dark, intense mood to the minor mode verse, and this made the chorus ("I want somebody to love up . . .") sound even happier when it came. When we had rolled the last note of the chorus, though, my friend Dexter next to me stood bolt upright, staring at me open-mouthed and wide-eyed. As I looked at him wondering what was wrong, he dove back into his pan to play the scintillating chromatic turnaround, while I, caught flat-footed, struggled to get my place again. Crap! I kicked myself mentally for missing Dexter's cue. I had learned my notes, but here on stage I was discovering a whole new dimension of drama that was crucial to Panorama performance. After variations on the verse and chorus that featured dramatic crescendos and counterpoint between the tenors and basses, the band settled into a groove, grounded by a bass line that Bradley had made to fit the words, "Somebody to love up!" Players and audience members sang the words along with the basses, as one exciting lick after another pealed out from the tenors over the steady vamp. This was the first "jam" of the arrangement, and it felt like we had arrived at a place where we could stay as long as we wanted, floating on the cycling sound waves of the intertwining bass, strum, and percussion. Then suddenly, SMACK! went the snare drum, and the bottom of the band dropped out, while the tenors went skittering up a chromatic scale. When the basses finally returned with "LOVE UP," I heard a delighted moan above the roar of the crowd, *Oh Gaaaaawd!*

So began my first experience playing in Panorama, and though I have performed on the Savannah stage a half-dozen times since, I never again felt quite the same excitement. For many steelband musicians, however, the thrill of playing in Panorama is a perpetually renewing and invigorating experience, no matter how they may complain about the competition's inequities and distortions. They come back not just to perform, moreover, but also for the sense of community and belonging they find in the panyard. One of the moments when the bonds of community touched me most warmly was playing football in the yard after carnival. For people who live in the same neighborhoods and come together for two months of intensive music making every year, these bonds are much more intense.

Bellyaching after Panorama is also an important part of the cycle of events. After Panorama, I heard disgruntled assessments of the judging and complaints about competition generally that resonated with some of my own impressions. The complaint that Panorama music was no longer good for dancing, in particular, reminded me of the music I had experienced listening to the single pan band from Belmont, or even moments of rehearsal with Pandemonium when a slower tempo and the informal panyard environment nourished a more relaxed sense of groove and well-being. I became interested in the way Panorama performances, like the pan-around-the-neck competition, tended to privilege complexity and speed over soulfulness, staged presentation over festive participation. Though this problematic aspect of competition was the furthest thing from my mind while I played on the Panorama stage, it was impressed upon me in a particularly memorable way when we performed in another context.

The Panorama finals took place on a Saturday night, and Pandemonium planned to play on the road the following Monday morning for J'ouvert, the opening of carnival celebrations. After Pandemonium placed a disappointing sixth in the final scoring, though, few members showed up at the Sunday afternoon rehearsal. For the few of us who came, Clive Bradley taught simple verse and chorus arrangements of two calypsoes, as well as a calypso-style arrangement of the progressive rock song "A Whiter Shade of Pale" by Procol Harum. The next morning I played mud mas'[6] with my landlord's friends and his coworkers, and I was covered in dried mud from head to toe by the time I joined Pandemonium, who were already pushing their pan racks slowly up Frederick Street. They were not playing "A Whiter Shade of Pale," though, or any of the other new songs because no one could remember them well enough. Instead, they played our Panorama arrangement, which felt uncomfortably out of place here on the road. Its intricate texture,

[6] J'ouvert Monday morning, the opening of carnival, is traditionally a time when people play dirty mas', smearing themselves with mud, paint, or oil in a ritual of transgression that contrasts with the pretty mas' (large bands of elaborate coordinated costumes) that dominates the streets later in the day, and especially on Tuesday.

modulations, and drawn-out variations did not move the crowd in the same way as the short catchy phrases, cyclical form, and exciting breaks of "Conga Line"—which now blared in its original recorded version from the massive speakers of DJ trucks, along with other hit songs of the season. Some spectators stopped to listen as we passed, but few followed us, preferring to jump up behind the more danceable and gut-wrenchingly loud music of the DJ trucks. When one of these trucks passed, we had to put down our sticks and wait until we could be heard again, a distinctly more humble position than we had enjoyed just a few hours before on the Savannah stage.

What had happened to the steelband, I wondered, to make it slip from favor as music for carnival dancing? How could steelband musicians be content with learning just one tune during the carnival season, a tune that people did not even want to listen or dance to once Panorama was finished? In subsequent conversations and interviews I heard many Trinidadians echo and add to these concerns, lamenting that the spirit of pan was succumbing to the politics of carnival; that bands were too concerned with Panorama to maintain a dance repertoire; that merchants and DJ trucks played recorded music too loud for the steelbands to be heard on the streets; that favoritism skewed Panorama judging; that judges with formal music training imposed inappropriate criteria; and that the government was subsidizing the steelbands too much or too little. All of these perspectives contributed to the impression of pan as a sort of embattled, stagnant, or even declining art form—a sad epilogue, it seemed, to the glorious story of the steelband.

AN INSTRUMENT OF SPIRIT

As a scholar, I struggled to understand how this rhetoric of nostalgia and decline related to the obvious passion so many Trinidadians maintained for pan and Panorama. I was inspired in my task not only by my own experience playing, but also by the ever-blooming enthusiasm of panmen and panwomen, who sacrifice family life and carnival season diversions to be in the panyard rehearsing every night for up to two months. Even when people appeared disillusioned with politics after Panorama was over, they returned the next year with fresh enthusiasm. In various presentations and publications, therefore, I worked to reconcile the daunting political constraints confronting the steelband with this optimistic and joyful spirit—by highlighting the agency of individual musicians (Dudley 2001; 2002b), by illustrating how steelband music reflects and speaks to political issues but also transcends them in important ways (Dudley 2002a), and by exploring the dynamic balance between constraint and creativity in competition (Dudley 2003).

My understanding of pan's renewing force was helped forward by the work of Trinidadian playwright and scholar Rawle Gibbons, who has researched the extensive overlap between the Orisha religious community and the steelband community at the time of the pan's inception (Gibbons n.d.). Gibbons identifies early panmen who were also Orisha men and who brought to the steelband their drumming techniques, their song repertoire, and their understanding of music as a vehicle for the manifestation of divine power. This influence of the Orisha religion is not stressed in most accounts of the steelband (apart from occasional citations of Orisha drumming as one of several influences, as by Blake, above, or in Stuempfle 1995: 39), in part because many Trinidadians still regard Shango practitioners with disdain or even fear. Nevertheless, Gibbons's assertion that "the pan is regarded by African-Trinidadians in particular as an instrument of 'spirit' " (n.d.: 2) helps to explain the peculiar reverence and zeal that so many Trinidadians show for pan, even those who have had no direct exposure to the Orisha religion. From this perspective, the common Trinidadian saying that "pan is a jumbie"[7] (a spirit that possesses people) can be understood as more than just a colorful metaphor. It is also, on some level of awareness, an indicator of the steel pan's cultural roots and spiritual power.

The element of Gibbons's argument that is most germane to this book is the connection he draws between the Orisha faith and the steelband's spirit of resistance. Many narratives of the steelband portray the panmen's defiant persistence as an analogue to Trinidad and Tobago's struggle for independence (Stuempfle 1995: 235), and Gibbons suggests that this persistence has taken spiritual sustenance from the Orisha religion. He notes that "the [Orisha] yards were a resource for the emerging steelband which shared their spirit of defiance" (n.d.: 14). The fearless and aggressive attitude of the steelbandsmen was, in this perspective, analogous to the behavior of Orisha devotees who are possessed by, or who "manifest" the Orisha deities, with the encouragement of drumming, singing, and dancing. "Oscar Pyle witnessed 'manifestation on the street,'" writes Gibbons, "while Prince Batson asserts that Tokyo used 'mounted drums' (African drum) among their pans and these could send people into a fighting frenzy"[8] (n.d.: 13). The analogy between spirit manifestation and resistance points to the deep connection between music and politics in Trinidad. Whether in relation to slavery, colonial domination, nationalism, or class and ethnic tensions, the tendency to reflect, resist, or transcend political circumstances is fundamental to the spirit of carnival music in general and pan in particular.

[7] Or "pan is meh [my] jumbie." A jumbie is a spirit or ghost, connected with mischief and malevolence, associated in some people's minds with African spiritual practices like Orisha worship.

[8] Oscar Pyle was the leader of the Casablanca steelband and Prince Batson was a founding member of the Trinidad All Stars steelband.

An important question, however, both for Trinidadians and for students of culture generally, is whether this independent and defiant spirit can be sustained now that pan has been adopted and promoted as *national* culture. Gibbons celebrates the steel pan's role in forging "an identity for Trinidad that is not class or ethnic bound but has become almost national in acceptance," and he suggests that Trinidadians today experience the spiritual dimension of pan as a "consciousness of the divine within and around our lives" that transcends institutional religion (n.d.: 17), given that steelbands include Hindus, Muslims, Orisha people, and Christians of various denominations. On the other hand, one could argue that the participation of Trinidadians from diverse class, ethnic, and religious backgrounds has diluted the steelband's cultural base, and that the cosmopolitan values of cultural nationalists have replaced the worldview from which the steelband first sprang. Has the steelband been co-opted, therefore, or is it still a force for resistance to elitist values and control? And as the steel pan assumes a less oppositional role in Trinidadian culture, through its institutionalization in schools and in other ways, what positive spiritual force does it exert?

NATIONALISM AND MODERNIST REFORMISM

Questions about the steelband's spiritual health, and especially the erasure of its social roots, link Trinidad's unique cultural history to a broader pattern of postcolonial nationalism that has been termed "modernist reformism" (Turino 2000). Modernist reform is a process by which middle-class intellectuals seek to modernize lower-class performance traditions and to put them on display in ways that conform more closely to cosmopolitan conventions, such as stage presentation. This ideology has an especially strong appeal to Caribbean nationalists because of the newness and hybridity of their societies, a condition which they are never allowed to forget. Trinidadian writer and Nobel laureate V. S. Naipaul, for example, famously wrote that "history is built around achievement and creation, and nothing was created in the West Indies" (1962: 29). And although nationalists decry Naipaul's intolerance (some might say self-hatred), less cruel echoes of his attitude are found even in the writings and speeches of Trinidadian patriots who, in their efforts to lift their culture up, implicitly put it down.

Labor leader, writer, and pan-Africanist C. L. R. James, for example, measured Caribbean art forms by the standards of what he saw as a more mature European civilization, questioning whether there was "any medium so native to the Caribbean, so rooted in the tight association . . . between national surroundings, historical development and artistic tradition . . . from which the artist can draw that strength which makes him a supreme practitioner" (1977: 184). James had a genuine enthusiasm for the possibilities of adapting European high art disciplines like modern dance to include local forms, and in this regard he particularly commends the work of Trinidadian choreographer Beryl McBurnie (see chap. 4). But this kind of enthusiasm tends to have a transformative effect on the very traditions it promotes. As Thomas Turino writes, "Because . . . reformers consciously engage with indigenous lifeways, and because they typically operate from a middle-class, modernist position themselves, their programs often have a more direct transformational effect than colonialist positions that disparage or simply ignore indigenous arts" (2000: 107).

The sort of cultural intervention that James advocated is part of the work of building a nation-state. In theory, this means a state in which people are bound not just by common geography and government but also by a common history, language, folklore, religion, and so on. A commonly cited precedent for this strategy is the work of Johann Gottfried Herder and other eighteenth-century European "romantic nationalists" who sought to articulate national culture through the collection and promulgation of stories, songs, and dances of the common people (W. Wilson 1973). This folkloric orientation generated an idealized view of the "folk" as a people and a culture untainted by education and modernization. For example, in his 1866 book, *An Introduction to the Study of National Music*, the English scholar Carl Engel wrote,

> In civilized countries . . . we find, as might be expected, the characteristic peculiarities of the National music most strictly preserved among the less educated classes, —much as we find the peculiar manners, customs, and prejudices of a nation more strictly adhered to by the common people than by the higher classes, whose education is more in accordance with that of the educated classes of other civilized nations. (3)

While idealizing the folk in this manner, romantic nationalists have generally reserved for themselves the right to decide how folk culture is to be promoted and disseminated, recognizing that "genuine peasants or tribesmen, however proficient at folk-dancing, do not generally make good nationalists" (Gellner 1994: 58). This tension between the elite and the folk reflects not just class conflict, but the fact that no state is ever culturally homogenous. Unlike folk dancers, that is, nationalists must manage diversity strategically, constructing cultural symbols that are inclusive enough, on the one hand, to compel a broad range of people, and exclusive enough, on the other hand, to distinguish their nation from other nations. At the same time, these cultural symbols must conform to cosmopolitan conventions of national culture (e.g., an anthem, a flag, a soccer team, a national dance troupe) if the nation is to be taken seriously by the rest of the world.

This balancing act, between local distinctiveness and international respectability is described by Turino as the "twin paradoxes of nationalism":

> A basic paradox of nationalism is that nation-states are dependent on cosmopolitanism [i.e., internationally shared values and institutions], but are simultaneously threatened by it: unless nation-states maintain their unique identity, they will disappear as distinct, and thus operative, units on the international scene. . . . A second paradox of nationalism is that nation-states celebrate and are dependent on local distinctiveness, but they are simultaneously threatened by it. . . . Nationalists' need to celebrate local distinctiveness carries its own dangers since culturally distinct groups within the state's territory could potentially claim a separate national status by the orthodox logic of nationalism itself. (2000: 15–16)

In twentieth-century nationalist movements, these paradoxes are exacerbated by colonialism. Because the boundaries of most postcolonial nations were determined by struggles and treaties between European states and had little if anything to do with cultural homogeneity, the task of articulating a national culture that simultaneously accommodates and restrains the diversity of an India, a Nigeria, or a Brazil is immensely challenging. Although Trinidad's society is relatively small and relatively new, its cultural diversity is hardly less impressive. The two largest ethnic groups in Trinidad are Africans and East Indians (the latter brought as indentured laborers by the British in the mid-nineteenth century, to replace the slave labor of the former), and there are significant numbers of people who trace their ancestry to China, the Middle East, and Portugal as well. Moreover, the island has known two colonial masters, Spain and England, and was strongly influenced by the culture of French plantation owners who immigrated to the island with many patois-speaking slaves in the late eighteenth century.

In addition to this internal diversity, Trinidadians contend, as do all decolonizing people, with a fundamental tension between the need to proclaim national autonomy and the need to justify this claim to their former masters—to justify themselves, that is, in terms of those same European Enlightenment values their colonial rulers used to justify their subjugation (Chatterjee 1986). The very idea of the nation-state as the normal and desirable condition for people to live in was exported from Europe to the rest of the world during the colonial enterprise of the nineteenth and twentieth centuries. At the same time, this and other values of the "enlightened" West (including individual autonomy, the privileging of reason over emotion, social justice, and representative government) have consistently been advocated by drawing a contrast with a "backward" East, or the non-European world generally (Said 1979). Even as they affirm their autonomy, therefore, people emerging from colonial rule have had to deny their backwardness, reconciling their own distinctive cultural values and histories with the irreversible technological, economic, and political developments of Europe and the modern world. In Trinidad, the steelband movement's concern with "progress" reflects this dilemma, as pride in pan's lower-class roots and African heritage is inextricably linked with ambition to refine the instrument and master new repertoires.

The imperative of progress exists in dynamic tension, however, with the imperatives of distinction and authenticity. This tension is especially evident in the arts, which often serve as a bulwark against total Westernization, even as European models of representative government, law, and capitalist production are adopted wholesale. Postcolonial nationalists in many countries have actively challenged the superiority of European art, literature, and music, and have endowed local cultural expressions with a new value and respectability, discouraging globalization in the cultural realm even as they embrace it in the economic and political realms.[9] In Trinidad, for example, criticisms of steelbands that played "foreign" music at carnival in the 1960s illustrate this aggressively protective attitude (chap. 5).

Even in the realm of expressive culture, however, nationalists promote changes they think are necessary to fulfill new symbolic functions, a project of reform that recasts indigenous culture in relation to cosmopolitan values. Examples of such reform abound in the literature of ethnomusicology and provide useful comparisons by which to evaluate the changing role of the steelband in Trinidad. In his description of folkloric dance companies that were created in communist Bulgaria beginning in the 1950s, ethnomusicologist Tim Rice explains how the stage, in particular, disrupts traditional processes and values:

> The basic form of Bulgarian traditional dance is the circle, closed or broken. While a wonderful form for creating group solidarity and interaction, it is a poor form for stage presentation, since the audience continually views the

[9] Partha Chatterjee observes that many postcolonial people respond to the dilemma of heritage versus progress by assuming the attitude "that the superiority of the West lies in the materiality of its culture, exemplified by its science, technology and love of progress. But the East is superior in the spiritual aspect of culture" (1986: 51). One of the most compelling ways to make such spiritual values tangible, moreover, is through expressive culture—literature, art, and music. And most students of nationalism would concur with John Hutchinson's view that "the paradigmatic figure of the national community is the artist" (1987: 15). The tendency to foreground expressive culture is obviously not unique to postcolonial nationalist movements, but the contrast between "modernization" and "tradition" is felt with an even greater intensity in postcolonial societies than in Europe (Chatterjee 1986: chap. 1).

dancers' backsides. The Bulgarian choreographic solution broke the circle into lines and reconstituted them into squares, matrices, phalanxes, and other geometric shapes, continuously changing to amuse a passive audience. Individual simultaneous improvisation in the line, a hallmark of village dance, was eliminated in favor of choreographed variations performed sequentially in unison by the entire company. (1994: 178–79)

Such disregard for folk aesthetics and values goes hand in hand with disregard for the folk themselves. Zoila Mendoza demonstrates, for example, that the very effort to preserve or "rescue" folk traditions in Peru has tended to marginalize the folk themselves, whose actual practices may appear corrupted or diminished when measured against intellectual constructions of "pure" folk traditions (2000: 54–55).[10] This erasure of traditional performers may occur even in more socially elite performance genres, as Matthew Allen demonstrates in his study of South Indian *bharata natyam* (1997). Beginning in the early twentieth century, this dance form was largely wrested away from hereditary temple musicians by members of the Brahmin caste, who adapted *bharata natyam* to the concert hall, downplaying the sensuality of temple performances in favor of a "more ancient" Hindu spirituality that was congruent with European orientalist views. Each of these examples demonstrates how modernist reformers, in their zeal to promote traditional performance genres as symbols of the nation, marginalize the communities in which those performance genres originally developed, and for which they had other meanings.

Notwithstanding this well-documented ethical problem, however, modernist reform is also a creative process in which artists, regardless of their class background, strive to create performances that are aesthetically meaningful. A central concern of this book, therefore, is to understand modernist reform in musical as well as ethical terms. By this I mean paying attention to the creative thinking of musicians, to specific musical sounds and structures, and to the broader community's participation in musical performances. This is important for two basic reasons. First, though music making is conditioned by ethical and political considerations, it is also guided by an exuberant logic of its own. Second, musical experience conditions political thinking in ways that are beyond the control of politicians and intellectuals. A focus on musical thinking and musical experience thus highlights

---

[10] Many other scholars have made the same observation. Turino writes, for example, "The apparently benevolent cry for preservation is part of the same message that portrays indigenous lifeways as disappearing, and indigenous social groups and occasions as invisible or irrelevant" (2000: 154). And Kate Ramsey argues that "rhetoric of ethnographic salvage almost always implies the 'disappearance' of the folk referent—an extinction that is presented as the rationale for ethnographic representation, when in fact it often seems more like its condition" (1997: 352).

both the artistic and political agency of musicians. Moreover, to the extent that audiences participate in performances, this agency is shared by broader communities. A study of politics and performance therefore requires particular attention to the extent and nature of communal participation.

PARTICIPATORY MUSIC

A fundamental task of modernist reform is the reframing of communal performances for presentation on the stage. Performances that were once part of participatory community celebrations and rituals, in which the line between participants and observers might be quite indistinct, are reconfigured as staged spectacles presented to a relatively passive audience. This shift has occurred in various ways and degrees in twentieth-century Trinidad. Carnival song leaders, or *chantwels*, were reinvented as stage performers in "calypso tents" in the 1910s, for example (Rohlehr 1990: 11, 40; Dudley 2004: 24–25), and steelbands that once played on the road now concentrate their efforts on the staged Panorama competition. Even in these stage venues, however, the participatory ethos of street carnival persists in important ways, competing with the more European-style concert hall etiquette. Panorama musicians, for example, respond as much to the crowd's enthusiasms as the judges' criteria, and this has resulted in a style of music and performance that could not have been predicted by Panorama's organizers.

The competing aesthetics of the street and the concert hall that merge in Panorama can be characterized as participatory and presentational modes of performance, respectively (Turino 2000: 47–57). Though participatory performance takes many forms, the presentational mode of performance has become increasingly standardized through the effects of colonial rule, cultural exchange, media, and education, to the point where today it often represents a broadly cosmopolitan worldview. This worldview, embraced to some degree by the educated middle and upper classes of every country in the world, favors uniformity over individuality, variety over repetition, hierarchy over homogeneity, and planning over spontaneity. "Within middle-class ethics, the lack of control, organization, pre-planning, variety, and lack of *distinction*—between sounds as well as between artists and audiences— make indigenous participatory style objectionable" (Turino 2000: 138). Turino's characterization of presentational performance values as antagonistic to community-based traditions parallels the concerns of some Trinidadian intellectuals. Anthropologist John Stewart, for example, writes that "under the patronage and control of the middle-class Creole leadership, carnival has evolved into a grand spectator event" (1986: 309). More than a simple observation about evolution, Stewart's inference is that carnival has been *reduced* to a spectator event and, furthermore, that the middle class is responsible.

Despite the truth of this observation, it is also important to recognize how projects of modernist reform, at least in the case of the steelband, reflect the interests of more than just one social class or constituency. Steelbands participate in elite-sponsored promotions of the national culture, but they are animated by the musicians' creative impulses and are constrained by the festive crowd's expectations, both of which are sometimes antithetical to the elite agenda. Though many Trinidadians are concerned about the constraints Panorama has imposed on the steelbands, it is important to recognize that those constraints are shaped not only by elite cultural activists but by musicians and their communities (chaps. 8 and 9). Panorama's contested meanings and its unpredictability complicate the notion that modernist reform, and nationalism generally, are driven strictly by middle-class intellectuals. Popular input into constructions of the "national music" must also be taken into account, and this input is predicated on participation.

My own understanding of the participatory dynamics in musical performance has been informed especially by the scholarship on black music,[11] which has been much more concerned with the social and processual dimensions of music than is traditional music theory. In part because prejudices against black music have been so obviously linked to prejudices against black people, black music scholarship has tended to link the analysis of music to a positive moral vision of black or African culture. This vision, which stresses communal responsibility as both an incentive and a constraint for music making, is summed up in the following passage from Samuel Floyd's *Power of Black Music.*

> The coexistence of . . . apparently contradictory processes—discouragement of exceptional achievement, on the one hand, and the veneration of it, on the other—was possible because of the prevalence of what [Basil] Davidson has described as a sense of "controlled freedom" in which "an inner tension and creativeness . . . emerged in artistic triumphs that were morally inspired." . . . This controlled freedom took place within a moral order in which daily interdependence was the normal state of affairs. It was, in Davidson's words, a "robustly collective" society. Based on collective responsibility, it was a society in which exceptional individual achievement was expected to serve the community. This was its moral imperative. (1995: 33–34)[12]

[11] Though the term "black music" conflates race and culture in a way that is problematic for some (see, e.g., Hall 1998), it has nevertheless acquired currency and meaning through its frequent use, especially in the discourse of African American scholars. It is related in important ways to the political movements of black nationalism and black pride.

[12] Representations of African and African American music have of course been "colored" by their as-

Paul Berliner fleshes out the musical implications of this moral imperative in his description of Shona music, which includes not only virtuosic instrumental performance on the mbira, but also singing, hand clapping, and
dancing. Berliner details the variety of vocal styles that participants can
choose from, ranging from simple to complex, and relates these choices to
an ethic of participation: "Active participation in the music is characteristic
of the *bira* [a music and dance event centered on spirit possession], and
reflects the communal nature of the music, in which highly talented or professional musicians can express themselves without restraint within the
same context as beginners" (1978: 191).

The reconciliation of exceptional achievement with universal participation is also theorized by Olly Wilson, to whom I am indebted for many of
the musical terms and analytical distinctions I use in this book. Wilson
notes, for example, that many African and African American musical ensembles can be described as having *fixed and variable rhythmic groups* (1974,
1992; see Dudley 1996) that correspond roughly to accompanying and soloing roles. The fixed rhythmic group is formed by the interlocking of several
contrasting and repeating parts (in a textural relationship that musicologists call "polyrhythm"), as exemplified by the drums, bells, and rattles in an
Ewe ensemble; or the clave, percussion, piano, and bass of a salsa band; or
the irons, congas, and background pans of a steelband. These interlocking
parts model the interdependence of individuals in a community and provide a consistent and compelling rhythmic character (what is referred to in
colloquial terms as "groove") that guides dance, song, and improvisation.
Individuals with exceptional abilities, such as instrumental soloists, dancers,
and song leaders, give form and energy to a performance by playing variable
parts that relate to the fixed rhythmic framework. Often this occurs through
the formal device of *call and response*, in which an improvising soloist alter-
nates with a repeated chorus, exercising leadership and virtuosity while responding (literally) to the community. An African predilection for timbral
variety (particularly buzzing and rattling sounds) also encourages the dis-

---

sociation with challenges to a Eurocentric musicology. The characterization of African music as a
more communal and participatory alternative to Western music, in particular, is tinged with un-
settling suggestions of white fantasy. The very attempt to characterize "African music" or "black
music" thus raises a problem of racial essentialism. Historically, however, some degree of essentialism was required in order to articulate a coherent system of African American musical aesthetics, without which it would have been difficult to challenge the Eurocentric bias of traditional musicology. Furthermore, even though flexible and changing definitions of blackness are important,
many black people continue to feel powerfully connected to their African musical heritage. The
use of polyrhythmic texture, call-and-response forms, and heterogeneous timbre (not to mention
specific African rhythms, melodies, or instruments) in so much music of the black Atlantic is evidence that important aspects of African cultural style have survived the traumas of displacement
to manifest themselves in new contexts.

tinction of individual voices within the ensemble. At the same time this *heterogeneous sound ideal* blurs the boundary between speech and song, instruments and voice, and ultimately, perhaps, between musical and nonmusical experience. These predilections—rhythmic contrast, fixed and variable groups, cyclical call-and-response form, heterogeneous timbre—which Wilson refers to collectively as "African conceptual approaches to music making," exemplify the aesthetic of controlled freedom that Floyd cites, and explain how social relations are both reflected and constituted through music making.

By expanding the conception of music to include not just formal structures but also *processes*, black music scholarship has helped to open up a dimension of music theory that is useful for the study of all kinds of music. Turino's theoretical distinction between participatory and presentational modes of performance, for example (2000: 47–50), draws heavily on African examples and bears the clear imprint of ideas that were earlier articulated by Olly Wilson. Earlier still, Charles Keil took inspiration from LeRoi Jones's 1963 book, *Blues People*, to challenge Leonard Meyer's influential writings on music theory, pointing out the limitations of studying the "embodied meaning" of music that inheres in the syntax of written scores. Keil advocated instead a focus on the "engendered feeling" that inheres in the process of making music, shifting attention from composition to performance ([1966] 1994). Keil later applied this paradigm, which was inspired by African American jazz, to various genres of what he calls "people's music," such as the polka (1992, 1993, 1995). Finally, Christopher Small (1998) brings a helpful focus to this whole line of thought by proposing that, since most of us experience music as an activity rather than a reified object, we should refer to it by the term "musicking" rather than music. Small demonstrates the value of this distinction by analyzing European art music as performance rather than written score.

My attention to musicking focuses both on creative innovation and on the way performance facilitates and responds to participation. Because I am especially interested in the ways steelband musicians adapt Afro-Trinidadian performance traditions to new contexts, I may sometimes seem to conflate black music with participatory music as I oppose them both to Eurocentric values. It should therefore be remembered that African music is not necessarily participatory and participatory music is not necessarily African. Nonetheless, many participatory performance conventions of Trinidad carnival have been profoundly shaped by African and Afro-Trinidadian musical practices, some of which are invested with racial symbolism, but most of which are simply taken for granted. My aim is not so much to convince readers of the steel pan's Africanness (a genealogical link that should be obvious) as to articulate some of the unspoken conventions that guide steelband performance, the better to understand how performance responds to and shapes ideas about culture.

A NEW NARRATIVE OF STEELBAND HISTORY

The attention given in this book to performance and musical thinking adds a new dimension to steelband scholarship, much of which has been concerned with the collective social and political struggle of the steelband's early development. Stephen Stuempfle points out that this struggle, culminating in the steelband's dramatic rise in cultural status, has become a "master narrative" that dominates "most oral and written discussions of the movement" (1995: 3). Folklorist J. D. Elder writes, for example: "We have traced the history of 'pan' all through the vicissitudes of change, the growth and adaptation of Negro music in a new land, integrating with the music of other peoples among whom it was cast, and yet maintaining its basic character. This is a stirring story of a great cultural adventure" (1969: 20). Vicissitude, change, growth, adaptation, integration, authenticity—as well as race, class, politics, and nationalism—are placed at the heart of the steelband's story by other writers as well (e.g., Aho 1987; Blake 1995; Goddard 1991; E. Hill 1997: 43–54; Stuempfle 1995; and J. Thomas 1990). These writers have thus paid a great deal of attention to one of the elements in this book's title, "behind the bridge"; yet little has been written about "music," an omission that dismays some Trinidadians. Journalist Kim Johnson complains, for example, that the steelband "fell to the social scientists by default, as if beating pan was some quaint folk practice, an aspect of ethnicity or national identity or pluralism—anything but a serious, modern art form" (1996: 4). Though I would avoid framing the steelband as "serious art" (a term that tends to devalue such things as festivity and collective participation), this book does foreground the experience of music and the creative impulses that generate performance, introducing issues of festivity, affect, and artistic ambition into the story of the steelband.

Another purpose of this book, closely related to the foregrounding of musical thinking and experience, is to suggest interpretive frameworks for the post-independence history of the steelband, a task that has received relatively little scholarly attention. Writers tend to construct the steelband's master narrative in reference to Trinidad's pre-independence history, when the most dramatic transformations in the steelband's social and musical status occurred. Little has been written about the Panorama competition, which began in 1963 and which has come to dominate the repertoire and the energies of most steelbands. The abundant popular and journalistic discourse on contemporary steelbands is often characterized by nostalgia for the time when steelbands had a more varied entertainment role, and by dismay at the creative stagnation or commercialization of Panorama (see J. Thomas 1986). Some studies have observed and catalogued emerging new issues, such as the participation of women, steelbands in the schools, or corporate sponsorship (e.g., Stuempfle 1995; Tarradath 1991). Nonetheless, scholars and other commentators have yet to find a compelling new narrative that accounts for the extraordinary creative energy of the Panorama competition.

One explanation for this lag in scholarship might be that, since Panorama's battles tend to be fought on musical ground, their analysis and interpretation require somewhat specialized tools. The master narrative of the steelband's earlier transformation is commonly recounted in terms of political demands and pitched street battles (e.g., Goddard 1991; Stuempfle 1995: 70–91), but Panorama's arguments are much harder to analyze without resort to a language of musical form, rhythm, texture, and harmony. This musical argument has always been a crucial part of the steelband movement, but it gets obscured in portrayals of the panman's determined and sometimes violent social struggle (see Aho 1987; Blake 1995: 86–95). Novelist Earl Lovelace, for example, writing about the importance of J'ouvert (the "opening" of carnival in the dark hours of Monday morning) as a commemoration of emancipation, says:

> Steelband was the Emancipation-Jouvay movement's new force. It had arrived at the beginning of a new epoch. The colonialist movement was on its last legs. Self-government and independence were around the corner. The Jouvay characters that had maintained their expressions of rebellion and resistance for 120 years were now largely taken for granted, the social conditions out of which they had grown, ignored. The steelband provided a new focus and challenge, not only because of its music but also the violence that accompanied it. Where the violence of the Jouvay characters had become formalized into ritual, the steelband presented a violence that was naked, that could not be ignored, that recalled the first fierce Jouvay revelers coming onto the streets just after Emancipation. (1998: 55)

Most steelband musicians with whom I have talked, although they identify with the *social* struggle of the panman, remember the early days of the steelband movement as a time of exciting *musical* discoveries and innovations. They also see themselves, therefore, as "pannists"[13]—creative musicians in the same category with guitarists, violinists, or pianists. This artistic

---

[13] This term is perhaps most frequently applied to steel pan musicians who aspire to perform as soloists or in small ensembles. It has the advantage of gender neutrality, and its usage has increased with the significant participation of women in steelbands since the 1980s.

self-identification is particularly strong among Panorama arrangers, who compose complex multipart music for a hundred players, not unlike the composer of a symphony. Thus Panorama, in part because it has so exalted the status of the arranger, challenges writers to give the pannist equal billing with the panman. Such a focus on artistic self-perception not only honors the musicians' views but also sheds light on the way that individual innovations and performances reshape collective notions of style and taste. Beginning with the creation of a musical instrument from junk metal, steelband musicians have taken pan in unpredictable directions at every step of the way, and the steel pan has always been, in the final analysis, what musicians make of it.

Attention to individual agency has become part of the common wisdom of contemporary ethnomusicologists (Rice 1987). This is due in part to a social sciences trend toward conceiving culture as a system of conventions that can be grasped only through their repeated reproduction in practice and that are subject to change and variation in every reproduction (Ortner 1984). As ethnomusicologists have embraced this social science paradigm, though, they have continued to mistrust the historical musicology paradigm that credits "great men" as the agents of such musical change (Shelemay 1987: 489). Thus, while ethnomusicologists have made important contributions to the understanding of many musical systems and to the ongoing reinterpretations and transformations of these systems, they are less likely than historical musicologists or even writers on popular music to consider the idiosyncratic ways in which individual performers or composers make such reinterpretations—the personal inspiration or genius, that is, that sparks collective musical change.

Of course, musical innovation cannot be viewed uncritically as the product of great men or great women; indeed, there are good reasons to mistrust this perspective. One must guard against the tendency in some musicological discourse, for example, to separate individual style from its collective social and performative context, or to glorify the composer over the performers and audience. But there are also good reasons to lower one's guard in appropriate cases. Bruno Nettl has noted, for example, that the tendency of ethnomusicologists to overlook individual genius and innovation reinforces a qualitative distinction between European art music and non-Western or folk music, and also reinforces "the long-held assumption that music in non-Western and folk cultures is stable and unchanging until polluted by the West" (1983: 278). To this list of pitfalls I would add the tendency to view music as being overdetermined by social forces, and thus to take for granted that important musical changes in the history of a particular culture were simply waiting to happen. The case of Panorama, where a few top arrangers make many of the musical decisions (reminiscent, indeed, of a symphony orchestra's hierarchy), demands that we also consider what *else* might have happened had different individuals been involved, and how the musicians of today may help to define the terms of tomorrow's cultural debates.

In addition to crediting the agency of individual musicians, my focus on their musical thinking brings into sharper focus the socially and historically constructed constraints within which musicians operate. Panmen's enthusiasm for "the classics" of European art music, for example, points not only to their need for validation, but also their lack of opportunities for formal musical training. Young people who wanted to learn more about music, but could not afford piano or violin lessons, seized upon the steelband as an opportunity to expand their musical knowledge and tools. In the late 1950s, steelbands began to arrange these classics for festive carnival performance, a practice that became referred to as "the Bomb." Public disagreements about this practice highlighted the differences between the musical thinking of steelband musicians and the political thinking of middle-class nationalists who were oppressed by the symbolism of European art music (chap. 5). More recently, steelband arrangers have challenged Panorama's conventions of musical form, which are shaped both by audience preferences and nationalist constraints, and the *way* arrangers make this challenge shows us where the priorities of intellectuals and Panorama audiences coincide or diverge, and the specific kinds of constraints they place on music (chap. 10). Such links between musical strategies and social history demonstrate the impossibility of fully understanding one without the other.

This book's music-centered narrative therefore embraces the sociological narrative of the steelband and goes beyond it, complementing valuable scholarship that has already been done. It also underscores the artistry and dignity that is so often denied in images of the steelband that are purveyed in North American popular culture, advertising, and tourism promotion. Most important, my narrative of the steelband makes room for the whimsy and playful spirit of music making that politics can never completely deny. Though accounting for the social constraints and motivations to which musicians respond, I also seek to treat music, particularly in a festive context, as a distinctive mode of human consciousness and behavior—to keep sight not only of the relationship between politics and music, that is, but also of the differences between politicking and musicking.

2

The Steelband Movement and Music

I definitely was from a poor family. We had nothing. And the onliest thing we get was this little thing to play. And the police was against that. Boy, and they woulda had to kill we, because it was all we had.

Carleton "Zigilee" Constantine, personal conversation, 1993

A fierce commitment of people in the poor neighborhoods of Port of Spain to make the most of their one opportunity, "this little thing to play," is at the heart of what is known as the steelband movement in Trinidad and Tobago. As a political and economic force, the steelband movement took its most tangible form during the first decade of independence, under the political patronage of Eric Williams and the People's National Movement (Lee 1997: 69). But as a commitment to struggle and progress, the steelband movement is as old as the instrument and has persisted in spite of the passing of colonial rule and the declaration of pan as Trinidad and Tobago's national instrument. Rooted in an experience of marginalization and struggle, the steelband movement in the postindependence era is still driven by a concern for acceptance, both social and artistic. This is illustrated in the following comments by Exodus steelband manager Ainsworth Mohammed. (Ainsworth and his late brother, Amin, founded Exodus and also became successful bankers.)

Even when we had gotten up to the position where we are now, we did not feel we could turn our backs on it at all. We feel that we have an obligation to the steelband movement in particular to lend, if we can, credibility and stature to the movement. . . . You must understand, long before our time people have worked hard. I mean . . . our part in it is just a stage of [the steelband's] development, so to speak. And it was a lot of hard work to get it to the stage to which it has reached. . . . But we are part of that process, you know; and one gets very emotional when that thing that you have worked for for so long is being threatened in some way. Whether being threatened by people kind of making a mockery of it, or feeling it's not a genuine instrument. You get all kinds of foolishness from people from time to time, feeling it's a frivolous thing, you know.

We never viewed steelband and steelband competition as frivolous at all; to us it's a very, very serious thing. Our families know full well—don't get between that and Ainsworth or Amin, you know? You don't get between it because it's something we live for, we live for Exodus, we live for steelbands. We get involved in a lot of other steelbands' business if we are asked to. And sometimes with Pan Trinbago, wherever we could support them you know. More because we want to further the development of the steelband movement. (personal conversation, 1993)

The Mohammed brothers' sense of mission, which is shared by many others, persists in part because the social advancement of the panmen has not kept pace with the instrument's popularity. Just as important, however, the steelband movement endures as a restless search for new musical possibilities: tuners look for new techniques and sounds, arrangers strive to surpass one another, and players promote new styles and new venues for pan. In all of these endeavors, contemporary steelband musicians take inspiration from a past which they keep alive through tellings and retellings of the steelband's early history.

TELLING THE STORY

The many stories of the steel pan's origins reveal conflicting claims about who invented the instrument and when. Comparison and verification of these claims has been undertaken by a number of researchers (e.g., Goddard 1991; J. Thomas 1990). Without trying to decide who was the first to beat pan, however, one can learn much from these stories by considering how and why they are told. A case in point is the story of Winston "Spree" Simon, whose claim to have invented pan was one of the first to become widely known and celebrated. Simon was the leader and tuner of the John John steelband, later named Destination Tokyo, from the John John neighborhood at the southern foot of Laventille Hill. His claim to the invention of pan rests partly on a report published in the Port of Spain *Gazette* of

March 5, 1946. The occasion was the first carnival celebrated in Trinidad following a wartime ban that had been in force since 1941, and the place was Marine Square in downtown Port of Spain:

> His Excellency the Governor and his party showed much amusement at the John John steel band led by "drummer Springer" who treated the crowd to varied musical tunes. Among the popular tunes this band played were "Lai Fung Lee," "Ave Maria" and ended with "God Save the King."

Despite this recognition in print (of which I have cited the full text), Simon's fame in the 1940s and '50s was not so great as it is today. He was an important panman, but compared to other leaders who guided the early development of the steelband from the 1940s through the 1960s, Simon enjoyed relatively little public recognition or influence during the years when he was active as a player and tuner. After he suffered a stroke in the early 1970s, however, Lord Kitchener (Aldwyn Roberts) wrote a calypso in his honor, and he appeared on the stage of the 1975 Panorama finals to receive a government award for his contribution to the steelband. Simon died in 1976.

Trevor Belmosa, Simon's biographer, has acknowledged that there are competing claims to pan's invention, but he justifies his version of history on the grounds that every nation needs its heroes.[1] The need for national heroes certainly helps explain Trinidadians' emotional response in 1975 to Spree's imminent passing. Of course it also explains the time, energy, and ink that has been spent exploring and arguing for other origin stories. Of the many stories people tell, some construct heroes that represent the nation, whereas others construct heroes that represent particular bands and neighborhoods. These stories function as myths of a sort, not in the sense of an exaggeration or an untruth, but in the sense of an origin story by which the tellers anchor their history and their place in the world. And although they differ in their names, dates, and plot details, consistencies in the manner of their telling underscore core values that Trinidadians associate with the steel pan. In the following comparison of the different accounts of pan's origins,[2] I therefore seek not only to establish a historical chronology, but also to underscore the values of musical progress and resistance to authority that these stories affirm.

One of the best storytellers I met in Trinidad was Carleton "Zigilee" Constantine. Zigilee was perhaps the first panman to achieve national fame in Trinidad when his praises were sung by Kitchener in his 1946 calypso,

---

[1] This is my paraphrase of remarks I heard him make on the television program *Calypso Showcase* sometime in 1993.

[2] Many of these accounts are more extensively rendered and compared in Goddard 1991.

Fig. 2.1. Carleton "Zigilee" Constantine speaking at the "Coming of Age" steelband exhibit in 1993, flanked by Andrew "Pan" de la Bastide (left) and Henry "Patcheye" Pachot.

Fig. 2.2. Tamboo bamboo. These boom and foulé rhythms are recounted by both George Goddard (in J. Thomas 1990: 76) and Carleton "Zigilee" Constantine. The cutter rhythm is recounted by Constantine. The cutter is struck with a stick, and double stops indicate beats on which the cutter is simultaneously struck against the ground. Both the boom and foulé are played by striking the bamboo tube against the ground.

"The Beat of the Steelband." He had an extraordinary musical memory and an eternally youthful spirit. Born in 1926, in the East Dry River near Calvary School, Zigilee's musical apprenticeship, as he called it, was served in Hell Yard (later to become the home of Trinidad All Stars), near the intersection of Duke and Charlotte Streets. After being arrested for playing pan in 1940, he founded Bar 20 on Bath Street in the backyard of his mother, who wanted to keep him closer to home. When I met him in Trinidad in 1993 he was visiting from London, where he lived and played in an old-time steel pan trio in a hotel restaurant. He was sixty-seven years old then, two years before his death, and he still spoke with innocent enthusiasm about a time when he and other young men found themselves in the midst of a musical revolution, with infinitely exciting possibilities to be explored.

The first carnival music that Zigilee learned to play was *tamboo bamboo* (from the French *tambour*), an ensemble that featured three types of instrument: the *boom* and the *foulé*, which played fixed rhythmic patterns; and the *cutter*,[3] which played more varied and improvised rhythms[4] (see fig. 2.2). The boom was the largest piece, and it was pounded on the ground to play a steady low-pitched foundation. The medium-sized foulé was both pounded against the ground and struck with a stick. The cutter, of similar size, was cracked lengthwise to give an edge to its sound, and either played like the foulé or held horizontally. Another important instrument in the bamboo

[3] "Cutter" is a term that is ubiquitous in drumming ensembles of the Anglophone Caribbean, referring to a high-pitched drum or percussion instrument that improvises over the fixed rhythms of the other instruments.

[4] See Jeffrey Thomas (1990: 75–78) for more description of tamboo bamboo instruments and playing style.

Fig. 2.3. A tamboo bamboo side from Gasparillo, including a two-note "dudup" pan (left), performs for the old-time carnival in Port of Spain (1993).

bands of Zigilee's time was the bottle and spoon. Gin bottles were the most popular, tuned to different pitches by filling them to a certain level with water, and played so as to "braid" their different rhythms together in a polyrhythmic texture. All of this percussion provided accompaniment to the singing of *lavways*, rendered in call and response between a chantwel (song leader) and a chorus.

Early steelbands functioned in much the same manner, but with the difference that metal instruments were substituted for bamboo and bottles, a transition that Zigilee witnessed and participated in. Zigilee's account emphasizes practical advantages of metal, such as durability and volume, and also the fierce competition that stimulated musical innovation. (See appendix I for more explanations and illustrations of individual instruments.)

> Now it had two *foulé*, two pieces. . . . The cutter would be longer, but this
> one you want a crack in it; and being it have a crack in it you'll find it has a
> *kack, kack*, a different sound. . . . This one playing the cutter, sometime they
> hold it "slow palms," you know like a guy hold a gun? But he have a next
> piece of stick. So you got the whole combination. He cutting, you know,
> he's improvising, to keep in harmony with that rhythm, so he keep the thing
> flowing. Then you have the gin bottle, sort of square but tapered. All these

guys who play the gin bottle they know their water mark. So you'll find they fill up the bottle with water then throw out till they get it right [i.e., get it to sound at the pitch they want]. You have several bottles, several guys with cutters, several guys with foulé. . . . It was easy to know a boomer, because when he drinking sometimes, well sometimes he get too drunk and forget to open a leg. It was easy, when you pass through a band and you see a guy with he toe tied, don't bother ask, you know exactly what went down.

This went on for quite a while. Then come the change. Now the boom of the bamboo it have tone but not plenty carry [volume]. That's why you find in the band you have five to six boomers. Then come the biscuit drum. The biscuit drum when it come in that's the first who invade the bamboo. When you hear that—more tone, easier to carry. So it went on a little while, just about for a few weeks. So out go the boom. All the rest hold on there for a little while, till a guy come with two piece of stick, and he start to rattle on the side of the biscuit drum there. . . . So after a few days the cutter on this biscuit drum it have more volume than the old cutter, so out he went too. So this biscuit drum, that is two set of damage what he done, to the boom and to the cutter. Pan start to come in now. Then you find the guy get a next, maybe a Vaseline drum, the same principle as the biscuit drum. . . .

So eventually now, the bamboo—problem. 'Cause we was young, and it had some older guys who like the bamboo. So what we used to do, they would be doing their thing in the yard, and we would come right there with the steelband, and we would blow them off. Because more volume, and when we start to pile the pressure on they start to sit down and quit, and all kind of names they call we. But eventually they give in to the long run, and all them they leave the bamboo and steelband pick up from there. (personal conversation, 1993)

Zigilee's account is compatible with the notion of a somewhat gradual and widespread adoption of metal instruments in tamboo bamboo, but other accounts suggest a more sudden and geographically precise beginning. The Newtown Boys Bamboo Band, from the west side of Port of Spain, is said to have replaced their bamboo instruments with metal all at once and changed the band's name to Alexander's Ragtime Band as a way of drawing attention on carnival day. This event is dated as early as 1935 in one account,[5] but George Goddard (himself a leader of Alexander's Ragtime Band in the late 1940s) cites newspaper articles and other evidence that date it to 1939, the year in which the American motion picture *Alexander's Ragtime Band* was released (1991: 37). Carlton Forde remembers advocating

[5] This date was provided by Carlton Forde, but in other accounts Forde contradicts himself, stating that the switch to metal occurred in 1936 or 1937 (Goddard 1991: 30–32).

for the change on behalf of the band's younger members, who had already begun experimenting with metal instruments:

> I went to the yard and told them that we would surprise town this Carnival if we let go bamboo. They fussed and grumbled, but Freddie Maroon said he liked the pans, and we moved over our instruments to the "Big Yard" at the corner of Tragarete Road and Woodford Street. . . . Ragtime Band was taken from the picture by the same name which was showing at the Empire Theatre at the time. When Carnival came on Monday morning we lined up. I, as "Alexander," was the leader of the Band. Every member was equipped with music sheets, and of course I had my baton. (quoted in Pierre 1962)

This account underscores the interconnectedness of music and masquerade in neighborhood bands that competed to make a dramatic impression at carnival time. Like Forde's conducting baton and his new identity as Alexander, "music sheets" were clearly part of the masquerade, since it is unlikely that any of these young men would have known how to read musical notation.

Though Alexander's Ragtime Band may have been the first to exchange all of its bamboo instruments for metal, these young men were not the first ones to play upon metal containers during carnival. A number of stories place the origin of pan not in Newtown but in the neighborhood of Gonzales, in the East Dry River, and one of the Newtown band's own members, Frederick "Mando" Wilson, remembers first hearing such music played by a man from Gonzales sometime before 1935. Wilson witnessed this event in the Queen's Park Savannah, an open park three miles in circumference that provides a recreational space for many neighborhoods, both east and west, rich and poor: "A fella from Gonzales they called 'Little Drums' [came] into the Savannah with a dustbin beating and the whole of his crowd and others who were in the Savannah followed him . . . with this pan beating. . . . And it is from there pan came into being" (quoted in Goddard 1991: 30). Calypsonian Raphael de Leon, aka the Roaring Lion, argues that the steelband began even earlier, with a type of junk metal ensemble called a "Bobolee" band that was popular around 1920 (Goddard 1991: 26). For that matter, the beating of "tin pans" is even reported in nineteenth-century accounts of carnival (Cowley 1996: 179–82), and a variety of metal percussion also persists in contemporary carnival. The blue devil masquerade, for example, is today danced to a distinctive rhythm beat on rectangular kerosene containers; and vehicle brake drums are beaten not only with the steelband but in many other contexts as well. Thus the question of when and how the steelband originated hinges on the definition of "steelband."

Goddard cites newspaper accounts from around 1940 that still described the metal instruments being played at carnival in terms that were not specifically musical, referring to "empty cans" and "biscuit drums and dustbins orchestras" (1991: 37). The advent of the terms "steelband" and "steel pan," on the other hand, correspond with the transformation of these simple metal containers into instruments that were capable of playing not just rhythm but melody. Many stories of the steelband's origin identify a particular moment when this transformation was either made or set in motion. This one about the Newtown Boys Bamboo Band, for example, suggests that the first pan was employed in the wake of a minor disaster:

> On Carnival Tuesday night 1934 the New Town Tamboo Bamboo band was coming down Nelson Street. . . . [As the band turned] into Prince Street, a bottle of rum fell and broke. . . . Many of the revellers took to flight thinking there was a fight, [a frequent occurrence] in those days. Later, the players, seeing there was no danger, re-assembled and began to play once more. . . . Victor Wilson, alias "Mando" . . . took up a green paint pan from the canal and started to beat it. This pan had been serving as a stand for a fruit vendor's tray which was overturned during the excitement. Young Mando started to beat the pan with the bamboo beaters. (Sylvia Gonzalez, quoted in Goddard 1991: 21)

Other versions of this story give different dates or credit a different member of the band with first taking up the pan (Goddard 1991), but its dramatic essence is consistent: a threat of violence and a sudden clearing of the streets revealed the instrument of the future lying in the gutter. The attribution of pan's origin to a moment of radical transition is common to many stories and contrasts with Zigilee's description of a more gradual progression through stages.

It is also significant that the story above credits pan's invention to something more akin to divine intervention than human ingenuity. In contrast to Carlton Forde's account, that is, which boasts of how he and other young men innovated with materials that had been in use for some time (in tin-pan bands or bobolee bands), this depiction of a serendipitous discovery of something altogether new is a more popular way of telling the story. This story's hero does not earn his place in history so much as he is chosen, a pattern which also characterizes other stories of the steelband's origin. The following account by steelband historian Austin Simmonds, for example, which credits an entirely different neighborhood and band, focuses similarly on a moment of startling and unexpected revelation. (The date given here is much too late to support any claims of first invention, but it is probably wrong; other accounts give earlier dates for the beginning of pan in Gonzales.)

The first record of a steel container being used as a musical instrument in Trinidad is to be had from . . . "the Lime Grove" in Gonzales,[6] one of the suburbs of Port of Spain. Sometime in early [19]45 the boys were beating a little bamboo. One of the bass bamboo burst, and a resulting gap in the rhythm was filled by the accidental striking of the gas tank of an old chassis. . . . The person who by this accident started a chain of events that has far-reaching consequences is still known by the humourously quaint sobriquet, "Mussel-Rat." He was a bass-bamboo man of no mean proportions, and on realising that the note of the empty gas-tank filled the breach left by the bursting of the bamboo, he kept on striking the tank. (quoted in Goddard 1991: 20)

Even Anthony Rouff's argument in support of Spree Simon's claim, which acknowledges that metal instruments had already been in use, focuses less on Spree's ingenuity than on a moment of accidental discovery:

The point is . . . [who] first placed musical notes on the oil drum. . . . I doubt anyone will be able to arrive at the exact day or month, when the first note was put on pan, because [Spree] himself does not remember. But he could remember the year, which was early 1940. A year which could not have been easily forgotten. The war had started the year before and it was the last Carnival before the war that he had made his discovery. . . . During the last Carnival before the war . . . tone was discovered accidentally by Spree, who told me he had loaned his 'kettle pan' to Wilson Bartholomew, who was nicknamed "Thick Lip." . . . After taking back his kettle pan . . . the face of the pan was beaten in and the tone or sound he was getting from it before, was gone. He then tried to punch out the face of the pan with a stone and in so doing got a different tone and notes from the pan. And so the convex, or the "Spree" fashion, came about, leaving evidence of his achievements as the first to place notes on pan. (quoted in Goddard 1991: 23–24)

Such depictions of pan's discovery as a sudden and fortuitous event underscore the radical change of fortune that the steelband brought to the black urban underclass in Trinidad. The steel pan was the first Afro-Trinidadian instrument that was widely acknowledged by the dominant classes to be musical. Drums, tamboo bamboo, or tin-pan bands may have been fun and exciting, but they did not play "music" as this word was understood in colonial Trinidad in the 1930s. Note, for example, the distinction between music and rhythm that George Goddard implies in his characteri-

[6]Gonzales lies in the hills east of the Dry River. I don't know if the Lime Grove was a stand of lime trees or simply a place where people gathered to "lime" (meaning to socialize and pass the time).

zation of the early steelbands: "For the Carnivals of 1935 to 1940 no mention is made in the print media, as far as I was able to ascertain, about any music supplied on Carnival days other than music supplied by string bands, bamboo and spoon bands and banjoes. However . . . in 1937 both daily newspapers did mention that old pots, old pans and tin pans were used to beat out crude rhythms" (1991: 34–37). Although Goddard credits tamboo bamboo with "music,"[7] he clearly attaches significance to the fact that metal instruments in 1940 were still not capable of rendering a melody by themselves.

Even when pans were tuned with multiple pitches, in fact, they were not necessarily considered to be fully musical in this sense. This was explained to me by All Stars tuner and leader Neville Jules, who underscored the significance of All Stars' accomplishment when it became the first band to play recognized calypsoes on the road. The songs that Jules played in 1945 on his new four-note ping pong were the Roaring Lion's calypso, "You Want to Come Kill Me," and another calypso by Radio.

NJ: Now you see in '45 . . . we were the only band playing a song on the road. Because the bands were allowed to play then; because during the war they had stopped all steelbands from playing on the street, there was no carnival. So for VE, Victory over Europe, we were allowed on the street. Also for Victory over Japan. And there were a lot of bands playing on the street, but our band was the only one playing a song.

SD: The only one playing a tune on pan, is that what you mean?

NJ: Yes.

SD: Other bands, they might have some sort of . . .

NJ: They had pans, but they were not playing, in those days they didn't used to play songs; everything was rhythm.

SD: And did you have some people singing a lavway or something?

NJ: Yeah, as a matter of fact, it was only one guy playing a pan, you know. Because after I tune the pan, I give it to Fisheye to play. And while he was playing that I was playing another pan, but not playing a song, I was playing what they call a tenor kittle, in the rhythm.

SD: Without different notes?

NJ: It have notes in it. But I was just playing rhythm. Because in those days you had the tenor kittle, you had the bélé, you had different pans, you know?

SD: So what would the tenor kittle play, can you sing the pattern it would play?

NJ: Yeah, something like [sings, fig. 2.4].)

---

[7] I assume that the "musical" aspect of tamboo bamboo was the singing. Early steelbands, however, also accompanied call-and-response lavways in much the same manner as bamboo bands. It may be that singing was less prominent or feasible, though, with the louder metal instruments and thus more strongly associated with tamboo bamboo.

Fig. 2.4. Old-time tenor kittle rhythm (recounted by Neville Jules).

In an interview in 2004, Jules cautioned me that this tenor kittle was tuned rather imprecisely, and that early steelband melodies took their more precise shape from the voices of people singing along. In terms of its exact pitches, therefore, the melody in figure 2.4 may represent later tenor kittles more accurately than it does the one Jules first heard played by Zigilee around 1940, or even the ones Jules was tuning in 1945.

More important, Jules's distinction between "song" and "rhythm" hints at a criterion for melody that was of particular importance to the panmen: the steelband's new musical competence was symbolized especially by the playing of "recognized" tunes. Ping pongs that could play melodies in this sense made the steelband an independent melodic ensemble, no longer limited to an accompanying role for singers. Because the melodies that early pan beaters and singers invented spontaneously to suit their instruments did not have the same status as melodies from other established repertoires, "Mary Had a Little Lamb" was one of the favorite steelband tunes in the very early years (Rouff, cited in Goddard 1991: 23; A. Williams 1988). The image of hardened young toughs swaggering through the Port of Spain streets playing a nursery rhyme may seem incongruous, but it satisfied the panmen's desire for musical recognition. Anthony Williams describes the procedure by which he and other tuners arrived at this song before almost any other:

> In those days, you know how it developed you're just pushing notes at random. We didn't know about diatonic or chromatic scales. You just play a tune. "Mary Had a Little Lamb" calls for four notes, you had to put in four notes. When you wanted to play another tune that called for a note you didn't have, you had to make a new pan, and push that in somewhere. (quoted in J. Thomas, 1990: 132–33)

Thus "Mary Had a Little Lamb" was popular with early steelbands because it was a widely recognized melody that could be played on an instrument with four notes, or perhaps even three.

If a children's song conferred cultural recognition on the panmen, one can understand why Winston Spree Simon's performance of "God Save the King" and Schubert's "Ave Maria" before the English governor in 1946 became a powerful symbol of the steel pan's musical legitimacy. For people who could not afford pianos or even guitars, and who lived in a society that did not recognize the sounds made by bamboo, bottles, and African drums as music, the steel pan provided, for the first time, something to proudly point to as their own culture. What Spree's story commemorates, therefore, is not merely the advent of a new instrument, but in an important sense *the first* instrument for the people who played it. Pan brought them recognition and musical opportunities that had previously been denied to them. This sense of opportunity was at the root of the panmen's fierce determination to protect their instrument from the police, to play it and develop it.

This passion was fueled in part by a desire to be included in the larger society, but it also reflected, somewhat paradoxically, an enduring tradition of challenging authority through music. Such a tradition of challenge and resistance has been documented for calypso and other carnival songs dating back to the nineteenth century. Both calypso and steelband also have their roots in the martial tradition of *kalinda*, a kind of stickfighting that is done to the accompaniment of singing and drumming. Kalinda battles between neighborhood bands, which often escalated into wider scale riots or "clashes," became a feature of Trinidad carnival soon after emancipation of slaves in 1834 (fully implemented only in 1938).[8] British authorities became increasingly nervous during the ensuing decades about unruly behavior at carnival, and tension came to a head in 1881 in a pitched battle with police known as the Canboulay riot.[9] In the aftermath of this disturbance, the Peace Preservation Ordinance of 1884 effectively banned the use of skin-headed drums,[10] which, in the minds of the English, were associated not only with kalinda, but with the arousal of group spirit and rebellion generally. Tamboo bamboo then emerged as the music of choice for lower-class carnival revelers, substituting the kalinda drums. Though bamboo percussion was likely played in Trinidad prior to the 1880s,[11] its use in carnival was a resourceful response to the British colonial administration's attempts to suppress drumming and other public music making.

---

[8] In 1834, emancipation was declared in all the English colonies, but actual emancipation was delayed by a period of "apprenticeship" that obligated most slaves (except young children) to continue working for a period of four to six years. Apprenticeship was ended earlier than planned in 1838.

[9] Canboulay is a patois form of the French "cannes brulées" (burnt cane). This carnival ritual originated as a reenactment of the forced marches of slaves from one plantation to another that occurred when a sugarcane field burned and extra hands were required to harvest it before it was ruined. Perhaps because such fires were often set intentionally by the slaves as a tactic of resistance, African Trinidadians continued to reenact the torchlight procession as part of the annual commemoration of emancipation in August. At some time in the mid-nineteenth century, the practice was shifted to carnival.

[10] Cowley (1996: 100) states that the Peace Preservation Ordinance gave the governor "powers to prohibit" the beating of drums and other "noisy instruments," as well as carrying of torches, dances or processions, and assemblages of ten or more people armed with sticks or other weapons.

[11] Bamboo percussion has precedents in many African and Caribbean cultures and is still played in rural areas of Trinidad for wakes and on other occasions.

Stories of the steelband's origins often relate pan to this musical subversion of colonial authority. Sociologist and calypso composer Pete Simon writes, for example, "Many decades ago a ban was placed on the beating of drums during the carnival celebrations. . . . Then something happened. On Carnival Monday morning—*Jour Ouvert* 1937, a band from New Town swept into the city. Paying tribute to the then current film hit, the banner proudly proclaimed, *Alexander's Ragtime Band* . . . a mass of jubilant humanity reacted ecstatically to its ample rhythm and noise" (quoted in Goddard 1991: 21). Other stories cite a 1930s ban on bamboo that parallels the 1884 restrictions on drumming, portraying pan as the most recent in a series of innovative responses to deprivation. Desperadoes elder George Yeates, for example, made this claim in his explanation of the steelband's origin:

> In 1937 the Police had forbidden Bamboo Tamboo stick bands because . . .
> the rival bands were getting into fights too often . . . and a ban was passed
> by the Police. . . . The young people wondered how they could celebrate car-
> nival without rhythm, but they refused to be discouraged. . . . The young
> people had to travel some distance to fetch water from a public stand-pipe.
> They used pitch-oil tins and zinc buckets, and on their way down to the
> stand-pipes they would keep a rhythm so that the distance was not felt;
> and, there we believe the thought of Steel Bands was originated. Within a
> few years the young men worked out a primitive steel band composed of
> garbage cans and brake drums from old cars. (cited in Goddard 1991: 23)

Yeates's reference to a ban on bamboo is not supported by any evidence of legislation that I have been able to find, and his explanation differs from the accounts of some early participants who suggest that what propelled the switch from bamboo to steel was a concern with musical innovation and advantage, not police repression. Zigilee, for example, clearly delighted in the competitive advantage that the louder biscuit drum gave him over older men playing bamboo, and Carlton Forde of Newtown Boys makes much the same explanation for his switch to metal instruments: "I was not so known to the Bamboo giants so I figured that if I could get my clique together only with pans the next year . . . we would be on top" (from Pierre 1962, cited in Goddard 1991: 24). Rather than circumventing a legal ban on bamboo, in fact, the advent of the steelband actually triggered new restrictions on music making. In 1945, when the louder metal instruments came into use on a wide scale, the Legislative Council amended the Summary Offences Ordinance "forbidding the playing of noisy instruments on the streets and other public places except during such time as the Governor shall proclaim or with the permission of the Commissioner of Police" (*Trinidad Guardian*, Dec. 3, 1945, cited in Stuempfle 1990: 91).

Whether or not a legal ban on tamboo bamboo was ever enacted, however, the claim has an important rhetorical function in the telling of the steelband's story. It draws a genealogical connection between the steelband and the 1884 Peace Preservation Ordinance, casting pan as the latest in a series of ingenious circumventions of colonial law. This particular explanation for the steel pan's invention persists whether or not it is historically accurate, that is, because it underscores a legacy of defiance and resilience that storytellers hold dear.

In summary, the different stories of the steel pan's invention reveal some broad outlines of its chronology and the manner in which it proceeded. The steelband developed in the late 1930s through the substitution of metal containers and brake drums for the bamboo and bottles of the tamboo bamboo ensembles. This innovation was made by young men who sought to distinguish themselves from older bamboo players and outdo their rivals during competitive music making and display. One band that was widely remembered for this innovation was Alexander's Ragtime Band (formerly the Newtown Boys Bamboo Band), which came out on the road with all metal instruments for carnival in 1939. Though this story about the Newtown band is recorded in several versions, other accounts point to a less public beginning for the steelband in the neighborhood of Gonzales, east of the Dry River, citing dates as early as 1935. There is no clear evidence, however, that metal bands in the 1930s featured melodic pans. A number of accounts, including Anthony Rouff's story about Spree Simon, suggest that the first melodic pans were tuned around 1941, just as a wartime ban on carnival began, and developed in relative obscurity until public performances resumed at the end of the war. Neville Jules remembers, on the other hand, that All Stars was the only steelband to play songs on steel pans for VE and VJ days (Victory in Europe and Victory in Japan) at the close of World War II in 1945. In March of 1946, the performance of several popular melodies on pans was unequivocally documented in newspaper reports of Spree Simon's performance at the first postwar carnival celebration.

Although these dates, people, and places are important to tellers of the steelband's story, the *way* in which they tell their stories also reveals important concerns about musical innovation and about the political symbolism of the steelband. In stories about the origins of pan, the transition from older types of percussion bands to steelbands as they are known today is dramatized as a moment of sudden revelation. The crucial musical element of this transition is not just the development of melodic instruments, but the ability to play "recognized" tunes. Thus early panmen were keenly aware of the connection between musical repertoire and cultural status, and the expansion of repertoire figures prominently in tellings of the steelband's story. Such tellings are also shaped, however, by pride in the panmen's resistance to authority. Even more than the specific musical strategies that shaped steelband performances, steelband origin stories stress the obstacles to performing (deprivation, prejudice, and police repression) and the refusal to be constrained, often invoking nineteenth-century carnival rebellions as a precedent for the more recent struggles of the steelband movement.

MAKING NEW MUSIC IN AN OLD WAY

Although the steelband could never have prospered without the panmen's defiant attitude, its advancement ultimately depended more on musical skills and innovations than on defiance. Since this part of the story has not received the same kind of attention as the question of pan's origins, my own telling of the steelband's story must stray a little from the master narrative at this juncture to underscore the element of craft and the importance of musical thinking.

The diverse musical styles that steelband musicians took on with their new instruments made them painfully conscious of all they did not know, and when I ask panmen about music in the early days, they almost invariably recall the challenge of learning about harmony, form, and texture through performance of the classics and other repertoires. This very important aspect of the steelband's development, in which musical curiosity and status concerns are sometimes impossible to distinguish, will be explored in chapters 4 and 5. "Recognized tunes" from the European tradition, however, were by no means the only model for this new ensemble in the 1940s. Early steelband musicians also inherited a vast knowledge of musical procedures from tamboo bamboo, Orisha drumming, and other Afro-Trinidadian traditions and adapted these procedures in less self-conscious but nonetheless creative and compelling ways.

The following story about Andrew Beddoe, a famous Orisha drummer who participated in steelbands, illustrates the interconnections between many kinds of recreational and sacred music in Afro-Trinidadian communities.

The Dead End Kids Steelband's panyard [in Tacarigua village] was just
next door to Mother Gerald's Orisha Shrine, and Parlay and most of those
Shango-cum-Steelbandsmen visiting Mother Gerald's found themselves at
the panyard during the daytime. Up until then, the steelband was made up
mainly of contraptions which provided rhythm for melodies delivered by
lead singers and basic background syncopation, but Andrew Beddoe, one of
the Orisha (Shango) visitors to the panyard, changed all that. It is said that

he automatically won the hearts of members of the Dead End Kids Steelband, because he took one of their pans, made a few indentations in the convex mould and started playing out simple melodies which mesmerised the
members. Incidentally, those tunes he played, were known by the members,
since they were all of the Orisha (Shango) ilk. The tunes he played included:

a) Bab Dev Oh, Baba Dev. Yea Kwame
b) Ogun L-la-I Hoo lay-Lay
c) Ah Jah-Jah Yea. A Re-Lav.

(Kenrick Thomas, quoted in Gibbons n.d.)

Though the playing of Orisha songs on pan may not have been the norm,
the participation of Orisha men in steelbands was certainly common at the
time, and they applied principles of religious singing and drumming to
steelband music. As noted in chapter 1, Orisha practitioners sometimes recognized spirit manifestation occurring in steelband performance on the
streets. More generic observations of a transformative or energizing power
in steelband music abound as well. Zigilee explains steelband violence, in
particular, in terms of a psychological transformation that was induced by
the music, in much the same way that Orisha drummers "enchant" the spir-
its into manifesting themselves in human form.

> In those days, man, because when that music really reach you . . . You take
> two drink-a lot of surprises. Well it had some guys from decent families, at
> least what we call decent. And in the band sometimes when you hear they
> cuff somebody down you can't believe it, because of the family's back-
> ground. The music. Because you coming down the road [*sings the old time
> steelband beat with the bugles on top, and stands to dramatize*]. Somebody
> stamp on your foot here [*he jerks around and strikes the imaginary offender a
> blow*], you ain't even conscious of what you do. That music, you understand?

This capacity of music to boost courage and martial spirit represents an important connection between the Orisha religion, kalinda stickfighting, and
the steelband movement.

In addition to spiritual energy—or perhaps as a foundation for it—many
steelband musical structures and principles of ensemble playing are also related to Orisha drumming, and to Afro-Trinidadian percussion ensembles
generally, especially tamboo bamboo. Neville Jules explained to me, for example, that the standard conga drum rhythm used to accompany steelbands
today used to be played by the foulé of the tamboo bamboo ensemble (fig. 2.5).

A more general principle shared by the steelband and other African percussion ensembles is the tendency to structure music in repeating and inter-

Fig. 2.5. Steelband conga pattern (said by Neville Jules to derive from tamboo bamboo foulé pattern).

locking parts, providing a constant background or groove. This procedure, which musicologists call polyrhythm, is described by steelband musicians as "braiding" or "plaiting" the rhythm, a technique that is particularly associated with the irons. Irons are vehicle brake drums that are not tuned to specific pitches, but, like gin bottles tuned with water, they are chosen and combined in such a way that their different sounds (pitch and timbre) complement one another in a pleasing way. They are the heart of the steelband's engine room, driving the rhythm of the whole band with their piercing ring (figs. 2.6 and 2.7).

I use a box notation[12] in figure 2.6 (and elsewhere) to draw attention to the temporal relationship between interlocking musical parts and the consistent polyrhythmic textures they form. These iron patterns also illustrate a particular quality of off-beat stress (typified by the cutter's rhythm) that distinguishes the rhythmic feel of a Trinidad steelband. Pattern (a) is the most common way of braiding, in which the high and low irons alternate double strokes, while the cutter weaves between them on the off-beat. This off-beat stress contrasts with the regular pulse (indicated as 1,2,3,4) of the dancers' feet, a pulse that is also reinforced by other instruments, especially the bass or kick drum in a steelband. At times the cutter may also play varied improvisations against the fixed patterns of the high and low irons. In pattern (b), a style of braiding demonstrated to me by Eddie Odingi of Starlift steelband, the high and low irons interlock in such a way that the composite of the two fixed rhythms produces a stress on the off-beat—that is, the two irons sound together, and hence louder, on the off-beats. With either of these styles of braiding, the person playing the cutter can vary his part to give variety and life to the music.

The first pans that were tuned to different pitches functioned in this way also, as Zigilee remembers it: "The cutter in the bamboo, you know how it used to cut? Well, that pan now, it something like it cutting. You keeping the whole rhythm section under control" (personal conversation, 1993). The cutter played exciting rhythmic patterns and variations, that is, on two or

---

[12]This type of "box notation" was used as early as 1970 by ethnomusicologist James Koetting, in his publications on Ashanti drumming (e.g., Koetting 1970).

(a)

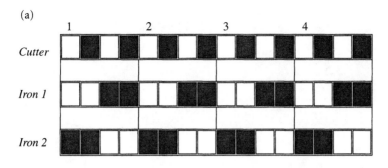

(b)

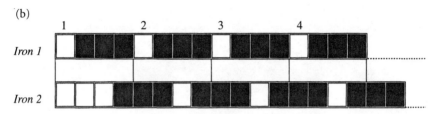

Fig. 2.6. Braiding the irons. This diagram shows two styles of braiding the irons, rendered in box notation. The "main beats" (labeled 1,2,3,4) are quarter notes that correspond to a dancer's steps, and each main beat is divided into four sixteenth notes, represented by individual boxes. Black boxes are sounded, blank boxes are silent. Boxes that are aligned vertically sound simultaneously. Irons 1 and 2 play fixed patterns that complement one another, while the cutter plays variable rhythms, or a consistent contrasting pattern like the one shown in (a).

three notes whose precise pitches were not important (fig. 2.8). This musical concept has a precedent not only in tamboo bamboo, but also in techniques of lead drumming in many African and African diaspora traditions, as well as African double bells.[13]

When panmen began experimenting further with the differentiation of pitches, however, it set off a frenzy of innovation that changed the character of the instrument and its musical role. "In those days from the time somebody do something and it was good, the word got around," recalls Neville Jules. "So from the time somebody says, 'Boy it have a little fella there in Woodbrook, sink the pan inside and put some groove. . . .' And in those days, now, everybody could tell how much notes each person have. And they say, 'Boy a man was playing a pan and it have ten notes in it.' And they say,

---

[13] The Ewe gankogui or the Brazilian agogo are well-known examples. Unlike the cutter, these instruments tend to keep a fixed rhythm or time line. However they also may be played in a leading role and used for improvisation, as in Ewe gamamla ensembles of bells alone.

Fig. 2.7. Concentration shows on the faces of iron men who anchor the rhythm for T&TEC Power Stars. The man at left plays a cutter held aloft; other irons are supported on a shelf (Nagahama 2000).

'Ellie Mannette have 13 notes in his pan,' and it keep going like that" (Jules, personal conversation, 1999). Zigilee also recalls the intensely competitive and rather haphazard process by which he and other panmen made the transition from using pan as a rhythm instrument to using it as a melody instrument, estimating that the entire process described here took place in the space of just one and a half years from 1941 to 1942:

It start off with like, this guy have a pan with two notes, you make one with three, and then a next one come with four and make your one into rubbish, and then one come with five, and you know we keep on. . . . And that definitely was the competition at that time. I can remember when I make it seven, I go and hide my pan beneath the old lady bed. Well at least I was lucky because it make about two days before it was rubbish, and then a guy come out with more. It had seven notes, so being it had seven notes, you didn't want to let anyone else see it, you just want to be the boss. Well, it make at least two days. And then it come out because it was rubbish. . . .

Now when we was looking for notes, we just looking for notes, different tones. We don't know what we looking for, just something different when you hit the pan [*sings a sequence of apparently random notes*]. And you buss on that [i.e., figure out a good pattern and jam on it]. You don't know what

Fig. 2.8. Early ping pong rhythms with two pitches (top recounted by Carleton "Zigilee" Constantine; bottom recounted by Daisy McLean).

the note was, but you just had seven. So that's why I find in the old time days, we had to create. The pans that we was making couldn't play the melodies about, you understand, that's why we had to create we own. . . . It was hard to copy from bands. Because I have a pan with eight notes, you have a pan with eight notes, but we can't play one another thing, you know [i.e., notes were not in the same key or arranged in the same pattern]. (personal conversation, 1993)

The earliest melodies and songs that Zigilee and other witnesses sang for me were not quite as haphazard as the above description implies; they tended, in fact, to emphasize triadic patterns (using the notes of a chord, that is). One model for this was the bugle, which was often played in steelbands at the time (fig. 2.9[d]). Figure 1.5 shows a bugle call that Zigilee remembers hearing played by pans. Anthony Williams also recalls that Victor "Totee" Wilson of Alexander's Ragtime Band tuned a pan to the notes of the Queen's Royal College clock tower chimes (Saldhena 1984: 10; Pierre 1962). Triads may have appealed to the pan players as a way to create an interesting melody with just three or four notes. Also, since they imply the harmonic effect of a chord,[14] triadic patterns provided interesting accompaniment to other melodies that could be sung or played on top of them. One of the first widely imitated steelband melodies, referred to by some of my informants as the "basic" or "long-time" steelband melody (fig. 2.9[a], basically the same as Jules's tenor kittle rhythm in fig. 2.4), played just such an accompa-

[14] The core structure of a chord is a triad. To put it simply, a triad is built by choosing a root note and adding the third and fifth steps of the scale above the root. Using the notes of a C major scale, for example (C-D-E-F-G-A-B), a triad of C-E-G can be built on the root of C; a triad of D-F-A can be built on the root of D; and so on.

Fig. 2.9. Early steelband melodies (recounted by Carleton "Zigilee" Constantine).

nying role. Many people I spoke with remember hearing this melody played over and over by early steelbands, a kind of repetition of brief fixed patterns that was still consistent with the tamboo bamboo's role of polyrhythmic accompaniment to singing. Zigilee recalls that when pan players improvised melodies over this pattern, people in the crowd sometimes put words to them to create lavways:

> Well you see the basic rhythm of the steelband was [*sings a melody, fig. 2.9(a)*]. You have a pan—that's the basic rhythm—now to play melody you have to fit in inside that. [*I sing the basic, and Zigilee sings on top, fig. 2.9(b)*]. You see that is the basic thing, and then eventually a next guy pass along and he say, "Give me little water please to quench me thirst." It hot. So that becomes a melody. Then you find like, um, same basic melody, but [*sings melody in fig. 2.9(c)*]. That's Alan Ladd, this gun for hire. I think you know that old flick. . . . But he was just playing that. But the spectators in the band—when you make the melody, it have some guy in the band, he like a writer then, he just come and he puts words to it and as he puts words to it the band start singing, you understand. "Alan Ladd, Alan Ladd, Alan Ladd this gun for hi-yar."

Zigilee's account suggests that, unlike the lavways sung with tamboo bamboo, melodies of early steelband songs were first conceived on the pan and then provided with words by a singer. This scenario matches Neville Jules's description of how All Stars was playing around 1945: one pan played "songs," while others accompanied the song with "rhythm" (in this case the basic tenor kittle pattern).

Broadly speaking, early steelband melodies were devised in relation to a performance context that had a long history in Trinidad carnival: dancing and singing accompanied by a percussion ensemble. When panmen turned their attention to other repertoires, they continued to be guided by many of the musical processes associated with this context, including call and response, polyrhythmic interlocking, and crowd participation. Panmen also continued to invent original songs even after they developed tunings that enabled them to play songs from other repertoires. The patterns in figure 2.9, for example, require more notes than "Mary Had a Little Lamb," and would therefore appear to have been invented and played even after the steelbands were able to play "recognized tunes."

As the range of notes available on steel pans expanded, so did the possibilities for differentiation and relationship between parts, and by the late 1940s steelband musicians were concerned not only with playing different melodies but also giving those melodies harmonic accompaniment. This could be done by adapting scores for orchestra and other ensembles, which became possible with the advent of fully chromatic instruments around 1950. But musically illiterate panmen also developed styles of orchestration that were idiomatic to the steelband. An important concept underlying this type of orchestration is the division of the steelband into "frontline" instruments and "background" instruments, which basically parallels the distinction Neville Jules made between a pan that plays the "song" and others that accompany it with "rhythm." In the 1940s and 1950s, different bands used pans with different names and note patterns (see appendix II), but most of them featured some type of ping pong, the highest pitched pan which played the melody. The ping pong and other instruments that reinforce its melody constitute the frontline. Instruments such as the *cuatro*, *bélé*, *grumbler*, or *grundig* (so-called because its powerful sound reminded someone of a German-made Grundig radio) provide harmonic and rhythmic support, and, along with the lowest-pitched *boom* or *bass*, constitute the background. Frontline and background pans are supplemented by the rhythmic support of the "engine room," which comprises non-pitched percussion instruments like the irons, scratchers, and drums that power the steelband.

During the 1950s, pans were modified and renamed—the ping pong evolved into the tenor, the background pans evolved into guitars, cellos, and other midrange pans, and the boom became the bass. Though names like "cello" and "tenor" reflect the panmen's interest in classical music, the more immediate model for steelband orchestration was calypso, in which a singer was accompanied by Venezuelan cuatro and/or guitar strumming chords in a consistent rhythmic pattern. Panmen adapted this concept of strumming to their instruments by voicing chords in just two notes (a player held one stick in each hand), or by distributing the notes of a chord between two or more pans that "strummed" them in interlocking rhythmic patterns. Figure 2.10(a) shows an example of a strumming pattern for the guitars and double seconds, playing a C chord and a G7 chord, and figure 2.10(b) is the same rhythm rendered in box notation. Note how the rhythmic composite of the second and guitar strums reinforces the iron cutter's off-beat stress notated in figure 2.6. This is an example of how Afro-Trinidadian principles of polyrhythmic ensemble guided the integration of such new musical concepts as harmony and strumming.

Steelband orchestration can also be related more specifically to the texture of the tamboo bamboo ensemble, in which cutter, foulé, and boom relate to one another in much the same way as the frontline, strumming pans, and bass of the steelband (table 2.1).

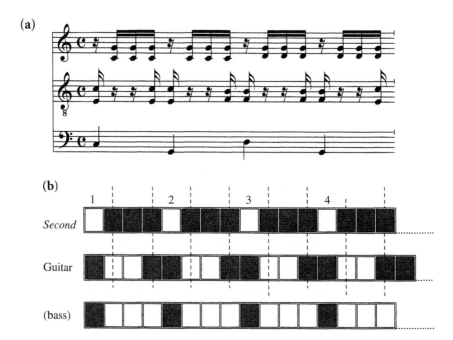

Fig. 2.10(a) and 2.10(b). Strumming patterns. This is a common pattern of interlocking strums played between seconds and guitar pans, each player taking two notes of the chord. Notice that the rhythms of these pan strums are almost identical to the braided iron rhythms in figure 2.6(b). Seconds and guitars begin each strum on an off-beat (marked by the vertical dotted line in [b]), and the two pans sound together on every other off-beat. This produces a composite rhythmic accent that resembles the off-beat pattern played by the cutting iron (fig. 2.6[a]) and contrasts with the on-beat bass. (In contemporary steelbands, it is also common for guitar pans to simply strum the off-beat cutter pattern by themselves, as in fig. 2.13.)

Table 2.1.   Three-part Textural Principle Common to Tamboo Bamboo
and Steelband

Steelband		Tamboo Bamboo
FRONTLINE	(variable rhythms and melodies)	CUTTER
STRUMMING PANS	(fixed rhythms, dense, off-beat)	FOULÉ
BASS	(fixed rhythm, less dense, more on-beat)	BOOM

The early steelbands' harmonic vocabulary was limited to some extent by the fact that the low-pitched bass pans could only be tuned with four or five pitches (lower notes required more surface area than high notes). Bass players found creative ways to support chords for which they did not have the root (see appendix I) and often played simple ostinatos like the ones in figure 2.11 with a variety of chords strummed on top of them. In contrast to the off-beat accents of the strumming pans, the bass in a steelband tends to stress the on-beat pulse of the dancers' steps.

Figures 2.12 and 2.13 show steelband arrangements from two different eras which, in spite of some differences, illustrate the persistence of the basic frontline/background approach to orchestration that took shape in the steelband's early years. Figure 2.12 is a piece called the "Syncopation" that was adapted from brass bands and widely played by steelbands in the early 1950s.[15] It consists of a series of riffs (some of which have breaks and call/response) played over a constant bass line and chord progression. This version of the syncopation is one that I reconstructed based on an interview with Zigilee, and on my own working knowledge of chord voicing and strumming techniques. It features a chromatically tuned bass (consisting of several separate barrels that stand on a stage, or are mounted in a rolling rack for the road), but Zigilee also remembers playing the syncopation with a single-pan bass (the alternate bass in fig. 2.12). A more recent example is the phrase shown in figure 2.13, which I transcribed with Ray Holman's help from Len "Boogsie" Sharpe's arrangement of his original composition, "Back Line," as played by Phase II Pan Groove (1986).[16] In this performance, the background pans sometimes interrupt their repetitive bass and strum patterns to play a break or response to the melody. This technique is com-

---

[15] For a few more variations, see Dudley 1997: 163. Also, a recorded example of brass band syncopation can be heard on the Smithsonian Folkways CD, "Calypso Awakening," (SFW CD 40453, 2000) in the first track, titled "Saturday Night Blowout."

[16] Here again I had to rely on my working knowledge of steelband arranging to sort out the parts and voicings, with help from Ray Holman.

Fig. 2.11. Bass pattern from Silver Stars' "Jean and Dinah" (Smithsonian Folkways

mon in modern steelband arranging, but such interruptions are momentary departures from what is still basically a fixed rhythmic accompaniment in the background pans (this consistency of background is less true for Panorama competition arrangements, discussed in chaps. 7, 8, and 10).

Many of the early steelband melodies are not well known beyond the shrinking cohort of Trinidadians who played and listened to steelband music in the 1940s. Nonetheless, the basic conventions of braiding, strumming, form, and texture described here, as well as some specific melodies and harmonies such as those of the syncopation, constitute a sensibility that is shared by all steelband musicians (with some variations between bands) and is remarkably conservative. Even more than the specialized musical knowledge many arrangers and players today have acquired, this unheralded common sensibility and its participatory ethic are the musical essence of a Trinidad steelband.

SUMMARY: THINKING MUSICALLY

A dynamic relationship between musical aspirations and sociopolitical resistance is embedded in the very stories of pan's origin, which foreground new musical opportunities as well as long-standing conflicts of class and race. Because of the steelband movement's imperative of "progress," accounts of the steelband's development tend to emphasize the acquisition of

Fig. 2.12. "Syncopation" (recounted by Carleton "Zigilee" Constantine).

Fig. 2.13. "Back Line" (composed by Len "Boogsie" Sharpe).

European repertoires and formal training, whereas the steelband's link to earlier Afro-Trinidadian traditions like tamboo bamboo and stickfighting is constructed more in terms of struggle and defiance. Nonetheless, an important aspect of the steelband's musical progress was the adaptation of Afro-Trinidadian repertoires and musical procedures (cyclical forms, polyrhythmic texture, call-and-response singing, improvisation, etc.) to the new instrument. Through their participation in Orisha religious drumming, tamboo bamboo, and other kinds of performance, steelband musicians internalized musical procedures such as braiding/polyrhythm, call and response, fixed and variable rhythmic groups, and improvisational strategies that were as sophisticated and subtle as the techniques of European art music, if less formalized and composition-centered.[17] This unself-conscious musical competence, rarely articulated or celebrated in the daily discourse of steelband musicians, continues to exert a dominant influence on steelband performance.

Some readers of this book may find it odd that I would feel the need to prove this connection to African music, since the steelband's association with Afro-Caribbean culture is hardly in doubt. I am not so much concerned to prove these connections, though, as to specify them as a foundation for arguments that I make later about how African musical principles

[17] For those who wonder whether this might be an exaggeration, whether banging on an iron in a steelband can really be considered as "sophisticated" as playing a violin in an orchestra, consider my experiences teaching steelband music to conservatory-trained music students. I use systematic pedagogical techniques—including simultaneously dancing, clapping a contrasting rhythm, and singing a melody, for example—and drill my American students intensively over the course of a year in hopes that they can make a plausible showing at their end-of-year concert. I keep the

have been either diminished or reclaimed in steelband practice. Also, teasing out the Afro-Trinidadian elements of steelband music is important for the way it gives names to aspects of the steelband musician's craft that are often ignored or undervalued in the vocabulary of European musical discourse. That said, one must be careful not to let such generalizations about "African" or "Afro-Trinidadian" music obscure the complexities of the steelband musicians' musical heritage. Steelband musicians regularly transgressed the boundaries that their larger society erected between musical repertoires, appropriating and adapting *both* African and European musical traditions in imaginative ways. These innovations cannot be fully understood as acts of resistance or accommodation to colonial prejudices (a point that will be further elaborated in chap. 5), because power and status do not inhere in musical structures. Every innovation begins with an individual who makes musical choices for reasons that may be hard to predict. In the next chapter, therefore, I will single out a few individuals who had significant influence on the development of the steelband, underscoring the spirit of exploration and creative rivalry that compelled them.

arrangements melodically and harmonically simple, so that they can keep their focus on rhythmic ensemble rather than technique or memorization. Many of these students make wonderful progress, and they benefit from the skills that they learn in steelband, but few of them are able to achieve the basic rhythmic sensibilities that are taken for granted in a Trinidad steelband, let alone the understanding that would be required to compose or improvise effectively. Whether "sophistication" is the right term or not, the point is that Trinidadian steelband musicians must master significant musical skills to play in the band at all, and they must have highly complex skills to take positions of musical leadership. These skills are not articulated and objectified in the manner of European art music techniques, but they constitute a complex and coherent musical system that is passed from one generation to the next in Trinidad.

3

An Unlikely Instrument

When I was in Casablanca I had a pan . . . but what another man coulda play on his own, I just couldn't play on mine. When I get to find the note he had, it was a G#, and we used to call these notes "in-between." Till a man was even trying between E and F, and B and C. Man was still trying to get something because he just feel it have something between everything!

Carleton "Zigilee" Constantine, personal conversation, 1993

On my first visit to Trinidad in 1989, my landlord, Jimmy Kissoon, took me to a Friday afternoon lime in a bar where he and his friends engaged in a sort of carnival trivia contest. Many of the questions posed were about carnival competition statistics—"Who was the first calypsonian to win both the road march and the calypso monarch?" (Sparrow, with "Jean and Dinah" in 1956); "Which steelband defied the Panorama boycott of 1979?" (Desperadoes). But some were also about important steelband innovations—"Who was the first to tune notes on a bass pan?" (Neville Jules of All Stars); "Who was the first to put pans in wheeled racks to play on the road?" (Anthony Williams of Pan Am North Stars). In this conversation and in many others I heard, the story of steelband innovation and progress was constructed in terms of the instrument rather than the music. Disputes about Spree Simon's contribution, for example, focus not on the question of whether he played "Ave Maria" or on how well he played it, but rather on whether he was the first to tune a pan that *could* play it.

Though their achievements have acquired new fame and importance through such historical retrospectives, tuners were always important people in their own communities. One measure of the tuner's importance around 1950 is the number of tuners that were appointed to the Trinidad All Steel Percussion Orchestra (TASPO), a group composed of stars from many different bands who were brought together to perform at the Festival of Britain in 1951. Of the eleven TASPO members,[1] only four were officially designated as tuners—Ellie Mannette, Philmore "Boots" Davidson, Sterling Betancourt, and Andrew de la Bastide (Blake: 160)—though Anthony Williams recalled in an interview with Stephen Stuempfle in 1988 that all of the players were tuners with the exception of Patsy Haynes. A great deal of the competition between early steelbands was decided by superior instruments, and since most bands jealously guarded their tuning techniques, any band of distinction had to have its own tuner. Like Spree Simon, many tuners were also leaders of their steelbands, with an important say in musical decisions and band discipline.

The improvement of tuning was the early steelband musicians' most passionate quest. Superiority was initially measured in numbers of notes, as Zigilee recounts above, but soon the innovation of new patterns and the refinement of timbre became important. Indeed, after an initial phase of expansion in the range and note patterns of the various steelbands, it was advances in timbre more than anything else that brought recognition for the steel pan as a legitimate musical instrument. The steel pan's contemporary sound is testament to the genius of curious young men who took pieces of junk metal and so transformed them that they could be mistaken for an organ when played together. This transformation was not the work of one person, of course, but of tuners from many different neighborhoods and regions who made important contributions along the way. Sonny Roach from St. James, for example, is credited for the prowess of Sun Valley and other West bands whose tuners learned from his style, including Anthony Williams of North Stars, Emon Thorpe of Tripoli and Crossfire, and even Ellie Mannette of Invaders. Celebrated tuners/leaders from the downtown and Laventille areas included Spree Simon of Tokyo and Neville Jules of Trinidad All Stars; and in a younger generation, Rudolph Charles of Desperadoes, Bertie Marshall of Hilanders, and Herman Guppy Brown. Partisans of different bands and neighborhoods argue about who should be credited for

---

[1] Jeffrey Thomas reports that there were as many as thirteen panmen originally chosen, but eleven sailed for England, and one of these, Sonny Roach, did not complete the trip because of illness (1990: 165). According to Thomas, the TASPO members included Andrew de la Bastide (Hill 60), Sterling Betancourt (Crossfire), Belgrave Bonaparte (Southern Symphony), Philmore "Boots" Davidson (Syncopators), Orman "Patsy" Haynes (Casablanca), Ellie Mannette (Invaders), Sonny Roach (Sun Valley), Winston "Spree" Simon (Tokyo), Dudley Smith (Rising Sun), Theo Stephens (Free French), Anthony Williams (North Stars), and Lieutenant Joseph Griffith. Blake also lists Granville Sealey (Tripoli) (160).

particular innovations. Marshall, for example, is often credited with having invented the technique of tuning the octave, fifth, and other overtones of a note independently, a technique known as "harmonic tuning" that gives modern steel pans their characteristic brightness. Mannette credits Marshall for this innovation but remembers the pans of Katzenjammers steelband, tuned by Percy "Lizard" Thomas, as being even brighter in sound (personal conversation, 2005). And Lloyd Gay, a prominent tuner from Gasparillo in the South of Trinidad, told me that the first person to do harmonic tuning was Allan Gervais, from in the south of Trinidad, who tuned for Cavaliers and Hatters in San Fernando, as well as other bands. Gay complains of the "town" bias in the construction of steelband history, whereby bands and individuals in Port of Spain have received more attention and credit than those in other parts of the island. Indeed, the number of prominent tuners who hail from the South is striking, including not only Gervais and Gay, but also Leo Coker, Bertram Kellman, and Lincoln Noel. Most of these tuners have made their reputations, however, through their work for town bands— Coker, for example, made the famously bright-sounding instruments used by Trinidad All Stars, Exodus, and Tokyo; Kellman tunes for Renegades; and Gay, Noel, and Kellman all tune for Phase II, as well as other bands, the majority of which no longer have exclusive relationships with a single tuner. In steelbands, as in calypso, reputations are made in Port of Spain, so the canon of great bands and great tuners often overlooks contributions from outlying areas.

I have chosen here to illustrate major tuning innovations through detailed profiles of four tuners: Neville Jules of the Trinidad All Stars, Ellie Mannette of Invaders, Anthony Williams of the North Stars, and Rudolph Charles of Desperadoes. These men exemplify the status of tuners in the early years of the steelband not only because they were major innovators, but also because they were musical and administrative leaders of legendary steelbands. Many other tuners, of course, some of whom are mentioned here and some not, helped bring about pan's spectacular transformation from makeshift percussion to a rich-toned and versatile melodic instrument. As in the case of the steelband's origin stories, therefore, it is sometimes difficult to determine which tuner was the first to do what, but the following biographies can serve at least to illustrate some of the most important steps in the development of steel pan tuning.

NEVILLE JULES

Born in Laventille in 1927, Neville Jules moved with his family to downtown in the 1930s and lived close by Hell Yard, an open lot on the west bank of the

Fig. 3.1. Neville Jules (left) with arranger Leon "Smooth" Edwards in All Stars' panyard in 2000.

Dry River just off Duke Street that is occupied today by the Trinidad All Stars. Hell Yard was a popular site for social gathering and recreation, including tamboo bamboo. After Alexander's Ragtime Band came out with metal instruments in 1939, the Hell Yard men followed suit and formed a steelband named Second Fiddle that accompanied the Bad Behavior Sailors at carnival in 1940. Jules frequented Hell Yard with other young men who enjoyed the music and sometimes got a chance to play. Sometime after the 1941 wartime ban on carnival, the older men in Hell Yard stopped playing, and the youth formed a steelband of their own called Cross of Lorraine, led by Rudolph "Fisheye" Ollivierre. Jules was the tuner. When Jules's mother moved to St. Joseph, he stayed in Port of Spain to be with this steelband. "I stay in town and I would sleep by Fisheye and them, I would sleep in Royal Theatre, I do whatever I want to do. . . . I gambling for a dollar, I hustling" (personal conversation with Kim Johnson, 1996).

Jules was first spurred to tune pan during the war when he saw Zigilee playing a tenor kittle with Bar 20 steelband and coveted his instrument. His determination to best Zigilee reflects the intense competition that fueled early tuning innovations:

> From the time I hear Zigilee playing that pan, I remember it was a Christmas-
> time, he was playing that pan, he was going over Gonzales. Zigilee beating a
> kittle pan. I follow him, I listen to him. Any time he stop, like the band fall.

And when he start back the band pick up again. So I ask him for a beat.
I could remember good: he just shake he head and he keep beating. Next day
I look for a pan and I tune one, and any time I see Zigilee it's war in he tail,
war! Sometimes the two bands meet and the two bands gone and me and he
in the road there. (personal conversation with Kim Johnson, 2000)

As both a tuner and a skilled player, Jules was a key member of Cross of Lorraine, and some young men soon approached him about forming a new
band under his leadership, hoping to recruit outstanding players from other
steelbands, including Zigilee. Although they never persuaded Zigilee to join
their new band, they did form the band, and they kept its ambitious name,
the Trinidad All Stars. All Stars developed an enduring reputation for discipline, thanks largely to Jules, who took pains to see that they did not get into
fights. His success in this regard was remarkable, given the violent culture of
the steelbands at the time and the fine line that separated musical rivalry
(including the "war" that Jules himself remembers waging with Zigilee)
from all-out brawls.

> I was the guy who decide what to play, what to do, and when I took over
> I continued that, along with a no-nonsense type of thing. If we say you got
> to be at rehearsal a certain time, you got to be there or else you're gonna be
> fined. We fine you X amount of dollars or whatever it is and at the end of the
> Carnival season, whatever money you work for, those fines will be deducted.
> Or sometimes according to whatever you do you're suspended. Like, for in-
> stance, we would tell our members do not go by another panyard to listen to
> music, the pan music, 'cause they figure you come to spy to hear what they
> playing and this could end up in a fight, 'cause lots of bands used to fight for
> less thing than that Carnival Day. Somebody just rub somebody the wrong
> way: big fight. So we try to get away from that. (interview with Johnson,
> May 1996)

All Stars' discipline not only kept them out of fights, it also made them one
of the most musically accomplished steelbands in Trinidad. The band became particularly well known for its performances of the classics, and was a
perennial powerhouse and frequent winner of the biennial Music Festival
from the 1950s onward. In the early days, Jules listened to classical records
and arranged the music for All Stars, even though he could not read music.
The even greater challenge at first, though, was to tune pans with all the
notes this music required. In his drive to give Trinidad All Stars a more complete and impressive sound, Jules created many of the early pans that became models for the expanded orchestration of the modern steelband. (See
appendix I for an overview of instrument types.) Jules remembers that

Cross of Lorraine was the only steelband playing "music" on the road for VJ day, and is quite certain that he tuned a melodic ping pong before Spree Simon. Even leaving aside the thorny question of who invented the first pan, however, Jules is credited with several important tuning breakthroughs, particularly in the invention of background pans.

Immediately following the war, many other tuners were still focused on the soloing or "cutting" function of the ping pong, increasing its range of notes so that it could play more intricate melodies over the steady rhythms of the cuff boom, dudup, and tenor kittle.[2] Jules, however, became interested in a more integrated steelband orchestration that would include harmonic and melodic roles for the lower pitched pans. In 1947 Jules made a biscuit drum with four large, low-pitched notes tuned to the first, second, fourth, and fifth steps of the scale (do, re, fa, and sol).[3] This pan, which was called the "tune boom" to distinguish it from the non-pitched cuff boom, gave a new harmonic definition to the low end of the steelband. Its four notes represented root and fifth of the most common chords (tonic, dominant, and subdominant) and were played in a limited number of rhythmic/melodic patterns. All Stars' tune booms created such a sensation that other steelbands came out the following year with large sections of tune booms (Jules remembers Katzenjammers in particular).

Jules next improved on the tune boom by using a caustic soda drum, which had a longer skirt than the biscuit drum, giving its low notes a more powerful resonance. This was the first "bass pan," which Jules tuned with either three or four notes. The caustic soda drum was brittle and didn't last long, but it was lightweight and easy to carry and play. Jules also invented the "cuatro" pan, whose sound he conceived to imitate the strummed chords of a stringed cuatro. Although he does not take credit for inventing the first strumming pan (he remembers steelbands using a "second pan" before his cuatro), the cuatro's distinctive low-pitched strumming became part of the steelband sound, and the cuatro was the model for later strumming pans, such as the "guitar" pan.

One of the very earliest pioneers of tuning, Jules is most well remembered today for his innovations in background pans. And his legacy as a disciplined and principled bandleader is perpetuated to this day by the Trinidad All Stars (with whom he continues to be affiliated, although he now lives in Brooklyn). His fame reached well beyond town, and he often sold

[2] A dudup is a two-note pan with a deep tone and an essentially rhythmic function. See appendix I for descriptions and pictures of the cuff boom and tenor kittle.

[3] Tuners did not tune to concert pitch at this time, so they did not choose a particular key or even know how to describe the notes in these terms. Pans were tuned to match the other pans in the band, but not to any absolute pitch standard such as a piano.

pans to other bands, especially before he took a full-time job as a dock worker in the 1950s. He even remembers tuning pans for some white boys in Diego Martin, which might connect him to one of the very earliest middle-class "college boy" bands (see chap. 4). His preeminence as a tuner was eclipsed, however, by a rival from the west side of town, Ellie Mannette.

ELLIE MANNETTE

Elliot "Ellie" Mannette was born in the village of San Souci in northeastern Trinidad in 1927, and moved to Port of Spain in 1931, living first in St. James and later in Woodbrook. He first became intrigued with pan by watching Alexander's Ragtime Band, and although he was too young to participate, he began playing on his own and experimenting with different metal containers in the late 1930s. The group of young boys who gathered to play with him eventually dubbed themselves "Oval Boys" because they practiced across from the Oval sports stadium where they all chased balls for tennis and cricket matches. Oval Boys later became the Invaders steelband.

Fig. 3.2. Ellie Mannette with U.S. first lady Hillary Clinton in 1999, at a ceremony in which he was honored with a National Heritage Fellowship from the National Endowment for the Humanities.

With the advent of melodic pans, Mannette began tuning, and dividing his time between school and panyard. Although his family was poor, he earned a scholarship to attend the Bishop Anstey High School in the early 1940s. Around 1945, though, he had a falling out with his teachers and stopped attending school. Afraid to tell his parents that he had forfeited such a coveted opportunity, he went to work in the afternoons in the machine shop of a friend, Mr. Robinson, to learn a trade and make a different career for himself. Mannette had worked as a machinist for a year[4] before his parents found out he'd left school, and Mr. Robinson consequently threw him out of the metal shop as well, at which point the only thing left for him was pan. "I have no trade and I have no school, my parents really upset," he recalls, "So I decide, well, I made a boo-boo here: I flunk out of school and I get messed up in the machine shop, well I'm going hogwild with the drums now. So I really started going behind the drums" (personal conversation with Kim Johnson, July 1996).

One of the tuning innovations for which Mannette is generally credited is sinking the face of the drum to make it concave (in contrast to the first pans which were hammered from below into a convex shape), which he claims to have done as early as 1941. Mannette also remembers being the first to put rubber tips on the pan sticks, although Neville Jules disputes this claim, asserting that Prince Batson of All Stars first came up with the idea. Mannette's account suggests that this innovation could possibly have occurred in two different bands simultaneously, since the panmen had sought ways to soften their sticks even before rubber:

> We used to cut black sage stem and pound the end of it and make it a little softer. Or we used to get coconut limb, the coconut branch, trim it down. Take it and cut a slice off it and use that but it was too soft. And we used to use everything possible—pound on the broom handle to try to make it softer because it was too much of a harshness on the top of the drum. I don't know how I came up with the idea, I just had an old bicycle tube sitting around, and I cut it and I wrapped the stick in 1944.

The use of rubber was an innovation in timbre, softening the percussive "harshness" in the sound of pan-beating. And once rubber sticks had been introduced, the challenge was to improve the timbre or "tone" of the pans themselves. In this realm even Ellie Mannette's rivals concede that he was the master. Compared to the confusion over who invented which style of

---

[4] Mannette claims to have learned something about working with metal from the fitters in the shop, who heated and tempered steel, and worked it with hammers (personal conversation with Kim Johnson, July 1996).

pan first, there is less argument about whose pans *sounded* best in the 1940s and early 1950s. Timbral quality was not copied as easily as note placement and patterns, and Anthony Williams recalled that Mannette "had a unique way of tuning his pans, he produced very good sounds. We used to call them the harps at that time, their harp-like sounds, also string effects" (personal conversation with Kim Johnson, 1996). And Neville Jules, though he does not concede any advantage in playing skill to the Invaders, is candid in his admiration for Mannette's pans. "People would say, 'Boy, all you beat better than Invaders, but Invaders pan tune better than you all. . . . Because when it coming to that, in those days nobody could touch Ellie. He had the best tuned pans, so men used to say, 'Boy, if All Stars had Invaders pan . . .'" (personal conversation with Kim Johnson, 1996).

Invaders also had many skilled players of their own, including Mannette himself. In fact, Neville Jules remembers that the first time he heard Mannette's name was when someone told him about a young fellow from Woodbrook who had beaten Spree Simon in a ping pong competition. Later, Mannette gave up playing pan because he was too busy tuning and arranging for Invaders, but he continued to play iron when the band played on the road at carnival. Ray Holman, who joined Invaders in 1957, credits Ellie with teaching him and other players how to get the best sound out of the pans by playing them with the proper touch. He also cited Mannette's iron playing as a foundation for the unique rhythmic feel of steelbands in the western neighborhoods of Woodbrook and St. James: "West rhythm, as I know it, I still seeing Ellie Mannette playing the iron, wearing a cork hat. . . . I hearing that man playing this iron. The rhythm of Invaders was a unique rhythm, you know. I ain't know what he did on that iron, but it used to give a certain feeling to the music" (personal conversation, 1993).

Mannette's legacy is based both on his exceptional skills and his exceptional willingness to share them. At a time when many steelbands were secretive about their tuning, Mannette made pans for several other bands, including Desperadoes and Starland, and he made no secret of his techniques.[5] Zuzie St. Rose, in contrast, told me that when people watched him tune, he would "tie their foot" (confuse them) by doing something wrong on purpose (personal conversation, 1993). And even when tuners were willing to work outside the band, their fellow band members often tried to discourage them. Vernon Headley remembers hiring a tuner named Croppy from Casablanca to make pans for his band, Nightingales, in Tunapuna in

---

[5] When I saw Ellie Mannette in the San Francisco Bay Area in the mid-1980s, he happily shared with me all the diagrams, including note shapes and sizes, that he worked from to design his pans, even allowing me to photocopy them. His generosity and openness was particularly remarkable because I was apprenticing at the time to another tuner, Cliff Alexis.

the 1950s. When other Casablanca members got wind of the plan, however, they stole Croppy's clothes to prevent him from going, and Headley had to pay for a new set of clothes and shoes before he could get his pans. Some bands were equally jealous about their musical arrangements, the most famous example being All Stars, who rehearsed their new carnival songs in an attic, playing with fingers instead of sticks so that the music couldn't be heard in the street (see chap. 5). But Invaders welcomed listeners at their rehearsals, and in fact their yard was a popular social gathering and entertainment spot for Woodbrook residents, including middle-class steelband enthusiasts.

The relationship between Invaders and the middle class began in the late 1940s, when Invaders were invited to perform at the Little Carib Theatre in Woodbrook. Invaders and Ellie Mannette soon became the darlings of the progressive cultural elite, a social connection that, combined with Invaders' musical prowess, had made Ellie Mannette the most renowned pan tuner in Trinidad by 1950.

> The Little Carib was an outstanding group in Trinidad, were most of what you call the so-called socialites, the affluents: Hannayses and the Procopes and the Woodings and the lawyers and doctors. All of those people affiliated to the Little Carib, and they had these so-called plays every so-and-so time, and we were the house band, and we played for the Carib day in and day out. So as a result of that, the people get to like me a lot, the so-called socialites. That's why I become such a favorite to the government. I'm popular in the government because all the big people of Port of Spain associate with the Carib, and as a result of that Ellie Mannette could have done no wrong. Whatever I do I could have got away with it on account the influence of the Carib so those are the people that really had me where I was in my standing in Trinidad. But, you know, I was just one of the bad boys also. (personal conversation with Kim Johnson, 1996)

Given his tuning prowess and his social connections, Mannette was an obvious choice for TASPO when it was formed by a government commission in 1951. TASPO brought together tuners and players from different steelbands under the musical direction of Lieutenant Joseph Griffith (a Barbadian who had worked with the Trinidad Police band before taking a job with the St. Lucian government), who required the tuners to tune chromatically for the first time. Mannette adjusted the pattern of his low tenor, which at the time already had twenty-eight notes, to make it fully chromatic, and this pan, usually referred to as the "Invader" tenor, remains popular today (though it has been surpassed by the fifths tenor—see appendix I). His experience in TASPO also inspired Mannette to create entirely new designs that were more systematic than his low tenor. In 1952, Mannette built a set of double seconds with complementary whole-tone scales in each drum (appendix I). Knowing nothing about whole-tone scales, Mannette came up with this pattern by "just trying to make the chromatic sound, left, right, left, right" (personal conversation, 2005). In the mid-1950s, he developed a similar chromatic pattern for three pans, which he called "cellos," featuring complementary diminished chords in each pan (appendix I). Mannette, who still had no theoretical understanding of chords or diminished and augmented intervals, told me he saw this pattern in a dream. Through a similarly intuitive and pragmatic process, he also tuned a tenor bass with four complementary augmented chords. All of these patterns became fundamental models for contemporary steel pans.

In the 1960s, Invaders' celebrity declined and Ellie Mannette eventually left Trinidad to live and work in the United States. His first extended stay in the United States came in 1961, when he went to South Carolina to work with the U.S. Navy steelband, but he soon became discouraged by the racism he experienced and returned to Trinidad. In 1962, Invaders was further hobbled when the band lost Ray Holman and many of its other best young players to Starlift. This occurred on the eve of independence, and the legendary Invaders never played an important role in the new era of Panorama steelband competition, which began in 1963. In 1967, Mannette left Trinidad for good, sponsored by the Graceland Shipping Company to build pans and teach steelband music to disadvantaged youth in New York City. This work was coordinated by Murray Narrel, whose son Andy later became an internationally renowned recording artist on the steel pan and an advocate for Mannette's instruments.

Mannette's work soon extended into the New York public school system, and in 1971 he began working with Jimmy Leyden, a music teacher at Horace Greeley High School in Westchester County. Leyden became an advocate for the steelband in school and university music programs, and he helped introduce Mannette to music educators all over the country (forming one of the branches of the steel pan genealogy where I locate myself).[6] By the end of the 1980s, steelbands had cropped up in dozens of high school and university music programs across the United States, and Ellie Mannette became the most sought-after tuner in the country. He was invited in 1992 to found the University Tuning Project at the University of West Virginia in

[6] I first played in a steelband in 1980 with three Horace Greeley High School graduates, Peter Mayer, Mike Geller, and Toby Gordon, who brought pans built by Ellie Mannette with them to Oberlin College. Ellie was the first tuner I met, and Leyden's arrangements formed the bulk of the early repertoire for our college band, the Oberlin Can Consortium (a name we came up with to fit the CC initials stenciled on the drums, which had originally stood for "Calliope's Children," the Horace Greeley steelband's name).

Morgantown, where he has worked ever since to build and sell steel pans and to train a new generation of American tuners. In 1999, Mannette received the National Endowment of the Arts prestigious Heritage Award. He returned to Trinidad and Tobago in 2000 (for the first time since his 1967 departure) to receive the government's Chaconia Silver Medal and an honorary doctorate from the University of the West Indies. At the time, there was grumbling in the steelband community about the lack of comparable attention for tuners who had remained in Trinidad and made important contributions to the art form, reflecting the very real frustrations of panmen who have seen Trinidadian politicians take their cues again and again from foreign "experts" who praise and validate the steelband. Nevertheless, Mannette was a key innovator in the development of the steel pan in Trinidad, and his role in establishing the steel pan as an international instrument has been unparalleled.

ANTHONY WILLIAMS

Anthony "Muffman" Williams was born in 1931 to a family that lived on Nepal Street in St. James. He was raised by his mother, who was hospitalized for mental illness when Williams was a teenager, and by his grandmother, who sold snow cones to support the family. Williams remembers staying away from school sometimes because he was embarrassed to go to class without shoes. He was a bright student, though, who even skipped a grade, and upon graduation from Mucurapo Boys Royal College at the age of fifteen he entered the Royal Victoria Institute for vocational training. But carpentry had to compete with pan for his attention.

Williams formed his own steelband during the war, then played in Harlem Nightingales and Nob Hill, and joined Sun Valley in Upper Bournes Road in the late 1940s. In Sun Valley, Williams learned from Sonny Roach, who was one of the highly regarded pan tuners at that time. Williams remembers Roach for his efforts to achieve a four-part steelband orchestration similar to the differentiation of ranges (soprano, alto, tenor, and bass) in a choir. Roach tuned a second pan to play just below the ping pong, and he introduced a "spring bass" in the 1946 Island Wide steelband competition that could play notes in the lower register before bass pans were invented (Roach's spring bass was actually a lamellophone, with plucked metal keys, not a steel pan).[7] Sonny Roach disbanded Sun Valley after a disappointing

---

[7] Roach's spring bass was modeled on what Trinidadians call a "bass box"—also called *marimbula* in the Spanish Caribbean, a large lamellophone similar to the African mbira or sanza—but Roach's instrument had a body made from a biscuit drum rather than a wooden box, and the plucked

Fig. 3.3. Anthony Williams speaking at a ceremony honoring members of the National Steelband that was formed in the early 1960s. Listening to him are (from left to right) Pan Trinbago Secretary Richard Forteau, Pan Trinbago President Patrick Arnold, and tuner Cliff Alexis (2006, courtesy of Cliff Alexis).

loss to Casablanca in a competition just after the 1950 carnival, so Williams and some of the other young members moved to a yard in Lower Bournes Road to form a new band called Northern Stars, which they later shortened to North Stars.

In the same year Williams, who had by then made a reputation for himself as a ping pong player, was chosen for TASPO. Although Williams was not officially appointed as a tuner, he was already tuning (as were most of the other TASPO members). In TASPO, he shared tuning techniques and ideas with other tuners, and he responded to Lieutenant Griffith's call for chromatic instruments by developing a new tenor boom. Williams made this new instrument from two 55-gallon oil drums instead of the Bermudez biscuit drums that were the norm at that time:

> The biscuit pan could only accommodate five notes at the time, and Griffith wanted seven, so when they try to put seven notes in the biscuit pan, the

tongues were made from a straightened gramophone spring. The information in this passage of the text comes from an interview that Kim Johnson conducted with Williams on Feb. 13, 2001, in Port of Spain.

notes didn't use to sound good—"plow, plow," kind of way. We were told
that Gerry Gomez, who was in charge of the Tourist Bureau, and others were
coming to hear the band for the first time, so I told a friend I don't like how
my pan sound. I had tuned oil drums with the same notes in the same positions to practice at home, and I had found that the oil drum produced a
better tone, so I told my friend I want to tune a new pan. He said all right,
he will come down, we will just go down to Cocorite, and he'll sink and I
will tune it. (personal conversation with Kim Johnson, 2003)

Lieutenant Griffith was impressed with Williams's new tenor boom, and
when Williams played it that same evening, the other tenor boom player,
Dudley Smith, refused to play his instrument, which was made from a biscuit drum. Williams was asked to tune another tenor boom from oil drums
for Smith, and this became the preferred instrument for TASPO. Fifty-five-
gallon oil drums also came to be used for TASPO's chromatic bass, which
was a set of three pans. Williams was thus one of the first tuners to experiment with the 55-gallon oil barrel, which subsequently became the standard
container for building all pans. Williams remembers sneaking onto the U.S.
Navy base to steal empty 55-gallon drums to experiment with in the late
1940s. He also purchased leaky Shell and Esso drums at a place on Wrightson Road.

Ellie Mannette, who tells similar stories, is frequently credited with being
the first to use a 55-gallon drum, but the innovation did not catch on immediately. Neville Jules, for example, first saw a 55-gallon drum played by a
man in a competition in Tacarigua, but he remembers that the crowd
laughed at this large and unwieldly instrument. The reason the 55-gallon
drum seemed ill suited for pan at the time was that it was much heavier than
the biscuit drum, and the same 18-gauge steel that allowed tuners to sink
deeper and tune stronger-sounding notes also made it difficult to carry and
play on the road. Panmen in the 1940s carried their pans on their shoulders,
playing with one hand, or hung them from straps like side drums (see appendix I). By the 1950s, sets of multiple pans, like the ones developed for
TASPO, were hung on stands for stage performances. On the road, however,
musicians continued to play with single pans suspended from neck straps
(by this time played with two hands). These were made from 55-gallon
drums for the higher range pans with short skirts, but biscuit drums or
caustic soda drums were still used for the low-range pans with long skirts.
Many steelbands in the 1950s thus had both a stage side that used sets of
multiple pans and a road side that used only single pans, which meant that
they could not play their full stage repertoire on the road. Williams, whose
North Stars had developed a formidable reputation for their stage repertoire, was frustrated that they couldn't play some of those tunes in the street.

The greatest musical limitation on the road was the range of the single pan basses, which could only be tuned with three or four notes, since lower notes required a larger surface area. Steelband music arranged for the road therefore tended to use just a few bass ostinato patterns (fig. 2.9). Williams improved the tone of these single basses by tuning the bottom of a 55-gallon drum and welding it onto the skirt of a caustic soda drum to make it light enough to carry; but this did not solve the problem of range. In 1956, however, Williams wanted to play a song called "Puerto Rico Mambo," which had an elaborate bass line, and he decided he had to find a way to bring North Stars' triple bass on the road. His solution was to put wheels on the bass pans: "It was just screw on, make a contraption to put on two wheels on the drum with a swivel so and we held it with one hand and played it with the other" (personal conversation with Kim Johnson, 2001).[8] The use of wheels quickly caught on, and before long all the steelbands were putting their pans on elaborate wheeled racks that were pushed by neighborhood supporters on the road, freeing the musicians to play with both hands just as they did on stage. Williams's innovation opened the way for a much greater variety of repertoire and arranging techniques on the road, an opportunity that steelbands quickly exploited for competitive advantage.

The single most significant tuning contribution that Williams made, however, was his "spider web" ping pong, the model for the modern fourths and fifths tenor pan. The spider web design was based partly on a principle that Williams discovered while working with TASPO. He noticed then that when notes an octave apart were placed next to one another they both sounded better, and he brought this principle of octave alignment to the attention of the other TASPO members. Williams wanted to understand more about such tonal relationships, and after TASPO he took private lessons in singing with a man named Moore in St. James, so that he could learn more theory and learn to read music. As the leader, tuner, and arranger for North Stars from 1953, he steered the band increasingly toward performance of the classics. He entered North Stars in the biennial Music Festival, and pored over the comments of the classically trained judges to learn whatever he could. In 1956, Williams heard one of the judges, Dr. Northcote, explain that he had a hard time learning to play the ping pong he had been given as a gift because it did not have a "balanced formation." This spurred Williams to perfect a new design that he arrived at by a painstaking process of discovery:

---

[8] Williams's description originally suggested to me that each of the three basses in a set was pushed separately, but a picture in Felix Blake's book (n.d.: 79) shows what seems to be a set of three bass pans on a single rack with one large wheel on each side of the rack; so the rack would have to be tipped and balanced to roll the pans on two wheels. More modern racks have three or more small swiveling wheels on which the rack rests squarely.

> The ping pong developed from a tenor kittle beat that was a major chord. . . .
> Soon the ping pong you had So-Do-Me there, so I counted the semitones
> from C to F (C-F-A is So-Do-Me, too). At that time I didn't know anything
> about F or anything like that, I just counted the semitones from C to F and
> found that there were six. And I counted from F to A and found it was five,
> so I put B flat there, and I kept counting six all the time and work out in the
> cycle of fifths. Without knowing the cycle of fifths we discovered the cycle of
> fifths. (personal conversation with Kim Johnson, 2001)

In other words, Williams measured the pitch interval from C ascending to F
and found it could be measured in terms of six notes (C, C♯, D, E♭, E, F),
each a semitone away from the next. This pitch interval is referred to in formal musical terms as a fourth. Following this pattern, Williams designed a
pan with all twelve notes of the chromatic scale placed in a clockwise circle
around the rim, each note a fourth above the last, or a fifth below:[9] C, F, B♭,
E♭, A♭, C♯, F♯, B, E, A, D, G. To this pattern, which in reverse order is commonly described in formal musical terms as the circle of fifths, Williams
then applied the principle of octave tuning, placing octaves directly adjacent
to each other in concentric circles. This is how he came up with the spider
web ping pong (appendix I), a consummately "balanced formation" in the
sense that one could, in theory, play the same pattern over and over and
simply rotate the pan to render it in different keys (in actual practice this
was not possible, of course, because the pan is played hanging in a fixed position). The spider web pan did not catch on immediately because it could
not be made to sound as nice as Ellie Mannette's Invader tenor. But
Williams's determination to impose a formal musical logic on the steel pan
spurred a fundamental advance in the development of the instrument, and
his work had a big influence on other tuners.

RUDOLPH CHARLES

Born in Laventille in 1938, Rudolph Valentino Charles grew up near
Desperadoes but did not at first aspire to join them because they were, as his
brother Gerald put it in an interview with me in 2000, "a rioting band."

---

[9] A fourth, when inverted, becomes a fifth—for example, ascending from C to the F above is a pitch
interval of a fourth, while descending from C to the F below is a pitch interval of a fifth. The spider
web pan's notes were not placed in a circle of consistently ascending notes because Williams was
trying to fit all twelve notes of a single octave in the outer rim of the pan. After going up a fourth,
therefore, he usually descended a fifth to the next note; but in two places on the circle he tuned suc-
cessive fourths in order to keep within the octave range (see diagram in appendix I).

Charles was the son of a respected prison officer, and his parents were determined to raise respectable children. Although his mother was herself a talented musician, she did not want her boys to have anything to do with steelband, as Gerald recalls:

> I made a pan when I was a child. We used to live near where the old bands would set up over by Picton Road. I made this pan there and tuned it and everything. Once you play pan you are a vagabond, or on your way to be. My grandmother knew and told my mother "Gerald beatin' pan." My mother came up and took an axe and destroyed it. . . . She stopped me, but couldn't stop Rudolph, even with extreme punishments. Eventually she appreciated his accomplishments. Even so, we appreciated her strict discipline, and even the fact that she kept us out of steelbands and out of trouble.

Apart from their reputation for rioting, Desperadoes (in those days known as the Gay Desperadoes) were mainly known for their historical mas' (a masquerade based on historical eras or civilizations, or epic stories), but their musical skills were unremarkable. When Rudolph began to play pan, Desperadoes was not an attractive choice, and instead he joined a steelband called "Thunderbirds" that had an enthusiastic following among Laventille youth, especially the girls. Thunderbirds was popular at Christmastime, when it "serenaded" in the streets of Laventille and Port of Spain. Impressed with Thunderbirds' music, Desperadoes' leader, Wilfred "the Speaker" Harrison, came to Rudolph one day in 1958 and asked him to become Desperadoes' new musical director. At first Rudolph declined, upon which Harrison explained that all of Thunderbirds' pans would in that case be destroyed. Rudolph's father had recently died, leaving him with no one to help him or to stop him, so he threw in his lot with the feared Desperadoes, first as tuner and musical director and later, beginning in 1961, as their leader. As bandleader and tuner, Rudolph Charles shaped Desperadoes into a powerful force both musically and politically.

Somewhat ironically, Charles also helped put an end to the leadership role of tuners in the steelband movement, because he defied neighborhood loyalties and brought together talented tuners and players from different bands. Charles brought Bertie Marshall from Hilanders steelband in Laventille to share his new harmonic tuning technique with Desperadoes. He crossed town to listen to Invaders in their panyard and talked about tuning with both Ellie Mannette and Anthony Williams. Charles eventually recruited Invaders' best player, Emmanuel "Corbeau Jack" Riley, to instruct Desperadoes players and also to tune for them, as a result of which Desperadoes developed a sound that is more often compared to the West style of Invaders than to East steelbands such as All Stars and Renegades. Des-

Fig. 3.4. Rudolph Charles receiving an award in Miami in 1977 on behalf of Desperadoes steelband (photo courtesy of the *Trinidad Express*).

peradoes was thus one of the first bands to model a new role for the tuner as freelance craftsman, a role that has since become the norm in Trinidad.

A talented tuner in his own right, Charles sought to achieve a differentiation of range and timbre between steelband instruments that would parallel the instrumentation of a symphony orchestra. One of the pans he invented was the twelve-bass (a set of pans made from twelve oil drums), which he modeled on the sound and range of an upright bass. Gerald, who played upright bass and lived downstairs from Rudolph in the family home, remembers his brother's obsessive pursuit of the right sound:

I remember one day he came in from Los Angeles, and he said, "Gerald, I want to make a new bass, a twelve-bass, and I want it to sound like an upright bass. So could you come and play for me?" So I went up. But the bass ain't sounding like how the professionals outside, like Ron Carter and Roy Brown, because I haven't got the proper strings. He say, "Well, what kind of strings would make the bass sound like that?" So I went inside, and I took out an envelope [of my best strings]. So he say, "Give me the envelope," so I give it to him. Two days after he say, "I makin' a trip, I comin' back just now." He went back to the States to buy a set of strings, the specific strings I recommended, to put on my bass to hear how it sound to create this new bass that he wanted! He was a madman! When I say mad, I mean musically mad. An inventor usually is like that, eh?

When he came back . . . he say, "Give me a few minutes of your time now." So I went upstairs, and he kept me there from about 6 o'clock in the evening until 11 o'clock at night, just playing the different notes, and he was tuning from the bass itself. . . . And then he said to me, "You would never realize how important this is to me. I wouldn't be able to pay you for this thing." And it is there the twelve-bass came from. That is why people found that the band was sounding very professional, like an orchestra. So this is the extent he used to go to tune a pan. Sometimes he wouldn't sleep for a whole week.

Gerald Charles told me that Rudolph also perfected the modern fourths and fifths tenor, based on Anthony Williams's spider web design, and he invented a number of new pan types. Many of these new pans contributed not only to Desperadoes' sound, but also to what can be fairly described as steelband architecture. The visual elaboration of the steelband that had begun with the construction of racks on wheels was greatly expanded after 1963 on the Panorama stage, where a hundred or more pans with canopied racks were arranged around an elevated float at the center of the band. Charles elaborated on this spectacle with instruments like the twelve-bass that bristled with full-size oil drums suspended horizontally like cannons (fig. 3.5); the rocket pan, a set of low-range pans with tapered skirts that flared out like rocket engines pointed toward the audience; and the quadrophonic (fig. 3.6), which included two pans hanging flat like a double second and two more tipped on edge above them at eye level, forming a right angle (appendix I). One of his greatest visual effects was created when he chromed all of Desperadoes' frontline pans in 1970, so that the band presented a glittering wall of silver to the audience at Panorama. This practice was quickly adopted by other bands, and chrome became standard for frontline pans.

Charles's tuning skills were equaled by his political skills. People who knew him recall his extraordinary charisma, which he used to charm im-

Fig. 3.5. Nine-basses in Tokyo steelband (courtesy of Aurélie Helmlinger).

Fig. 3.6. Quadrophonics being played by a member of Phase II Pan Groove (2000).

portant political and business patrons. He helped Desperadoes to acquire wealthy sponsors, first Coca-Cola and then the West Indian Tobacco Company, who helped pay for his extravagant tuning ambitions. He also represented a crucial constituency for the People's National Movement (PNM), which depended (and still does) on the solid support of poor black voters in Laventille for its political power. Charles is rumored to have had access to Prime Minister Eric Williams whenever he wanted to talk, and he and other members of Desperadoes' leadership mediated between the government and Laventille residents in the allotment of jobs through the Special Works Program, as well as other favors, including housing (A. Lee 1997; also see chap. 5). Although another Laventille band, Hilanders, was commonly referred to as the "PNM band" in the late 1950s because of its frequent performances at political events, it was Desperadoes and Rudolph Charles who really traded upon their influence in the community to become political power brokers.

On the Hill, Charles's word was law, backed not only by Desperadoes' money and muscle but by the tuning hammer he always carried and which gave him his nickname. If people made trouble in the band, Rudolph would talk to them first, as his brother Gerald recalled, but "if they didn't listen they would get knocked out. . . . The hammer do the communicating." Upon Charles's untimely death in 1985, David Rudder eulogized him in the calypso "The Hammer," which was a runaway favorite for the 1986 carnival; it won both the Calypso Monarch competition and the Panorama competition. Charles's funeral drew thousands of mourners, and his body was carried in a coffin made of 55-gallon oil drums.

SUMMARY: NEW OPPORTUNITIES

Inevitably, disagreements will remain about who did what first, and some will dispute aspects of my account; at the very least, however, these individual stories underscore important innovations that differentiated the steelband from tamboo bamboo and other traditions that preceded it. Those innovations include the development of melodic and eventually chromatic instruments; a reconceptualization of texture by which background instruments acquired roles that were more versatile than rhythmic accompaniment to a "cutter"; the refinement of timbre to correspond more closely to a bel canto aesthetic; the accommodation of theoretical notions of balance and symmetry in note placement; cultivation of middle-class audiences and supporters; procurement of political and business sponsorship; sharing of talent and information between different bands; and the spectacle of steelband architecture. The history of these developments is more complex than what is represented here, since many individuals contributed. Nonetheless, every innovation was ultimately predicated on an individual breakthrough, and the tuners discussed here exemplify the genius and vision that gave shape to a most unlikely musical ensemble.

Individual tuning innovations also responded, of course, to broader social and cultural pressures that the panmen experienced. The transformation of the steel pan's percussive sound into a more smooth, sustained timbre, for example, helped steelband musicians prove their worth through the performance of classical music and other established musical repertoires. There was nothing that a trained musician could tell tuners about *how* to change their sound, because it was a unique and emergent technology requiring a sculptor's eye, a blacksmith's strength, a musician's ear, and an elephant's patience. For this reason, the panmen and their communities are rightfully proud of an invention that was entirely their own. Nonetheless, criticisms and encouragements from outsiders helped steer this invention, as pan tuners responded to comparisons between the steel pan and conventional instruments. Anthony Williams was stung, for example, by Dr. Northcote's 1952 complaint that steelbands were unable to play sustained notes convincingly (Stuempfle 1995: 106). Choir director Pat Bishop, who has rehearsed and directed some of Trinidad's most successful steelbands in the festival competition, compares the pan tuner's task to that of a choir director; in both cases, she suggested, "basically what you're trying to get is bel canto" (personal conversation, 1994). It was not coincidence, therefore, that by the 1970s the clarity and sustain of the steel pan's sound permitted comparisons to an organ, a choir, or even a symphony orchestra.

The transformation of the steel pan's timbre is almost invariably portrayed as an improvement to the instrument. Just as it has enabled new repertoires and performance techniques, however, it has undermined others, as steelband arranger Clive Bradley points out:

I think [in] the enthusiasm of tuners to "perfect" the sound, they're losing some of the more rustic sound that made those pans what they were. For example, there was a strumming pan long ago called a grundig. Now, the grundig is a pan that had a rough masculine-*Ara Bum, gara Bum, gara Bum, gara Bum*—that's what you used to hear out of them. Now that seems to be disappearing except in bands like, Solo Harmonites would still have that sound; their guitars and their four-pans sound rough and crude, which I love to hear—it gives me goose pimples!

With the strum, what I do is you split the strum in two, and you give the four-pan two notes and the guitar two notes. [The four-pan] plays *ga-rum*, on the beat [i.e., *rum* is on the beat] and the guitars strum, and they answer that [*sings the off-beat guitar strum*] so you get *ga-ru-pum, ga-ru-pum*

[*"-pum" is sung at a higher pitch; see* fig. 3.7]. It's a beautiful lilt that goes along with the combination [of] the high-hat and the cowbell. . . . Some bands I try to use that grundig strum, and it doesn't work because the cellos are not masculine enough, so I put them all together, let them strum the chord *pram*, all at once. But if I have some nice gruff pans down there: *ga-ru-pum, ga-ru-pum,* and the bass just walks along with them. Beautiful!

Bradley's observation demonstrates how tuning "perfections" like sustain and timbral uniformity have compromised the techniques of timbral and rhythmic contrast that early steelbands exploited. It is a reminder of the more general truth that the panmen's love affair with European art music has caused losses as well as gains.

The typical steelband musician in the 1950s, however, had little to lose and much to gain from the new opportunities that his instrument presented. Advances in the panman's social position were achieved in much the same way as advances in tuning and musical knowledge—through the agency of energetic individuals who seized new opportunities. Such a notion of individual opportunism complicates the master narrative of the "steelband movement" as a collective struggle characterized by class and neighborhood solidarity. This narrative is inspired both by the steelband movement's metaphorical relationship to the Trinidadian nation, and also by the values of band and neighborhood loyalty that many steelbands continue to hold dear. Even in the fiercely partisan early days of the steelband, however, exclusive neighborhood loyalties did not prevent disputes and differences within bands. This is clearly demonstrated by the incessant splitting off of rebellious factions to form new bands.

Intraband disputes arose not only from rivalries over leadership but also from different artistic or social visions. A case in point is the formation of Trinidad All Stars, discussed above, who wanted to base membership on

Fig. 3.7. Traditional steelband strumming technique (as recounted by Clive Bradley).

musical ability rather than neighborhood status. This was related in part to the problem of violent steelband clashes at the time, which tarnished the reputations of steelbands in the 1940s and 1950s, and which some panmen claim were instigated primarily by neighborhood supporters rather than by the musicians. Harold Headley, for example, recalls how the influence of "strongmen" or "badjohns" continued to hold back the steelbands even into the 1960s, when he began playing pan: "Those fellas did really like fighting because they figure that was their power, and because of that it killed the steelband to a point" (personal conversation, March 1993). Individuals who saw music as their power, therefore, sometimes broke ranks when appeals to band solidarity took the form of a call to physical violence. This is not to deny that musical rivalry generated its own kind of solidarity but rather to point out that panmen have been subjected to the same pulls that, in varying degrees, influence musicians in other cultures—individual reputation, professional opportunities, or the chance to learn and create—and that compete with group loyalty. From a musical perspective, individual ambitions and visions complicate the kind of monolithic social identity that is sometimes ascribed to particular steelbands or to the steelband movement generally.

Thus, when the steelband became an important site for the lowering of social barriers between the lower and middle classes in the 1950s, it was not only because of government officials concerned with antisocial violence, or middle-class progressives who identified with the new art form, but also because of the initiatives that individual panmen took to improve their musical knowledge and their social position. As more and more panmen actively cultivated contacts with middle-class people who were able to teach them music or provide them with new performance venues, steelband leaders found themselves working to make a place for the steelband in the same sociocultural establishment that lower-class carnival performers had tenaciously defied for a hundred years. The musical and social consequences of this sometimes paradoxical collaboration are explored through the next several chapters.

4

The National Instrument

*Pan, calypso, and carnival are the only things we have to make us proud today and
in the future; and of these, the only one we can claim entirely is pan. This is the
cornerstone of our culture.*

Masquerade designer Francisco Cabral, quoted in Ganase 1993

Francisco Cabral's description of pan as "the only [thing] we can claim entirely" implies pride in the accomplishments of panmen like Zigilee, who
himself described pan as "all we had." Despite the similarity between these
two men's statements, however, they are separated by distinctly different
conceptions of who "we" are. For Zigilee, as quoted at the opening of chapter 2, "we" are persecuted outcasts trying to make the most of the few
scraps that society has left us. For Cabral, "we" are a nation trying to define
its culture. The conceptual distance between these ideas—of pan as the
persecuted invention of poor black people, on the one hand, and pan as the
national instrument of Trinidad and Tobago, on the other—was bridged in
the late 1940s and 1950s by intellectuals and steelband supporters who
effectively integrated the steelband movement with the nationalist movement. A decisive factor in this integration was middle-class participation in
steelbands, which produced a transformation in the social and cultural status of pan that was dramatic not only because of its speed, but also because
of the deeply ingrained prejudices and class barriers that were challenged
in the process.

SOCIAL AND MUSICAL STIGMAS

The most obvious reason why many Trinidadians despised the early pan-men is that they were seen as troublemakers, engaging in frightfully violent clashes with each other and with the police that persisted into the mid-1960s. The stigma of violence that attached itself to the panmen had much older roots, however, in European fears of African expressive culture. From the earliest days of slavery, African music was perceived by European slave-holders as threatening because of its potential for communication and spiritual empowerment, and drumming was prohibited or regulated by law in various ways throughout the American colonies (see, for example, Cowley 1996; Epstein 1977; Handler and Frisbie 1972). Such fears persisted in Trinidad even after emancipation in 1838 and were probably even exacerbated by the entrance of Afro-Trinidadians into public carnival celebrations at that time. Concerns about carnival violence came to a head in the 1881 Canboulay riots, but the resulting restrictions on drumming and stickfighting did not put an end to violent rivalries. The stickfighter's place was taken by other belligerent carnival performers, including the Pierrot, a nobly dressed speechmaker armed with a lead-filled whip and a steel pot helmet. As folklorist Andrew Carr describes it, confrontations between individual Pierrots could erupt into large-scale brawls that were similar to stickfighting battles (and to the steelband clashes of later years):

> Like the stick-fighting gang of former years in their relation to a district, each Pierrot assumed overlordship of a territory consisting of a couple streets or more, and resented intrusion by another into his domain. One of them is still remembered for his opening speech: "I am the King of Dahomey, but I also rule over many countries that I have conquered. Do you now visit my dominions to offer your subjugation, or do you come as an enemy to dispute my rule?" . . . Fighting became so frequent and severe among these maskers that a law was passed in 1896 making it necessary for a special license to be obtained from the police, in order to play this type of mask, accompanied by a deposit of £5 against good behaviour. Frequently, the followers also of each Pierrot would enter the fray with sticks in a general free-for-all, aided and abetted by women armed with bottles and stones. Pressure, through numerous arrests and gaol sentences, finally resulted in the disappearance of this princely belligerent on the Carnival scene. (Carr 1956: 282–83)

With the decline of the Pierrot, violent rivalry took new forms again with the tamboo bamboo bands and continued to be a concern.

Oral and written accounts of the steelband's early history suggest that this tradition of carnival violence intensified with the emergence of the steelband in the 1940s. Increasing labor unrest around the time of the steelband's advent and frustration over economic conditions following World War II may have contributed to increased carnival violence. At the close of the war, with American troops still stationed in Trinidad, soldier and sailor masquerades were also popular with the steelbands, a dramatic theme that heightened their martial spirit. Many of the steelbands took their names from American war movies and westerns: Desperadoes, Bar 20, Tripoli, North Stars, Casablanca, Destination Tokyo, Invaders, Renegades.[1] The steelband's distinctive musical dynamics—louder sound and intense competition to innovate—may also have contributed to a new level of violence during carnival. Whatever the reason, Steelband Association leader George Goddard writes, "I find it difficult 40 years afterwards to convey to the reader the senselessness of the steelband clashes. There has to be some sociological explanation above the head of a layman like myself. The violence left the society bewildered" (1991: 49).

The following depiction of steelband mayhem is just one of many that appeared in newspapers between the late 1940s and early 1960s.

A steel band riot which marred carnival celebrations in the city yesterday afternoon, resulted in the injury to nine persons. . . . It is understood that the members of the Invaders Band were marching along Park Street with two or three other bands playing mask and had just swung into Charlotte Street when they were confronted with a barrage of bottles and stones and quickly took to their heels only to be followed by their pursuers who rushed them from several points in the Park Street Hill. Masqueraders and spectators alike fled in terror. . . . Some less fortunate were cornered and assaulted. One of the victims reported that even a policeman, near whom he sought protection, was also forced to seek safety, leaving him at the mercy of an assailant who struck him with a sharp-cutting instrument. A number of steelbandsmen were forced to abandon their instruments. The instruments were said to be destroyed. One of the persons involved stated that a number of the bottles thrown at them contained corrosive fluid. Besides bottles and stones, cutlasses are reported to have been used. (*Trinidad Guardian*, Feb. 21, 1950, cited in J. Thomas 1990: 161)

Despite Goddard's own disgust at such violence, he also felt that media accounts exaggerated the problem, noting that "the newspapers gave extensive

[1] The epilogue to Goddard 1991 includes a table that lists the names and dates of the movies that these and other steelbands took their names from.

coverage to these steelband clashes. Sometimes the incidents were reported in a sensationalised style" (1991: 49).

In fact, as Trinidadians began to contemplate the prospect of political independence, both detractors and supporters of the steelband foregrounded the problem of violence to make very different arguments about the national culture. The energetic condemnations of steelband violence during the 1940s and 1950s can thus be read, on the one hand, as an outraged response to liberal sympathizers who defended the steelband as a native art form. A writer to the editor of the *Guardian* newspaper in 1953, for example, seemed agitated not just by steelband violence but also by government efforts to organize and control the steelbands, which he obviously viewed as misguided:

> Steel band fanaticism is a savage, bestial cult and must be recognised as such and completely wiped out, for there can be no compromise with unlawful killings. Control is not the answer, for it would only stop for awhile and then break out again worse than before. Steel bandsmen are 90 percent the loiterers and the unemployable who do not want to work. They are able to obtain cash by robbery and violence throughout the year, and are bound together by hatred, jealousy, violence and unnatural rivalry. (letter to the editor, *Trinidad Guardian*, June 23, 1953, cited in Stuempfle 1990: 167)

This kind of alarmist commentary in the press, on top of the truly frightening violence of steelband clashes, led many Trinidadians during the 1940s and 1950s to associate panmen with mayhem and crime more than music— a stigma that has not been completely erased even today.

Steelband violence is cast in a more positive light, on the other hand, by people who seek to portray the panman as a cultural hero. Although some middle-class steelband supporters may have taken this stance in the 1940s and 1950s, it really came into fashion after the most violent era of steelband history had ended. Such an interpretation of steelband violence was easiest to make, that is, at a safe distance from its real ugliness; it also reflects sympathy with the panmen, however, and a view of carnival as a forum for popular resistance to authority that is especially popular with intellectuals. Sociologist Ann Lee writes, for example, "In the absence of political representation, [poor people's]culture became their main weapon in the struggle against oppression" (1991: 423). Similarly, most defenders of steelband violence portray it as a response to official repression, and to the larger social forces that discriminated against poor blacks in Trinidad. As journalist and former Starlift steelband member Eddie Odingi explains:

You had to fight. Because it was in the colonial days, it was in the war days. . . . You have to remember, you'd come through slavery into colonialism, and one of the things that was banned was the drum. In the early stages you had the Baptists, who used to dance and sing and shout, and that was banned. Most of the local culture was banned. And here it is, this instrument, this pan just coming through, this culture just coming from nowhere, and to them it was just noise. (personal conversation, 1993)

Like Odingi, many supporters of the steelband movement justify or even glorify physical violence as a kind of cultural resistance waged against the Eurocentric establishment and thus as a metaphor for Trinidad's independence struggle.

Apt though this metaphor is, it obscures some of the more banal realities of steelband violence. Violence in steelbands, as in other walks of life, was often a symptom of humiliation. Fights over women, in particular, are often cited as a cause of steelband clashes.[2] Zigilee also recognized, despite his defiant attitude toward the police, that many physical battles were fought after musical battles had been lost:

We had a sort of temperament built in us: from the time that you could play sweeter than me, you is a better band than me, let we say. The onliest thing I could do was to hate your ass, you know. [Nowadays] if a band playing good, you willing now to go and listen to them and try and learn from them. Well, you must remember it's primitive stage we were in, it wasn't like that. Because you could play better than we, we ready to break in your ass. That is how it was. We would break in your ass. You coming in and playing sweeter than we and making people watch you, and watching we skeptic. We used to break in . . . go and bust your pan. Every pan you had, you get it busted up. That is how it was. It ain't nothing to be proud of, but that's how it was.

Zigilee's view of such behavior as "primitive" was shared by other steelband musicians who came to see violence as an obstacle to their musical progress. These musicians also resented police persecution, however, and were keenly aware that the authorities' intolerance was symptomatic of a deeper cultural bias by which their music was judged to be "just noise." It was one thing to be called loiterers or badjohns, that is, but panmen were more deeply wounded by condescending dismissals of their music. Just as musical performance enhanced the panmen's reputation among their peers, therefore, it became the central means for the panmen to establish their rep-

[2] I have heard this explanation in many conversations and interviews, and it was also one of the conclusions of a 1949 Youth Council investigation (Stuempfle 1995: 87).

utation in the wider society and to overcome the stigma of violence and degeneracy associated with the steelbands. The following commentary, a letter to the editor, is a vivid example of this stigma, a Eurocentric view of steelband music that was shared by many educated Trinidadians in the 1940s and that defined the battle lines of the panmen's musical endeavor:

> We must put up with the transformation of earth into bedlam, to the utter disgust of parents, students, tired workmen, troubled people and invalids. Can beating is pan beating in any language and in any form. It does nobody any good, and when it is indulged in all day all night, day in and day out, it is abominable. Why is there no legislation to control it? If it must continue and if by virtue of its alleged inherent beauty and charm it will someday bring popularity and fame to the island and a fortune to the beaters, then by all means let it go on—but in the forests and other desolate places. (*Trinidad Guardian*, June 6, 1946)

Although the panmen associated negative judgments like this one with a certain middle-class perspective, they also encountered a more sympathetic middle-class mind-set—the very mind-set, indeed, to which the above writer's cynicism is directed. The romantic view of folk music ("inherent beauty and charm") and the concern for foreign opinion and tourism ("popularity and fame to the island") at which this writer pokes fun were hallmarks of a cosmopolitan cultural attitude shared by a significant number of educated Trinidadians in the 1940s. Here again, therefore, the writer's vehemence can be understood in part as a reaction against middle-class advocates for the steelband, who had already made their voices heard in 1946, the very year in which Spree Simon's performance before the governor symbolically inaugurated the new instrument. Who were these advocates, why were they interested in the steelband, and what influence did they have on its development?

MIDDLE-CLASS INVOLVEMENT

As early as the 1930s, middle-class intellectuals in Trinidad made concerted efforts to document and promote local folklore. Key figures in this folklore movement included Andrew Carr, who did some of the first field research and publishing on Trinidadian folk culture, and with whom choreographer Beryl McBurnie first began her folkloric dance research. J. D. Elder, of a younger generation, promoted local arts as a member of the Trinidad and Tobago Youth Council, earned a Ph.D. in sociology and folklore, and wrote extensively about calypso and other Afro-Trinidadian performance arts. Prominent artists with formal training in European music and dance also helped promote Trinidadian folklore, including the steelband. One of these was Edric Connor, a baritone who included Trinidadian folk songs in his repertoire and performed them internationally. For a presentation of Trinidadian folklore in 1943, Connor is also reported to have invited what must have been a fledgling "Gonzales steelband" to take part (E. Hill 1972: 49). A few years later, in 1946, choreographer Beryl McBurnie arranged for the Invaders steelband to play at the anniversary dance of the Trinidad and Tobago Youth Council, an organization whose members contributed significantly to the promotion of local culture, including the steelband.

The activities of folklorists and artists were closely intertwined with the interests of political activists who viewed expressive culture as an essential component of national identity. These activists were influenced by ideas about folklore that they had absorbed through their British education and cosmopolitan intellectual formation. In 1944, for example, Charles Espinet and Harry Pitts published the first scholarly treatise on calypso, which was radical because it asserted the African roots of Trinidadian culture (Rohlehr 1990: 389), but it did so from a distinctively European ideological perspective. Espinet and Pitts's opening sentences set forth the romantic nationalist criteria by which educated Trinidadians at the time measured themselves against people of other nations:

> No study of a people can be complete without reference to their folk-music—the melodies and rhythms which, handed down orally from generation to generation, remain for centuries as much a part of their country as its hills and valleys, its rivers and lakes. The Irishman has his jig, the Scotchman his reel, the Spaniard his bolero. So too, the Trinidadian has his calypso and to listen to and understand the calypso, even in its present commercialised form, is to get an appreciation of the mentality of the Trinidad Creole and an understanding of many of his customs. (1944: 13)

Espinet and Pitts's apology for calypso's "present commercialised form" underscores their interest in a pure and untainted cultural essence. At the same time, however, they complimented innovators like the Lord Executor who were thought to "improve" calypso in a way that made it more appealing to respectable audiences. They even praised an instrumental calypso performed by a foreign wind quintet, expressing hope "for the further musical development of the calypso along classical lines" (1944: 22). With respect to its purism as well as its concern for improving folk culture—both of which reflected a certain disdain for the vulgarity of the actual folk—the cultural nationalism espoused here adhered to a cosmopolitan ideology of modernist reform that was typical of nationalist intellectuals throughout the colonial world.

Folklore promotion in Trinidad was shaped by local circumstances as well, though, especially by its relationship to carnival and tourism. During the 1930s and early 1940s, calypso records sold quite well in the United States (Eldridge 2002), which made money for Trinidadian businessmen such as phonograph merchant Eduardo Sa Gomes and attracted tourists to carnival (D. Hill 1993: 131–35). In 1939, the government formed the Tourist and Exhibition Board and the Carnival Improvement Committee, one of whose charges was "to lift Calypso" (Rohlehr 1990: 328). It can be no coincidence that Espinet and Pitts's study followed quickly on the heels of these developments, and their disdain for commercialization belies the fact that the political and business establishment in Trinidad had a financial interest in projecting calypso as a vibrant folk music. Just as Trinidadian nationalists viewed commercialization in calypso as inauthentic, they assumed that it would disappoint tourists who came to see the "real" Trinidad. Espinet and Pitts wrote, for example, that "today Trinidad's foremost calypsonians are . . . almost obsessed by the idea of making 'big money' and their art has suffered by this change" (1944: 21). These disparaging remarks about commercialization were ironically related, however, to a concern for calypso's marketing as an "authentic" national music.

The imperative to support local culture was genuinely patriotic as well, and it required nationalists to engage in the project of articulating and in some ways creating a local culture that Trinidadians could be proud of. This was not an easy task for colonial subjects who had been educated in British schools and had been expected in almost every walk of life to value European speech, manners, and of course music. Hugh Skinner, who served as president of the Trinidad and Tobago Youth Council in the mid-1950s, remembers wrestling with this problem:

> You couldn't divorce politics and culture. In those days, the two things went hand in hand. Because you're answering the white man. You're talking about independence, and he says, "Your grandfathers were climbing around in trees, you wouldn't know what to do with it if we gave you independence." The word "culture" was being bandied about, but no one really knew what was meant by that. Is culture *bélé* and tamboo bamboo and calypso? Is that what you mean by culture? So we wanted to know the answers to some very fundamental questions. And, for me, a deeper yearning to know the origins of myself, not only as a member of an ethnic group but also as a human being. . . .
>
> [The strategy was] putting it on stage, getting it out of the shadow of night. That was when most of these things were performed: rada, shango, bongo. Putting it on stage, incorporating it into concert form, and finally getting it onto the radio, which was the ultimate—once it reached there,

it gained respectability. But we were all amateurs. . . . We had a couple of programs, but of course the political taint, the red smear, soon caught up with us in the youth movement because we were working in both fields. I was politically active as well as being in the Youth Council. So they withdrew the program eventually. Shell was the sponsor, which was a bad thing for us. Here we were talking about kicking out the foreigners, and they were one of the main representatives of the foreigners. But before it was done, we put on some good programs, afternoon programs on Radio Trinidad. (personal conversation, July 1993)

Prominent Youth Council members of the 1940s and 1950s included dramatist Errol Hill and lawyer Lennox Pierre, who in 1947 arranged for the first broadcast of steelband music on the Youth Council's "Voice of Youth" radio program. (Older people today still remember Ellie Mannette's ping pong performance of Brahms's Lullaby on this show [Pierre 1962].) These activists' cultural views were influenced by pan-Africanism and by leftist politics and social ideologies that circulated internationally through labor and anticolonial movements. Not surprisingly, therefore, they were supported and even joined in their efforts by progressive politicians like trade unionist and Legislative Council member Albert Gomes, and future Prime Minister Eric Williams. As Skinner explains above, culture was something these activists and politicians sought to *display* in order to expose people to new ideas and to challenge the dominant cultural icons. Thus the *proscenium stage* became a crucial venue for folklore performances. This cultural frame gave new status to Afro-Trinidadian culture, but it also constructed the steelband and other music and dance practices as "art forms" that could, and perhaps even should, be separated from the social processes that had generated them in the first place.

Beryl McBurnie and the Little Carib Theater

The staging of folklore in Trinidad was influenced by international models that ranged from the work of European nationalist composers, to North American Negro spirituals, to the performances of budding national dance companies in the Caribbean, Africa, and elsewhere. One artist who not only implemented such models in Trinidad but also influenced their development and dissemination in the Caribbean and North America was Beryl McBurnie. An examination of her career and the community of interest that gravitated to her work provides insight into cosmopolitan ideologies of folklore promotion that helped shape the relationship between panmen and middle-class cultural activists. At the same time, the inclusion of steelbands

Fig. 4.1. Dancer and choreographer Beryl McBurnie (photo courtesy of Molly Ahye).

at McBurnie's events gave panmen the chance to shape a new experience of "Trinidadian culture" for middle-class intellectuals, artists, and politicians.

Beryl McBurnie was born in Woodbrook, a neighborhood on the west side of Port of Spain, whose middle-class residents included black people and "coloured" people (of mixed African and European race), with some Portuguese and Chinese as well, and who were upwardly mobile and ambitious. At an early age, she developed a passion for putting on plays, concerts, and other shows that led her to an interest in Trinidadian folk dance. She received particular encouragement in this interest from folklorist Andrew Carr, whom she accompanied on many trips to observe and document folk music and dance in rural areas of Trinidad during the 1930s. During her three years as a schoolteacher, McBurnie was able to recruit other young people to join her in staging performances that integrated elements of the folk dances she observed with European musical and dramatic conventions. Thus, by the time she traveled to New York in 1938 to study Creative Arts at Columbia University, she was already an experienced performer and choreographer of Caribbean dance and had a growing following in Trinidad.[3] In New York, McBurnie studied modern dance with Martha Graham and other luminaries, and she taught American dancers who were fascinated by the exotic novelty of Afro-Trinidadian forms. One of her early students in New York was Katherine Dunham (Ahye 1983: 4), whose method of Afro-Caribbean choreography would eventually become part of the language of modern dance generally.

Not only was McBurnie a pioneering contributor to this field, she also seems to have identified with the view of Western dance students such as Dunham who saw authentic ethnic traditions as a resource for the development of dance as a universal art form. Even as she instructed American dancers in Afro-Trinidadian idioms, therefore, she integrated dance genres from Haiti, Cuba, and other parts of the Caribbean into her own repertoire. Such variety of repertoire is not typical of folk practice, but it is a hallmark of folkloric performances, whose patrons expected an entertainment spectacle (Turino 2000: 109). Disparate dance traditions were linked in these concerts by a relatively uniform style of movement and choreography and by dramatic themes such as "Spirit of Shango" (1945), "Isles of Rhythm" (1948), and "Cannes Brulées" (1958) (Ahye 1983: 19, 27, 48). More than simply representing the localities from which they came, the dances McBurnie choreographed also served a larger goal of representing the African diaspora to an international audience.[4]

The following review (published in the *American Dancer* of January 1942) of McBurnie's presentation of a show titled "Antilliana" at New York's Museum of Modern Art in 1941 gives an idea of the way McBurnie's work was perceived by American audiences: as exotic and refreshingly unpretentious, but at the same time comparable with international idioms of dance that could be evaluated as "important," not just entertaining. (McBurnie is referred to here by her American stage name, Belle Rosette.)

> The cast, composed of Belle Rosette, the Haitian Rada Group and Gerald Clarke's Calypso orchestra, was a variety of shades of black, all superb performers of this specialized folk art, whether exuding a cabaret species of

---

[3] Much of the biographical information here is gleaned from Ahye 1983.
[4] Indeed, McBurnie was participating in an international movement to promote folkloric dance that was even more broadly dedicated to representing the human condition in its diversity and unity. In this regard Matthew Allen (1997) provides a good discussion of Western choreographers' interest in "Eastern" dance traditions, and the impact this had on Bharatnatyam dance in India in the first part of the twentieth century. Turino's discussion of presentational performance norms (2000: 47–57), which he applies to analysis of African dance companies, also underscores values shared by many "national" dance companies—values that constitute an international, or "cosmopolitan," culture of folkloric dance production.

glamour as did Belle Rosette, or a nonchalance which was hilarious to watch
in some instances among members of the group. . . .

From the point of view of dance interest, the first part of the programme
was the best and most important, including besides the two voodoo rituals
mentioned, two dances (with song) by Belle Rosette, of an *Obeah Woman*
and a *Trinidad Bourroquite Dance,* as well as two other group numbers of
Haitian origin, exuberantly performed by the convulsively jerking Haitian
Rada Group. The Calypso orchestra was warmly received by a warm audience. (quoted in Ahye 1983: 14)

Despite her promising career in New York, in 1945 McBurnie returned to
Trinidad to pursue a cultural mission.[5] In 1948, she inaugurated her Little
Carib Theatre in Woodbrook, which would become an enduring cultural
institution. The list of luminaries who attended the Little Carib's opening
show, titled "Talking Drums," underscores the intersection of politics and
culture in McBurnie's work, and its international significance. Among those
present were Albert Gomes, Eric Williams (who wrote a preface to the program notes), Charles Espinet, Andrew Carr, Canon Max Farquhar of the
Anglican Church, and the commissioner of police. Academics and artists
from New York also sent congratulatory messages (Ahye 1983: 34). The highlight of the evening was a laudatory speech and a recitation of Langston
Hughes's "The Freedom Train" by the African American singer and political
activist Paul Robeson, who happened to be in Trinidad on a performing
tour of his own. This was followed by a performance of the Invaders steelband, led by Ellie Mannette.

The Little Carib thus became the first venue in which lower-class panmen had regular face-to-face encounters with Trinidad and Tobago's most
influential culture brokers. Events at the Little Carib commonly concluded
with a steelband (usually Invaders or Merry Makers) playing for dancing, in
which audience members were invited to participate:

Common folk rubbed shoulder to shoulder with the elite as the music after a
performance became the magic ingredient for mixing. Usually at the end of
a performance there was a ritual which became the custom. As the dancers
left the stage they made their way into the audience and took individuals

[5] McBurnie was undoubtedly under pressure from Trinidadian friends and colleagues to resist the
pull of the commercial entertainment world. Critics in Trinidad heralded McBurnie's success
abroad, but their nationalist pride made them all the more concerned that McBurnie's work be
perceived as more than simple entertainment. Eric Williams, who would later become the leader of
the People's National Movement and the first prime minister of Trinidad and Tobago, said as much
even in 1949: "There was one disturbing aspect of Miss McBurnie's rise to fame. Many people
tended to regard her as an entertainer" (quoted in Ahye 1983: 38).

picked at random, to dance on the stage. In the meantime the others would
stack the chairs to the sides and the "fete" would begin for the audience.
(Ahye 1983: 49)

As word spread of this post-performance dancing, attendance at the Little
Carib surged, and extra shows were scheduled. For cautious middle-class
Trinidadians who ducked into side streets when they saw a steelband coming on the road, the Little Carib afforded an opportunity to enjoy steelband
music in a safe environment. And notwithstanding all the praises that were
heaped on McBurnie's choreography and staging, it was dancing with the
Invaders that forged a powerful affective bond between the cultural progressives who frequented the Little Carib.

The panmen, for their part, were confronted with middle-class anxieties
about international cultural standards. Eric Williams, for example, referred
to the Little Carib as "the Albert Hall, the Carnegie Hall, the Opera of
Trinidad," and heralded its international visibility as a turning point for
West Indian culture:

> Until recently it was fashionable to deny the existence of West Indian culture,
> or to disparage it when its existence was admitted. Beryl McBurnie has given
> to one aspect of that culture a local habitation and a name. The Little Carib is
> now an essential feature of our contemporary West Indian scene. It is assured
> of an honoured niche in our West Indian history when that comes to be writ-
> ten. For Beryl McBurnie has not only established herself in the hearts of her
> people. The Little Carib now has an international reputation. The members
> of the Caribbean Commission, and of its Interim Tourism Committee, Ja-
> maican businessmen, His Excellency the Governor and Lady Shaw, the high-
> est in official and professional and business circles in Trinidad—all, in the
> words of His Excellency, came, saw, and were conquered. (E. Williams 1949)

Williams's remarks reinforce the notion that West Indian "culture" can
begin to be valued only when it is put on stage and displayed for viewing by
non–West Indians. This was a message that steelband musicians had of
course heard loud and clear as early as 1946, when Spree Simon was lauded
for his performance before the English governor.

The Little Carib, however, presented panmen with a strange new twist on
this message: they experienced a new welcome from progressive middle-
class audiences at the Little Carib, but at the same time their separation
from the staged dramas and their position at the end of the show relegated
them to an entertainment function that was not praised in the same terms
that were used to praise McBurnie's stage presentations. Steelband performances were kept largely separate from McBurnie's carefully choreo-

graphed and dramatized presentations, playing "only for the dancing after-wards, or for the last item if it was a calypso or spicy number" (Ahye 1983: 50). Reviewing one of the few pieces for which McBurnie integrated the In-vaders steelband with her dancers, Albert Gomes was unenthusiastic:

> Many of McBurnie's dance creations . . . seem like mere fragments placed into programme pattern by an imagination too casual and furtive to sustain and co-ordinate its efforts. This is a criticism that applies particularly to her "Jour Ouvert" number which ended just when it should have begun. Because of this failure to pursue an idea until it has been made to give optimum re-sults, many of her dance creations have been weak in dramatic structure and, therefore, artistically unsatisfying. . . .
>
> There is no creative achievement in lifting a bit of life from its natural context—the bizarre cry of the street vender or the wayside beggar. Repro-duction is not art. It is the aesthetic meaning that the artist imports to his material that is important and that seems to define the boundaries that sepa-rate art from life. (*Trinidad Guardian,* May 22, 1949, quoted in Ahye 1983: 36)

What is particularly significant about this criticism is its source. Albert Gomes was a great champion of the steelbands and of indigenous culture generally. A former trade unionist and influential member of Trinidad's elected legislative council in the 1940s and 1950s, Gomes was instrumental in the work of the government steelband committee, and he wrote newspaper columns championing the steelband and berating "prissy milksops" who could not appreciate their own indigenous culture (Stuempfle 1995: 80). Nonetheless, Gomes criticized McBurnie for presenting something that was too close to an actual carnival performance. It was one thing, in other words, to jump up with a steelband after the formal presentation had con-cluded, but to include it as part of that presentation—as Art, Culture, or "The Dance"—violated an important boundary. Even for its supporters, therefore, the steelband apparently did little to resolve what Ahye describes as "the problem of music for the creative effort of local choreographers. While the dance was moving ahead, the local musicians were not yet ready to keep abreast." (1983: 45). Ahye's criticism of "local musicians" was proba-bly aimed at musicians with formal training in Western music. But if trained musicians were not deemed capable of keeping up with the new West Indian art, where did that leave the lower-class steelband musicians? Simply put, it kept them in their place as folk musicians who provided enter-tainment and inspiration but were too ignorant of cosmopolitan standards to create true art.

The various examples above show how cultural ideology, not just con-cerns about public safety, guided government and middle-class efforts to control steelband venues and performance style during the 1940s and 1950s. Intellectuals who promoted local culture felt a sense of responsibility, that is, for how that culture should be presented, both to appeal to Trinidadians' patriotism and to make a good impression on the global stage. Despite their new affective affinity with steelband music, therefore, and their sincere efforts to dispel prejudices against the steelband, most intellectuals and politicians were not ready to turn over the responsibility for national culture to the panmen themselves. The separation at the Little Carib between McBurnie's choreography and the Invaders' performance was symptomatic of a general concern that steelband performances needed to be properly framed if they were to reflect well on the nation, and that steelband musicians needed the guidance of middle-class intellectuals and artists.

Trained Musicians and Classical Music

Whatever misgivings they may have had about middle-class appropriation and meddling, the panmen were generally eager for musical guidance, because their reputations increasingly depended on the mastery of repertoires and skills that were not transmitted within their own sociocultural milieu. Anthony Williams's story of seeking out a singing teacher (chap. 3) is repeated with variations by many panmen who actively sought the kind of musical training—including written notation, harmonic theory, tone quality, and articulation—that was usually available only to middle- and upper-class Trinidadians in the 1940s and 1950s. Entire steelbands developed long-term relationships with formally trained musicians. Casablanca became a potent musical force in the late 1940s with the arranging help of police band musician Anthony Prospect, for example. Tripoli's members received musical instruction from Father John Sewell, an English-born Anglican priest, and toured internationally with the pianist Liberace in the 1960s. The Trinidad All Stars benefited from the musical direction of Jeremy Jemmot, who devised a simplified kind of musical notation on a chalkboard to help them learn parts (All Stars member Clive Telemaque, personal conversation, 1993). The satisfaction of these collaborations was often mutual, as working with steelbands became a passionate hobby for some middle-class musicians. Youth Council activist and lawyer Lennox Pierre, for example, took his violin to the panyards of Invaders, Casablanca, and other bands in the late 1940s and 1950s to instruct them in chromatic tuning and classical music performance practice.

Pierre also helped pave the way for the panmen's influential encounter with TASPO musical director Lieutenant Joseph Griffith (see chap. 3). In 1948, Pierre initiated a Youth Council investigation into steelband violence after discovering that Invaders' ongoing war with Casablanca had interfered with his efforts to raise money to send Ellie Mannette to England for music study (Stuempfle 1995: 87–94). Pierre took his conclusions to Albert Gomes, and Gomes and the other members of the Executive Council established the steelband committee in 1949. The committee's charge was, in the words of the acting governor, "to carry out a sociological survey of the steelbands in the Port-of-Spain area, and to make recommendations whereby the cultural and recreational potentialities of the steelbands may be encouraged" (Stuempfle 1990: 133–34). In April 1950, the committee organized the Trinidad and Tobago Steel Band Association (which later became the National Association of Trinidad and Tobago Steelbandsmen, and finally Pan Trinbago). TASPO was established as the performing arm of this association and comprised representatives from most of the major steelbands. With Lieutenant Griffith in charge, members received the formal musical theory and training they had been seeking, and they carried new musical ideas from TASPO to their neighborhoods, including chromatic tuning, new repertoire, and professional standards of rehearsal and performance. Although TASPO's new tuning designs were largely created by the tuners themselves, since they best understood the technology of making and playing pans, the relationship between Griffith and TASPO's members was generally perceived as one in which formal musical knowledge was transmitted from the trained police band director to the panmen. This is illustrated in the following remarks by tuner Zuzie St. Rose. St. Rose was not a TASPO member, but he was active in steelbands in the early 1950s, and his attitude reflects the panmen's humility, gratitude, and eagerness to obtain such musical knowledge:

> The man who really teach us pan was a Bajan [Barbadian], Griffith. . . .
> We would just tune a pan and put any note, but we didn't know what was that note. So then is he come and make we know about this C, C#, F#. . . .
> We didn't have no six-bass, . . . so when he come to do "Tennessee Waltz" in musically, we could not have do it with a single pan, so then he have to show us the notes what we have to get. . . . Then when we start to play this tune, and we start to understand it, then we get to know that we were real behind time, we were dunce in music. . . . Musically, we did not know no music comes from pan. But when they hire Griffith, and he came, and he see the kind of pan we have—a dudup, a one thing—he say "no!" And is then he start to tell we we must have to get this note, because C, C#, F#, and then teach we the scale of *music*. (personal conversation, 1993)

The notion that the panmen were, as St. Rose puts it, "dunce in music" was soon dispelled, not only by improved instruments, but by enthusiastic reviews for a series of performances that TASPO gave to raise money for its upcoming trip to the Festival of Britain. The band's repertoire in these concerts included light classical, calypso, Latin dance music, and film music (see table 4.1). A newspaper review of TASPO's first public performances in 1951 touted the attendance of prominent members of society, as well as the novel and civilizing use of music stands and scores:

> Before an audience whose numbers brought forth visions of the White Cliffs of Dover, 10 steel bandsmen comprising TASPO . . . gave their first public performance at the Globe Theatre, Port-of-Spain, last night. Their crude, unpainted pans stood in sharp contrast to their shiny musician's stands and printed scores, which were being used for the first time by a steelband. But the music they played had all the polish and brilliance which their instruments lacked. . . . All were unanimous . . . in the thought that TASPO must play at the Festival. (C. Yip Young, *Trinidad Guardian* June 30, 1951, cited in Stuempfle 1995: 96–97)

When TASPO played at the Festival of Britain later that year, it won rave reviews from the English press, which bolstered the steelband's image back home and galvanized nationalist sentiment. Calling TASPO's Festival of Britain performance "a grand day for the steelbands," journalist John Grimes wrote in the *Trinidad Guardian*, "The story should be written in octaves, semi-quavers and the sharps of the sambas, rhumbas and calypsoes. It is the all-time success story of Trinidad. From rags to riches; from the Dry

Table 4.1. Concert Program, TASPO, 6/25/51

Return of the Allies (march composed by Lt. Joseph Griffith)
Tennessee Waltz (film music)
Mango Walk (rhumba)
Enjoy Yourself (samba)
Drink to Me Only (traditional English tune)
Cradle Song (Brahms)
Parang (rhumba)
Sonny Boy (fox trot)
Johnny (calypso)
Golden Earrings (bolero, film music)
Serenata (Toscelli)
Figare (calypso)
Mambo Jambo (mambo by Perez Prado)

Source: From Stuempfle 1990: 146. For more information on individual compositions, see appendix II.

River to the Albert Hall; from intolerant non-entity to world-wide recognition" (July 7, 1951, in Stuempfle 1995: 98).

Following TASPO's triumph at the Festival of Britain, a steelband category was created in Trinidad and Tobago's annual Music Festival, which was
mainly dedicated to the performance of European art music. The festival
not only encouraged steelbands to expand their repertoire of classics, but
also gave them more opportunities for feedback from formally trained musicians, especially the judges. Anthony Williams credits the festival for much
of the steelband's progress in the 1950s, claiming that it "caused improvement in making and tuning the pans, improvement in arranging and orchestration, improvement in playing the pans and improvement in the appearance of the instruments. All of these things came about because of the
adjudicators' comments which were very helpful. And that helped improve
the steelband movement in general (quoted in Stuempfle 1990: 161). Williams's internalization of Dr. Sydney Northcote's concern for "balance" in
the tuning pattern of the ping pong (chap. 3) is one example of the way
judges' feedback influenced the panmen.

Northcote, himself an Englishman, also infamously suggested that steelbands should deemphasize the classics, a piece of advice that he framed in
the rhetoric of nationalism: "The progress of the steelband," he was paraphrased as saying in a 1956 newspaper article, "has been phenomenal. But if
only because it was the one thing that Trinidad had which was unique and if
only because it was truly indigenous to the island, they should concentrate
on playing the type of music around which the steelband was built" (*Trinidad Guardian,* March 20, 1956, quoted in Thomas 1990: 226). Like the separation between art and entertainment at the Little Carib Theatre, Northcote's
comments implied that the panmen had an important but circumscribed
role to play in Trinidad's national culture—that, as the custodians of a
uniquely Trinidadian music, they should not aspire to master cosmopolitan
musical skills and repertoire.

The panmen actively challenged this notion, however, by investing extraordinary pride and effort in their performances of classics at the Music
Festival. When disagreements arose between the National Association of
Trinidad and Tobago Steelbandsmen and the organizers of the festival in
1964, the steelband association organized a festival especially for the steelbands so that they could continue to compete in the performance of European art music (Goddard 1991: 117). The new name given to this event in
1980, "Pan Is Beautiful Too," advertised the steelband movement's artistic
mission and challenged stereotypes of pan as merely fun, exciting, or rustic.
The competition format continued to include a test piece composed for the
occasion, and a "tune of choice," which was usually a calypso or other popular music genre, but it was (and still is) conceived by the steelband musi-

cians primarily as a venue for classical music, in contrast to Panorama and other competitions. Selections I heard performed at the 1992 Pan Is Beautiful competition included such classical favorites as Mozart's *Eine kleine Nachtmusik* (performed by Simple Song) and Rossini's *William Tell Overture* (Cordettes), as well as more challenging works such as Wagner's *Tannhauser* Overture (Tropical Angel Harps), Gustav Holst's *Jupiter* (Laventille Sound Specialists), Rimsky Korsakov's *Capricio Español* (Harmonites), and Smetana's *Bartered Bride* (Desperados). The institutionalization of classical music performance in the Music Festival has made it part of the training of virtually every pannist, and has enshrined classical music as the model for playing techniques like dynamics and articulation; for compositional techniques of form, harmony, and polyphonic texture; and for the timbre and sustain that pan tuners strove to perfect in their instruments.

College-Boy Bands

In contrast to the promotional and advisory roles played by middle-class cultural activists, or the instructional roles played by formally trained musicians, a more active form of middle-class participation in steelbands emerged in the early 1950s, when boys from some of Port of Spain's most prestigious schools began to form their own groups. These so-called college-boy bands[6] were formed around 1950 by boys daring enough to defy their elders but not quite daring enough to join one of the feared grass-roots bands like Casablanca, Desperadoes, or Invaders. The new middle-class bands were sometimes referred to also as "white-boy bands" because some (though by no means all) members were light-skinned. At first discouraged by alarmed parents and schoolteachers, the popularity of college-boy bands surged in the wake of TASPO's triumph at the 1951 Festival of Britain (Stuempfle 1995: 94–100, Thomas 1990: 170–73), and they quickly became the darlings of middle-class Trinidadians who hired them to play at fêtes and danced behind them on the road at carnival.

Before the advent of the college-boy bands, the idea of jumping up with a steelband on the street had been too frightening even for many people in town, let alone middle-class Woodbrook residents. Vernon Headley told me that the more violent steelbands in the 1950s were as likely to scare people off as attract them, because no one wanted to be around when a fight started between steelbands: "From the time they look up and they see that banner coming up and it's Desperadoes, that part of the street clear. Casablanca

---

[6] "College" in Trinidad refers to high school, and sometimes more generally to exclusive private schools (i.e., schools where students pay tuition).

coming, that part. Coming down Park Street, you know the people will go into the side streets until that band pass because they realize that somebody may say something and antagonize one of those strongmen, and there it [the fight] is" (personal conversation, 1993). Jumping up behind a group of one's own sons and neighbors beating pan, on the other hand, felt both exciting and safe for middle-class Trinidadians. The college-boy bands were therefore embraced in large part because they lowered the barriers to middle-class participation in carnival. Nationalistic feelings in the wake of TASPO's success were augmented by festive exuberance, and steelband fever swept across a broad social spectrum in the 1950s.

The first college-boy band to make a name for itself was Dixieland, which began as Melody Makers in 1950 in Ernest Ferreira's yard in the Corbeautown area. Curtis Pierre, who became the musical leader of Dixieland, remembers his mother's reaction when he first brought a pan home—her horror at the thought that her French creole son (i.e., a Trinidadian of French ancestry) could be associated with the common rabble.

> I'll never forget it. It was a green and black Casablanca tenor pan. And I was amazed, and I was fascinated by it. . . . So that I took the pan home. Well, my mother didn't see a pan. She saw a symbol of "rabs," as she used to call it. "I don't want you mixing with the rabs—that is not for you." And I said, "You know, everybody is going to like this eventually." She said, "I don't care if the King's son beat pan. . . . I don't want you beating pan." (quoted in Stuempfle 1995: 101–2)

Pierre was not dissuaded, but he and his friends had a hard time making much music out of their instruments at first. All of their pans were tenors (ping pongs), and they didn't know how to play them properly anyway. So they screwed up their courage to ask help from members of the Red Army steelband, which had its yard close by. Dixieland really got started musically when Red Army lent the college boys some more pans, and one of Red Army's members, Alfred "Sack" Mayers, instructed the Dixieland boys (Stuempfle 1995: 102).

Close on the heels of Dixieland, other college-boy bands formed, including Nightingales, Stromboli, Starland, and the most popular of all, Silver Stars. Nicky Inniss, Silver Stars' captain for many years, initially played with Nightingales, but he left in 1951 after the band had a frightening clash with the grass-roots band Rising Sun. Inniss joined a band named Valentinos, which rehearsed in the yard of Ronnie Chan on Picton Street. When the band moved to Woodford Street the next year, it changed its name to Silver Stars. All of Silver Stars' members attended St. Mary's College (secondary school), where they had to conceal their steelband participation at first. Inniss remembers that his parents had no problem with his interest in pan, but some of his teachers threatened expulsion for students who joined steel-bands. Some parents objected strongly to this policy, however, and the excellent academic performance of Silver Stars members made the threat difficult to carry out (personal conversation, 2000). In any case, their teachers' disapproving attitudes soon changed, and Silver Stars was invited to perform at St. Mary's graduation ceremony in the mid-1950s (personal conversation, 1993, with steelband arranger Edwin Pouchet, whose brother, Junior, arranged for Silver Stars in the 1950s and 1960s).

In a short time, Silver Stars tapped into and greatly expanded the middle-class following that Invaders had already begun to cultivate in Woodbrook. Silver Stars' pans were made by Ellie Mannette, and Inniss was especially proud the day Silver Stars drew away some of Invaders' audience and Ellie Mannette himself came to hear what people were so excited about. The band became even more popular when it began to organize spectacular masquerade bands to accompany the steelband on the road. By 1955, Silver Stars counted more than two thousand members, and in 1963 they became the first and only steelband to win the Band of the Year award for best masquerade, with the theme of Gulliver's Travels. This steelband mas' on the road was a thrilling new mode of carnival participation for middle-class people, who had until then played mas' only in more circumscribed venues, such as private masked balls, the Queen's Park Savannah, or occasionally in flatbed trucks that insulated them from the "rabs" on the road.

Silver Stars was popular not just for their mas' but also for their beautiful music, commonly credited to the skill of arranger Junior Pouchet. Pouchet was from Cocorite, just west of Port of Spain, and benefited from musical parents. His father was a parang musician, and his mother, who played violin, was open-minded enough to buy Junior the instrument he so desperately wanted for his thirteenth birthday—an Ellie Mannette tenor pan. Pouchet's parents did not want him associating with Invaders, though, and after first forming a band named Gold Coast in Cocorite, he joined Silver Stars around 1955 (personal conversation with Edwin Pouchet, 1993). Pouchet was an avid fan of classical music, and the introductions and key changes that he sometimes included even in his calypsoes set a new standard for steelband arranging. Some of Silver Stars' most well remembered hits were classical or film songs that Pouchet arranged in dance tempo for the road (which became known in the late 1950s as "Bomb" tunes), including "Salud d'Amor" and "Waltzing Matilda." Nicky Inniss remembers Pouchet especially for his elaborate bass lines, which he composed for the new triple basses that Ellie Mannette had learned to make in TASPO (personal conversation, 2000). Pouchet also became one of the first arrangers to work for more than one steelband, arranging for Tripoli, and even for the fearsome Renegades, who were the antithesis of Silver Stars' college-boy image at that time.

Pouchet's case provides evidence that, just as the college boys were indebted to the grass-roots panmen for instruments and instruction, the grass-roots panmen were indebted to the college boys for certain musical influences. These men from different social backgrounds bonded in the fraternity of the steelband, a bond that is still evident today at functions and social gatherings where veteran panmen gather to commemorate their achievements and renew their camaraderie.[7] At the same time, there were and still are significant tensions between the college boys and the grass-roots panmen. In the 1950s and 1960s, for example, Silver Stars and Dixieland got a disproportionate share of the work playing at private fêtes, and lower-class panmen could see that the steelband's popularity was paying more dividends to middle-class newcomers. The disparity in their fortunes persists even today. Nicky Inniss, for example, lives comfortably in Trinidad as the retired CEO of Fernandes Distillers Ltd., and he proudly points out that many of his Silver Stars comrades have been as successful as he. Many grass-roots panmen, on the other hand, continue to live in poverty. Among the few who have continued to make their living from pan, however, the steelband has been something of a leveler. For example, Ellie Mannette eventually became director of the University Tuning Project at the University of West Virginia in Morgantown (see chap. 3), while Junior Pouchet, from a middle-class family, arranges and performs day in and day out with a steelband at Disney World in Orlando. Thus, although the story of the college-boy bands in the 1950s is riven with issues of class conflict and appropriation, it is also a story of musical enthusiasm that forged genuine bonds of camaraderie and shared fortunes between Trinidadians of very different social backgrounds. This social integration accelerated over the ensuing decades.

Women in Pan

The 1950s also saw the beginning of gender integration in pan, a less visible and less widespread development than the college-boy phenomenon, but one that presaged dramatic changes to come. Because it does not fit neatly with the steelband's masculine image, the participation of women is an aspect of steelband history that has yet to be confronted squarely and fully un-

---

[7] I am thinking here of specific events I attended, including liming in the VIP seats at Panorama, Pan Trinbago functions, an opening function for the Birth of Pan museum exhibit in 1993, an annual lime hosted by Hugh Borde at his home in Belmont, and various other occasions.

derstood.[8] Trinidadians commonly illustrate the steelband's marginalization in the early days by pointing out that no responsible father would have allowed his daughter to associate with a panman, which takes for granted that no woman would play pan herself. On my first trip to Trinidad in 1989, I perceived this lingering prejudice when I heard a bass player in Pandemonium steelband holding forth loudly about the proper place of women, which he said was raising "pickneys" [babies]—this despite the fact that at least a quarter of the players in Pandemonium were female. In 2000, I received another memorable lesson in manliness while playing with Phase II Pan Groove. It was the night before the preliminary round of Panorama, and I and the rest of the band had been waiting in the panyard for more than an hour after rehearsal to receive our jerseys for the competition; I was growing tired of idle banter and wishing for my bed, so I tapped the shoulder of Black Holman, the double seconds section leader, a powerfully built man who bragged that he hit the pan so hard he "played for two," and I asked him if he would be handing out the jerseys soon. To my consternation, Holman wheeled on me angrily, brought his face close to mine, and snarled, "Panyard is a masculine thing—this ain't no girlie thing!" I took this to mean that standing around in the panyard talking with your bandmates at one in the morning is something that sets men apart from women (despite the fact that Phase II's ten or fifteen female band members were waiting for their jerseys, too). In any case, Holman's reaction made an unforgettable impression, and his gendered view of the panyard was not unique. Others communicated to me in more subtle ways that the panyard should be a place for camaraderie between men, unfettered by the domestic obligations (or the need to get up for work in the morning) that women respond to.

Though the panyard was clearly viewed as an inappropriate environment for women in the 1940s and 1950s, there were a handful even then who played alongside the men, and there were others who formed steelbands of their own. The most famously celebrated women in early steelbands, however, were jamettes,[9] women of loose morals and hot tempers who were matrons to a panyard or who waved the flag at the head of a steelband on the road and occasionally even fought. One of the most famous of these is Yvonne "Bubulups" Smith, who waved the flag for Bar 20 in the 1940s. A

[8] A recent series of articles and biographies published on the Panonthenet Web site is the most comprehensive single resource I know of for information on women in pan (http://www.panonthenet.com/woman/2005/index.htm). Another important resource for me has been a senior thesis by one of my undergraduate students, Eiko Nagahama, who did research on women in pan in Trinidad in 2000.

[9] From *diametre*, referring to people who are outside the margins of social acceptability. Depending on context, the term *jamette* may refer to the underclass generally, or specifically to underclass women whose ostentatious behavior in carnival and other public events drew moral disapproval from "respectable" people.

prostitute who was as feared as any man for her fighting ability, Bubulups was immortalized in calypso[10] after she went to jail for knocking a police officer flat (Johnson n.d.: 141). Another Bar 20 flag waver was a vivacious pipe-smoking brothel-keeper named Muriel White, who was older than Bubulups and assumed a more matriarchal relationship to the panmen. Bar 20 rehearsed in front of her house on Bath Street, where she often fed and sheltered the young men and limed with them (Johnson et al. 2002: 152).

These and other jamette women had to transgress conventional morals and gender roles to participate with steelbands, not only because of the violence of steelband culture, but also because of a long history of middle-class efforts to improve carnival and rid it of "bad behavior." For women in the early twentieth century, even participating in the street carnival was likely to be seen as bad behavior. Dating at least from the 1880s, following the Canboulay riots, the debate about how to contain and control carnival featured a disproportionate emphasis on the licentious behavior of women or of men dressed as women (Cowley 1996; Rohlehr 1990: 31). Organized competitions sought to enforce respectable norms of dress and deportment as correctives to these kinds of behavior. Gordon Rohlehr also suggests that the paucity of women in calypso tents throughout much of the twentieth century reflects a middle-class creole concern for respectability and was a departure from earlier carnival practices in which women played an important role as singers (1990: 89–90). Like calypso, the steelband is an art form that many Trinidadians prefer to see as a male domain. This view was nurtured during the colonial era by a concern for making carnival more respectable, and later reinforced by the master narrative's emphasis on confrontation and resistance.

The stories of early female pannists remind us, however, that the steelband movement was driven not just by social pressures but by musical talent and passion. One of these stories is that of Daisy McLean (née James) (fig. 4.2), who began playing pan in 1944 when she was only six years old. Even though her mother forbade her to go in the panyard or to leave the house on carnival day, she began practicing on a three-note ping pong her brother brought home from Casablanca. Recognizing that she had talent, her brother took her one day to play with Casablanca before a gathering of tourists, and the tourists were so taken with the little girl's performance that they showered her with tips. Her brother kept the money, but she didn't care because she so loved playing. Later her brother and some other Casablanca players formed City Syncopators in the Jameses' yard. Daisy sneaked away to

---

[10] I have not found the name of the calypso, but both Stuempfle (1995: 60) and Kim Johnson refer to calypsoes about this incident. Johnson quotes this Kitchener lyric, "Bubulups darling, why you beat the officer? Bubulups darling—six months hard labour" (n.d.: 141, sec. 4).

play with the band for a few hours on carnival days, and she reveled in the attention she attracted on the road. Even with grown men begging her for a turn to play, she never wanted to stop. "I had my own pan, and I would play it whole day. I wouldn't get tired or anything. Yeah, whole day. I didn't have to go for anything either because people giving me a little sweet drink, a little snow cone, chicken, anything. You wouldn't see me, because the amount of people who were around me, just watching me play whole day" (personal conversation, 1993). One day McLean was attending a steelband concert with her parents when someone in the band unexpectedly invited her to play a solo. She played "Somewhere over the Rainbow" and "Indian Love Call" to a standing ovation, after which her parents looked more favorably on her pan playing (Nagahama 2000). In recounting these stories to me in July 1993, McLean downplayed the issue of sexism. "I was accepted," she told me, "I was treated well. If we go somewhere, I would always get the best seat, the best of everything. They would make sure that someone drop me home, this type of thing always, and they show respect." She also insisted that most panmen were, like herself, more interested in making music than in fighting, although she remembered the mischievous delight they took in heckling fearful middle-class masqueraders: "They used to play mas' in truck, you know, they ain't want to come down on the ground with we. Sometimes we used to stone them (well, not me, I playing pan). Pelt orange peel and fig [banana] skin and thing." But McLean's accounts generally evince a passion for music rather than for confrontation, and her story is a reminder of how important music was to steelband musicians generally, and how it created some common ground on which she could participate with men. She also remembers, however, that there were almost no other women like her who played in the established steelbands,[11] and the exceptional nature of her experience is proof that there were significant barriers to the participation of women.

Whereas McLean overcame these barriers with talent, enthusiasm, and good luck (including her brother's and parents' support), it was more common for women to play pan in all-female steelbands where they were free from both violence and gender prejudice. In a sense these were counterparts of the college-boy bands, but there were significant differences. The girls' steelbands did not play for carnival, for one thing, and they also tended to have supervision from adult women with formal musical training. The first all-female steelband was the White Stars, organized in the early 1950s at the Girls' Industrial School, a correctional institution (Stuempfle 1995: 178). Though other all-female steelbands of the 1950s through the 1970s were also

---

[11] Other exceptions were Norma Callendar of Hill 60 in Belmont, and Gemma Worrell of Desperadoes and Savoys (Nagahama 2000: 18).

institutionally based, they were generally composed of middle-class girls. (This means that Daisy McLean's experience was doubly exceptional, since she was from a lower-class neighborhood.)

In 1951, Hazel Henley founded and directed the most famous female steelband, the Girl Pat Steel Orchestra.[12] Henley was a product of the middle-class folklore movement. She had received folk dance instruction at Tranquility Girls School from Umilta McShine, and also danced and played piano at Beryl McBurnie's Little Carib Theatre. Some other members of Girl Pat also participated in folk dance groups, and in general they were daughters of culturally progressive middle-class Woodbrook residents who viewed the steelband as a positive musical opportunity, despite its dangerous social environment. "It was a bad time for steelband at that time," Henley remembers, "because they were behaving so badly, fighting and so on. But I always said, music is music and we love music. So I asked my mother what she thought. She said, 'Yes, you can do it, but you are not going into the panyards, please bring it here. And bring your friends. So I went to my friends and my friends . . . wanted to do it too, their parents let them" (Nagahama 2000: 27).

Girl Pat found a niche playing for a variety of social and cultural events, including Beryl McBurnie's shows at the Little Carib and folkloric performances by Olive Walke's group, La Petite Musical. They also played for government functions, fundraisers such as the Red Cross ball, and concerts at the Roxy Theatre. With the help of manager Bruce Procope, Girl Pat even toured abroad, performing in Guyana in 1951 and with Beryl McBurnie in Jamaica in 1952. Girl Pat played a wide variety of music and became known especially for their steelband renditions of the Castillian, a genteel society dance from Venezuela with a waltz rhythm. Most members of Girl Pat played piano and read music, and many contributed in some degree to the band's arrangements. This musical expertise gave Girl Pat a certain advantage, and also made middle-class girls in general useful to the male steelbands as adjudicators, arrangers, and coaches.

Women served as adjudicators at the Music Festival from early on, and Umilta McShine composed some steelband test pieces for the festival (Nagahama 2000: 22). Girl Pat alumna Jocelyne Pierre, who served as a steelband adjudicator for the festival and later for Panorama, was invited by the Invaders to arrange "In a Monastery Garden" for the 1960 Music Festival, and the band won second place (Tarradath 1991: 382). Other women have since been called upon for help with preparation of classical music arrangements for the festival. Notable among these is Pat Bishop (another product of Tranquility Girls School, as well as of Bishop Anstey High School for

---

[12] The band's name was taken from a yacht (Nagahama 2000).

girls), who studied music and art in England in the 1960s and returned to Trinidad to take a leading role as a choir director and arts advocate from the 1960s on. During the 1980s, she took on a high profile in the steelband world as coach and arranger for the Desperadoes in a variety of classical music performance venues, and she has since been in demand as a coach for numerous steelbands, both in the festival and Panorama. As director of the Lydian Singers, Bishop also developed a steel orchestra to accompany her choral performances.[13] In the modern era, when so many women participate in steelbands, Bishop's high profile may be taken for granted by some, but her directing role (as opposed to playing) points to important differences that existed in her generation between the musical opportunities for boys and girls.

These differences are also illustrated in the story of Merle Albino de Coteau. Albino de Coteau grew up in Laventille in a musical family, and both she and her brother began piano lessons at an early age. Her brother soon gave up formal instruction to play pan with Savoys steelband, an option not open to her. As a girl in the late 1950s, Merle was not permitted to play pan, and the pressure to stick to respectable music only increased when she began playing the organ in church at age 13. She was fascinated, though, by the music she heard from her brother's steelband and on the radio, and she learned it on her own. When she won a music competition at her school, playing a film song called "The Night Has a Thousand Eyes," she was rebuked by a nun who whispered, even as she handed Merle her prize, "You never played the right thing." Her piano teacher also tried to discourage her popular music tastes and to mitigate the influence of her brother, who helped her learn popular songs by ear. As Albino de Coteau explains it, "He was not reading something. She said to him, 'Don't show that to [Merle] at all,' because she didn't want to spoil my technique" (personal conversation, 1993). Thus Merle was initially denied the opportunities her brother had to learn pan and explore popular music freely. The boys eventually recognized her reading ability and musical knowledge as an asset, however, and they recruited her to arrange classical music and Bomb tunes (classics in calypso style) for Savoys in the mid-1960s. Merle Albino de Coteau went on to become the first woman to arrange for a steelband in the Panorama competition, in 1972, and she subsequently became a regular adjudicator for Panorama.

Women have thus been involved in steelbands from its inception, as jamette consorts, flag wavers, matrons, players, arrangers, coaches, and judges. Middle-class women played an important role in introducing steelband in-

---

[13] Much of this information is included in Pat Bishop's curriculum vitae, which is posted at http://www.panonthenet.com/woman/2005/pbbio.htm.

Fig. 4.2. Gathering of steelband pioneers and friends in 1993. Front row, from left: Daisy McLean, Henry "Patcheye" Pachot, Merle Albino de Coteau, author Earl Lovelace, steelband historian Felix Blake. Back row, from left: Ethnomusicologist Mervyn Williams, David "Little Sweet" Edwards, Andrew "Pan" de la Bastide, Carleton "Zigilee" Constantine, Ossie Campbell, Calypso Princess Hendrickson-Campbell, Pan Trinbago officer Keith Diaz.

struction in schools, which in turn opened the way for greater female participation in established steelbands to the point where some steelbands in Trinidad today have as many women members as men. The notion of the steelband as a male domain persists, but it competes with the reality of extensive female participation, and with what one might call the modern domestication of pan (to which I return in chap. 11).

SUMMARY: NATIONALIST IDEOLOGY VERSUS PEOPLE'S CULTURE

The steel pan became an increasingly compelling symbol of the Trinidadian nation during the 1950s (as witnessed, for example, in its pervasive iconography, figs. 4.3–4.5). This national identification with the steel pan was stimulated by the foreign recognition achieved by TASPO and other bands, and also by middle-class participation at home. As its symbolic importance increased, however, so did efforts to control the emergent art form. Middle-

Fig. 4.3. Original logo of the state-owned British West Indies Airline.

Fig. 4.4. Advertisers like to associate their products with the popular image of the steel pan, as seen in the design of this condensed milk can.

class intellectuals touted the panmen's creativity, but felt responsible for guiding and framing steelband performance in ways that would enhance the image of indigenous culture in Trinidad and abroad. The pride they took in the steelband's rebellious vitality, and the new pleasures they discovered participating in steelband performances, went hand in hand with a sense of embarrassment about the prospect of uneducated panmen representing them to the rest of the world. As a result, many middle-class advocates for the steelband were concerned not only to preserve the indigenous reper-

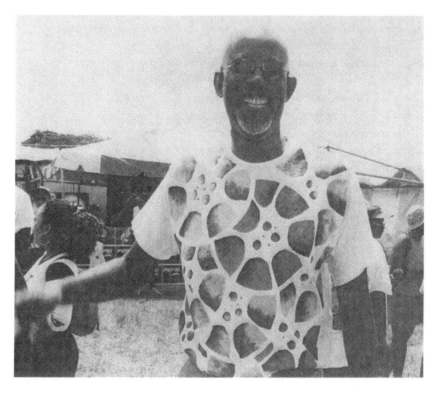

Fig. 4.5. This Panorama fan sports a shirt with a steel pan motif.

toires of the steelband, but also to preserve a distinction between festivity and art.

In this perspective, the efforts panmen made to learn classical music and other repertoires were more than a capitulation to hegemonic pressure. They were also a way to resist the limitations that nationalists imposed on them—a way to resist the notion, that is, that they were good only for festive entertainment. By learning foreign repertoires and adapting European techniques and aesthetics to the steel pan, the panmen claimed control of their instrument and guided its development for themselves. Although this idea is paradoxical, it is a key to understanding the panmen's agency—an agency that is evident not only in the ways they challenged European hegemony, but also in the ways they actively incorporated and reconfigured European cultural practices for their own benefit.

Simple oppositions between resistance and assimilation are also complicated by the new affinities that the steelband forged, beginning in the 1950s, between people whose identities had previously been quite separate. The more people from diverse backgrounds participated together in steelband performances, the less easy it became to predict aesthetic preferences by distinctions of class, race, or gender. Whereas it would be a great mistake to ignore those social distinctions, it would also be a mistake to treat them as reliable predictors of the musical or political opinions held by any given individual. Indeed, as more individuals found themselves shoulder to shoulder with people from other neighborhoods and communities, in steelbands and in the streets, their aesthetic affinities created new social bonds that competed with or even redefined older social categories—bank tellers and day laborers could make common cause beating pan together in a steelband.

With these considerations in mind, we are ready to consider a defining moment in the history of the steelband. The years before and after Trinidad achieved independence in 1962 saw an intense contest over steelband repertoire and venue. Arguments in this contest, made in the language of colonialism and nationalism, depicted it as a struggle between European and indigenous Trinidadian cultural models, focusing particularly on the question of whether steelbands should play European classical music at carnival time. At a deeper level, however, it was a struggle to balance the competing priorities of elite ideology (which valued indigenous calypso) versus people's culture (which valued festive engagement and poking fun at the elite) in articulating the character of the new nation.

5

Dropping the Bomb

What we want is the Trinidad image . . . the projecting of our own culture[,]
not someone's else's. If we are going to achieve a higher level musically, the basic
raw material should be our folklore.

Trinidadian folklorist J. D. Elder (quoted in Rouse 1966)

At the time of Trinidad's independence from England, the most popular
and hotly contested carnival performance venue for steelbands was the
"Bomb," in which steelbands played arrangements of foreign repertoires
performed in calypso style. Especially popular were carnival arrangements
of European classical music. The projection of such colonial icons by the
national instrument at the national festival brought together highly charged
and seemingly incongruous symbols, and contributed to heated debates
about the national culture that persist in important ways up to the present.
This chapter outlines contrasting interpretations of the Bomb to analyze the
aesthetics of the steelband's diverse constituents and to sort out some differences between musical thinking and political thinking.

Many arguments about the Bomb focused on the *meaning* of music, and
to understand musical meaning one must focus on the act of interpretation
(Feld 1994: 79). When a steelband plays a Beethoven minuet, that is, Trinidadians will interpret its meaning differently than English or German listeners might. Indeed, different Trinidadians interpret it differently. Despite
the uniqueness of each listener's interpretation, however, meaning is also
socially constructed, and we can identify certain broad interpretive tenden-
cies or possibilities that influenced the way individuals ascribed meaning to

the Bomb in 1960s Trinidad. I will refer to such possibilities here as "interpretive stances." This term acknowledges, for one thing, that any given statement about music can be understood as a stance taken in relation to particular problems and arguments, and may not represent the full complexity of an individual's thinking and feeling. The concept of interpretive stance also gives me a way of acknowledging certain solidarities of upbringing and ideology, while at the same time allowing that opinions about music are not reducible to social class. In carnival music, where participation and collective performance are the norm, people of different classes often enjoy dancing to the same music, and affective affinities bridge social and ideological divides. The Bomb was thus experienced and understood not only in relation to political debates or social class, but also in relation to shared sensibilities of style, movement, and pleasure.

PERFORMING THE BOMB

The steelband most famous for its Bomb tunes is the Trinidad All Stars. Neville Jules remembers how All Stars' rivalry with Invaders led All Stars to develop elaborate rituals of preparation and public confrontation.

> In the late '40s, [Invaders] would leave Woodbrook, and they would come into the city, and when they leave, it is everybody from the city going back into Woodbrook, you know, following the band, enjoying the music, you know. At that time, our band was at Charlotte Street in the heart of the city. So we just figure, look man, we got to do something about this. We want to have at least a little piece of what they having, you know. So we would try to arrange or play our music so that the people could compare our music with theirs. As a matter of fact, it went on that way until we used to be sending out scouts, like come carnival time we would have guys from the Green corner of Park Street on the lookout where Invaders are after they leave Woodbrook and they come into the city. So we can meet them on the streets and play together with them so that the public would see, hear, and judge the music. . . .
>
> And it went on like that for a couple of years, and then I decided well, you know what, I am going to surprise them. I am going to learn something, play something that they don't hear, even the public wouldn't hear. And we started rehearsing secretly at night. . . . The first tune was a tune named "Skokian." That was one of the first tunes that we did with that. And from there on it went on like that. And I guess it catch on because all the other bands, you know, because at that time too, we started to get popular. And the Bomb tune that we playing, the other bands start to see if they can outdo us

also. But at that time the name wasn't Bomb, you know, because it was just we playing any song that we would like to play in the calypso flavor. But . . . the supporters of different steelbands would meet at times in the street and they would argue who was the better band and whatnot. One of our players told a guy, "Wait until J'ouvert morning when we drop the bomb." So there is where the Bomb talk comes into being. (personal conversation, 1999)

A turning point in this competitive tradition came when All Stars was unexpectedly bested by another West band, Crossfire. One of the top steelbands in St. James, Crossfire was an offshoot of Tripoli steelband and was led by tuner Emon Thorpe. In 1957, they licked up the competition in town with an arrangement of the film song "Another Night Like This," catching All Stars off guard in front of a big crowd and sending them off humiliated. Jules resolved that the following year All Stars would avenge this defeat with something extraordinary. The piece he chose to arrange was Beethoven's Minuet in G, which the band rehearsed while touring in Guyana. In the 1958 carnival, All Stars surprised Crossfire with a rendition of the popular piano composition in calypso rhythm: "In the morning we sent our scouts out, and we heard [Crossfire] were coming down on Frederick Street. We caught them on the corner of Frederick Street and Duke Street, and we were playing Minuet in G, and there was no more talk about Crossfire again" (personal conversation, 1999).

Minuet in G created a precedent for the competitive performance of classics on J'ouvert morning, and fueled a passionate ritual of musical rivalry. Bomb tunes were rehearsed in secrecy so as to enhance their impact when they were unveiled on the streets in the early hours of J'ouvert Monday morning (the opening event of Trinidad carnival). All Stars, for example, rehearsed their Bombs in the attic of a downtown building, using pencil erasers instead of normal sticks to make the music quieter. The most intense rivalry in the Bomb was between bands from the East of Port of Spain (especially All Stars from downtown and Hilanders from Laventille) and bands from the West (especially Invaders and Starlift, both from Woodbrook). On J'ouvert morning, spectators anticipated the showdown eagerly, lining Park, Charlotte, and Frederick Streets and Marine Square in the wee hours to see the steelbands pass. Winners were judged informally by these crowds; Neville Jules remembers that "you would know how well you playing by the talk of the people listening" (personal conversation, 1999). Starlift arranger Ray Holman also remembers the influential commentary of big dock workers with loud voices whom he called "the pundits of pan" (1999). Sometimes the panmen could tell right away when they had been beaten, as Starlift member Eddie Odingi recounted (see appendix II for identification of these and other musical titles):

I remember in 1961 when we came up with "Ave Maria," All Stars stopped
and listened to us. Rain was falling. We played "Ave Maria," and we felt good
because the great All Stars had stopped and listened to us. And then we
stopped to listen to them, and they dropped Muzetta Waltz, and they followed that with Anniversary Waltz. In quick succession, they dropped
them—one, and then two that morning. I went home in tears. The following
year when we played Dance of the Hours and Hallelujah chorus they ran.
That was '62—they ran, boy! Then I felt good. (personal conversation, 1993)

The repertoire of the Bomb consisted of foreign tunes, most often classics. Although foreign in origin, the tunes panmen chose to arrange for the
Bomb tended to be well known in their communities. Even lower-class
Trinidadians had significant exposure to classical music through Sunday
radio programs, steelband performances at the biannual Music Festival, and
other venues. They heard foreign popular music, like Perez Prado's mambos, on the radio, and enjoyed American film songs and soundtracks in
movie theaters.

What distinguished the Bomb, though, from other steelband performances of the classics was that it was arranged in calypso rhythm; or, more
precisely, in the style of a steelband "road march," suited to the processions
of dancing masqueraders.[1] Figure 5.1, for example, shows my transcription
of Minuet in G based on the RCA single that the Trinidad All Stars recorded
in 1958. In contrast to the Beethoven original, the melodic phrasing is transformed to fit a duple meter, and the pianist's left hand is replaced with walking bass and strummed chords. Though not fully realized on the recording,
the street performance would also have featured accompaniment by the
steelband's usual battery of interlocking irons (vehicle brake drums struck
with bolts) and *shac shacs* (maracas).

After the initial "dropping" of the Bomb on J'ouvert morning, rivalry
generally gave way to revelry. During most of the Monday and Tuesday carnival celebrations, steelband supporters danced to the strains of Beethoven, Mozart, and Handel, as well as calypsoes by the Mighty Sparrow and

[1]Calypso bands, with string and wind instruments, have always conformed to some of the same
basic carnival dance sensibilities as the steelbands, but calypso is also performed for seated audiences in the "tents." Steelband music features some rhythmic conventions (strumming and iron
patterns, for example) as well as voicing and arranging techniques, that are not necessarily found
in calypso bands, and vice versa. This is an important distinction to keep in mind in relation to
claims that calypso is carnival music and is therefore the "natural" repertoire of the steelband. In
historical perspective, calypso is only one of several kinds of carnival music, including styles that
are specific to particular masquerade characters and their dances. Some steelband musical conventions are unique to the idiom, others can be traced to a variety of Trinidadian sources (Stuempfle
1995: 32–44), and many, as I argued in chapter 2, are innovative interpretations of African musical
principles that predate both calypso and steelband.

(a) All Stars

(b) Beethoven's piano score

Fig. 5.1. Minuet in G.

Lord Kitchener, mambos by Perez Prado, and popular songs from film and radio—all rendered in a consistent carnival rhythmic feel by the steel pans, irons, and other percussion. The revelers' exclamations and the rhythmic "chip, chip, chip"[2] of hundreds of leather soles on pavement joined with the music as steelbands wound their way through the city. The diverse "foreign" repertoire of the Bomb was thus rendered in a distinctively Trinidadian style that expressed itself in sound, performance, and participation.

[2] This sound is remembered fondly by older steelband musicians as an integral part of the music, and provides the name for a typical style of Trinidad carnival dancing, called "chipping." It can be heard on some of the recordings made by Emory Cook in the streets of Port of Spain in 1956 (1994).

Former Starlift member Eddie Odingi remembers the late 1950s and early 1960s, when the Bomb was at its peak of popularity, as "the best time in my life. We used to look forward to it. All steelbandsmen used to look forward to this Bomb" (1993).

CALYPSO NATIONALISM

In counterpoint to the panmen's enthusiasm for the Bomb, an intellectual discourse on the importance of calypso intensified in the 1950s and 60s, partly in reaction to the steelbands' penchant for playing foreign tunes. In this discourse, European art music was portrayed both as a model and as a problem for the development of Trinidadian culture, reflecting the more general colonial dilemma of reconciling cosmopolitan ambitions with pride in local culture. As discussed in the previous chapter, Espinet and Pitts's 1944 study promoted the calypso as Trinidadian heritage music[3] while simultaneously advocating for its improvement. Trinidadian writer, political activist, and pan-Africanist C. L. R. James, who also viewed Caribbean culture as relatively immature compared to European culture (see chap. 1), nonetheless celebrated the potential of calypso, writing in 1959 that, "when our local dramatists and artists can evoke the popular response of a Sparrow,[4] the artists in the Caribbean will have arrived" (1977: 188). Thus in the years leading up to independence, Trinidadians generally were concerned that their indigenous musical forms should not only be valued, but should develop and improve—priorities that were potentially contradictory.

Although the steelband's progress had gone hand in hand with the mastery of diverse repertoires, many intellectuals at the time of independence (not to mention many calypsonians) expressed concern that their national instrument should play their national music, at least at carnival time. Steelband musicians were criticized for abandoning calypso in their pursuit of progress. Debates on this topic began as early as 1955, when the five most popular steelband choices turned out *not* to be calypsoes, and "the preference of the public (or the musicians) for foreign melodies was the subject of much commentary after carnival" (Rohlehr 1990: 437). One explanation for this problem was that calypso offered little musical challenge for the steel-

[3] The concept of "heritage music" is discussed at length by Barbara Kirshenblatt Gimblett (2002), who uses it in relation to the folk revival movements of the 1960s and 1970s in the United States, and in particular to the institutionalization of folk culture as heritage that was made possible by government funding during this time. With regard both to ideological and institutional promotion, the term is useful to describe the status of calypso in Trinidad and Tobago.

[4] The Mighty Sparrow (Slinger Francisco), whose extraordinary popularity and longevity began in 1956 with the song "Jean and Dinah," is still viewed by many as Trinidad's greatest calypsonian.

bands (see chap. 10), but efforts to solve the problem eventually focused less on changing calypso and more on pressuring steelbands to play it.

In a panel discussion on the topic of steelbands and classical music in 1966, for example, folklorist J. D. Elder urged: "By all means play the classics, but what we want is the Trinidad image . . . the projecting of our own culture[,] not someone's else's. If we are going to achieve a higher level musically, the basic raw material should be our folklore" (Rouse 1966). Pressure on the steelbands to play calypso had its most significant expression in the creation of a new competition called Panorama in 1963 that required steelbands to play calypsoes. Panorama eventually became the most important venue for steelbands, while the Bomb, though it never completely died out, ceased to inspire the steelband musicians' best efforts and lost its hold on the public imagination. The Bomb's decline and Panorama's ascendance can be explained by a variety of factors that will be explored in later chapters, but ideological arguments about the Bomb fundamentally shaped the institution of Panorama, and influenced the steelband at a pivotal moment in its history. Any analysis of the modern steelband in Trinidad must therefore take into account the meanings Trinidadians attached to steelband performances of classical and calypso repertoires in the 1960s.

INTERPRETING THE BOMB

Sophistication

The easiest interpretive stance to identify in published accounts and opinions during the 1960s was a tendency to dismiss the Bomb as a pitch for status and sophistication, a view closely related to the "calypso nationalism" described above. Leaving aside for the moment the question of whether such ambitions were unseemly, it is clear that the cultural status of a work was an important consideration for its selection as a Bomb tune—that Beethoven's compositions offered more cultural firepower, so to speak, than those of local calypsonians. Beyond the need to vanquish rival steelbands, mastery of European art music (and "recognized" tunes generally) had from the start been one of the most effective ways for steelbandsmen to enhance their reputations in Trinidadian society. Because steelband musicians took pride in their musical sophistication, the suggestion that they should concentrate on calypso was not always welcome, and was seen by many as an attempt to cast them in the role of rustic folkloric musicians. Therefore, in response to J. D. Elder's exhortation (cited above) to project "our own culture[,] not someone's else's," Pan Am North Stars' leader Anthony Williams argued that the panmen still needed to expand their musical abilities:

By interpreting the classics the steelband achieved many things. . . . We began
to get ideas in modulations. . . . The classics play an important part in steelband development. Right now we are not mature enough to experiment in
folklore, which is limited and simple. It is a case then of going to the masters
to acquire knowledge, not so much a case of rejecting our own, which, like
I said, offers no challenge. In time, we should be able to come back to our
folklore and do a good job on it. (quoted in Rouse 1966)

In the view of nationalists, however, such comparisons between calypso
and classical music seemed to privilege European ideals of harmonic, melodic, and formal complexity over musical strengths that one might associate with carnival musicians and calypsonians (such as rhythm, phrasing, or
wordplay), devaluing Trinidad's indigenous music. Opposition to the steelbands' eclectic carnival repertoire was led in the press by Pete Simon, a journalist, musician, and cultural activist. Simon resented the intrusion of classical music into what he felt should be a celebration of local culture: "Isn't this
preference for the classics by steelbandsmen during this tempo-setting period of our National Festival a clearcut attempt to downgrade the calypso? To
relegate it to second choice? To give it an inferior place?" (Simon 1970). While
taking care to praise the art form and the musicians, Simon suggested that
panmen were being manipulated by competition promoters, and he noted
that "semi-classical" melodies such as Minuet in G that were "recognisable
and singable" had given way in the late '60s to more obscure works whose
only virtue was their supposed musical sophistication: "The titles of the
bombs tell the story of snob appeal and the names of the composers are cast
in the same mould. One is not surprised to hear of "The Seventh Movement
of the Sixth Concerto" by Janislav Bumbumkoski, or "The Last Overture of
the Twelfth Opus" by Igor Ronskoopoofpoof!" (Simon 1969).

Echoing Simon's disgust, an "ex-J'Ouvert fan" wrote to the *Guardian*
newspaper complaining that steelbands were pursuing a musical agenda
that was antithetical to the spirit of the occasion:

The past two years were a miserable experience, longing for the band to
play a calypso and all they play are these classical pieces, leaving the crowd
to walk away thoroughly disgusted and dissatisfied. This is all well and good
for Queen's Hall at the Steelband Festival which I would sit for hours and
thoroughly enjoy, but definitely not on J'Ouvert morning, dressed up in old
clothes and the spirit set for the beginning of "The Carnival Bacchanal," only
to have a great disappointment. It amounts to a Ball with a Mantovani orchestra and the guests waltzing in jeans and hot shirts. (Feb. 8, 1969)

This attitude about the appropriate time and place for the performance
of the classics, expressed frequently in public debates about the Bomb in the

1960s, suggests that opponents of the Bomb did not disapprove of the performance of classical music per se. Simon and others supported and enjoyed local efforts to render the works of European composers, but they felt a need to separate the musical experiences of the concert hall and carnival. "We feel ten feet tall, and rightly so," wrote Simon, "to boast that our panmen can play anything from Calypso to Chopin, but it must here be emphasized that where the Great Masters are concerned, the elements of Time and Place must be the determining factors" (1969). In the previous chapter, I suggested that some middle-class nationalists were uncomfortable with the panmen's ambitions to be considered "artists." Debates about the Bomb demonstrate, furthermore, how such intellectuals were invested in their own identification with the "folk," and wanted, therefore, to keep carnival free of any reminders of their elite European heritage. The preservation of carnival as a domain of cultural expression that was ostensibly indigenous and off-limits to the encroachment of European "high art" thus helped educated Trinidadians to reconcile their cosmopolitan cultural identity with their sense of national pride.

While it may be true, then, that panmen dropped the Bomb partly to prove themselves by colonial cultural standards, middle-class nationalists who opposed the Bomb were burdened in their own way by the same dilemma of European cultural domination. Raymond Williams notes that this dilemma is a fundamental dynamic of hegemony and warns that "it would be wrong to overlook the importance of works and ideas which, while clearly affected by hegemonic limits and pressures, are at least in part significant breaks beyond them" (1977: 114). This caution is underscored in many ethnomusicological explorations of the interface between "traditional" or "local" music systems and "Western music" (e.g., Nettl 1985; Guilbault 1993; Barber and Waterman 1995) which demonstrate how Western forms are given new meanings, or made to serve local aesthetics and values. Indeed, if we take Pete Simon's judgment with a grain of salt and look more closely at the experiences of the people involved, we can find evidence that lends itself to more empowering and positive interpretations of the Bomb.

Resignification

In contrast to Pete Simon's view of the Bomb as a capitulation to colonial values, it could be argued that the Bomb was consistent with a broader practice in Trinidad carnival by which symbols of colonial power were either mocked or appropriated for the empowerment of the performers. This second interpretive stance is one that I have not seen taken explicitly in relation to the Bomb, but it has been used to explain the significance of other carni-

val arts or of carnival in general, and is especially popular in academic discourse. Many scholars have characterized carnival as an occasion for invert-
ing the normal order of things and of subjugating symbols of power and social respectability to the pleasures of the vulgar masses (e.g., Bakhtin 1984;
DaMatta 1991; Kertzer 1988). The Bomb appears in some ways to be a particularly vivid validation of this theoretical interpretation: the work of a
revered European composer is removed from the concert hall and wedded
to the kinds of instrumentation, dancing, and licentious behavior that are
commonly viewed as antithetical to the values of the classical music concert.

The popularity of the Bomb among the general public also suggests to
me that the thrill of this resignification had some resonance beyond intellectual circles. In contrast to the irritation of the "ex-J'Ouvert fan quoted
above, the following excerpt from a 1964 newspaper article by Austin Simmonds titled "Calypsoes versus Classics" paints a picture of enthusiastic
public reception for the Bomb. Simmonds attacks attempts by "purists" to
enforce the performance of traditional ("old minor") calypsoes through
formally judged competitions, and he implies a social distinction between
the middle- /upper-class venue of the Queen's Park Savannah and the
"people's" carnival downtown (Frederick Street or Independence Square).

> Nothing but "indigenous melodies" are judged at Carnival competitions.
> Do these judges ever leave the judging arenas, where the entire audience is
> seated and bored stiff after the first two hours, and travel along the streets?
> If they do, they will be able to judge for themselves what makes Jack jump.
> Travel along Frederick Street or Independence Square on Monday morning,
> and listen to what the bands are playing before they arrive at the Grand
> Stand where the judges sit. Look at the faces of the throng of paraders and
> spectators. Those who line the pavements cannot stand still. There is a great
> difference between these spectators and those who sit at three o'clock in the
> Grand Stand at the Savannah. The "Minor-key" no longer establishes rap-
> port with those who have come to participate in the enjoyment. Casablanca
> did it long ago with "Bells of St. Mary's." Ebonites set the town ablaze with
> "Roses From the South," Dixieland brought down the house at Queen's Hall
> with "Estudiantina"; North Stars did it with "Voices of Spring." Listen for
> Silver Stars with "Elizabethan Serenade" this year. This is the pattern.
> (Simmonds 1964)

Simmonds clouds the issue slightly by conflating Queen's Hall concerts
("Estudiantina," "Voices of Spring") with Bomb tunes performed on the
streets, but his contention that the Bomb was "what made Jack jump" on
J'Ouvert morning is consistent with oral accounts I have heard. Unlike Pete
Simon, then, who felt that the classics were out of place in carnival, many

Trinidadians found the Bomb to be delightfully consistent with their conception of carnival festivity.

Many scholars have promoted the idea that such festive enjoyment is rooted in Trinidad carnival's historical role as a venue for protest. This perspective is announced unequivocally in the titles of works like Hollis Liverpool's *Rituals of Power and Rebellion: The Carnival Tradition in Trinidad and Tobago* (2001), or Ana Maria Alonso's "Men in 'Rags' and the Devil on the Throne: A Study of Protest and Inversion in the Carnival of Post-Emancipation Trinidad" (1990). Given this view of carnival generally, the Bomb could reasonably be interpreted as a form of resistance to colonial authority, an act of transgression, a defilement of dominant cultural icons. For example, Pete Simon (exemplifying once again the conflicting impulses of local and cosmopolitan cultural identification, and the situational nature of interpretation) accused the steelband of defiling the great works of the European "masters," arguing that the appropriate setting for classical music was the Music Festival rather than "a bawdy, loud, raucous, shouting, giggling, cavorting, hippie-minded, oil-drenched band of revellers in different stages of ridiculous undress and various degrees of drunkenness, throwing decorum and conventionalities to the wind. Is this the setting for listening to the Masters? This is nothing short of sacrilege" (1969). For steelband musicians and their supporters, criticisms like this only increased their zest for flouting the conventions of high culture. This perverse delight in defying decorum is a thread that runs through all the carnival arts, expressing itself in calypso and masquerade as well as in steelband music.

Perhaps the most pervasive symbol of this kind of defiance in Trinidad carnival is the character of the devil, which takes many different forms. Calypsonian and historian Hollis Liverpool suggests that the devil masquerade was a way for black people to mock white authority by embodying negative characterizations of the black race (2001: 263–64), a psychology that could be applied to the Bomb as well. Mitto Sampson's account of an 1870s stick-fighting song, *Djab sé y ô neg, Mê Dié sé nom-la blâ* ("The Devil Is a Negro, but God Is a White Man"), shows that identification with the devil was a way to convert derogatory stereotypes into attributes of power. The stick-fighters "came to feel that since God is a white man and the devil is a negro every negro has that devilish ferocious quality in him, and it whipped them up" (Pearse 1956: 257). Whether by coating themselves with black oil, behaving lewdly, clashing violently with rival bands, or terrorizing middle-class people in the streets, Trinidad carnival performers through the years have embraced images of evil and mayhem.

It is important to note, though, that these "devils" were engaged not only in defiance and mockery, but also in a symbolic appropriation of power. The appropriation of attributes of high status by people of low status certainly defied the notion of European superiority, but it did not necessarily defile the icons of European power. Through the practice of the Bomb, for example, musicians and supporters gained satisfaction not from deriding the authority of classical music, but from wielding this authority themselves. The cultural power or weight of classical music is acknowledged in the phrase "dropping the Bomb." And since they get to do the dropping for a change, this Bomb gives people a sense of exhilaration rather than oppression. A similar kind of appropriation can be seen in the carnival character called the Book Man. The Book Man, with goatee and horns, armed only with a feather quill and a book titled "The Golden Rule" on one cover and "The Royal Law" on the other, confronts a fearsome dragon on the street. While the Book Man writes with devilish glee, the Dragon writhes in agony (fig. 5.2). Onlookers to this drama must have some empathy for the hapless dragon, struggling in the web of the Englishman's law, and the Book Man's white face seems to cast the Englishman as the devil. On the other hand, people can also identify with the devilish Book Man and vicariously experience the thrill of usurping the oppressor's role.

Like classical music or legal erudition, another important symbol of power in colonial Trinidad was the English language, and the use of English in calypso is also an important part of the carnival tradition of appropriating symbols of power. Soon after 1900, English, the language of the colonial

Fig. 5.2. The dragon is subdued by the Book Man's furious writing, in a volume titled "The Golden Rule" on one cover and "The Royal Law" on the other (1993).

administrators and the educated, replaced French *patois* in carnival songs. This happened as chantwels (the singers for neighborhood bands, who were often stickfighters as well) began to perform for paying audiences in tents, where they became known as "calypsonians." The use of extremely florid English by calypsonians was a weapon with which they cowed rivals and boosted their prestige, as illustrated below in the lyrics to "Iron Duke in the Land," sung by Julian Whiterose in 1914. Whiterose was one of those calypsonians who made the transition from chantwel to tent singer, and he spices his lyrics with the patois boasts of the stickfighter:

> At my appearance upon the scene
> Julius the devil play the Chord
> And still I am the head of fraternal order
> Calling, sweeping to all the agony
> Achieving my surprising majesty
> In blending, beaming and swaying
> Jumping this way, bawling, "Clear de way, Whiterose *joli*
> *Djable ré-ré'o*" [Handsome Whiterose the devil king]
> (transcription from *Calypso Pioneers*, Dick Spottswood and Donald Hill,
>   producers, 1989)

It is significant that Whiterose's English is *not* entirely "correct," or even entirely English. Just as classical music was modified in the Bomb, literate-sounding English had to remain subservient to an established complex of calypso aesthetics (which includes devilishness). This is implied in politician and cultural activist Albert Gomes's mild criticism of Attila the Hun, made in the 1930s (Atilla, aka Raymond Quevedo, was an educated calypsonian who insisted on proper English):

> The ideal Calypso, to my mind, would be one combining the bawdiness of
> the Lion with the wit and intelligence of Atilla, whose only fault is that his
> compositions are apt to become too tendentious. In spite of my political sen-
> timents, I should not like to see the Calypso a mere propagandist form of ex-
> pression. It is essential—very essential indeed that it retain its swing, and its
> sly, sensuous humour, qualities with which songsters like the Lion are pri-
> marily concerned. (*Trinidad Guardian*, Jan. 29, 193?, cited in Rohlehr: 332)[5]

The calypso, then, like the Book Man masquerade or the steelband Bomb tune, may evoke symbols of colonial power to bolster the performer's au-

---

[5] Because of a typographical error, the date of this citation is missing in Rohlehr.

thority, but it privileges a local carnival aesthetic. And in Trinidad, an important part of the carnival aesthetic *is* the resignification of establishment icons and the defiance of colonial authority.

To view the Bomb in terms of resistance is still problematic, however, because accounts of the Bomb's reception give little evidence that the classics' cultural authority was being subverted. An instructive example is the performance of Handel's *Messiah* at carnival, which was done by Hilanders and some other bands in the early 1960s. These steelbands were sharply criticized by citizens who objected to the spectacle of such explicitly sacred music being profaned by performance during carnival. Panmen reacted by playing other movements of the *Messiah* the following year, but their defiance in persisting seemed directed more at their prudish detractors than at Handel, or the *Messiah,* or the cultural values it represented. The music of Handel's *Messiah*, and the classics generally, continued to be admired and appreciated by steelband musicians. Therefore, if the popularity of the Bomb did derive to any significant extent from redefining the authority of elite cultural icons, it probably had more to do (at least from the musicians' perspective) with the chance to identify with symbols of power than a desire to mock them. The thrill of wielding Beethoven's cultural authority is suggested in Neville Jules's account of All Stars' feud with Crossfire; and, in general, the association of the Bomb with interband rivalry and belligerence suggests that the classics retained their power to intimidate in these carnival performances.

Aesthetic Pleasure

Despite the classics' elevated cultural status, however, Bomb performances meant much more to their participants than status or intimidation, and the interpretive stance most frequently taken by steelband musicians is primarily aesthetic—focusing, that is, on the relative beauty, value, or appropriateness of different compositions and arrangements. By naming it "the Bomb," by rearranging its sound, and by dancing to it, Trinidadians claimed European art music as a repertoire that they could enjoy in their own distinctive way, as an experience of pleasure, and as a thing for aesthetic contemplation. Some contemporary scholarship debunks the aesthetic as a concept that, while cloaking itself in the innocent guise of personal sensibility is in fact a socially constructed ideology that is implicated in the maintenance of order and authority (Eagleton 1990; Said 1993). The depiction of large-scale musical forms like sonata form, for example, as being more intellectually interesting than cyclic call-and-response forms may be implicated in a larger

argument for the intellectual superiority of Europeans over Africans.[6] Terry
Eagleton notes, however, that the aesthetic is "radically double-edged" because its glorification of individual sensibility can easily generate resistance
to conformity (1990: 9). In the case of Trinidad carnival, I have argued that
performances may be understood both as negotiations of social status and
as satire or projection of personal power, suggesting that aesthetic judgments about classical music do indeed cut both ways—valuing both accommodation *and* resistance to dominant norms.

This kind of analysis can sound pretentious, though, to people who care
about the music and who would not agree that their aesthetic judgments
can be reduced to mere political opinions. Indeed, the fact that ideology
and affect are entangled with one another in every aesthetic judgment does
not mean that ideology and affect are the same. Eagleton reminds us that
the term "aesthetics" was originally applied not just to art but to "the whole
region of human perception and sensation, in contrast to the more rarefied
domain of conceptual thought" (1990: 13); and if we insist upon this affective dimension of the term (as many of us still do), we can talk about how
aesthetic judgments relate to emotion, movement, and an experience of joy
and well-being. While such experiences may be intensely personal, in festive events like carnival they also involve a communal feeling of being "in
sync" (Turino 1993: 111) which may transcend barriers that divide people at
other times.

As Trinidadian steelband musicians and their audiences embraced the
classics, therefore, it is clear that their internalization of European values
was partial and situational. Performances of the Bomb were guided by a
Trinidadian social and musical style that departed decisively from the aesthetic of the European concert hall, integrating individual expressive fulfillment with communal in-syncness. In contrast to the formality of European-style stage performances, Bomb performances required steelband
musicians to put people at ease, to make them dance and enjoy themselves
unselfconsciously. For a steelband's reputation and status, this skill could be
just as important as symphonic finesse. In this regard, steelband arranger
Ray Holman implies a distinction between two different *kinds* of status (associated with stage concerts and the road, respectively) when he compares
his own band, Starlift, with the Pan Am North Stars: "When we talking
about, 'old chap': Pan Am. See what I'm saying? Status: Pan Am. Girls, limin',
who will get women: Starlift. . . . It was a different thing. They never had the
following we had" (personal conversation, 1999).

---

[6] See, for example, Charlie Keil's critique of Meyer's argument contending that deferred gratification
in music "is a sign . . . that the animal is becoming a man" (Keil 1994: 74–75).

Starlift was one of the most popular bands for carnival during the late 1960s and early '70s (known as a good group to lime with, as Holman says—meaning to hang out, talk, party, or otherwise enjoy the company of friends). Compared to North Stars' polished stage performances of the classics, where traditional European concert etiquette dictated a separation between active performers and passive audience, Starlift's Bomb tunes were enjoyed in a very different way: "There was a great respect for classical music. So if a band play that in the road, it used to sound nice. You know this tune, and you could dance to it; because in the Queen's Hall you can't dance to it. So the same nice tune, the same nice melody and chords, you're getting it that you could dance. And Trinidadians love to dance. So it was more appreciated" (interview, 1999).

Holman thus appreciated the Bomb for the way it enhanced the appeal of a music he and some of his listeners already liked. Some other Trinidadians, however, really enjoyed the classics *only* in the context of the Bomb, where they could and did participate in the performance through dancing, shouting, playing a bottle and spoon, or chipping along in time. Crowd participation in these street performances bridged the gap between performers and audience that was such a powerful aspect of the sacralization and distancing of "high culture" as experienced in the concert hall (Levine 1988; Small 1998). All Stars member and arranger Leon "Smooth" Edwards explained how the performance context of the Bomb helped many people to relate to the classics in a more familiar and comfortable way:

OK, the Festival it was played as written. If it's legato, if it's andante, if it's whatever. So you listen to it in its true form. Carnival time it was played in a dance form where you could chip and dance and have fun with it. Probably slightly altered, or rephrased slightly, but left enough so that you could recognize it. So it's just something unique, you know, the mere idea that you could dance to a Classic. A Classic to most people is something that is normally boring or too high for them. And the mere idea, it's simplified enough that you could dance to it, you know, it brought about a new novelty. It brought about a new meaning to classics. It made people appreciate classics now, in the sense that they could sing it, you know. A lot of people knew classics by the Bomb, by listening to the band playing it. It became accessible to the people. (personal conversation, 2000)

Just as the Bomb gave steelband supporters a chance to relate to the classics in a way that came more naturally to them, the musicians also enjoyed the chance to adapt these works to a style of playing with which they could more fully identify:

When you hear a tune, you used to try to take that tune and turn it from
a waltz to a mambo, from a waltz to a samba, or from a waltz to a kaiso
[calypso]. And it takes a lot of doing to do that. . . . You're disarranging the
whole of the fellow's composition. You are disarranging it and rearranging it
to suit your mentality. . . . You break down the foundation of the tune all
over and you start re-building it with some sort of magical growth of yours.
(All Stars member Big Mack Sandiford, quoted in Stuempfle 1995: 163)

The excitement that musicians and supporters felt in making the classics
their own was clearly related to the status of European art music, but in at
least two different ways. As argued in the preceding sections, the Bomb was,
for some people and in some contexts, about conforming to or appropriating the authority of the "Great Works." However, in the context of carnival
festivity, many people also enjoyed the Bomb for the way it *neutralized* the
authority of the classics and their ability to make them feel alienated or inferior. For musicians and supporters alike, the Bomb provided relief from
judgments about high and low culture that were associated with other experiences of listening to European art music. This ability to immunize oneself
against the oppressive authority of colonial culture may in itself be an act of
resistance, but it also sets the stage for a much more psychologically diverse
range of experiences and emotions, as Veit Erlmann argues in relation to the
isicathamiya performances of South African factory workers:

In an environment that imposes denotative precision and the one-
dimensional functionality of "labor units" on the individual, the production
of such abundant, overflowing meaning is not only a creative process but
also an enormously political act of resistance. By concentrating on this
abundance, the analysis of the politics and praxis of performance can move
beyond the construction of accommodation and resistance as dichotomous
categories and lead us to a better understanding of performance in the logic
of its own praxis. (1992: 705)

Like South African isicathamiya, the Bomb's appeal—indeed the affinity
that steelband musicians felt for classical music generally—had to do with
aesthetic choices that cannot be fully accounted for by considerations of accommodation and resistance, or sophistication and resignification. A case
in point is this amusing story told to me by Ray Holman in 1993:

Ellie [Mannette] come on the pan, and he play, and he say, "Well, that is A
minor—how you playing D?" He couldn't understand it. "G, and you playing

D. E minor, and you playing D." So they call Mr. Pierre. Big thing, you know, when he say send to call Mr. Pierre. So they call Mr. Pierre, Mr. Pierre come in the yard. But in the meantime, now, I say, "Listen," I jump on my bicycle, eh? And I head down Petro Street. It had a fella called Blackman; they were music teachers, and the fella used to go to school. I say, "Listen, I want you to help me with something. Tell me what this is." And I play for him, we going on the piano now [sings the tune]. I say, "What you call that? What it is I doing there?" And he go, and he bring out his sister. (He didn't know.) When I play it, she says, "That is a pedal point." I say, "What it is you say—a pedal point? What is that?" She say, "Just what you're doing there, playing one note, even if the chords change." I say, "Uh-huh, well, they dead now!" I gone now, boy!

I jump on my bicycle, man, and I gone up in Invaders yard. I have my two sticks in my pocket. When Mr. Pierre start to talk, he say he can't understand this thing. "But Ray. . ." I say, "Mr. Pierre, you don't know what is a pedal point?" Boy, all the young fellas in the yard, they watching me like I know this amount of music! That was kicks, boy! I feel like a big, big man now, because I teach them this thing. I say "Mr. Pierre, you don't know what is a pedal point?" Well, you see that? Mr. Pierre lost all credibility then. Because some other man who was in the yard listening—a gentleman—came and he say, "What the boy saying is correct." And he speaking proper English, eh? "What the little fellow said is correct: it's a pedal point."

On the one hand, this story demonstrates the power and authority that steelband musicians attained through formal knowledge of music. On the other hand, Holman used the pedal point before he had any idea that he could claim it as a sanctioned technique of European art music. This suggests that steelband musicians like Holman were interested not only in status, but in the possibilities for new sounds that the classics offered them. In their decisions to use certain classical works or techniques, they were guided by considerations of craft as well as of status.

It is important to remember that, for most Trinidadians in the 1950s, classical music was not an exotic experience but rather a part of their routine soundscape. Steelband musicians performed classical music at the biennial Music Festival and other venues, and the panmen were familiar with some pieces as standards in their repertoire. Beethoven's Minuet in G, for example, was a favorite solo piece for the festival competition for several years before Neville Jules decided to arrange it in calypso rhythm for carnival. People of means often played songs like Minuet in G in piano lessons (or heard it played by their sisters, since girls were more likely than boys to be encouraged in music lessons), and most households were exposed to a wide repertoire of "light" classical music on the radio, particularly on Sunday mornings. Smooth Edwards, for example, who grew up in the humble neighborhoods of John John and Laventille, remembers:

> In my days growing up, Sunday morning you were sure to get some program of classics and hymns, you know, standards, from way back when. You would hear it. Not necessarily sit down to listen to it, but you would hear it. The same way you would hear a hymn at church service. Somewhere along the line you would hear—it was sort of what the people in the area thought was soothing, relaxing music, and they thought that was the time of the week to feature it. It may not have been the harsh [sound] or the big symphony, you know. It might have been just the lighter classical forms, the Bach, you know . . . pleasing to the ear. (personal conversation, 2000)

And although European art music was an important influence and re-source for steelband musicians, the classics (notwithstanding Pete Simon's complaints about the works of "Janislav Bumbumkoski" and "Igor Rons-koopoofpoof") did not dominate the Bomb repertoire overwhelmingly. This can be seen in the list of tunes in appendix II, and is borne out even more convincingly in a broader investigation I did of more than fifty Bomb tunes,[7] roughly half of which were European art music compositions. Many of those, furthermore, were "light classical" pieces that did not have a partic-ularly elevated stature. Status, therefore, was not the only consideration, and perhaps not even the main consideration in choosing pieces for the Bomb.

One important consideration for steelband musicians was the sheer di-versity of musical material that the classics, film music, mambos, and other genres offered them. This contrasted with the relatively narrow range of harmonic and melodic patterns in calypso, a song genre in which text is often the focus of interest (E. Hill 1971; Dudley 2004: 23, 46). Steelband arrangers are by no means oblivious to text, but they are also interested in the way a given composition can be made to fit the rhythmic sensibility of their band, how they can bring it alive for dancers, the emotions that melody and harmony invoke, and many other affective considerations. Mu-sicians thus have distinct opinions about what kinds of music "work" in a steelband arrangement. Teddy Belgrave, for example, told me a story of how Hilanders once tried to arrange an excerpt from Bizet's opera *Carmen*. Even though the first part of the arrangement turned out nicely, they eventually scrapped it entirely because they came to a spot that they couldn't arrange to suit their style (Belgrave 2000). By contrast, Carleton "Zigilee" Constan-tine believed that Perez Prado's mambos were popular with steelbands in

---

[7] This survey included Gideon Maxime's review of steelband competitions (n.d.) and other tunes mentioned in interviews and newspaper articles.

the 1950s because they were so well matched to the idiom: "That music was just definitely like he make it for pan" (Constantine 1993). For Ray Holman, the "groove" that he valued, the urge that the Bomb gave people to dance in a particularly sweet and satisfying way, had to do with melody and with a quality of sadness that some songs had:

> I would look for a nice melody. That way I could make them groove.
> The Bomb was to groove. Or to make you feel in heaven—Hallelujah chorus wasn't a groove, that was heavenly [*sings*]. But when we play Accelerations Waltz, it was groove [*sings*]. . . . Melody, and a certain feel that people would want to cry when they hear the song. It is a certain feel, I don't know how to describe it. The tune must have a certain melancholy in it. That is the important thing, for the Bomb. When they played "Liebestraum," people used to cry. (personal conversation, 1999)

Holman's perception that "groove" depends on melody and poignancy contrasts with the tendency in much ethnomusicological literature to explain danceability in terms of rhythm (e.g., Dudley 1996; Keil 1995; Washburne 1998). It is also an important reminder that musicians of the African diaspora are capable of experiencing an aesthetic affinity not only with African or neo-African musical forms, but also with European art music. Steelband musicians, then, were not just making a calculated appeal to someone else's standards of beauty and value when they chose to play European compositions—they were making music that they and their audiences enjoyed dancing to.

Holman and other steelband arrangers respond to an aesthetic of carnival dancing that is defined in terms of both movement and emotion, and is expressed in phrases like "free up," "break away," or "leggo" [let go]. Indeed, like the trope of agitation or heat (*anraje, chofe*) that Gage Averill identifies in Haitian carnival music (1997: 21), the trope of "freeness" pervades Trinidad carnival (see, for example, Miller 1991; Regis 1999: 42). Part of the freedom of the Bomb, as Smooth Edwards noted, was that dancing made the classics less alienating. In addition to jettisoning the repressed behavior of the concert hall, however, carnival dancers relied on a particular style of melody and rhythm to free themselves up. Big Mack Sandiford's reference to "disarranging [a Classic] and rearranging it to suit your mentality" speaks about the need to generate a musical structure and feeling (kaiso) that were more familiar and energizing to carnival dancers than were the structure and feeling of the original (waltz).[8] This responsiveness to a style of carnival dancing constitutes an essential Trinidadian musical aesthetic that links steelband music closely to other kinds of carnival dance music. The differ-

---

[8] See Dudley 1996 for a discussion of calypso's "rhythmic feel."

ences between this local musical aesthetic and foreign aesthetics are under-scored by steelband musicians' need to restructure European compositions.

Attention to dance reveals distinctions not only of local and foreign, how-ever, but also a variety of affective distinctions *within* Trinidad carnival music. Moving to the music of a steelband playing a Panorama arrangement slowly in the panyard, for example, dancers project a particular kind of free-ness. In the panyard, you may see swaying bodies, waving arms, twirls, and other dramatic movements that contrast with the more consistent move-ments associated with calypso and soca on the road: stepping steadily for-ward ("chipping") and winding the waist ("wining"). The panyard way of dancing relates to the programmatic quality (suggestive, that is, of an unfold-ing story or drama) in both Bomb tunes and Panorama arrangements, and to the sort of wistful abandon that Ray Holman implies by his use of "groove." This contrasts with the sexual abandon and physical intensity of people danc-ing to the "jam and wine" music that dominates modern carnival.

Abundant complaints about the dissolution of modern carnival might give the impression that "jam and wine" is displacing "groove" as the young generation takes over from the old (see Ahye 1991; Miller 1991). "Groove" and "jam and wine" represent more enduring Trinidadian distinctions of affect, though. Indeed, commentaries on the carnival of the nineteenth cen-tury are replete with complaints about moral and aesthetic dissolution that echo the outrage of modern carnival critics (see Cowley 1996). Similarly, the "soothing, relaxing" qualities that Edwards associates with classical music, or the "melancholy" Holman heard in "Liebestraum" surely had early prece-dents in carnival—in the music of Venezuelan string bands that were popu-lar for carnival entertainment around the turn of the century, for example, or the quadrilles danced even by lower-class revelers in the nineteenth cen-tury (Cowley 1996: 113–24). The Bomb thus resonated with preexisting aes-thetics of carnival music and dance, even as it reshaped them. To some ex-tent, that is, steelband appropriations of the classics at carnival time during the 1950s and 1960s filled an established affective niche in carnival, coexist-ing with other kinds of music and other kinds of affect. "The Bomb was to groove," said Ray Holman, and the Hallelujah chorus "to make you feel in heaven"—and he could have added that a Kitchener road march could make you "jump up," "get on bad," and "wine your waist." Different ways to free up, with different kinds of music.

SUMMARY: MUSIC AND POLITICS

The temptation to analyze the Bomb in terms of accommodation and re-sistance has its parallel in the scholarly debate about whether carnival functions as a "steam valve" that ensures social stability, or whether its unbridled energy subverts the status quo in lasting ways (see Alonso 1990; Kertzer 1988: 125–50). The commentaries of steelband musicians suggest that this is not the only important question, however, since the Bomb was musically satisfying on a level that power relations cannot fully account for. Even though the experience of the Bomb was conditioned by a variety of social concerns—class distinction, political resistance, or the affective unity of emotion and movement in a carnival band—its meaning was greater than any one interpretive stance. The different messages that people heard in the Bomb could be compared to what anthropologist James Fernandez calls an "argument of images": contrasting images that tell us little individually, but which, by their repeated juxtaposition in ceremony and ritual, collectively help us sense the "complex whole" with which we yearn to connect (Fernandez 1986). The images of the devil and the dragon, fancy costumes and mud mas', sailors and steelbands, are consistently juxtaposed in the bacchanal of Trinidad carnival. In performance, the visual dimensions of these images are vastly expanded, linking them to an argument of sound and movement, of which the Bomb is a part. Christopher Small points to such an argument when he writes, "Through musicking humans have the power to explore and articulate . . . contradictions and paradoxes simultaneously, in ways that verbal language cannot" (1998: 204). For some people, the Bomb meant status; for some, it meant romance; and for many people its different messages were surely experienced simultaneously, integrated so that they made sense in a deeply felt way.

In contrast to this abundance of meaning, however, public discourse about the steelband at the time of Trinidad's independence focused overwhelmingly on its significance to national identity. Official strategies for the steel pan's promotion thus favored practices that reinforced its nationalist symbolism and actively discouraged other meanings, exemplifying what David Guss argues is a tendency of nationalist promotion generally:

> Events that were not only structured by local histories and conflicts but that also celebrated them now become symbols for a nation at large, a purpose for which they were never intended. To accomplish this has required that the hallmark of festive behavior, its superabundance of symbols and meanings, be shrunk as much as possible to a handful of quickly and easily understood ideas. (2002: 13)

The founding of the Panorama competition in 1963 has to be understood, at least in part, in terms of this nationalist strategy. It was intended, that is, to restrict the range of meanings that could be communicated and experienced in festive steelband performances, particularly through its requirements that steelbands play calypso music instead of classics and that they perform on the Queen's Park Savannah stage instead of the street. Though its rules stressed the national symbolism of musical forms (calypso versus classics), they disregarded the processes that produced these forms (street participation versus staged presentation). Nationalist logic thus focused single-mindedly on the problem of playing Beethoven during carnival, and it ignored the problem of removing steelbands from the participatory performance environment of the street. In an important sense, this disregard for the performative process represented a disregard for the musicians and communities who had created the steelband. As I will demonstrate in the following chapters, however, these people refused to be disregarded, significantly shaping the Panorama competition—and, by extension, the understanding of Trinidadian culture—through their active participation.

6

A Showcase for Pan

Panorama is what we panmen live for.
　　　Tuner and steelband leader Patrick Arnold, personal conversation, 1990

Perhaps because it is a relatively young instrument, or perhaps because of its history of trouble and misbehavior, the steelband is often discussed in the anthropomorphic terms of birth, growth, and maturation. A 1994 exhibition on the history of the steelband presented by Trinidad and Tobago's Ministry of Culture, for example, was titled "Coming of Age." Chapters of George Goddard's chronicle of the steelband movement (1991) have such titles as "Birth and Infancy of the Steelband," "The Early Years: The 1940s," and "Growing Up: The 1950s." Everyone likes to tell the story of the steelband's disadvantaged origins, its fierce determination to make something of itself, and its happy coming of age as a nationally and internationally acclaimed art form. Less often is it noted, however, that the steelband has spent most of its adult life obsessed with the Panorama competition. Although Panorama does not figure prominently in most narratives of the steelband's development, its constraints—not only artistic, but political and financial as well—have shaped steelband music more than any other performance venue; and the notion of a mature and stable steelband movement is belied by constant expressions of concern about Panorama's impact on the art form. The story of the steelband is not yet over, therefore, and any useful assessment of its future in Trinidad must begin with an understanding of Panorama.

Beginning as it did, in conjunction with Trinidad and Tobago's independence, the Panorama competition was from its outset an important symbol of national culture, and it linked the new government to both the musical excitement and social promise of the steelband movement. Its attraction for steelbands and their audiences can be explained by a variety of factors, including its active promotion by government agencies, the decline of other steelband venues and repertoires, the artistic possibilities it presented to steelband musicians, and its grand spectacle. Soon after Panorama began in 1963, at the first carnival following independence, the popularity of the Bomb waned. Then, in the 1970s, steelbands began to lose work to DJs who played recorded music on massive sound systems for carnival fêtes and for masquerade on the road. During this time, the islandwide Panorama competition, which unfolded over several weeks leading up to carnival, attracted more and more bands, and by the 1980s the competition generated much more public interest, prestige, and remuneration for steelbands than masquerade, fêtes, or any other performance venue.[1]

With this popularity came incentives and constraints that have had a profound influence on steelband music in Trinidad. Many important norms of steelband style, repertoire, and organization today—including the dominant role of the arranger, a premium on speed and excitement, structurally complex calypso arrangements, and a virtual absence of improvisation—are direct results of Panorama, which has wrought these changes through the diverse and sometimes contradictory input of different groups. Politicians and sponsors played an important role, especially at the start, in shaping Panorama and redirecting the steelband's trajectory. On the other hand, arrangers, who became the new stars of the steelband in the Panorama era, also directed this trajectory in ways that Panorama's founders could not have predicted. Players and audiences, for their part, enforce conventions of carnival festivity and give their support (or not) to new musical ideas. This chapter will focus on the motivations and constraints that sponsors imposed through this new performance venue, as a point of reference by which to understand the responses of other constituencies.

VENUE AND REPERTOIRE

From the point of view of its organizers, Panorama brought the steelband into the fold of the national arts, providing it an official showcase alongside

---

[1] There are still alternative venues for the steelbands, including fêtes and playing on the road at carnival time; parties, functions and concerts throughout the year; and non-carnival competitions such as Pan Is Beautiful, or the Pan Ramajay competition, which features small ensembles with improvisation. However, they do not constitute substantial opportunities for steelbands, largely because of competition from DJs and amplified bands that usurped the steelbands' role in fêtes and masquerade beginning in the late 1970s (Thomas 1986).

calypso and masquerade. As Ronald Williams, the chair of the Carnival Development Committee (CDC), recalled later:

> To give steelbands more prominence and status Panorama was brought into the official programme of the CDC with the finals of the competition being held on Dimanche Gras together with Calypso King and Queen of Carnival contests. To give the National Association of Trinidad and Tobago Steelbandsmen more prominence and status the preliminaries and Panorama were held under the joint sponsorship of NATTS and the CDC, with the CDC providing all the finance, doing all the work and sharing the profits with NATTS. I should mention that no charge was made against the Panorama shows for the use of the CDC facilities. (1980)

The steelbands' new prominence and status came with strings attached, though, because Panorama took steelbands into a venue where their performances could be more effectively framed and controlled by sponsors. Williams's account is also misleading with respect to the first few years of Panorama when the finals were *not* scheduled on Dimanche Gras night. This did not occur until 1968. When the competition began in 1963, Panorama's final round was paired with the semifinals of the Carnival Queen competition on the preceding Friday night, providing the steelbands a "prominence and status" that were qualified, to say the least.

To play second string to the Carnival Queen competition, of all things, would have been irksome to the panmen. The Carnival Queen was generally regarded in the working-class communities of steelband musicians as a symbol of the elite carnival, defined as such by more than a century of separation and antagonism between the downtown "people's carnival" and more exclusive celebrations that took place in the Queen's Park Savannah. The separation between downtown and uptown carnivals began in 1834,[2] when emancipated blacks first participated in Port of Spain's carnival in large numbers, and French creoles retreated to private venues for their celebrations. For the remainder of the nineteenth century and into the twentieth, Ann Lee notes that "it would not be an exaggeration to say that . . . there were two carnivals. Whites were hardly a part of the downtown carnival. Their circuit was the Queen's Park Savannah" (1991: 427). The symbolism of these spaces was reinforced by a rivalry that began in 1919 between alternative carnival competitions sponsored by the *Argos* and *Guardian* newspapers. The *Argos*, run by middle-class coloured businessmen, positioned itself as the champion of the people's carnival, holding its event downtown in Marine Square, and casting the *Guardian*-sponsored event in the Savannah as elitist.

---

[2] Emancipation took place in stages over a period of "apprenticeship" between 1834 and 1838.

Accusations of elitism were leveled particularly at the *Guardian's* Carnival Queen competition, which began in 1946 and gained prominence as businesses eagerly competed to attach their names to the event's list of sponsors (Rohlehr 1990: 418). The queen contestants' light skin made clear to lower-class Trinidadians, however, that this event did not represent them. On the contrary, the popularity of the Carnival Queen competition was a sign that the social elite, uncomfortable with incipient efforts to valorize lower-class carnival arts such as the steelband, wished to maintain their distance from the lower classes. A 1950 *Guardian* editorial, for example, defended the queen competition on the grounds that "there is no reason why Carnival should not gain in attractiveness what it loses in vulgarity" (Rohlehr 1990: 416). Given such attitudes, most steelbands and their supporters viewed the Savannah as enemy territory during carnival. Tokyo steelband's attack on Invaders during the 1950 carnival, for example, was rumored to have been motivated by Tokyo's disgust over Invaders' participation in the Dimanche Gras show (Rohlehr 1990: 418).

In 1957, the Carnival Development Committee acquired stewardship of the Savannah carnival shows, after the *Guardian* abdicated its organizing role amid protests by calypsonians and others over the queen competition (Stuempfle 1990: 176). The CDC members were not neutral mediators, though, between supporters of the downtown and uptown carnivals. They supported chamber of commerce efforts to suppress the downtown Bomb competition for steelbands, on the pretext that it was causing congestion at Green Corner, where the steelbands customarily dropped their bombs. Although this concern over congestion may have been real, there is no evidence that the CDC or the chamber of commerce sought other solutions before proposing that the competition be moved to the Savannah. Not surprisingly, this proposal was vigorously resisted by NATTS president George Goddard, who observed in a 1969 newspaper article titled "Come Hell or High Water the Bomb Stays" that Pete Simon's anti-Bomb rhetoric had found sympathetic ears among carnival sponsors and organizers. Goddard identified Simon and another journalist, John Grimes, with an influential school of thought that was at odds with the panmen: "The Bomb did not meet with the approval of certain people who felt that a similar cash prize should not be awarded for the non-calypso contest as that for the Panorama contest which was a calypso contest" (*Trinidad Guardian,* Feb. 9, 1969). In his memoirs, Goddard also includes CDC chairman Ronald Williams and folklorist Andrew Carr in the list of influential opponents of the Bomb (1991: 180).

As Goddard's complaint implies, the influence of these cultural activists and organizers was exerted especially through prize money. Steelband musicians had long been encouraged to think that if they focused on music and desisted from violence, they would be taken seriously not only as artists but also as professionals, and so financial incentives were important. George Goddard himself, regardless of his resentment over outside meddling, made clear on many occasions that his job was to secure financial opportunities for steelband musicians, a priority shared by the majority of poor panmen who hoped that the steelband's new social position would bring them some financial relief. This vision of social welfare for the steelbands is reflected in NATTS' 1958 constitution, in which the first concrete priority specified is "to obtain employment for the steelbandsmen" (Goddard 1991: 92).

Panmen also continued to be concerned, of course, with rivalry and reputation, but it was not initially clear that Panorama was the place to enhance their reputations. Even though Ronald Williams touted the "prominence and status" of Panorama, this didn't amount to much of an incentive in the early 1960s, when demand for steelbands was at its peak, and the steelband was the heartbeat of carnival. The relatively low status of the Panorama competition compared with other carnival entertainment roles is reflected in newspaper coverage at the time, which focused on steelbands that were associated with popular masquerade bands. The *Guardian*'s front-page article on the eve of the 1963 carnival was titled "Despers go to Zululand"; another article, on page 11, discussed Silver Stars' masquerade theme, "Gulliver's Travels." In contrast, there was no commentary on Panorama until several days after it was over. The $1,000 prize that CDC offered for Panorama was necessary to compensate for this initial lack of prestige, and to offset the concerns of popular steelbands that they might actually lose earnings from masquerade and fêtes if they devoted time to CDC-sponsored events.

What was most important for Panorama's organizers was that the competition's financial incentives should lure steelbands away from the Bomb. Thus when Citibank agreed in 1964 to award a prize for the Bomb that would be commensurate with Panorama's first prize, it came under pressure from the CDC and reduced the prize to $500 ("Interview with George Goddard," *Trinidad Guardian*, Feb. 17, 1969, p. 12).[3] Starland captain Selwyn Griffith agreed with Goddard that such financial pressure to participate in Panorama was the result of a calculated strategy on the part of carnival sponsors: "They brought the Panorama competition in 1963 to sort of put on a greater muzzle and guideline now on the ability of the steelbands" (personal conversation, 1993). Sensitive to such criticisms, perhaps, organizers initially avoided characterizing Panorama as a calypso-only competition. As late as 1967, a newspaper description notes that, in addition to calypso, steelbands performed a Bomb and a test piece called "Is Paris

[3] By 1968, the first prize for the Bomb had dwindled to $200 ("Come Hell or High Water the Bomb Stays," *Trinidad Guardian*, Feb. 9, 1968, p. 5).

Burning?"[4] These last two categories, however, are described as "optional" (*Trinidad Guardian*, Feb. 5, p. 3). Eddie Odingi recalls that the winner of the first Panorama of 1963, Pan Am North Stars, was the only steelband to really understand this; North Stars put virtually all their preparation into the calypso arrangement. While other bands prepared a variety of tunes, as was their custom for carnival, the North Stars walked away with the $1,000 prize.

> The panmen didn't really take it that seriously, but North Stars did. Starlift played for the people, on the ground[5]—"I Feel Pretty," and everybody ran over to the band, big favorite band, all right. Going down the straight, Starlift played a Sparrow calypso, "Spend Your Money Wise." North Stars played "Dan Is the Man in the Van," another Sparrow calypso. But Tony [Williams], being the man that he was, had an arrangement of "Dan Is the Man in the Van" that was prepared for the competition, and he won. (personal conversation, 1993)

Beverly Griffith, arranger for Desperadoes and other bands, also describes how increases in prize money after 1963 (see table 6.1) contributed to a narrowing of the steelbands' repertoire:

> The Panorama was brought in more or less to push the calypso forward. . . . The prize money didn't start out the way it is now. [In the early years of Panorama] an arranger would go into a panyard and do six tunes—do two Bombs, three calypsoes, and then one Panorama tune. When the Panorama tune goes up to $10,000, $15,000, $20,000 but the Bomb isn't rising along with the Panorama, why do you take your time now to do a Bomb tune when the Panorama is $20,000? The Bomb competition is still one or two or three thousand dollars. (personal conversation, 1993)

POLITICAL PATRONAGE AND THE RACIALIZATION OF CULTURE

While the increase in Panorama prize money served the sociocultural aim of controlling steelband repertoire and venue, it also served the PNM government's political imperative to garner votes in the communities these steelbands represented. Sociologist Ann Lee (1997) documents how this PNM, beginning with the legislative election of 1956, relied on steelband leaders in Laventille to get out the vote, and even to provide protection and intimidation during the tense rivalry between the PNM and the Indian-

---

[4] This was the title of a popular 1966 movie (Goddard 1980).
[5] Odingi contrasts the "straight," a track that passed by the judging stand, with the "ground," meaning areas of the Savannah further away from the stands where the steelbands might stop and play before or after passing the judges.

Table 6.1.   **Panorama Prize Money**

These are the amounts (in Trinidad and Tobago dollars) only for first prize in selected years. Appearance fees, prizes for zone winners, and other remuneration (total amounts indicated for selected years) provide additional incentives for steelbands to compete in Panorama and add significantly to the amount of money that the government invests in Panorama.

1963	$1,000	(plus other prizes totaling $1,250)
1970	$1,500	
1975	$5,000	
1977*	$15,000	
1980	$19,800	
1989	$20,000	(plus other prizes and fees totaling $237,000)
1998**	$38,000	
2000**	$140,000	
2006***	$400,000	

Source: Figures are from Thomas 1990 (304–39) unless otherwise indicated, as follows:
* *Trinidad Guardian*, Feb. 19, 1977, p. 1.
** Terry Joseph 2001.
***Hewitt 2006.

dominated Democratic Labor Party. In return, steelband members were given preferential access to government work programs, community and youth development programs, and other material benefits.

The PNM originally treated steelbands more as gangs than as musical organizations, and granted them favors and material rewards but not identifying particularly with their culture. In 1970, however, the Black Power movement in Trinidad produced serious disturbances, including a brief mutiny by members of the Defense Forces, which put pressure on the PNM to take a more Afrocentric cultural stance (Oxaal 1971). Prime Minister Eric Williams responded by making highly publicized weekly visits to panyards, dubbed a "Meet the Panmen" tour (Harris 1975: 6), and spoke with new enthusiasm about the cultural value of pan. Although the Black Power movement thus forced the PNM government to identify itself somewhat more explicitly with Afro-Trinidadian culture, the nationalist movement had from its inception embraced a vision of "creole"[6] culture that amounted more or less to the same thing.

---

[6]The term "creole" was generally used in the colonial Americas to refer to people born in the New World, in contrast to European-born newcomers. In Trinidad this usage is seen in the term "French

Afro-Caribbean folk dances, not Indian dances, were the foundation of Beryl McBurnie's repertoire, for example; and the carnival arts of calypso and masquerade had been projected as the national culture for several decades before independence, for both commercial and political reasons. Playwright and cultural activist Errol Hill's explanation for this vision of Trinidadian culture reflects the view of most Afro-Trinidadians:

> Of all ethnic groups, only the African ex-slaves were forced to accept Trinidad as their new home. The white and educated coloured classes looked to Europe for their cultural heritage. Their contribution to native Trinidad culture would for years continue to be coincidental rather than fundamental; they did not need a native culture and sought often to obstruct its development.
>
> The Asiatics, when they arrived, retained their language and customs; even under the demeaning conditions of the indenture system they remained spiritually a part of India or China, not Trinidad, and they had the promise of eventual repatriation at the end of their contract even though, as it turned out, few would opt to return home. But for the Blacks, the possibility of return to an African homeland from which they or their ancestors were torn was so remote as to be non-existent. They had to adapt and develop a language and customs to the new environment, in the process accommodating aspects of the dominant ruling class culture. It was they, therefore, who were primarily responsible for creating the new indigenous culture. (1976: 60)

The basic logic of Hill's argument—that Indo-Trinidadians have been somewhat ambivalent about their identification as West Indians, whereas Afro-Trinidadians have embraced and shaped this identity—has also been deployed by creoles to question the commitment of Indo-Trinidadians to political independence. Sociologist Selwyn Ryan, for example, cites evidence that some Indo-Trinidadians in the 1950s viewed the prospect of independence with trepidation, particularly if it were to mean a West Indian federation with other English-speaking islands that had much smaller proportions of Indians (Ryan 1972: 99).

Any such reluctance would have to be understood, of course, in the con-

---

creole" in Trinidad, which draws attention to the Caribbean ancestry of French planters (many of whom came to Trinidad from other Caribbean islands in the late eighteenth century), in contrast to more recently arrived English administrators and merchants. More commonly, however, especially in contemporary Trinidad, "creole" distinguishes black and coloured people from East Indians or whites.

text of the bitterly racialized politics of the late 1950s, as a result of which many Indian leaders came to view the policies of the ascendant PNM as "Negro nationalism" (Brereton 1989: 241). Sensitive to this perception, and to the need to win over at least a small number of Indo-Trinidadian voters in tightly contested elections, Williams and the PNM originally adhered to a cultural ideology that promoted neither pluralism nor Afrocentricity, but a creole melting pot. This ideology, according to anthropologist Kevin Yelvington, effectively "constructed 'Trinidadian' and 'national' as Afro-Trinidadian-derived 'culture' and labelled practices such as 'East Indian culture' which deviated from such a process as 'racist' and 'unpatriotic' " (1993: 12–13). Even when the PNM began to identify itself more actively with the steelband as a cultural icon in reaction to the Black Power movement, therefore, it tended to portray pan as a multiethnic art form. A 1965 report from the government's Committee on the Role of the Steelband in National Life gives an example of this official portrayal of the steelband's ethnic inclusiveness: "Racial integration has perhaps been the most resounding sociological achievement of the steelband movement. Born in circumstances rather confined to one ethnic group—the Negro—it has spread to every ethnic group in society" (quoted in Aho 1987: 49). This assessment is not literally false, but its inference of racial integration and harmony represents wishful thinking more than reality.

Indian responses to the PNM government's promotion of pan included efforts to identify Indian contributions to the steelband, as in Noorkumar Mahabir's book *The Influence of the Tassa on the Making of the Steelband: The East Indian Contribution to the Trinidad Carnival* (1987), which draws attention to the history of multiethnic participation in both steelbands and tassa drumming[7] in neighborhoods such as St. James. More commonly, however, Indians rejected the creole vision of Trinidadian culture as too exclusive. Indian resentment of the PNM's cultural ideology was still strong in 1992 when Prime Minister Patrick Manning finally made official the steel pan's status as Trinidad and Tobago's national instrument. In reaction to Manning's declaration, Satnarine Maharaj, secretary general of Sanatan Dharma Maha Sabha (an organization that promotes Indian language, religion, and culture in Trinidad), made the following protest:

[7] The tassa drum was associated originally in Trinidad with the Muslim festival of Muharram, which Trinidadians call "Hossay." It has become a more pan-Indian instrument, played also at Hindu weddings and secular festivals. In the Hossay celebration of St. James, which is driven by a core of devoted Muslims who build and parade beautiful tajs (large and ornate representations of Persian-style tombs), tassa drumming groups include many creoles who enjoy the music without regard to its religious association. Mahabir (1987) argues that this multiethnic participation was so significant as to make tassa the primary model for the steelband, but that is a long stretch.

What happened to the dholak?[8] What happens to those people who do not play pan? How can we talk of an equal place for every creed and race[9] and of unity in cultural diversity when the State is imposing a special musical interest on us?

I am shocked at the Prime Minister's declaration. . . .

Tassa is used in Carnival more than even steelpan. It is used by the Indian and non-Indian community also. Why wasn't tassa also made the national musical instrument? (*Express*, Sept. 1, 1992, p. 1)

Tassa drumming is associated especially with the Muslim festival of "Hossay" (Muharram), celebrated most famously in St. James, where many creoles do indeed play alongside Indians. Tassa has had a less significant role in carnival, so Maharaj's claim might be plausible only in relation to a broad spectrum of carnival-type occasions. In any case, most Afro-Trinidadians regarded Maharaj's complaints as ridiculous. Their endorsement of the PNM's vision of a creole national culture is exemplified in this letter to the editor:

Since when is the steelpan associated with Africa or African culture? For your information, Mr. Maharaj, the steelpan is the only musical instrument to be born in the 20th century that was invented right here in T&T. This is an achievement of which every Trinbagonian, whether African, Indian, Chinese, or other descent should be proud. It is not African culture, but the culture of T&T. (Mrs. Roseman, *Trinidad Guardian*, Sept. 8, 1992, p. 8)

By the 1990s, this view of pan had become so naturalized that even politicians of the Indian-dominated United National Congress felt obligated to support steelbands. When, in 1995, UNC leader Basdeo Panday became Trinidad and Tobago's first prime minister of Indian descent, government subsidies for the steelbands and for carnival generally were maintained (while subsidies for Indo-Trinidadian arts and media representation were substantially increased). By the late 1990s, many UNC campaign rallies also featured steelbands (Diethrich 2004), and Indian participation in steelbands had increased by this time, thanks to steelband programs in the schools, and to the example of successful Indo-Trinidadian steelband musicians like Jit Samaroo (see chap. 7). Nonetheless, the persistence of government support

[8] The *dholak* is a North Indian drum popular among Trinidadian East Indians for use in devotional music and also "chutney" music, a folk genre that has been transformed in contemporary practice by the use of electronic instruments and by many influences from both Indian film music and creole soca and calypso.

[9] Maharaj refers here to a line from Trinidad and Tobago's national anthem: "Here every creed and race has an equal place."

for steelbands in the post-PNM political era confirmed the dominant position of Afro-Trinidadians in the national culture, notwithstanding official ideologies of cultural mixing or "creolization." Aggressive support and subsidy for Panorama (as well as other carnival competitions) by the PNM government played an important part in establishing this Afro-Trinidadian cultural dominance. In the long run, however, this patronage also transformed steelband music in significant ways.

BUSINESS SPONSORSHIP

In addition to doling out political favors and prize money, the PNM government also supported steelbands indirectly by encouraging private sponsorship. When the PNM took over from the British in 1962, Eric Williams became an advocate for the steelbands with private businesses, as well as government enterprises like British West Indian Airlines (who sponsored the BWIA Sunjets in 1964) and the T&TEC power commission (who sponsored the T&TEC Power Stars in 1967) (Harris 1975: 4). Such arm-twisting was directed especially at multinational corporations who were eager to curry favor with a new government (Taitt 1972: 13). One of the first sponsored steelbands, for example, which predated the PNM's rise to power in the 1956 elections, was the Esso Steelband, created in the early 1950s. In 1956, Shell sponsored the "Shell Symphony" for the Music Festival (Taitt 1972: 6). These steelbands did not advertise an independent name or community affiliation, though they consisted of experienced players from established steelbands.[10] In 1960, however, Shell sponsored the Invaders, and set the precedent for private business sponsorship of independent steelbands.

In the early 1960s, other businesses and steelbands rushed to follow suit. By 1966, twenty-six of the ninety steelbands registered with NATTS had private sponsors (Stuempfle 1995: 145), and in 1968 the only unsponsored band to make the Panorama finals was All Stars; the following year even it had acquired a sponsor, the Catelli company. At some point, pressure from the PNM became less important than the opportunity for businesses to associate their names with a popular spectacle. Sponsoring companies such as West Indian Tobacco (Desperados), Shell Oil (Invaders), and Solo Beverages (Harmonites) had their names featured prominently on the banners and pan racks of steelbands at Panorama. Beginning in 1969, steelband sponsors

---

[10]Anthony Taitt (1972: 6) says the Esso Steelband was an offshoot of Dixieland; Stuempfle (1990: 189) says the players came from Southern Symphony, based in San Fernando. Perhaps the Esso Company worked with a variety of musicians, because the company doesn't seem to have simply offered its sponsorship to an already-existing band as later sponsors generally did. Neither Stuempfle nor Taitt gives a precise date for the beginning of the Esso Steelband.

reaped further advertising rewards by banding together to fund a special "Steelband Supplement" magazine in the *Trinidad Guardian* during Panorama time, featuring historical articles on individual steelbands and touting the sponsors' role in helping them.[11]

Sponsorship of steelbands has been credited with many positive influences. For one thing, sponsors applied pressure on the steelbands to desist from violence (Aho 1987; Stuempfle 1990: 191–92; Taitt 1972: 11). The resulting improvement in behavior helped to break down the social stigma that many in the general public had long associated with steelbands. Sponsorship also was a stimulus to tuning and arranging innovations that helped to consolidate the new social position of the steelband, as explained by North Stars tuner and leader Anthony Williams:

> [Sponsorship] helped in the development because steelbandsmen wanted to experiment. We wanted pans to experiment. So if the sponsor just supplied drums alone, that was good enough. And, of course, paint and things like that—the other accessories to help. Later on, they assisted in paying for tuners and, in this way, a tuner then could do that work full-time. . . .
>
> The festivals demanded expert arrangers because the adjudicators started to condemn steelbands for playing the classics, because the way steelbands played the music, playing bad chords and so on. So steelbands had to look for musicians, good qualified musicians, to arrange for them. And, with the sponsors, they were able to pay for that service. Before that, they couldn't afford that. . . . But Trinidadians at the time, I don't think they were interested to be associated with steelband. . . . But by the sponsors coming in— giving a different image to the steelband and of course putting out money— this provided a different sort of atmosphere. So they could come in and assist in the steelband. (quoted in Stuempfle 1990: 191)

Largely because of sponsorship, steelbands have also continued to dream the impossible dream of employment for every steelbandsman. Every player who performs in Panorama receives a small sum of money for the season, and some make extra money for other kinds of work in the panyard, including painting and welding.

This sharing of the wealth is offset, however, by inequities that sponsorship has created among bands and within bands. In contrast to the self-sufficiency of the early neighborhood bands, which drew tuners and arrangers from their own ranks, sponsors encouraged steelbands to hire these services from outside the community. Wealthy bands thus have been able to hire the best arrangers and buy the best instruments instead of de-

---

[11] This annual supplement was published for several years, at least until 1975.

pending solely on the skills of their own members. The resulting advantage in competition breeds new advantages: bands who do well in Panorama receive more money from sponsors, and they also attract top players who would rather enjoy the Panorama limelight playing for Desperadoes, Renegades, Phase II, All Stars, or Exodus than be eliminated in the first round of competition with a small neighborhood band. Efforts to address these inequities have included the creation of a small-band category in Panorama; restricting arrangers to a single band so that their loyalties are not divided and clouded by money (done in 1994); and creating alternative competitions such as Pan Ramajay, which features small combos with improvisation (begun in 1990). These measures have done little, however, to correct the imbalance of prestige and wealth caused by Panorama.

The profound influence of the Panorama competition on steelband organization can be illustrated by the story of one new band that tried to establish itself outside the Panorama star system in the mid-1990s. A group of former members and supporters of Starlift steelband began organizing a new band named Odyssey, which they envisioned as a relatively small group that would play a broad repertoire of music for carnival masquerade and other entertainment occasions. They sought musical leadership from their former arranger Ray Holman, an outspoken critic of Panorama's narrowness and conservatism who was interested in alternative performance opportunities. The first job for Odyssey's organizers was to raise money for pans, which were becoming increasingly expensive as demand for them increased in Trinidad and abroad. Initial funds were raised through an official launching of the band and appeals to fans of Holman's music. Between 1998 and 2000, while Holman was a visiting artist at the University of Washington, this money was used to commission pans from various tuners, and the new instruments were stored in the home of Noel James.

When Holman returned to Trinidad, he worked intensively to raise more money for instruments and operating costs, trading on the reputation and connections he had developed as a top Panorama arranger. He soon became convinced, however, that participation in Panorama was necessary in order to attract funding and players, and he proposed to merge Odyssey with an established band, Hummingbird Pan Groove, for the 2001 competition. This caused an acrimonious disagreement between Holman and other organizers of Odyssey, who saw the plan as a negation of Odyssey's fundamental mission to model musical alternatives to Panorama. Some members of Odyssey complained bitterly that Panorama's limelight had seduced Holman into betraying their hard work. Holman maintained, however, that it was not he but the sponsors who were seduced by Panorama, and that the only way he could garner financial support was if he agreed to participate in the competition. Regardless of who is right, this story shows how Panorama's money and prestige exert a gravitational force that suppresses alternatives. It is one of many stories that underscores the downside of the attention and money that were lavished on the steelband in the years following Trinidad's independence.

SUMMARY: INSTITUTIONAL CONSTRAINTS

Panorama provided financial rewards for the steelbands (through prize money, appearance fees, and private sponsorship) and a kind of prestige through their inclusion in the "official" carnival. Along with these benefits, however, steelbands who participated in Panorama subjected themselves to certain kinds of control and restriction that served the interests of government and business sponsors. They were required, for example, to perform in the regulated environment of the Queen's Park Savannah and to prioritize calypso in their repertoire. As the competition's popularity and financial incentives increased, preparation for Panorama became more and more intensive, and steelbands found themselves with less time to play in other venues or to cultivate the varied repertoire they needed for dances and masquerade. In this way, Panorama eventually contributed to a transformation of the steelbands' role in carnival. This transformation entailed some losses (a narrowing of repertoire and entertainment roles), but it also opened up new musical possibilities. The next chapter in the steelband's history is the story of how steelband musicians responded to those possibilities.

7

The Rise of the Arranger

I sometimes call the steelband my university.

Arranger Clive Bradley, personal conversation, 1993

Panorama produced a new category of steelband hero. For all its political and artistic constraints, the new competition offered a scope for arranging and composition that was unequaled, not only in the experience of steelband musicians but also of Trinidadian musicians generally. One of the earliest and most significant changes that Panorama brought about, therefore, was an expanded role for the arranger, who was elevated to a level of importance that is analogous to (and, one could argue, modeled on) the European orchestral composer. Influential arrangers helped to shape Panorama's conventions, and their artistic ambitions continue to represent an important counterbalance to the controlling influence of government and sponsors. Just as tuners were the champions of the steelband in its early years, therefore, the spotlight after independence shifted to arrangers.

Prior to Panorama, most steelbands drew members from their local neighborhoods. Although some bands recruited formally trained musicians from outside their communities to arrange classics, the role of the arranger at this time was usually not as important as that of the tuner or even the best player. Even in the early days of Panorama, Ray Holman recalls, there was a sense of collective input in the band he arranged for, Starlift, that contrasts starkly with the hierarchy of a symphony orchestra: "You see everybody from one yard, it's like a culture. All I have to do is start the tune, and they just bring it alive" (personal conversation, 1993). For dance music at carnival, especially, arranging was often an informal process. Zigilee described to me how he and some other members of the City Syncopators in the 1940s and '50s could "catch a tune" after hearing it just once on the radio and then teach it to the others. Seconds player Kenny Hart would find the right chords to match the melody, and then the arrangement would take life from a shared sensibility of texture and rhythm: off-beat chords strumming against a pulsing bass and a battery of irons.

Similarly, Holman remembers how Invaders' music in the late 1950s took shape through collaborative arranging and individual improvisation:

> You would come in the yard and Jack[1] would be playing, people playing informally then. I would go on the second pan, Roy and them fellas on the bass, so we backing Jack, Jack was the soloist then. Then in the night now, we're learning a tune and Ellie might come, and he would call out. . . . Ellie might play it on the tenor pan, then go on the second and play something— nothing elaborate like it have now. He might do one or two tunes, and Zephrine might do a couple of tunes. (personal conversation, 1993)

These informal arranging processes described by Zigilee and Ray Holman corresponded to the carnival practice of playing on the move. In this context, dancers who chipped along with the band wanted a consistent mood and groove, and perhaps a recurring chorus to sing. Through moving and singing they took an active role in animating the music themselves, complementing the soloing role of pan beaters like Zigilee or Corbeau Jack who spiced and varied the music with their improvisations. Even stationary spectators who watched from the sidewalks could only listen for as long as it took a steelband to pass, and thus did not appreciate musical forms that took a long time to unfold. This was a mode of performance that favored repetition.

In contrast to the repetitive musical forms employed on the road, how-ever, Panorama's stage performances required steelbands to vary the melody, add new countermelodies, new chords, and even create new sec-tions altogether. In the 1960s, as now, most steelband musicians were unfa-miliar with the harmonic progressions, voice leading, and other musical procedures that might allow them to create such variety, so this new trend made it important to have an arranger with formal musical training. Even before Panorama, steelband arrangers had begun to introduce more large-scale formal shape to their stage performances, sometimes taking these arrangements onto the road at carnival time. Edwin Pouchet identifies his brother, Junior Pouchet, as an innovator in this regard, arranging for Silver Stars steelband in the 1950s:

---

[1] Emmanuel "Corbeau Jack" Riley was Invaders' most famous player; Ellie Mannette was its tuner and leader; Errol Zephrine played seconds; and Roy Rollock was a teenage friend of Holman's.

They were one of the bands that started all these things, you know. They were really into this thing where they didn't want to just play a calypso verse and chorus—[Junior] found it monotonous. So you had to arrange an introduction, verse, and chorus; change key; put in a bass arrangement. And we're not talking about a Panorama tune here. Every piece of music he put down, you had something to talk about in it. (personal conversation, 1993)

This perception of verse and chorus repetition as "monotonous" corresponds to a kind of listening that is more characteristic of seated audiences than of dancers on the road, and (generally speaking) to the aesthetics of middle-class Trinidadians like Pouchet who became increasingly involved in steelbands during the 1950s and 1960s. Turino suggests that such privileging of variety over repetition in postcolonial societies is a sign of Western or cosmopolitan influence:

Community participatory occasions do not require the same variety of styles to maintain the interest of participants, since interest is in the doing. In cosmopolitan stage, film, and TV settings, however, variety is crucial to maintaining audience interest—both because of the lack of active audience participation, and because prolonged repetition (lack of contrasts) is not generally valued within modernist-cosmopolitan aesthetics. (2000: 109)

In Panorama music, the need for variety expresses itself not so much in different styles[2] as in the use of complex and lengthy formal procedures that suggest the influence of symphonic models. These forms contrast starkly with the participatory call-and-response lavways of kalinda, tamboo bamboo, and early steelband music, and with the repetitive and participatory formal procedures of contemporary soca road marches as well. In adapting to a new performance context, steelband arrangers drew upon established musical forms from the classics, from calypso and soca, from jazz, Latin music, and other idioms, and recombined them in innovative ways. A review of the work of some influential arrangers during the first decade of Panorama will help to understand both the logic and the idiosyncrasies of the choices they made.

I have pieced together the following accounts of these early arrangers and their contributions from a variety of sources: personal conversations with arrangers, interviews with listeners, biographical works, and recordings.[3] It

[2] All Panorama arrangements are based on calypsoes, so in a sense they are all one "style." Within an overall calypso style, however, arrangers sometimes quote other styles to create variety and effects. Some examples are discussed in relation to particular arrangers later in this chapter and in chapters 6 and 8.

[3] Unlike popular music traditions like jazz, rock and roll, salsa, or even calypso, in which recordings

should be remembered that, though I listened to archived recordings of all the *winning* Panorama arrangements over the years, I have less direct knowledge of the broader repertoire before the mid-1980s when I became involved performing in steelbands myself. Panorama music is ephemeral in the sense that it rarely receives a repeat listening in recordings, nor is it preserved in notation, so in reconstructing its early development I have relied heavily on the memories of other listeners. Some of my consultants described arrangements that they had heard only once, perhaps twenty or thirty years earlier, and although the detail of their musical memories is extraordinary, they have not undergone the process of re-listening and reconsidering that helps aficionados trace patterns of innovation and influence in other genres of popular music. My reconstruction of stylistic developments and influences here is not definitive, therefore, and the claims I present about who did what first are relatively untested. Nonetheless, these brief biographies collectively provide insight into some of Panorama's important musical paradigms and the creative processes that shaped them.

ANTHONY WILLIAMS

In addition to being an innovative tuner (see chap. 3), Anthony Williams, Pan Am North Stars' captain, was also a disciplined director whom many people credit with taking the steelband to a new level of musical achievement. In the opinion of steelband arranger Harold Headley, for example, "the only thing the bands have today on Pan Am North Stars is tone of pan. 'Cause when it comes to voicing, orchestration, arrangement, you would realize that they haven't really moved away from Tony" (personal conversation, 1993). Though he came from a family of humble means, Williams acquired some formal tutoring in singing during his childhood in St. James (Saldhena 1984: 35), and he enforced rigorous standards of musicality and execution when he became the captain of North Stars in 1950. North Stars was especially famous for performances of the classics, as exemplified by the band's accomplishments at the Music Festival. North Stars' rendition of Strauss's "Voices of Spring," for example, which earned them first place in the 1962 Music Festival, took them six months to rehearse to Williams's satisfaction (personal conversation with Kim Johnson, 2001). North Stars also

---

are an important medium for sharing and remembering the music, Panorama music is relatively ephemeral. In reconstructing its early development, therefore, I have relied on the memories of listeners who may have heard a given piece only *one* time—but I have often been astonished at the detail and accuracy (which I discover in cases where I also hear the recording) of those memories!

made some of the finest steelband recordings of the 1960s, including a 1969 album recorded with Trinidad-born concert pianist Winifred Atwell. In addition to their classical music performances, North Stars also distinguished themselves by polished performances of calypso, mambo, and other popular music genres that were suited to a concert setting. Alvin Daniell, who heard North Stars perform in his youth, remembers that they demanded attentive listening even in informal street and open air performance contexts: "You don't get on with Pan Am North Stars, you listen. You're forced to listen. Everything—the way they begin, the way they end, the crescendos and decrescendos and that sort of thing—is so masterful" (1993).

As a band that didn't play for people to "get on" (that is, dance or otherwise react excitedly), the North Stars were especially well prepared to play calypso for classically trained judges in the first Panorama competition. In the first few Panoramas, bands still played on the move, and many played the same variety of tunes they would normally arrange for carnival. At a certain point along the Savannah procession route, though, they were judged on their calypso arrangement by a panel of formally trained adjudicators. Williams was the only arranger in the first Panorama to fully grasp the new musical opportunities that this format presented. Eddie Odingi[4] recalls how Williams mixed some of the rhythm and excitement of the road with conventions of more formal stage performances, such as introductions, codas, modulations, and counterpoint:

> Everybody prepared, but they weren't expecting that standard. He did things that people hadn't thought of. Just the way he arranged. Those days calypso was just verse and chorus. You play your tune, you might put in a rev,[5] but just [strum] chords. Tony wouldn't play just chords. [Starlift's] second pans would be strumming, right? But he wouldn't do this, he was running up and down, countermelody and thing. So they won, and everybody sat up and took note. . . .
>
> By the following year, 1964, he won with "Mama Dis Is Mas'." . . . Tony changed three keys! First time ever in a Panorama competition. Before that they used to change keys in festival. Because we used to do calypsoes in music festivals. We used to change keys in music festival, but not on the road, because on the road is something you dance to, you just moving and dancing. But Tony changed three keys in "Mama Dis Is Mas'." Gone again. So he set the pattern. By then Panorama took a kind of classical outlook, because Tony was a sort of classical man. (personal conversation, 1993)

[4] Odingi was a member of Starlift in the 1950s and '60s and had the most phenomenal memory for musical detail that I have ever encountered.

[5] A fast run or some other lick.

Williams's arrangements set a precedent for more complex forms and modulations to new keys. He also employed textures that departed from the road march convention of bass, strum, and melody. In Williams's 1963 arrangement of Sparrow's "Dan Is the Man," for example, the background pans play arpeggios instead of strumming, an Anthony Williams trademark that creates an illusion of counterpoint. Steelband veteran George Yeates recalled that Williams's 1964 arrangement of Lord Kitchener's "Mama Dis Is Mas,'" "really signaled [that] pan was going to do serious orchestration" (personal conversation, 1992). In this arrangement, Williams did a variation, for example, in which the low pans played the melody of the Kitchener calypso while the frontline pans played new melodic figures on top. This technique, as well as others pioneered by Anthony Williams, was widely adopted in Panorama after North Stars' success in 1963 and 1964 served notice to other steelbands that they would have to develop similarly elaborate arrangements.

BOBBY MOHAMMED

If the North Stars' victories in the first two Panorama competitions set a precedent for polish and sophistication, the Guinness Cavaliers' success in 1965 and 1967 affirmed the fundamental importance of excitement and drama in Panorama. Hailing from the southern city of San Fernando, Cavaliers introduced a strikingly different style to the aficionados of pan in "town" (Port of Spain).[6] Their leader was a young Indian Trinidadian named Lennox "Bobby" Mohammed, who had begun arranging in 1960 for Cavaliers' parent band, Gondoliers. Mohammed was an admirer of Silver Stars arranger Junior Pouchet, which showed especially in the way he featured the basses (personal conversation, 1993). His approach to arranging was also novel, though, and he was remembered as the antithesis of Tony Williams's "classical" orientation, featuring a powerful sound with exciting rhythmic breaks and changes in texture. Alvin Daniell recalls that the Cavaliers' winning performance of Lord Melody's "Melody Mas'" in 1965 "just blew everyone's mind when they came into town, and again everybody knew that was that" (personal conversation, 1993).

Just as North Stars' arranger Anthony Williams exploited the scope that Panorama offered for formal complexity, Mohammed recognized that a stage performance before a seated, stationary audience presented new op-

---

[6]No band from southern Trinidad has made such a significant impact since the Cavaliers. The only other steelband from South to win Panorama was the Hatters, in 1975. Fonclaire, another San Fernando steelband, tied for second in the 1989 Panorama and was considered a strong contender until arranger Ken Philmore left the band in 1994.

Fig. 7.1. Bobby Mohammed (photo courtesy of Norman Darway).

portunities for large, spectacular musical gestures and effects. Arranger Kenrick Headley remembers Cavaliers' impact vividly: "Here you had a nice flow, a nice melodic kind of thing, and then it changed from there to a guy who came and just thundered down the place. He was using drama. To me that's what it sounded like" (personal conversation, 1993). Mohammed's drama was generated especially through variations of texture and dynamics. He would have the basses drop out suddenly, then come roaring back in; or have the percussion stop for a moment while the high pans played through. This is how he described his technique to me:

> We used to cut the rhythm. Bands used to play kind of straight down. We started, and music band [brass band] and everybody doing it now. We used

to cut off all the bass and thing and have the high pans and all the harmony pans and them play. You see, cut off all the low pans and bring the low pans back and bring this kind of heavy sound. And cut off all the rhythm and bring the rhythm back. Really effective. And another sound . . . how the band can crescendo; bands didn't used to play crescendo then, you know; now everybody play crescendo. I used to have the band playing up and down all the time, the band used to rise and fall, this kind of impact. Even in the engine room.

[David] Rudder sang a song about me, you know, "Bobby Mohammed on the bell," I don't know if you heard it. "The Engine Room"[7]—you never heard it? He sing "Bobby Mohammed on the bell." I used to control the whole band with the bell, bring the rhythm real strong with that. With that bell I used to bring the crescendo, control the band, you know. We used to rise and fall. We were one of the only bands to play with that kind of effect, you know. We had a real effect. . . .

I just cut the rhythm, right? And let all the high pan and them carry and just drop bass, sometimes let the grundig pan and them go through, but I just cut off the bass, and then bring in the iron with the bass and thing. And sometime I just let the iron go, real easy, and then raise everything together. (1993)

What Mohammed calls "cutting the rhythm," other musicians might call a break, a sudden stop that leaves a breathtaking space which may be filled by a solo or unison lick. An important part of the effect is the reentrance after the break, bringing back the full polyrhythmic and harmonic texture and a "heavy sound," as Mohammed describes it. The break continues to be a favorite means of generating excitement in today's Panorama performances, as explained by arranger Beverly Griffith: "Excitement is one of the key things in today's Panorama; you hear that on every judge's scoresheet: 'It could do with a little more excitement.' They wouldn't tell you exactly what it is. And that's the reason for these breaks, the reason you put these four or five breaks in the song" (personal conversation, 1993).

CLIVE BRADLEY

Desperadoes first won Panorama in 1966, beginning a tradition of dominance that continues today. (At the time of this writing, Desperadoes' record of ten Panorama titles is rivaled only by Renegades' nine, with Desperadoes' wins spread out more evenly across the competition's four

---

[7] This song is on the David Rudder album titled *Haiti*, London LONLP 60.

decades.) Their arranger that year was Beverly Griffith, who came to Desperadoes with experience as a keyboard player and arranger for dance bands, and who enhanced Desperadoes' sound with sophisticated harmonic voicing and balance. When Griffith left Trinidad in 1968 to study abroad, he brought in another dance band musician, Clive Bradley, to replace him.

Fig. 7.2. Clive Bradley strikes a characteristically dashing pose (1989).

Born in 1936 in Diego Martin (a valley just west of Port of Spain), Bradley was a quick learner and a self-taught musician who acquired a guitar as a teenager and discovered the rudiments of musical notation by matching words to notes in a church hymnal. He began his career as a mathematics teacher but defied both his colleagues' disapproval and his strict Catholic upbringing by playing in clubs at night, getting his start in the music business when Fitz Vaughn Brian hired him to play piano in his dance band. Bradley's talent and ambition soon earned him other music work, including playing and arranging for Choy Aming's big band in the Salvatori building's Penthouse nightclub. Arranging became Bradley's new passion, even though Aming's band played what he viewed as a rather bland repertoire for upper-class Trinidadians and foreign oil workers. When Desperadoes offered him an arranging job, he saw it as an exciting opportunity. "I sometimes call the steelband my university," he told me in 1993. "Because I used to play in a band, play keyboards, had fun, but I never had the chance to write the music for the bands for which I was playing." Bradley's analogy to a university underscores the fact that Panorama's opportunities for musical composition were unique in 1960s Trinidad.

The university analogy also reflects Clive Bradley's uniquely studious and analytical approach to steelband arranging. As he saw it, the distinctive challenge of arranging for the steelband was the ensemble's uniformity of timbre, as compared to a brass band.[8] To achieve separation between like-sounding instruments, Bradley divided the different types of pan into "envelopes," defined by their different ranges and functions. The result is a clarity of sound that is one of Bradley's trademarks.

> The general rule in a big band is you double your lead. Now in the steelband I had to learn with whom to double the lead, and the steelband taught me you double the lead with the second pan. And the double tenor plays the harmonies in between. So for the top of my band I arrived at a plan where I had a top envelope where the tenor is the lead at the top, highest frequency; the double tenor is the middle; and the bottom of the envelope is the second pan, which plays an octave below the tenor. And all the harmonies happen in between there. . . .
>
> The second envelope, which is the lower frequency—now when I got to Desperadoes . . . the second pans used to work both strumming and bottom of the top envelope, and playing connecting lines. They used to work real hard. And I had reduced that to the top envelope, and I had taken the

---

[8] The term "brass band" is used in Trinidad to mean the kind of band that plays for dances or backs up a calypsonian, with a horn section of trumpets and saxophones, but also keyboard, bass, guitar, and drums.

guitars out of the whole thing, and I said, the thing is, this means the guitar, you've got to do all the strumming. I'm not going to use my top pans to strum.

But the problem there was which two notes of the chords are you going to put on the guitar? And from experience working and listening I discovered that the third is the most important note in the chord for a steelband. The fifth is the second most important note, and any note which alters the chord is the third most important. So when I started with Desperadoes, the third and the altered note I used to leave those on the guitar pan. The cello Desperadoes didn't have, but I used to arrange the top envelope so the note that was missing in the strum, it was somewhere in there. It took a little time to work it out, but that is what I came up with.

So that's Desperadoes' formula: the tenors on the top, double tenors almost invariably harmony, second pans octave down from the tenors. If the movement is slow where the guys can play with two hands, I might give the guys on seconds two notes.[9] The guitar is exclusively strum, except sixteen bars I might put something down where I would use the guitars with the lower register pans to do something. The tenor bass, I used to do two notes with him; one note belonged to the bass, and one note belonged to the guitars. That is how I used to help the guitars.

And one year when I was doing a tune called "Party Tonight." . . . I put the tenor bass and the bass both playing the same note. I didn't give the tenor bass any harmony, nothing, just the same as the bass. And it was very successful soundwise, and when they played, I said, "Damn, they're giving me the separation I needed all the time." And that is the formula I'm using today. As a matter of fact a lot of steelbands have come to that formula now.

In 1970, Bradley led Desperadoes to its second Panorama title, playing Kitchener's "Margie." This arrangement included, among other features, a four-chord vamp in the middle of the second chorus, with a riff in the front line played in cross rhythm against a repeating bass (Dudley 1997: 185–86). This was an early precedent for what is called the "jam" in Panorama music: a section of cyclical form, polyrhythmic texture, and exciting riffs. Like Mohammed's breaks and textural variations, Bradley's jam played on the crowd's thirst for excitement, but it drew more on an African aesthetic that privileged repetition over formal development, and rhythmic interaction over extended melody. The large scale form of theme and variation was interrupted, that is, by a moment of groove. The jam, for which Clive Bradley

---

[9] Pannists always play with two hands, of course, but what Bradley means here is that at slower tempos they can play in double-stops, striking two notes simultaneously rather than playing a single melodic line in which the right and left hands alternate.

set influential precedents, is a formal technique that has since become standard in virtually all Panorama arrangements.

EARL RODNEY

In 1968, Solo Harmonites overpowered the competition in Panorama, much as the Cavaliers had in 1963. Harmonites, a steelband based at the eastern foot of Laventille Hill in San Juan, went to Panorama with 210 pan beaters (*Trinidad Guardian*, Feb. 1, 1970), which prompted rule changes that limited steelbands in Panorama to 100 players.[10] George Yeates also lamented to me that the band's 1968 performance of Kitchener's "The Wrecker" set a precedent for the fast tempos that distinguish today's Panorama music and make it less suitable for dancing (personal conversation, 1993).[11] With respect to size and speed, therefore, Harmonites seems to have prevailed by brute force. Another important factor, however, was the band's talented arranger, Earl Rodney.

Earl Rodney was born in 1938 in Point Fortin, in the south of Trinidad, where he began playing in a steelband at the age of seven. As a teenager, he received some formal music tutoring (Blake 1995: 249), and formed a band called Tropical Harmony with tuner Allan Gervais. Through his immersion in steelband music, Rodney learned to arrange and also became an expert double seconds player, distinguished especially by his unusual technique of playing with two sticks in one hand. Rodney also learned to play acoustic bass and complemented his steelband experience with a stint as bassist for the San Fernando–based Dutchy Brothers dance band from 1965 to 1968 (Hackett 1984). In 1968, Rodney became the arranger for Solo Harmonites, and under his musical leadership they became the most dominant steelband of the era, winning Panorama four times between 1968 and 1974.

Trinidadians often associate Rodney's arranging style with Latin music influences. Such perceptions of "Latinness" in steelband music need to be understood partly in their Trinidadian context, where listeners are sensitive to subtle departures from calypso melodic phrasing, harmony, or rhythmic structure. Bobby Mohammed characterized as "Latin," for example, the syncopated bass patterns he used in "Melody Mas' " (fig. 7.4). For non-Trinidadians this bass rhythm tends to be perceived as generically Caribbean (it is used in Harry Belafonte's "calypso" recordings, for example, and in

[10] A 1977 letter to the editor protests the "new" size limit for Panorama imposed by Pan Trinbago, suggesting that this is when such limits were first imposed (*Trinidad Guardian*, Feb. 16, 1977).
[11] In the recordings I have heard, the Cavaliers' 1967 performance was actually faster than Harmonites' version of "The Wrecker" (135 beats per minute versus 118), but the Harmonites' recording was not made at Panorama, and competition tempo may have been significantly higher.

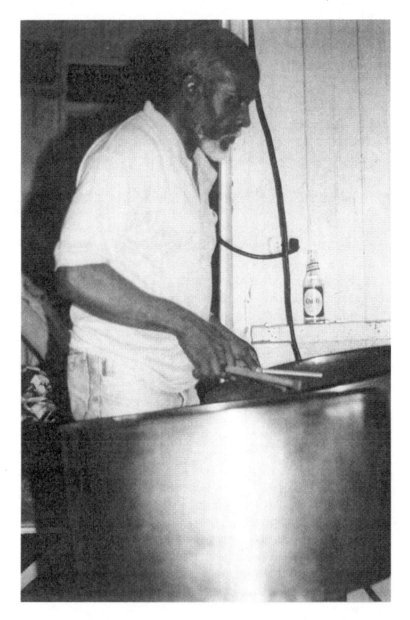

Fig. 7.3. Earl Rodney playing the double seconds, with his trademark technique of holding two sticks in the right hand (photo courtesy of Jocelyne Guilbault).

Fig. 7.4. Bass line from Cavaliers' "Melody Mas'," 1965

Jimmy Buffett songs like "Margaritaville"), but it contrasts markedly with the typical walking bass of early steelbands in Trinidad. Similarly, Rodney's choice of the minor mode for his jam in "The Wrecker" may have evoked a Latin flavor for Trinidadians.[12]

Also, the concept of the jam in general was probably influenced by Rodney's exposure to such Latin genres as mambo and salsa, in which call-and-response improvisations are a central feature of performance. Although there are ample Trinidadian precedents for call-and-response structure (like the carnival lavway or Orisha songs), its use in Panorama arrangements seems also to have been influenced specifically by Latin popular music. For example, I have heard both Clive Bradley and Robert Greenidge use the word "montuno" to refer to the jam section, a term borrowed from the Cuban *son* (*montuno* was first used in Cuba to describe the call-and-response section of the *son montuno* genre, and later came to refer also to the distinctive piano ostinatos that structure such a section). "The Wrecker" in 1968 was the first winning Panorama arrangement to feature a clearly demarcated jam section, and whether or not there were earlier precedents in other Panorama arrangement, it seems plausible that Rodney's use of this formal device was inspired by his interest in Latin music. Compared to "The Wrecker," Latin models are more obvious in Rodney's later Panorama arrangements. Figure 7.5 shows the background parts in a jam from "St. Thomas Girl" (1972), in which the syncopated bass and arpeggio patterns are suggestive of Cuban-style *montunos*, and contrast distinctly with the steelband's more typical bass and strumming texture. Rodney's use of Latin music elements in general represents a continuation of the eclectic borrowing that characterized steelband music from its very start. Even when required to play "calypso" in Panorama, that is, arrangers like Rodney continued to indulge their wide-ranging tastes through these kinds of borrowing and transformation.

---

[12] Calypso in the early twentieth century was typically sung in the minor mode, often using a standard chord progression that is referred to as "old minor" or "sans humanité." This represented an influence from Venezuelan genres like the *pasillo*, because Venezuelan string bands were popular at Trinidad carnival around the turn of the century and set influential precedents for instrumentation and musical structure in early calypso. In the 1930s and 1940s, however, calypsoes came to be sung mainly in the major mode, and this has been the norm since. For Trinidadians, therefore, the minor mode is associated both with early Venezuelan influences in calypso and also with genres such as salsa whose relatively common use of minor harmonies contrasts with the predominance of the major mode in contemporary calypso.

Fig. 7.5. Background patterns from jam in "St. Thomas Girl," Harmonites, 1972.

RAY HOLMAN

After Harmonites' victory, the Panorama title was brought back to the West in 1969 by Starlift. Based near the Roxie Theatre on the border between Woodbrook and St. James, Starlift had a sound that was shaped by arranger Ray Holman. Born in Woodbrook in 1944, Holman got involved with pan at the age of 12, when he and his friend Roy Rollock got the chance one day to experiment with a set of pans at the Little Carib Theatre. The Little Carib belonged to Rollock's aunt, Beryl McBurnie, and was a safe environment for college boys like Holman and Rollock. Just a few months later, however, the two defied their families' and teachers' warnings and became the first boys from a middle-class family to join the Invaders steelband. The participation of Holman and his friends boosted Invaders' middle-class following, which was already substantial thanks to the band's Woodbrook location (on Tragarete Road, opposite the cricket oval), its association with the Little Carib Theatre, and tuner Ellie Mannette's charismatic leadership. Holman's early experience with Invaders rooted him in this band's distinctive sound and rhythmic sensibility:

> Well, West rhythm, as I know it, I still seeing Ellie Mannette playing the
> iron,[13] wearing a cork hat. . . . I hearing that man playing this iron. The
> rhythm of Invaders was a unique rhythm, you know. I ain't know what he
> did on that iron, but it used to give a certain feeling to the music. . . . So we
> know that. Starlift used to sound more like Invaders than Invaders when I
> started to arrange for them, I know that rhythm so good. . . . [Iron players]
> Nicor Best and Mai Fan were in Starlift when I was there. That's why that
> band was so good, too. We had a good rhythm. You see everybody from one
> yard; it's like a culture. All I have to do is start the tune, and they just bring it
> alive. The iron fellas, boy. (personal conversation, 1993)

[13] The iron is a vehicle brake drum played with an iron bolt. It keeps a steady rhythmic pattern, usually "braided" with several other irons, and its loud, high-pitched sound serves as a time reference for the whole band.

Ray Holman left Invaders in 1962 and joined Starlift, eventually bringing many of Invaders' best young players with him, and Starlift developed a devoted following under his musical leadership. In addition to Panorama, they played for masquerade and for numerous carnival fêtes, and Holman and the other young players reveled in a glamorous reputation and the attention of girls. Starlift's reputation was enhanced by the recording of multiple albums, a distinction shared by only a few other steelbands (including North Stars and Silver Stars) during the 1960s and 1970s.

Holman's musical formation paralleled that of Earl Rodney in interesting respects. Both, for example, started on pan but also studied another instrument. Holman learned to play the guitar from his cousin Leslie Holman, a professional guitarist who played with calypsonians and dance bands. He also had a record player in his home, and he borrowed many classical music records from a neighbor to listen to at night. Holman especially loved Schubert and learned how to modulate from listening to his symphonies (personal conversation, 1999). Like Rodney, Holman made his mark early as a virtuoso pannist, winning the solo ping pong competition at the Music Festival of 1964 (fig. 7.6). Also, while studying at Queen's Royal College, Holman regularly took his pan to play in an after-school combo directed by local jazz musician Pilgrim Scofield, and many people describe Holman's arranging style in terms of borrowing from jazz.

Holman arranged for Starlift in the first Panorama and, like other arrangers, he responded to Tony Williams's challenge after 1963, making increasingly complex calypso arrangements in subsequent Panoramas. Since Starlift was a popular band, some of Holman's arrangements were influential even before they won Panorama. For example, Holman's 1966 arrangement of Kitchener's "Mas' in South" included a variation in which the bass played the original melody below counter-melodies in the tenors (expanding on Williams's trick of using of background pans for the melody in his 1964 Panorama arrangement). Other arrangers picked up on this device, and it has become standard in Panorama since. In 1969, Holman's winning arrangement of Kitchener's "The Bull" was notable for the way it transformed the mood of the original song, in which Kitchener threatens to beat disorderly steelbandsmen with a "bull" (a blackjack made from a bull's foreskin), singing, "Since they have no kind of behavior, I gon' lick them till they surrender!" Through slight reharmonizations, changes in phrasing, and new variations, however, Holman calmed Kitchener's belligerent tone and infused his steelband rendition with something of the sweet melancholy he liked so much in the Bomb.[14] This determination to pursue his own aesthetic sensibility eventually led Holman to turn his back on calypsonians al-

---

[14] See Dudley 2001: 193 for transcription and analysis of "The Bull."

Fig. 7.6. Ray Holman, in tie and jacket, celebrating his victory in the 1964 ping pong soloist competition with other members of Starlift steelband (photo courtesy of Ron Emrit).

together and to compose original music for the steelband, providing one of the most dramatic illustrations of the arranger's power to shape Panorama (chap. 10).

JIT SAMAROO

After Starlift's victory in 1969, no new steelband powers emerged in the Panorama competition in the 1970s. The big bands in Port of Spain did receive a shock when a band from the south of the island, Maritime Hatters, won Panorama in 1975 with an arrangement by Steve Achaiba. But apart from this anomaly, the only new band to join the Panorama winners' circle was the well-established Trinidad All Stars, who won in 1973 with Rudi Wells as arranger, and again in 1980 and 1981 with Leon "Smooth" Edwards. A new musical force was germinating, however, in an unlikely quarter. The Renegades, based in the La Cour Harpe neighborhood by the Dry River and generally thought to be good for nothing but rioting, made a bid for musical credibility in 1971 by hiring a young Indian arranger named Jit Samaroo. Samaroo's discipline, talent, and knack for success were soon to make Renegades the most dominant band in Panorama, which the band won nine times during the 1980s and 1990s. Although Samaroo did not play the same formative role in Panorama as the arrangers profiled above, he learned from all of them and consolidated a style that became a paradigm.

Born in 1950, Jit Samaroo grew up listening to many kinds of music in the multiethnic community of Lopinot in the northern mountains of Trinidad. When his mother died in 1961, Jit was the oldest child still living at home, and as a way of keeping the family together he taught his siblings to play parang,[15] a type of Christmas music enjoyed by all Trinidadians but associated especially with Venezuelan migrant workers, who were concentrated in cocoa-growing areas like Lopinot. He and his siblings sang and played guitar, cuatro, and shac shac (maracas). Later, Jit learned to play pan with Scherzando steelband in Tunapuna, walking several miles from Lopinot to play. He brought this new musical interest back to his family as well, and they played their debut concert in 1967 as the Samaroo Kids, later changing their band's name to Samaroo Family and, finally, Samaroo Jets. In 1970, they signed a contract with the Trinidad Hilton in Port of Spain, where they have played virtually every Sunday afternoon up until the time of this book's writing, an extraordinary testament to Jit Samaroo's leadership and professionalism. These qualities, along with his community-building mindset, help explain how Jit Samaroo was able to transform one of the unruliest steelbands in Port of Spain into a disciplined musical powerhouse.

Samaroo was introduced to the Renegades in 1971 by Birch Kellman, a close friend and the tuner for both Samaroo Jets and Renegades. Though he was intimidated at the prospect of leading a town band with such a rough reputation, he was reassured by Kellman's confidence, and he soon succeeded in galvanizing a new kind of musical family on Charlotte Street. "It have a lot to do with how you treat people," Samaroo told me by way of explanation for how, as both a geographic and ethnic outsider, he succeeded as Renegades' musical director. "Once people playing pan start to feel wanted and let them know they are as much a part of what's going on as I, that's when the band will really come together" (personal conversation, 1993).

---

[15] This is a Trinidadian version of the Spanish word "paranda," which refers to a group of musicians that walks from house to house singing and playing and hoping for refreshment at Christmastime.

Fig. 7.7. Jit Samaroo (right) with University of Washington research assistant
Eiko Nagahama in 2000.

Samaroo also brought considerable musical training to the job of arranging for Renegades. Though he grew up virtually penniless, he took advantage
of every opportunity to expand his formal knowledge of music, first learning to read music from Landig White, an Englishman who served as musical
director for Scherzando, and Gordon Maliphant, a professor at the University of the West Indies who was a choir master and organist at Aramalaya
Presbyterian Church. White subsequently paid for Jit to take a correspon-
dence course in music from Oxford University. Later, Samaroo formed a relationship with Father John Sewell, the Anglican priest who had provided
musical direction for Tripoli steelband, and Sewell performed classical
music concerts on piano with the Samaroo Jets on many occasions (Johnson
et al. 2002: 87). With only six players, Samaroo Jets began to play in Music
Festivals in the 1970s, where they honed their classical skills and competed
successfully with much larger bands to reach the finals repeatedly. Jit himself
won the soloist prize in the 1972 festival. Though the Samaroo Jets was distinguished early on by an extensive and varied repertoire that included calypso, Latin music, North American popular music, and even Indian music,
Jit was proudest of the band's renditions of European classical music, and he
developed a special enthusiasm for Bach (personal conversation, 1993).

The dense counterpoint of Samaroo's Panorama arrangements reflects
this affinity for Bach, but it also represents his strategic approach to Pano-

rama and to steelband leadership. Samaroo admired the music of Ray Holman, Clive Bradley, and Earl Rodney, but he also knew he had to do something different to set him apart in the competition. "What I really did was
look at what they wasn't doing," he told me. "And up to now that is what I
do." One of the first things he did was to compose long complex runs for the
tenor pans, and later he added runs in the lower pans, even the bass. The result was a dense contrapuntal texture that distinguished Renegades from
other steelbands and impressed Panorama judges. No less important for
Samaroo, his arrangements posed a formidable technical challenge to Renegades' players, keeping all the young people in his charge busy and out of
trouble during their nightly rehearsals. They could master Jit's arrangements only through unflagging attention and effort, for which Samaroo
himself set the example by demonstrating the parts he expected them to
learn. His hard work paid off in 1978 when Renegades made the Panorama
finals for the first time. In 1982, a decade after Samaroo's arrival, Renegades
won its first Panorama title.

Samaroo's arrangements are sometimes criticized as being formulaic
and overly busy. Whereas some Indian Trinidadians complain that this
reflects the racism of creoles who resent Samaroo's success,[16] Samaroo de-
fends his arrangements on musical grounds. He notes that his music is
complex and that many of its nuances are lost on those who do not take the
trouble to listen carefully and repeatedly, and he disagrees that he is any
more formulaic than other arrangers. It is true that Samaroo's arrangements tend to be quite regular in their formal pattern of theme and variation (see chap. 10), but this and many other aspects of the Panorama "formula"—the jam, the minor section, the inversion of melody in the bass,
and so on—were pioneered by other arrangers. In any case, if Jit Samaroo
uses a formula, it is a winning one. His virtuosic counterpoint gives players
the chance to shine and impress both judges and audience. His melodic
phrasing is exciting, crisp, and never obscured in the dense texture. He has
also succeeded in getting the percussionists in the engine room, a bastion
of steelband tradition and conservatism, to change their rhythm to a zouk
or merengue beat at dramatic moments in the arrangement.[17] Thus Sama-

[16] I heard this complaint expressed in casual conversations with several Indian Trinidadians, even
though it is something most people would be reluctant to discuss publicly.
[17] I have seen both Ray Holman and Clive Bradley try to introduce new rhythms in the engine room
to no avail. Although most steelband drummers will take instruction from the arranger, the iron,
conga, scratcher, and cowbell players generally know how to play one rhythmic feel well and seem
reluctant to depart from what they know. In 1989, I saw Bradley dress down the Pandemonium
iron players for their failure to catch breaks and changes in the arrangement, using the most in-
sulting terms possible to embarrass them, but to no avail. They returned the next night to play in
exactly the same way.

roo's arranging style represents innovation, as well as consolidation of earlier developments.

SUMMARY: FROM INNOVATION TO INSTITUTION

Within ten years after Panorama's beginning, a distinctive new genre of
steelband music had taken shape. This new music can be viewed as a response to large-scale social changes, insofar as it was constrained by the nationalist and commercial interests of its sponsors. Its particular forms, however, were worked out by a handful of ambitious arrangers. Most of these
arrangers were blessed with some kind of musical opportunity in their
youth: private lessons, a relative who was a music professional, or other
kinds of access to formal musical knowledge. This may be evidence that
arrangers as a group enjoyed a higher degree of socioeconomic advantage
than most steelband musicians, but that is not uniformly true of individual
arrangers. A more important link among the arrangers discussed here is the
sheer audacity it took to parlay scraps of musical knowledge into symphonic compositions for a hundred musicians.[18] Panorama music is an expression of their hunger to create on a grand scale.

Eventually the unpredictable and imaginative innovations of these arrangers contributed, ironically, to what some regard as an all-too-predictable
Panorama "formula." The essence of this formula is a balance between Bobby
Mohammed's excitement and crowd appeal with Tony Williams's idea of
theme and variation with key changes. Panorama arrangers today are keenly
aware of, and sometimes frustrated by, the need to reproduce essential aspects of this formula, which includes introduction and coda, verse and chorus followed by variations, modulations to new keys, a rendition of the original melody in minor mode, and an exciting jam or two. The Panorama
formula is catalogued in Godwin Bowen's 1993 song, "Raising Dust":[19]

First they start off with the intro
Then the rhythm start to leggo[20]

[18] I have to credit this insight to bass player Andy Gonzalez, who attended a presentation I gave at
the 1997 conference, "Musical Migrations," at the University of Michigan. Gonzalez had heard a recording of what we decided might have been Ray Holman's "Pan Woman," and without even
knowing its historical or performance context he was blown away by its "sheer audacity."

[19] This song was written by Bowen for Panorama, where his steelband, Pamberi, played his arrangement of it. It was recorded in a vocal version first, but had very little distribution (mainly radio
play), and I do not have a citation for the recording.

[20] The term "leggo" is sometimes used to refer to calypsoes or carnival songs that used to be sung in
the street at carnival. More generally it refers to the spirit of shedding restraint, "freeing up," and
being carried away by the music.

Then the verse and chorus follow
Then the variation come so
Now we go into the minor
Then they raise the key up higher
By this time the stage on fire
Dust fuh so[21] in the Savannah

Although the Panorama competition gave arrangers a relatively free hand to create at its inception, their innovations shaped the expectations of listeners, and the more specific these expectations became, the more they constrained the music. In the next chapter I will show how the Panorama formula responds to the pleasures of players and audience, and suggest ways in which arrangers are both constrained and empowered by the requirements of communal festivity.

---

[21] "Fuh so" is a Trinidadian expression that indicates intensity, quantity. "Lots of dust" is a sort of limp translation of what this phrase means.

8

Community Participation

If somebody really analyze the music that most bands play around Panorama time—
if you listen to it after carnival—then you would realize that what these guys play
around Panorama, some of it really don't make sense.

Arranger Harold Headley, personal conversation, 1993

In contrast to the arrangers' conception of Panorama as an opportunity to
explore and innovate, the expectations of players and supporters constrain
innovation and sometimes frustrate arrangers. The drama, rivalry, and
wordplay that shaped early steelband music (and which can even be traced
to the nineteenth-century carnival) constitute modes of performance[1] that
undergird Panorama's modern fashions of staging and arrangement. And,
as witnessed in the "Panorama formula" (chap. 7), new modes have also developed within the Panorama competition itself. By perpetuating these
modes, the players and audience exert a conservative influence that shapes
Panorama performances as much as modernist reform or arranging innovation. In this chapter I analyze Panorama's modes of performance based
on a somewhat generic portrayal of the competition as I experienced it between 1989 and 2000.

My decision to lump players together with the audience requires some
explanation. Despite the important differences in their roles during per-

[1] The concept of performance "modes" that persist despite changing forms and fashion was proposed by Terence Ranger (1975), for example, to argue that the "modern" attributes of *ngoma*
dancers in the emergent nations of East Africa—including European military instruments, uniforms, and ranks—are only the latest fashions in a mode of competitive display between rival moieties that dates to precolonial society.

formances, players and their supporters share certain expectations that are rooted in a model of the steelband as an extension of community that prevailed in the 1940s and 1950s, when players rarely participated in steelbands outside their own neighborhoods, and carnival performances were an occasion for neighborhood rivalry and festivity. In such performances, people who had no expertise beating pan could still make music through the sound of their chipping feet or the singing of spontaneous lyrics. This level of integration is not possible in Panorama, where players are separated from the audience by the stage, and where audience members not only come from different neighborhoods and different social classes, but from entirely different countries. Players today are also freer to join a band from outside their neighborhood, and some play in more than one. Nonetheless the sense of solidarity between the players on stage and their "supporters" in the audience is a potent force, a bond that today is constituted on the basis of taste as well as neighborhood. Popular bands such as Phase II Pan Groove, Trinidad All Stars, or Renegades, for example, are supported by fans from all over Port of Spain, or even other parts of the island, who share an appreciation for their music or who identify with their success and their style.

Many steelbands also continue to play important roles as neighborhood social and cultural organizations. Panyards that have been transformed from vacant lots into community centers (Desperadoes, Renegades, and Exodus are good examples among the larger bands) host not only steelband rehearsals and performances but other kinds of events, and they generate profit through concession stands. Most steelbands also draw the majority of their players from neighborhoods close to the panyard, even if they have a number of players who come from farther away, and some retain a particularly strong neighborhood identity. Exodus, for example, which is based in the eastern town of Tunapuna, has inspired regional pride through its successful challenge to the dominance of Port of Spain bands (Exodus won Panorama in 1992, 2001, 2003, and 2004). Exodus's leaders (including Ainsworth Mohammed and his late brother, Amin) have deep roots in the neighborhood and insist that neither their players nor their arrangers may compete in multiple bands for Panorama (a practice that is not uncommon for arrangers and top-notch players).

And then there is Desperadoes, which, when they descend from Laventille to play in the Savannah, bring "The Hill" with them. Their supporters line the stage and fill the stands at Panorama, foiling the officials' efforts at crowd control and raising the level of noise and excitement when Desperadoes perform. After Desperadoes won Panorama in 2000, for the second straight year, I came across the band in the parking area outside the grandstand where members had reassembled in the wee hours of the morning to play for throngs of happy supporters. Spotting a foreigner, a young woman

Fig. 8.1. Desperadoes fans swarm the stage at Panorama 2000 (Eiko Nagahama).

shouted to me as I passed, "Come and see the best steelband in the world!" and she raised her cup and closed her eyes in a joyful surrender to the music. She did not beat pan, but it was clear to me this was her steelband and her victory, too. Such identification between pan beaters and their supporters helps to bridge the distance between stage and audience, despite the presentational constraints imposed by Panorama, and is a fundamental aesthetic consideration that influences the arrangers and the judges.

STRUCTURE OF THE COMPETITION

In a given year, sixty to eighty large bands participate in a series of elimination rounds culminating in the Panorama finals just before the opening of carnival proper. While there are separate competitions for small bands, and for single pan bands that use old-fashioned instruments suspended from the neck, the term "Panorama" is synonymous for most people with the competition for large bands, which consist of approximately one hundred players each. The increasingly prominent place of the Panorama competition in relation to other carnival activities is reflected in its scheduling over the years. The first Panorama final, in 1963, was held on carnival Friday night alongside the carnival Queen semifinals; by 1968, Panorama finals were moved to Sunday night before carnival, as part of the Dimanche Gras show that included the prestigious Calypso King and Carnival Queen competitions; and by 1976 Panorama finals were held separately on carnival Saturday night, indicating that interest had grown so much that it was impractical to combine it with the other competitions. Indeed it is impossible to imagine the contemporary Panorama finals being combined with anything else, since the time it takes for setup, performance, and departure from the stage of approximately ten bands (that number has varied at different times) keeps patrons waiting for the judges' results until the wee hours of the morning.

Table 8.1 shows the schedule for Panorama in 2000, an example that is fairly typical of how the competition was structured through most of the 1980s and 1990s (changes made after 2000 are discussed in chap. 11). Bands are grouped by region, and venues include Shaw Park in Tobago, Skinner Park in San Fernando, and the Queen's Park Savannah in Port of Spain. (In 2000, presumably as a cost-saving measure, the preliminary rounds were used to choose zone winners as well as to select national semifinalists; the exception being the North Zone, which had a separate zone final, as had been true for other zones in previous years.)

Despite the importance of choosing a winner in the finals, some fans prefer the preliminaries. Many of those who consider themselves connoisseurs of steelband music spend the day of preliminaries on the track (see fig. 1.2), where they can stand close to each band and hear it running through its arrangement while it waits for its turn on stage. Here debates are waged about who is sounding good, who is likely to advance, and which of the less established bands might surprise the judges this year. Other fans prefer to watch from the stands, where they have two quite different options. The grandstand on the south is where the judges sit, where the best players are

Table 8.1. 2000 Panorama Schedule

Date	Location	Event
Sat. 2/19	Skinner Park	Preliminary round and zone finals (South and Central)
Sun. 2/20	Queen's Park	Preliminary round and East zone final (North and East)
Tues. 2/22	Shaw Park	Preliminary round and zone final (Tobago)
Wed. 2/23	Queen's Park	North Zone final
Sun. 2/27	Queen's Park	National semifinal
Sat. 3/4	Queen's Park	National final

positioned, and where ticket prices are highest. Here one generally finds those people who consider themselves "serious" listeners at Panorama. In the North Stand, on the other hand, a temporary structure erected for carnival each year, tickets are cheaper, and the atmosphere is boisterous. Here groups of friends make a lime with coolers full of food and drink, talking, dancing, and moving about freely on risers that are cleared of chairs for Panorama preliminaries. Enthusiastic beating on diverse drums, irons, and scratchers in "rhythm sections" scattered throughout the North Stand at times competes in volume with the steelbands on stage. This festive atmosphere lingers in the North Stand even during the semifinals and finals when the chairs go up.

The two stands therefore attract different kinds of people: North Stand fans are rowdier, younger, and less likely to identify themselves as diehard steelband enthusiasts, whereas the grandstand is populated by a mixture of well-to-do Trinidadians, tourists, and veteran steelband musicians and aficionados. The "serious listeners" of the grandstand and the "partiers" of the North Stand nonetheless represent two aspects of the same experience. Even music connoisseurs sometimes opt for the party atmosphere of the North Stand, especially during the preliminaries; and fans in the grandstand also drink, dance, and move about to greet friends and acquaintances. In short, Panorama is a place where people come looking for both musical and social excitement, and even though some listeners are truly intent on every note of the music, the onus is on the steelbands to get the crowd's attention.

MUSIC AND COMMUNITY

Even in the modern era, when star arrangers sell their services to the highest bidder, every arranger's artistic vision is constrained by his responsibilities to the steelband and its community. Most important, arrangers must compose music that the players will be enthusiastic about playing, as Daisy McLean explained to me in the simplest of terms:

> You see, there's no sense in putting down music for somebody and they
> don't like it, because they wouldn't play it properly. That happened to me
> when I used to play my pan, and we playing a tune. If I don't like the tune,
> but not with this love . . . you have to like the tune and enjoy playing the
> tune. So if you have a part that you don't like, you wouldn't play it well.
> (personal conversation, 1993)

Depending on individual style and band culture, arrangers may intuitively sense their players' tastes and accommodate them, they may actively solicit player input, or they may be pressured by players and band leaders. Jit Samaroo, who helped Renegades dominate Panorama in the 1980s and 1990s, makes a point of consulting his players about the choice of tune and about certain stylistic decisions because he wants to keep them engaged and working hard. In contrast to Samaroo's active concern for the players' involvement, Clive Bradley made changes at the request of Desperadoes captain Rudolph Charles several times because, as Daisy McLean put it, "Rudolph was a man—if you didn't take advice, you had to leave" (1993). In 2003, Desperadoes (no longer led by Charles) fired Bradley just before the Panorama finals over a disagreement about the ending he had arranged. In the same year, Ray Holman backed out of his agreement to arrange for Invaders because band leaders were not happy with his decision to go to Panorama with his own composition and insisted instead that he arrange a calypso of their choosing.

Such confrontations between band members and arrangers are not uncommon, and highlight their contrasting conceptions of steelband performance, which might be described as "communal" and "artistic," respectively—an experience of communal solidarity and rivalry, that is, versus an outlet for personal artistic ambitions. Neither of these conceptions is unique to players or arrangers, but arrangers are inevitably more invested in the artistic conception of Panorama, as witnessed in the comments of Birdsong arranger Harold Headley:

> What I like about Panorama is it gives you a chance to put your ideas into a tune for about eleven minutes, which you wouldn't get a chance to do during the year. And it also gives you a chance to listen to the ideas of the other arrangers. It also gives you a chance to hear the balance of different bands, and how the arrangers put their ideas together. What I don't like about Panorama is the judging, definitely. . . . And then too because of the surroundings, the noise that takes place around Panorama time, your music generally isn't really heard. If somebody really analyze the music that most bands play around Panorama time—if you listen to it after carnival—then you would realize that what these guys play around Panorama, some of it really don't make sense. (personal conversation, 1993)

Headley, who as a youth in the 1960s toured internationally with Tripoli steelband and later earned a master's degree in music at Northern Illinois University, implicitly invokes cosmopolitan standards of good music to judge what "makes sense." In his artistic perspective these standards are violated in the heat of Panorama competition.

In the communal conception of Panorama, on the other hand, the competition imposes its own distinctive standards of excellence. This is particularly obvious in the case of a band like the Trinidad All Stars, which has a distinctive style regardless of the arranger. During one Panorama, after All Stars scored poorly in the preliminaries, players confronted the arranger (whom I won't name) and demanded that he adhere to their traditional way of rendering the music. All Stars captain Clive Telemaque's justification for this confrontation underscores the aesthetic acuity of players and audience members:

> All Stars is famous for a particular styling, and I think the people probably not ready to accept a different styling right now. I not saying that we supposed to be playing all the things that Smooth play [i.e., hold the new arranger to the style of their previous arranger, Leon "Smooth" Edwards], but All Stars supposed to be this kind of band that even if you don't like the band, once you hear the band they supposed to make you move. They supposed to have that driving force within the rhythm and the tune itself. . . .
>
> [Certain arrangers] have the kind of mentality—they went and learn their music, and they figure that nobody who don't have their papers in music shouldn't be able to guide them, you know. But the panman come just like the people who paying their money to go in the stands, right? They know what they accustomed to, and they know what is a good arrangement. They mightn't be qualified papers-wise in music, but . . . I will always have this argument that I don't think that 20,000 people wouldn't pay their money to go in the stands if they doesn't have a concern for pan and understand it to some extent, you know? (personal conversation, 1993)

Telemaque's juxtaposition of formal music training and folk sense suggests that Panorama performances are guided in important ways by the un-schooled criteria of players and audience. These criteria are grounded in the thrill of community and musical synchrony, a thrill that keeps players and audiences coming back to Panorama year after year. Telemaque explains this feeling, especially as it is experienced by players:

> I think it's one thing that you can't get anywhere else outside of Panorama—it's that sense of being where you belong. I feel that, you know. Now it have some fellas that plays pan—you don't do it for a time because you have other responsibilities, and you have a family and different thing. But when that time comes around, them guys playing. And them don't even look for money. If the band make a million dollars, them wouldn't even come in the panyard and look for money after carnival, but they want to be there just to play on stage then after that, you know . . . So I think that nothing could substitute for that ten minutes there.

"That ten minutes" refers to performance on the Panorama stage, underscoring the fact that a musical bond is at the core of a steelband's social bond. Even I, playing in a steelband as a visitor with no sense of continuity or of a return to old friends (at least initially), had experiences of musical connectedness that peaked at transcendent moments. One such moment occurred during the 2000 carnival season, while I was rehearsing with Phase II Pan Groove (a particularly dysfunctional social group, but a musical powerhouse). Arranger Len "Boogsie" Sharpe had decided that year to arrange the pans in a new configuration, placing the quadrophonics directly in front of the engine room float, instead of off to the sides. The quadrophonics, which have two pans hung horizontally and two vertically, formed a wall separating the engine room from the tenors and double seconds in the frontline. This configuration muted the sound of the drums and percussion for me and other frontline players. Eventually the problem was solved when the quadrophonics were returned to the sides of the band; but in the meantime, I decided to try playing in a seconds rack on the opposite side of the engine room, and the difference was astonishing. Standing next to the engine room and closer to the basses and strumming pans, I was filled with a different energy. My hands were light and fast, and my brain directed them effortlessly and accurately from one passage to the next of the complex arrangement. At a tempo that had been uncomfortably fast the night before, I now played easily, not simply hitting the notes but channeling the exhilarating spirit of the music. It was the spirit of a hundred other people, more powerful than anything I could muster on my own, surging through me in the suddenly unfettered sound.

A successful Panorama performance is one in which the collective musical energy peaks, allowing everyone to play at the height of his or her concentration, spirit, and technical ability. Sound is fundamental to this communion; not only in its acoustic quality, but also in its musical feel, which depends on the players' expressive skills, their touch and timing. Visual communications of gesture and movement also intensify the steelband's collective synchrony (Helmlinger 2001).[2] On the competition stage, as op-

---

[2] Helmlinger (2001) demonstrates how players take cues from the gestures of their neighbors playing the same parts, and may even become disoriented without those visual cues. I have heard steelband musicians explicitly acknowledge the importance of both visual and auditory connectedness to one's band mates on various occasions. When I was rehearsing with the Northern Illinois University steelband, for example, Cliff Alexis reminded the players that this was not an orchestra, where the conductor showed everyone what to do, and that players needed to help one another remember the form, by looking up and making visual contact with their band mates at important transitions or breaks. In 2000, when I played with Phase II, the band was hosting an English tenor player who was very skilled but who loved to improvise. His section leader reprimanded him several times, telling him to stick to the part everyone else was playing. When we reached the stage on the night of the preliminary competition, I did not see him, and afterward I asked what had happened.

posed to panyard rehearsals, the audience contributes new dimensions to this collective energy. The sense of community is expanded here to include supporters and spectators, and the power of sound is amplified by the exhilaration of rivalry and spectacle.[3]

PANORAMA AESTHETICS

Panorama is a holistic experience that includes drama, movement, display, intertextual references, and audience reactions. Sound is central to this experience, but it is not enough by itself to guarantee a transcendent performance; especially since the Panorama stage, raised and open on all sides, is not the best acoustic environment for the steelband. Indeed, many people feel that they can better appreciate the music listening in the panyard or on the track, where they stand close to or even inside the band, and where the tune is sometimes run at a slower tempo that favors the intricacies of the background and inside parts. Many of the beautiful details that steelband arrangers put into their music are best appreciated in this more intimate and relaxed environment; but arrangers also know that ultimately they succeed or fail on the Panorama stage, where different modes of listening and participation prevail. To be successful, a Panorama arrangement must give play to the kinds of expressivity and participation that link performers and audience in a festive collectivity. I analyze these festive performance modes here in relation to the overlapping aesthetics of *drama, rivalry, song interpretation,* and *excitement.*

Drama

Viewed in the broader context of carnival spectacle, Panorama's "symphonization" of the calypso (like the Bomb's calypsofication of the symphony) resonates with the epic themes of modern masquerade bands, from "Gulliver's Travels" (Silver Stars 1963) to "Homer's Odyssey" (Peter Minshall 1993). More specifically, the large-scale formal procedures that inform Panorama arrangements, including theme and variation and sonata form,[4]

I was told that the Englishman had been improvising again on the track, during the last few run-throughs before the competition, and the section leader threw him out of the band because he could not risk having this fellow confuse his neighbors.

[3] Helmlinger also makes the important point that steelband recordings are rarely played on the radio or elsewhere, and suggests (correctly, I think) that this is precisely because they lack the visual aspect that makes live performances so compelling (2001: 200).

[4] Even though Panorama arrangements are essentially theme and variation, the use of modulation

create a programmatic quality that is largely absent from more repetitive carnival music like soca. Such steelband music invites both players and audience to imagine a dramatic development (program), and to enhance the drama with their individual gestures and display. As Aurelie Helmlinger puts it, "La musique crée un canevas chorégraphique sur lequel toutes les initiatives personnelles sont bienvenues" (the music creates a choreographic canvas that welcomes all personal initiatives) (2001: 200). I remember a spectator in the 1992 Music Festival, for example, who pretended to conduct a steelband while it was playing a classical selection.[5] The fellow obviously had spent time with the band in rehearsal, because he cued entrances and accents and amplified the climaxes and changing affect of the music with flailing arms, leaps, and turns. Although I sat on the opposite side of the large stadium from him, his gesticulations were so grand that the people all around me laughed and cheered at his antics, more riveted by his performance, it seemed, than by the steelband's. At the conclusion of the piece, this "conductor" collapsed exhausted in his seat, and the crowd gave him a standing ovation.

At Panorama, the players, even more than the fans, dramatize the music (figs. 8.2 to 8.5). The most entertaining players go far beyond mere mastery of their notes, rendering the music with facial expressions, gesticulations, and movements that amplify its drama—"gallerying" for the crowd, as they describe it. Almost every steelband selects one or two players who can not only execute their parts flawlessly but also have a flair for embodying the drama of the music, and places these players outside of the racks at the front of the band. The featured frontline players of Trinidad All Stars, including Johann Popwell, Clive Telemaque, and Dane Gulston, are unrivaled in this regard, intensifying the arrangement's excitement, pathos, romance, and fury through facial expressions and communications that make the most technically daunting passages of music look like spontaneous outpourings of feeling. Other players dance in place, spin around, circle their pans to play from the opposite side, leap on top of their racks, or even jump about on the stage during breaks (especially bass players, who are located on the ends). In 1993, I saw a tenor player in Hummingbird Pan Groove simulate spirit possession, rolling his eyes up into his head and trembling as he played a climactic passage. At the next moment, he broke into the butterfly dance, a Jamaican dance-hall style, indicating that it was all for show. This literal reference to spirit possession nonetheless hints at the porous boundary be-

---

and motivic development suggest to me that steelband arrangers have internalized certain aspects of sonata form. They often end in a different key than the one they started in, however, which negates sonata form's large-scale tonal logic.

[5] I think the band was Simple Song, but I've forgotten the piece they were playing.

Fig. 8.2. Starlift bass player puts on a show at Panorama 2000 (Eiko Nagahama).

tween drama and ritual generally (Hagedorn 2001: 67). The fact that it is "staged" does not necessarily diminish the emotional and spiritual intensity for the performer or the audience.

Everyone at Panorama may contribute to the intensely dramatic performance. Arrangers need to compose music that gives the players room and inspiration for their gallerying. Flagmen, who dance on stage waving a banner on a short pole, also act out dramatic moments of the arrangement for the pleasure of the crowd. Flagwomen (who either work in pairs to carry the band's headline banner or dance individually like the flagmen) also do some dramatic interpretation, though their performances usually consist more of wining their waists—either at a steady and elegant pace as they circle the band, or in more wild and provocative bursts that fire up the audience (fig. 8.5). Costume and decoration also contribute to Panorama's drama. Players wear matching jerseys and (if their sponsor pays enough) more elaborate hats, vests, and pants for the finals. Their visual displays sometimes depict a theme of some kind. In 1994, for example, Renegades' hard hats and orange jump suits represented the business of their sponsor, the Amoco oil company, and Exodus's silver face glitter and dust masks dramatized its song "Dust in Your Face." In 2000, All Stars sported red sailor suits that recalled the sailor mas' of the 1940s and 1950s (fig. 8.3), and Desperadoes paraded portraits of famous panmen to dramatize their song,

Fig. 8.3. All Stars four-pan players "gallery" on the Panorama stage in 2000, watched by Neville Jules at right (Eiko Nagahama).

Fig. 8.4. The visual spectacle of Cordettes' Panorama performance is enhanced by chroming and layered elevation of four-pans and by the dramatic gestures of players (Eiko Nagahama, 2000).

Fig. 8.5. This flag girl adds movement, color, and sex appeal to Renegades'
Panorama performance in 2000.

"Picture on my Wall" (fig. 8.1). At the 2000 Panorama, I also observed that spectacular carnival characters shared the stage with some steelbands, something I had not seen ten years earlier; carnival queens with huge glittering costumes, children's bands, and moco jumbies (stilt walkers) added to the entertainment.

The very appearance of the pans also plays a part in the visual drama. Tinsel fringes and other decorations line the roofs of the pan racks and float. Bass pans are painted festively, the larger sets with several full-size barrels splayed out horizontally, like cannons blasting sound at the audience (fig 3.5). At the center, the float rises above the rest of the band, its rows of chromed tenors rocking to and fro with the pulsing of the engine room. Some bands also elevate some background pans at the front of the band to enhance this architecture of chrome that trembles and flashes with the musicians' energy (fig. 8.4).

Rivalry

Given that Panorama is inherently competitive, it may be unnecessary to point out that rivalry is an important aspect of performance. Beyond simply winning the competition, however, the participants in Panorama are concerned with symbolically asserting their power and domination in much the same spirit that once characterized face-to-face musical contests and even pitched battles between steelbands from different neighborhoods. Thus writer Simon Lee evokes the excitement of Panorama by reference to instruments and players of old, violent clashes with bottles and cutlasses, and even spirit possession (being "ridden" by a pan jumbie):

> An is lights blazin an dus flyin an beers drinkin man bawlin an flag 'oman winin up in me face an is pongin we pongin an is beatin we beatin we beatin we beatin we flyin we flyin pan jumbie pan jumbie is ridin we ridin we check for de melody easy nuh easy nuh. An tonight is de night we go buss up dey arse all dem Despers Renegades Phase II Invaders dey go humble, dey go buss dey go mash up tonight.[6]
>
> . . . . We is tamboo and bamboo an Totee and Big Head, we is Mud Mout and Cobo Jack Scorpion and Salt.[7] We comin wid biscuit tin, paint can an oil drum and when bugle blowin is tunder we rollin and big stone and bottle we peltin and only cutlash choppin and razor singin and slashin an man oman and chile runnin dey runnin. Wid we rum in we head we go beat and fight till we dead. (1993)

[6] "Buss" (bust) and "mash up" describe the destruction or musical collapse of one's rival.
[7] These are names of famous panmen of yesteryear.

Even during the era of violent steelband clashes, battle was most often engaged symbolically and performatively. This is seen in the early association between steelbands and military mas', and in steelband names that were borrowed from war movies and westerns:[8] Desperadoes, Renegades, Destination Tokyo, Casablanca, North Stars, Invaders, Tripoli, Crossfire, Bar 20. Newspaper photographs show that during the first few years of Panorama steelbands performed on the Savannah stage in sailor dress; and some steelbands, such as Trinidad All Stars, continue to this day to play sailor mas' on carnival Monday.

In addition to names and masquerade themes, musical symbols evoke power and battle. In the 1950s and 1960s the choice of "Bomb" tunes, as discussed in chapter 4, entailed considerations of cultural power and authority. Similarly, in contemporary Panorama, musical complexity is valued for the way it confers prestige and power. Thus the gallerying described above not only adds dramatic expression to the music, but also, by the effortlessness with which complex passages are executed, asserts the players' prowess and cows their rivals. My friend Michael Robinson told me, for example, that when he heard Phase II execute a long chromatic pattern in the 1988 Panorama finals, he knew immediately that his own band, Pandemonium, was beaten, and he turned around and headed for home without listening to the rest of Phase II's performance. This sort of pyrotechnic arranging has become a pet peeve of some steelband aficionados who complain, for example, that rapid runs in the bass pans are virtually indiscernible and clutter up the music. Though that is true, it may be beside the point. A fundamental requirement of Panorama music is that it have a level of technical complexity that permits players to flaunt their prowess not only before the judges but also before the crowd and other bands.

Lyrics and intertextual reference are another way rivalry is expressed in Panorama. An obvious example is David Rudder's 1993 calypso "Dust in Their Face," which uses metaphors of war and gunplay to describe Panorama's excitement:

Chorus:
When you see we come down, is war declaring in town
Dus in deh face, Dus in deh face
Guns will be blasting for sure, in this musical war
Dus in deh face, Dus in deh face

We lookin' for fight
It's trouble tonight

---

[8] A list of band names and the movies they came from is provided by Roy Thomas in the epilogue to Goddard 1991 (246).

We feelin' all right
There's a pan man war
Yes me bruddah

We come on for war
To settle a score
The tenors sawed off
So it's buyaka, buyaka[9] ooh, mama!

Dus, in deh face it's
Dus, in deh face it's
Dus, in deh face it's dus, dus, dus!

Calypsoes like this one that are written for steelband arrangement constitute a genre unto themselves, often referred to as "pan tunes," whose texts
usually comment in some way on the steelband. Steelband musicians particularly enjoy pan tunes that invoke the power and excitement of pan and
which lend themselves to aggressive interpretations in steelband performance. To illustrate this with a negative example, Tokyo member John Murray explained to me that the very title of the song Ray Holman arranged for
his band one year did not bode well. "'Plenty Lovin''?!" he said to me in an
incredulous tone. "You coming into Panorama with a tune called 'Plenty
Lovin''?! You understand." By contrast, "Dust in Your Face" so fired the
imagination of steelband musicians that it was arranged for Panorama by at
least a dozen bands in 1993. Many of these arrangements evoked confrontation and battle with intertextual references to other music. Ken Philmore's
arrangement for Potential Symphony, for example, included brief statements of the theme music from two Westerns—*Bonanza* and *The Good, the
Bad, and the Ugly.* And Trinidad All Stars brought down the house by quot-
ing "Shot Call," General Grant's dance-hall hit of the same year, which described a gun battle at a dance.

Rivalry is also reflected in Panorama's premium on sheer volume. The
need for volume in modern Panorama is related, no doubt, to the way DJ
trucks and massive speaker systems have transformed carnival's overall
soundscape since the 1970s. But volume was a musical weapon for the
steelbands long before the advent of amplification. The reason steel replaced bamboo in the first place was that it was louder, and even when
melodic pans were later developed, Zigilee recalled that it was the ear-split-
ting sound of the iron that musicians depended on in confrontations with
rival steelbands.

[9]The word "buyaka" is used by Jamaican dance-hall singers to represent the sound of gunfire.

Band coming down, and band coming up. So both of you alongside, and it's firing, all band firing on all cylinders. Well is your iron man have to pull you through, man. Sometimes it have iron man—they could be tired and thing, yes? And sometime they have their woman in the band, they want to go and hug up, they want to drink and thing. But when the band going down so, and you sight a band coming up of repute, all man you see they leave they girl and taking the iron from everybody, because this is business, the business part of the fete. You only hear the whole rhythm [i.e., the non-pitched percussion] because band passing. We going down, you going up. And boy, everybody face serious, you know. This have no laugh. This come like superiority, you know, class. (personal conversation, 1993)

The irons are still the mainstay of the engine room today, their piercing sound an indispensable rhythmic reference for the whole band. In Panorama, however, where the elaborate arrangements require a much higher ratio of pans to irons, the best way to make the band louder is to use more pans. In the 1960s and '70s, steelbands took as many players to Panorama as they could provide pans for; Harmonites, as mentioned earlier, sometimes went to Panorama with more than 200 pan beaters. In response to this phenomenon a limit was imposed on the number of players allowed on stage (this has varied over the years between 100 and 120 players),[10] so that smaller bands would not be at such a disadvantage.

Once a band reaches its limit of 100 players, increased volume can still be achieved by using louder pans or playing more forcefully. Steel pan tuners in Trinidad, who in the 1950s and 1960s responded to the challenge of playing the classics by increasing the sustain and "sweetness" of their instruments, have responded to the challenge of Panorama by giving their pans more power. The difference can be illustrated by comparing instruments made by Ellie Mannette, for example, with those of Lloyd Gay or Herman Guppy Brown. Mannette was arguably the most influential tuner in Trinidad in the 1950s and early 1960s, but he left Trinidad in 1964 and has lived in the United States since then, where he continues to perfect his style without much concern for Panorama. He takes great care in the tuning of overtones and matches their resonance to the fundamental in such a way that a note sounds rich, bright, and warm when struck lightly. The purity of his sound makes his pans well suited to the microphone, for amplification or recording. If you strike a Mannette pan hard, though, especially the lower notes, it feels as though you have dug too deep and hit the bottom, where a metallic

---

[10]The limit has been changed from time to time. In 1994, it was reduced from 120 to 100, a move that was protested by the larger bands, who already had to cut players, but welcomed by many smaller bands who had difficulty attracting enough players to compete in sheer size and volume.

"wanking" detracts from its sweetness. This effect can be noticed in any pan, but it is less marked in pans tuned by Gay or Brown, which may actually need to be struck harder for their brightness to fully emerge. The notes on these pans also have less sustain than Mannette's and a timbre that some people would characterize as less sweet than Mannette's. (I would describe it as harder, and, particularly in Gay's case, more explosive.) Players and bands must consider the relative importance of sweetness and power when choosing which pans to play. For example, Boogsie Sharpe told me that although he loved the sound of Lincoln Noel's pans, he decided to supplement them in Phase II with more powerful pans made by Lloyd Gay.

Phase II players also beat these pans within an inch of their lives. Black Holman, the hard-hitting double seconds player who was my section leader in Phase II, told me, "I play for two!" and he demonstrated techniques that I could use to play louder, such as using longer sticks and alternating hands whenever possible on repeated notes. As a result of this kind of playing, Phase II's timbre is often characterized by a certain wankiness, an effect that Sharpe's arranging accommodates in interesting ways, especially in the low pans, where it is most noticeable.[11] Ray Holman, who also arranged for Phase II in 1994 and 1995 during Sharpe's absence, tried to discourage rather than accommodate this style of playing. He was exasperated by Phase II's concern with power, and he saw it as part of a trend toward heavy-handed playing that diminishes the sound of the pans (it also puts them out of tune more quickly, requiring more frequent and extensive blending by tuners). At present, however, Holman and other like-minded connoisseurs[12] seem to be fighting a losing battle, as the demands of rivalry and excitement favor powerful pans and loud playing.

Song Interpretation

The audience's enjoyment of musical quotes, sounds, or gestures that make reference to the lyrics of the original song is an important aspect of Panorama music. Unlike drama and rivalry, which have some precedent in older steelband practices and in carnival generally, the concern for song interpretation is a new aesthetic generated within the Panorama competition itself. The earliest steelbands functioned not to interpret the song, of course,

---

[11] Very heavy playing distorts the timbre of the lower pans, especially, and many of the inside parts on the six-pan or the quadrophonics in Phase II stand out more prominently because of this. Sharpe achieves creative sound effects from the entire band, such as chromatic slurs or rapid alternations between octaves, agitated sounds that are not enhanced by sustain and sweetness.

[12] Holman told me that some bands (including Desperadoes, All Stars, and Exodus) insist more than others on proper playing technique, constraining their players from hitting the pans too hard.

but rather to accompany it, playing interlocking rhythms to support the singing of chantwel and chorus. But even when steel pans became capable of rendering popular calypsoes and other songs in instrumental versions, their carnival performances were enlivened by the singing of dancers and revelers. Emory Cook's 1956 recording of a steelband playing Sparrow's "Jean and Dinah" on the road provides an example of this kind of performance (Smithsonian Folkways 2000). This steelband arrangement transforms Sparrow's original song to make it more closely approximate the participatory aesthetic of the carnival lavway: steel pans play the chorus over and over, omitting the verse entirely, while people in the crowd join in occasionally to sing its words. They also participate by dancing and shouting.

To give life to a performance on the Panorama stage, a steelband must to some extent replace this kind of spontaneous variety with planned variations and effects. This is not to say that Panorama audiences are passive; on the contrary, audience members frequently sing a catchy line of the chorus, sometimes urged to join in by the players' example, and also dance and shout their excitement. Compared to the road, however, spectators at Panorama are more interested in seeing what the steelband will "do with the song" (which spectators know from radio and tent performances), rather than doing something with it themselves.

The audience's enjoyment of song interpretation is rooted in the aesthetic tradition of calypso, an aesthetic that can be best appreciated in the "tents" (today they are theaters and auditoriums) where calypsonians perform live every night during the weeks leading up to carnival. Popular tents include Spektakula, Kaiso House, and the Calypso Review, each one boasting a stable of twenty or more calypsonians who take turns on stage singing two songs each, with a house band to accompany them. As performed in this context, calypso is above all a narrative art, in which word play and meaning are prized. The audience shouts and claps approval for a singer when he or she tells a good story, acts out a humorous parody, or makes witty criticisms and commentaries on current social and political events. Even though calypsoes for the road (called "road marches") may be relatively more concerned with danceability and tunefulness, this love of word play is an important aspect of carnival festivity generally. In Panorama, therefore, where some festive components of steelband performance, like dance and movement, have been diminished, arrangers have discovered that the audience appreciates playful manipulations and shadings of textual meaning, much as they do in the calypso tents.

Steelband interpretations of David Rudder's "Dust in Your Face," discussed above, provide examples of this. Ken Philmore's use of themes from popular westerns, referencing the shoot-out described in Rudder's lyrics, drew roars of appreciation from the crowd when he unveiled it in the

Panorama finals. Similarly, All Stars, who had scored poorly during the semifinal round, so inspired the crowd with their quote in the finals from General Grant's "Shot Call" that they jumped up to third place, and many people were disappointed that the band didn't win. Not all intertextual references are aggressive, of course, and they need not bring the crowd to their feet to be appreciated. In Starlift's 2000 arrangement of the song, "Picture on My Wall," for example, arranger Anise Hadeed quoted the opening motive from "Mona Lisa" to call attention to the title. This went over the heads of some listeners, but others surely appreciated it for the way it challenged their musical acuity and esoteric knowledge.

In addition to intertextual references, onomatopoetic sound effects sometimes underscore the original song's lyrics. All Stars brought kettle drums on stage, for example, to give sonic reinforcement to their interpretation of Lord Kitchener's "Earthquake" in 1994. Renegades used a kind of large African shaker and a tangle of repeating arpeggios to imitate the sound of rain during the introduction of Jit Samaroo's 1993 arrangement "Mystery Band," a Lord Kitchener song about the sound of bottles and cans in a rain-swollen river. Clive Bradley, in his 1988 arrangement of Mighty Trini's "Sailing" for Pandemonium, also imitated the sound of rain in a passage of the song that described sailing through a storm; he did this by having players reverse their sticks to play with the wooden end (instead of rubber), creating an unusual percussive patter along with the melody. And Alvin Daniell (a radio and TV commentator who judges calypso and has organized seminars for Panorama judges) explained to me that in Phase II's 1988 performance of "Woman Is Boss," Boogsie Sharpe made an even more abstract sonic representation of the word "totolbay" (referring to a love-struck man's state of mental confusion) by inserting a chaotic passage where each player rolled on two notes of his or her own choosing (personal conversation, 1993).

Clive Telemaque describes how these kinds of song interpretation are important not only in the arranging of the tune, but in the choosing of it as well, as All Stars players and arrangers accommodate the taste and festive pleasures of their audience:

> We put this part in the tune, this "Shot Call," because we always . . . depending on whatever a calypsonian say in his tune, we arrange the tune to suit that, you know. Like, Smooth[13] did "Curry Tabanca," and he bring the tassa and things in it because we have it here in the Caribbean, and "Curry Tabanca" is related to the Indian thing. The calypsonian is singing about that too, you know. So we introduce the tassa and different things within the

---

[13] He is referring to when Leon "Smooth" Edwards arranged for the band.

music because we was trying to create what the calypsonian was trying to say, you know.

He did "Woman on the Bass," he put a lot of bass solo and have it lively in the back there. "Dus in Yuh Face"—you find at some parts of the tune we try to create a storm, like it have some parts where you could picture the breeze coming and things like that. In "Soucouyant" he had a part imitating—well, we think down here a soucouyant is a thing that fly like a ball of fire—he had a part that sound like a fire engine. If you listen to it you could hear a fire engine coming, you know [*sings a chromatic passage*] like something coming and driving by.

So All Stars always choose a tune, especially when Smooth take over, we tend to go for more lively songs than the laid-back one. The more road march type songs, you know, and arrange according to what the calypsonian say. Because people using that tune to party, they want to hear it on the radio, all about. They party with it so they understand it, they understand all the lyrics that the people saying in the song, so when the band play it, they would expect that you would create some kind of a thing . . . well, we call it a hook line—some interesting part in your tune and things like that, you know. (personal conversation, 1993)

Arranger Beverly Griffith uses a visual analogy to explain how he enhances the lyrics: "My music is more like trying to paint a picture. I pay attention to lyrics, I try to form musical passages based on what the calypsonian is saying" (personal conversation, 1993). This points beyond intertextuality and onomatopoeia to more subtle calculations of musical mood and sentiment that reflect the text.

Griffith's metaphor of a painting presented to the viewer suggests a fundamental contrast with the participatory mode of steelband performance in the streets, and shows how Panorama's programmatic quality is created not only through abstractly dramatic musical gestures and forms, but also through various kinds of reference to the lyrics and meaning of songs. Such a programmatic conception of composition could be explained as yet another influence of European art music. Alvin Daniell believes, however, that it cannot be ascribed to the influence of formally trained judges, because they often miss the intertextual references in Panorama music. As an example, Daniell cites All Stars' 1993 arrangement of "Dust in Your Face," in which General Grant's "Shot Call" is quoted:

Somebody said, "Maybe this is why All Stars didn't win—because maybe the judges didn't even understand what was meant by "Shot Call." And it was true. The judges on that night were not even aware that there was a person called General Grant, they didn't know that he sang a tune called "Shot Call." So they didn't appreciate the relationship of what they were doing to "Dus in Yuh Face." They just thought it was the normal All Stars razzle-dazzle.

. . . . Now these are the little subtle things that I think are going over the judges' head, because, again, they're not into the culture of the instrument. They are pure musicians who feel "I know how to do my job, I have a good ear, I recognize things, I can hear things, I can recognize what's better than what musically." End of story. I think a lot more is needed than that for adjudicating Panorama. I think it is necessary to go into the panyards, to feel the culture; it is necessary to come to terms with the calypsoes being chosen, from the point of view of knowing them inside out. I cannot understand a judge going into Panorama and telling me he is hearing the calypso for the first time that night. (personal conversation, 1993)

The Panorama practice of song interpretation is rooted in a specifically Trinidadian love of word play and double entendre, and has evolved as a response to the aesthetic preferences of the audience, rather than any classical music bias the judges might have. (This is a point to which I will return in the discussion of formal procedures in chap. 10.)

Excitement

While song interpretation per se may sometimes go over the judges' heads, the general level of excitement in the audience is something they cannot ignore. Indeed, as arranger Beverly Griffith points out, "Excitement is one of the key things in today's Panorama; you hear that on every judge's score sheet" (personal conversation, 1993). Excitement is commonly evoked as an element that distinguishes Panorama music from other steelband repertoire and performance practice, as in Clive Telemaque's explanation of how Panorama differs from the Music Festival:

We want to move the people, and if the people sitting down and listening to it, we want that if we playing, people should be getting off their seat, and their mouth open, you know? Listening and enjoying themselves. We don't want people sitting and listening as if it was a music festival; we figure Panorama is not a music festival. (personal conversation, 1993)

Much of Panorama's excitement can be attributed to its atmosphere of drama and rivalry, as explained above. But Panorama also has a quality of excitement that neither drama (in the "programmatic" sense in which I have defined it here) nor rivalry completely accounts for.

Musicologist Pat Bishop references this quality when she asserts that in Panorama, "The whole thing is to raise the stand" (1993). Radio commentator Dave Elcock lists some of the ways this can be done, noting that steelbands "need to get a response from the audience by the use of various musical devices, whether it's crescendos or stops and starts, or rolls and runs and so on." Panorama arrangements are thus characterized by all sorts of exciting "effects," as Eddy Odingi explains:

> The pannists have become more versatile. They keep thinking of new things, new ways to defeat others. So they're always coming up with something new, more effects. Boogsie [used] Indian drums, he also used Shango drums. They try to make the pan sound like different things. Once [Bradley] took the sticks and hit the side of the pan to make it sound like rain falling. . . . So people do different things with the pan to get effects. Right now Panorama is about effects. (personal conversation, 1993)

Whether it is a chromatic run that dazzles with its virtuosity, a sudden break that sets off the listeners' adrenaline, or a clever and unexpected trick like beating the sides of the pan, Panorama arrangers must produce effects for an audience that expects novelty and excitement.

The particular quality of excitement in Panorama can be understood by contrasting it with music for dancing on the road. Clyde Inniss compares contemporary Panorama music with the early days of the competition, when the same music played on stage Sunday night would be good for playing on the road Monday morning, with a few adjustments (such as removing the modulation, or "change key"):

> In old times you could jump up with the Panorama tune. Even with what they put in. We used to call it the change key, where you change key, and you come with a different chord there. The change key is the tune for the stage, but when you come on the road, you ain't use no change key, and you got the music. So the next morning is the same, and this is the tune you looking for. The steelband music in the Sunday night, Monday morning that is the tune you want, and that is the tune you get. . . . But these Panorama tunes, you can't—I think it was about two years ago, the tune that Boogsie Sharpe win, you couldn't jump up with it. People was asking, "What is that tune?" When I hear it beating, I couldn't believe that is the Panorama tune. People askin' what tune that is, and a man say, "That is the tune they win with last night," and people hear it and they gone.

Daisy McLean likewise observes that "when you play [your Panorama tune] on the road, it have this set of Tchaikovsky this, and long run. You can't

jump to it." "Jump," in this case, means to dance generally, McLean's implication being that Panorama music is not good for dancing. Sunilal Samaroo
(drummer for the Samaroo Jets and other steelbands) uses the same word,
however, to describe the physical response that Panorama arrangers do try
to elicit by including a "gimmick, breakaway thing for people to jump up
and get on" (personal conversation, 1993). And recall that Clive Telemaque
judges All Stars' success by whether people get out of their seats and move.
Despite McLean's implication that one can't dance to Panorama music,
therefore, it could be said that Panorama music is conducive to a more excited *kind* of dancing, distinguished from dancing on the road both by
tempo and by its relatively less consistent groove. Thus a "Tchaikovsky this,
and long run" that would discourage dancing on the road does not prevent
Panorama audiences from jumping up excitedly with the music.

The difference between dancing on the road and jumping up at Panorama is important, nonetheless. Though I have been concerned up to now
with showing how Panorama perpetuates and adapts earlier traditions of
carnival festivity (such as rivalry and drama), and also how it generates new
traditions of its own (such as song interpretation), when discussions about
Panorama turn to dance they gravitate toward the problem of endangered
and lost traditions. This is a topic that, for older Trinidadians in particular,
evokes nostalgic recollections of chipping behind a steelband on the road,
and frustration with the stationary performance and frenzied tempos of
modern Panorama. Ray Holman, for example, insists that his Panorama
music should be just as danceable as the music he arranges for the road, but
recognizes that this priority is difficult to uphold in the competition:

> I don't like to stand up on a stage. I find that kind of kill the whole thing,
> too, you know. Pan is for moving. What is nice is hearing a steelband on the
> move playing. It's a beautiful thing, you know. . . . If you can't dance to the
> music, you might as well forget it. Is rhythmic music we playing. But if you
> going to have the music on a stage and everybody stand up and play now,
> the dancing really not coming so important. And there's a whole lot of
> things that cause the music to get stupid. It get wild, it have no groove in it.
> But if you had to move and play, the music would have to be arranged in
> such a way that it would have a swing in it. So the music would sound better,
> it would be better music, because it's moving. (personal conversation, 1993)

The concern of steelband veterans for the danceability of Panorama
music points, in musical terms, to the preoccupation of younger steelband
musicians and audiences with melodic, harmonic, and formal variety that
makes it hard for them to conceive of a steelband music whose primary attraction is rhythm and groove. Tokyo member John Murray, for example,

explained to me that rhythm was not something that he felt he needed to study actively: "You know, as a pan player, basically you could fit in any part of the rhythm. Playing the drum set is a more specialized skill. But basically once you're a pan player you're so much with rhythm, you understand? So it wouldn't be hard for you to take up a iron and beat a rhythm, or a cowbell and keep a tempo, or with a tambourine. You could fit in" (personal conversation, 1993). Murray's view is typical of many younger players who are so focused on mastering the technical complexities of the pan that they take other percussion instruments for granted.

A somewhat opposite perspective is provided by pan pioneer Neville Jules, however, who saw pans develop out of non-pitched percussion and conceives them as performing a similarly rhythmic function. Jules finds that younger players lack the ability or interest to learn certain rhythmic techniques on a pan:

If you listen to how they play the congas in the bands these days (we were the first band to bring congas on the road, you know), part of that is from the tenor kittle and the bele [*sings*] that is some of the beats we used to get long time. That is before we get any melody. So I used some of those same beats now on the grundig, with chords. . . . The reason why we don't have grundig in the band today because I find the guys and them, they couldn't play the rhythm I wanted, because some of them they wasn't around when these things was happening, so they have no idea what I want them to do, really. So even though I show them, they taking too long to do it, the younger guys. So they couldn't really do it, so I just abandoned the plan. (phone conversation, 1999)

Jules's observation reflects not just the changing styles of a new generation, but also the fact that ambitious young players tend to be more preoccupied with acquiring melodic and harmonic knowledge than consciously exploring the intricacies of rhythm. This is not to say that Panorama music is not rhythmically intricate. The polyrhythmic and cyclic conception of musical structure that characterizes other Afro-Trinidadian percussion ensembles continues to structure the jam section, in particular (chap. 10). Nonetheless, Panorama's particular qualities of excitement have helped to distance the steelband from the rhythmic conception and the dance function of the tamboo bamboo that was its original model.

SUMMARY: GAINS AND LOSSES

During the time that I experienced Panorama as a participant and observer between 1989 and 2000, its music appeared to me as a relatively stable idiom, characterized by drama, rivalry, song interpretation, and excitement. I have argued that this stability is imposed mainly by the festive traditions of pan beaters and audiences, who, despite being separated by the stage, continue in many ways to celebrate steelband performances as an expression of community identity and solidarity. In contrast to the changes in repertoire and venue imposed by sponsors, or the new musical paradigms proposed by arrangers, this communal conception of Panorama has been a conservative influence on the music.

Despite this conservatism, however, Panorama is often discussed in terms of alarm and loss by steelband veterans like Daisy McLean, Clyde Inniss, and Ray Holman, who view the steelband in a longer historical perspective. The perspectives of older players and fans are not exclusively nostalgic, since many see gains as well as losses. For example, Inniss is disappointed at the poor showing of contemporary steelbands on the streets but excited about their accomplishments on stage. Referring to the recent introduction of laptop computers for Panorama judges, he told me, "Ray Holman, this boy Jit Samaroo, these fellas and them—I think that music right now is real advanced. It come like computer have to work now to help the adjudicators and them. This is great!" (1992). Similarly, Zigilee, who, like Jules, recognizes the loss of the old-time steelband rhythm, recognizes that pan has made great gains in melody (by which I would guess he means timbre, harmony, and form as well): "The old-time rhythm, it gone. If anybody ask me, I will say that . . . 'the years that you know pan beating, what you think went on now from then?' We lost rhythm, but we gained melody, more melodious" (personal conversation, 1993).

While appreciation for the technical advances of the steelband may compensate for certain musical losses, negative feelings prevail when conversation turns to the steelband's larger role in carnival and in society. Clyde Inniss complains, for example, that concerns about money have eroded the loyalty even of rank-and-file players: "When we used to beat pan, it was for nothing. When we collected money we used to . . . make a nice cook [meal] for all the panbeaters and them. But now you have to give pan beaters $200, $300. So this is the real crash of steelband now." Inequalities in money and prestige also create a hierarchy by which a few prominent bands dominate Panorama, especially from the 1980s onward (see appendix III). The more the focus of steelband enthusiasts turns toward the national stage of Panorama, the fewer attractions small community bands can offer to young players. Compounding these changes, the steelband's role in carnival masquerade was largely usurped by DJ trucks and amplified brass bands by the late 1970s.

Many musicians and enthusiasts therefore regard the 1950s and '60s nostalgically, as a golden era when steelbands ruled the road and held their rightful place as the favorite music for carnival festivity. This nostalgia responds to modernizing trends that link the problems of the steelband to national and global pressures on Trinidad carnival generally, trends that include increased levels of official promotion, displacement of neighborhood masquerade bands by large commercial bands, and the interpenetration of calypso and soca with the world music market. For steelbands, the single most significant condition of modern carnival is the pervasive staging of culture in formally adjudicated competitions that privilege spectacle over participation. Questions about how Panorama has affected the spirit of the steelband—the relative influence of audience versus organizers, for example, or the potential for creativity in Panorama—may be most productively answered, therefore, by first considering the role of competition in Trinidad carnival generally.

9

Contest and Control

Is dis Panorama ting dat helping to kill steelband. Tuners and arrangers chargin'
too much money and dem judges judging some bands out of existence. Dey only
care about de big names and de majority ah people like winners. . . . Dey killing
de goose dat lay de golden egg.

Eddie Odingi, "Pan Jumbie," 1992

A fundamental change that Panorama introduced to the steelband tradition
was the substitution of formally adjudicated competition for the informal
rivalry of the Bomb and other kinds of carnival performances. Panorama
was not the first adjudicated competition for steelbands, of course; steelbands had competed in the Music Festival since 1952, and there were other
sponsored steelband competitions in the 1940s and 1950s.[1] What was unprecedented about Panorama was that, by the late 1970s, it was virtually the
only venue for steelbands, rather than one of many. In the absence of alternatives, like playing for fêtes and masquerade, the constraints of formally
adjudicated competition became oppressive for many steelband musicians
who began to wonder whether Panorama was stifling the creative spirit that
had produced the steelband in the first place.

---

[1] An islandwide competition called Steelband Bacchanal (or Carnival Bacchanal), for example, preceded Panorama, instituted in 1959 (Ann Lee 1997). And many others were organized on both islandwide and local scales from the very inception of the steelband. Thomas (1990: 218) even cites a
1942 steelband competition, which is so early in the steelband's development that it was probably a
continuation of an earlier tradition of organized tamboo bamboo competitions.

Arranger Ray Holman, for example, contrasts the Panorama experience with his memories of an earlier time: "We used to play pan because it's a pride you have—you want to play this tune. It didn't have no judge, the people is the judge. You would know when you play well. But now you have to sit down in front of these five people, and they pushing [their agenda]. I hate to hear this thing now" (personal conversation, 1993). Holman's frustration is part of a broader pattern of disillusionment over the demise of community control over carnival performances. Many Trinidadians feel that the ideal conception of carnival as a community-based celebration is threatened today by middle- and upper-class participation, expensive fees for mass-produced costumes, staged performances, growth in carnival tourism, and the international marketing of carnival music and masquerade. Novelist Earl Lovelace, for example, warns of "the horror of the vision of a Carnival torn from its political and social roots, gutted of its power and presented as a neutral aesthetic creation" (1998: 59). This vision of *presentation* of the steelband, calypso, and masquerade contradicts an ideal view of carnival performance as an occasion for creative and unfettered *participation*. In this chapter I will look at how this ideal measures up to accounts of carnival performances from the nineteenth century to the present, and assess the nature and limitations of elite control through competition in the Trinidadian case.

Questions about elite control in Panorama can also be considered in relation to other kinds of musical competition, however, and to the phenomenon of competition generally in human culture. To the extent that Trinidad carnival competitions provide opportunities for intervention and manipulation, they may invite comparison with the oppressive aspects of Western art music competitions. These, according to Christopher Small, are not for nurturing talent but rather "for restricting entrance to the big-time concert circuit." And while such competitions may favor the best competitors, they do not always favor the best musicians, causing Small to observe wryly that "it is in this way that the culture gets the artists it deserves" (1998: 31–32). A similarly negative pronouncement about music competitions is posted on the wall of my daughter's piano studio: "All one needs to know about prizes is that Mozart never won one." Cursory consideration of many less institutionalized traditions, however, from jazz cutting contests to Indian powwows, reveals that competition is more than a tool of elite regulation. Johann Huizinga argues, indeed, that competition is a formative playful impulse in human culture: "The two ever-recurrent forms in which civilization grows in and as play are the sacred performance and the festal contest" (1950: 48).

The creative and antihierarchical influences of competition are as intuitively obvious as its capacity for constraint. One commonly cited benefit of competition, for example, is that it spurs performers to new heights of excellence. This value may be fraught with problems of how "excellence" is defined, and by whom, but it is nonetheless true in music, as in sports and in war, that competition is an important stimulus to effort and achievement, and indeed to creativity. Moreover, in paradoxical relationship to the impulse to prevail over one's opponents, competition also enforces powerfully egalitarian values. The sports metaphor of a level playing field, for example, stands for fairness and equal opportunity. Similarly, in contrast to the notion of carnival competition as a tool of elite control, Roberto DaMatta argues that the pervasive role of competition in carnival is congruent with carnival's propensity to level the everyday world's hierarchies:

> The very idea of competition, of a contest between equals, is incompatible with hierarchized social systems and therefore seen as something that should be banned from them. There no one should rise by means of tests, which place *performance* above other criteria of greater importance (such as birth, residence, skin color, etc.). But in Carnival everything happens through competition, so much so that the idiom of the society is transformed. From a hierarchical language and style, we pass to a competitive and egalitarian code, since now open contests provide opportunity for all. (1991: 112)

Because competition is associated both with institutional control and egalitarian play, its analysis may provide important insight into the balance between elite domination and popular expression in the performing arts.

COMPETITION AS PLAY

As demonstrated in my account of the Bomb controversy and Panorama's beginnings (chaps. 5 and 6), adjudicated competitions can be used by elite minorities as a tool of control over popular expression. Before opposing the rules and rituals of such competitions to less "formal" modes of communal rivalry, however, one must consider that competition is a ubiquitous mode of human interaction with a complex logic and organizing impulse of its own. Many constraints of carnival competitions result as much from popular consensus as elite imposition, and one of carnival's paradoxes is that meticulously organized preparations are made for an event that is commonly thought to defy structure. Victor Turner calls attention to the elaborate rules and hierarchy of the Mangueira escola de samba in Rio de Janeiro, for example, noting that "it takes an awful lot of order to produce 'a sweet disorder'" (1987: 84). Turner argues that, if carnival at its best is characterized by a community bonding or "flow" which we might experience as spontaneous, "people need framing and structuring rules to do their kind of flowing. But here the rules crystallize out of the flow rather than being imposed on it from without. . . . [Mangueira's structure belongs] to the domain of *ludus* and not to the politico-economic order" (1987: 84).

Play (*ludus*) is a distinct mode of human experience whose function, according to Johann Huizinga, "can largely be derived from the two basic aspects under which we meet it: as a contest *for* something or a representation *of* something" (1950: 13). Huizinga cites the tendency of human societies to organize themselves in rival moieties, and the dualism that infuses many cosmologies, as evidence of a fundamental human penchant for representing the world in terms of rivalry and contest (1950: 53–54). This tendency to structure social groupings around play and rivalry is exemplified by steelbands in Trinidad, who represent larger neighborhood communities. Indeed, the violent steelband clashes of the late 1940s through the early 1960s were particularly intense manifestations of a kind of intergroup rivalry that has a long history in Trinidad carnival.

When the British first came to Trinidad around 1800, for example, they were alarmed to discover that slaves of the French planters were organized into groups called regiments or *convois*. Each *convois* had an elaborate hierarchy of officials with titles like king, queen, dauphin, ambassador, and prime minister (J. Cowley 1996: 13). With emancipation in 1838, these *convois* took to the streets at carnival time, and often clashed with one another in public. Carnival historian John Cowley presents an account of a confrontation between the Damas and the Wartloos, for example (who, he surmises, identified themselves with the French and the English, respectively—Wartloo deriving from Waterloo),[2] that escalated from song and masquerade into pitched battle (1996: 30–32). Over the ensuing decades, rivalry between kalinda bands became a cause of increasing alarm, culminating in the famous 1881 Canboulay riots where police battled stickfighters. Like the *convois*, stickfighting bands also had kings and queens, as well as hierarchies of musical specialists, such as the song leader, or chantwel, and drummers.

Terrence Ranger, who documents a similar pattern of festive contest between social groups in East Africa, argues that such ritually elaborate competitions represent a distinctively African strategy for defining social relationships. He explains how *Beni* societies of coastal Swahili-speaking people incorporated modern symbols of power and authority, such as European military uniforms and band instruments, into a mode of intergroup rivalry that predates these particular symbols—an argument that could be extended to the royal titles and costumes of Trinidad carnival bands. Ranger's

---

[2] At the 1815 Battle of Waterloo, the French army, led by Napoleon, was decisively defeated by the English, led by the duke of Wellington, effectively reversing French imperial expansion.

work shows that the organizational sophistication of these bands also extends beyond their hierarchies of rank, as illustrated in this description of a dance competition in the Tanzanian town of Bukerebe in the early 1900s (the narrator translates *ngoma* as "game" and uses this term to refer to the opposing groups):

> Competing games, always two in number, selected a mutually agreeable time and site. Each game was assigned a location approximately one half mile in distance from the other. Playing and dancing began at noon and stopped around five o'clock. . . . The winning game was determined by the number of observers who happened to be watching one of the games at the end of the afternoon. . . . Each game maintained its own internal organization complete with officers assigned to specific duties. (Ranger 1975: 114–15)

Music and dance competitions between rival social groups are also common elsewhere in contemporary Africa—in the *isicathamiya* singing of South African factory workers (Erlmann 1996), in the dance clubs of the Anlo Ewe in Ghana (Avorgbedor 2001), and in many other cultures (Gunderson 2000)—indicating an African precedent for the kind of musical and social rivalry seen in Trinidad carnival bands. Indeed, in the nineteenth century some of these bands still claimed African tribal identities (Cowley 1996: 32), and the European titles, names, and costumes they sported were relatively superficial embellishments on a more fundamental festive and competitive pattern.

Twentieth-century steelband musicians can be compared with Ranger's *Beni* examples in their use of militaristic language and images, and their methodic preparations for musical confrontations. During the 1940s through the '60s, especially, when carnival processions were the steelbands' main performance venue, it was a mark of success (as in the *ngoma* competition described above) for one steelband to draw supporters away from another as they passed each other in the streets. The secret rehearsal and strategic planning of parade routes described by Neville Jules in relation to the Bomb (chap. 5) also represent rules of planning, performance, and contest that developed in Trinidad carnival out of community play, without direction from government agencies or other "outsiders." The same might be argued for mas' camps, where costumes are planned and manufactured through an intricate division of labor (Scher 2003: 88–112), or the elaborate rituals of verbal and physical dueling between chantwels and carnival characters like the Midnight Robber or Pierrot Grenade. Direct African precedents for such competitions, and the ubiquity of the competitive impulse in human culture generally, remind us that organized competitions in Trinidad carnival do not in and of themselves represent colonial or elitist control.

On the other hand, Frank Gunderson, in his overview of musical competition in East Africa, notes: "Because of their impressive communicative potential in communities, music competitions are often targets for appropriation by larger social forces to include the needs of government and organized religion" (2000: 17). This kind of elite appropriation has been particularly obvious since Trinidad and Tobago's 1963 independence, and the historical record also suggests that it was an important dynamic in Trinidad carnival well before then.

COMPETITION AS INSTITUTION

Over the several decades since independence, the government's role in organizing carnival and supporting official cultural competitions has prompted complaints from various quarters that the expressive energy of the "people's carnival" is being eroded. Ana Maria Alonso, for example, asserts that "the creativity, profanity, ebullience and defiance of carnival have been neutralized; carnival is, in some sense, dead" (1990: 118). Trinidadian anthropologist John Stewart puts part of the blame explicitly on competitions, noting that their "inducements and constraints, along with easy access to the broadcast media and control of the main venues by the [Carnival Development Committee], have brought about a uniformity in the carnival which some find unrewarding" (1986: 307). Stewart speaks of a "sterile masquerade put on largely for [tourists'] benefit" (310). Similarly, Donald Wood laments that Trinidad carnival has become "one of the nice and pretty events needed by all countries as a symbol of their nationhood" (1968).

Despite the sometimes urgent tone of such criticisms, the process of institutionalizing carnival has a long history in Trinidad, and similar concerns have been expressed in other eras. Consider, for example, this assessment of carnival music by the calypsonian Duke of Albany (Charles Jones), made in 1950: "Calypso not being commercialised as it is today, there was a greater feeling of enjoyment on the whole" (Rohlehr 1990: 420). Jones made this observation during a time that Trinidadians today view nostalgically as a golden era of calypso, when Lord Kitchener was pioneering a new sound in London; the "Young Brigade," including Lord Melody, Pretender, and Spoiler, were singing in Port of Spain; and the Mighty Sparrow was soon to burst upon the scene (Rohlehr 1990: 457–532). From Jones's perspective, however, the performance of calypso for paying audiences in tents[3] repre-

---

[3] The term "calypso tent," which once referred to temporary structures, has come to mean a hall or auditorium that hosts a roster of calypsonians who perform there every night during the carnival season.

sented a corruption of the tradition he remembered from earlier days, in which chantwels composed songs for their neighborhood carnival bands. The chantwel was a song leader who improvised verses in call-and-response with a chorus, guiding the energy and excitement of the music and entertaining with his verbal wit. Though chantwels and drummers were people with specialized musical skills, everyone present could participate by singing the chorus, dancing, or playing an accompanying rhythm. In some respects, the calypso tent is to the chantwel what Panorama is to the steelbands of the 1950s: an institutional appropriation of lower-class folk practice, propelled by middle-class interest and commercial opportunities.

A key instrument in both of these appropriations was formally adjudicated competition, by which I mean competition that is judged by specified criteria (giving special power to those who do the specifying) and often by judges who are outsiders to the performers' communities. The choice of competition criteria and the social position of the judges raise obvious questions about hegemony and the invention of tradition.[4] On the other hand, this sort of elite interest and framing has influenced the lower-class carnival arts for so long that it could itself be considered part of carnival tradition in Trinidad. Formally adjudicated competitions date to at least 1900 and have functioned not only to control but also to valorize the carnival arts, and (in recent times) even to challenge nationalist hegemonies.

Some of these complex motivations and effects are illustrated in a 1919 competition for calypso and masquerade bands sponsored by the *Argos* newspaper in Port of Spain. At the time, calypso tents had only recently become popular as places where middle-class patrons could pay to hear carnival songs in a safe and respectable environment. The rules of the *Argos* competition reflected a concern for the sensibilities of these middle-class audiences, explicitly prohibiting ensembles of bamboo stamping tubes (tamboo bamboo that included gin bottles struck with a spoon. Their announcement read in part:

> We look forward to good behaviour . . . and will entirely discountenance
> the assembly of any stick playing band and things of the kind. . . . Those
> employing the use of bamboo and bottles will not be admitted into the

---

[4] "The invention of tradition" is a term coined by Hobsbawm and Ranger (1983) to refer to official rituals, pageants, etc. that are intended to legitimize the prevailing power structure by portraying it as timeless and unchanging. Hobsbawm underscores "the contrast between constant change and innovation of the modern world and the attempt to structure at least some parts of the social life within it as unchanging and invariant" (2). More generally, many scholars have come to recognize that the sanctity of "tradition" is often invoked to privilege one view of the past over others, and to reinforce the authority of certain groups over others (e.g., Handler and Linnekin 1984; Mendoza 2000; Raymond Williams 1977).

competition. Bands taking part in the musical competition must have at least eight pieces or ten performers and [their] members must be uniformly attired. (Rohlehr 1990: 96–97)

These cautions make clear that stickfighting violence had not disappeared from carnival with the banning of drums in the 1880s and that it continued to be associated to some degree with the tamboo bamboo bands. The professionals and merchants who sponsored the *Argos* competition not only regarded tamboo bamboo as distasteful, but also as a dangerous element of the lower-class *jamette* carnival. In Gordon Rohlehr's words, the *Argos* competition rules "made it clear that what they required was a de-Africanization of the music, the final abolition of its percussive Jamette elements. . . . The proud aim of all these people was to abolish the Ole Mas [masquerade] of the unwashed and put in its place the pretty Mas of the respectable" (Rohlehr 1990: 96–97).

What seems at first to be an obvious example of elite appropriation and constraint, however, takes on another meaning when compared to a carnival competition sponsored at the same time by the *Guardian* newspaper. The *Guardian* competition was to be held in the Queen's Park Savannah, a venue for horseracing and other elite diversions that was favored by the British colonial administration as a place where carnival celebrations could be more effectively contained and controlled. By contrast, the Marine Square location of the *Argos* event associated their competition with the downtown public celebrations of the lower classes. Just before carnival the *Argos* published a song that derided the notion of moving carnival celebrations to the lawns of the Savannah, using working-class dialect to advocate the tradition of a downtown carnival for creoles (a term that could refer to black or coloured people, or even white people of French descent):

Savannah side will be stale in a way
So keep de Carnival down-town

Razor grass does cut Creole foot
So keep it down-town

Tram and cab-horse all clear de way
So keep de Carnival down-town

To make room for Johnny at the break of day
So keep de Carnival down-town
(Rohlehr 1990: 93–94)

In relation to this division—both social and spatial—between the exclusive carnival celebrations of the elite and the public celebrations of the common people, the *Argos* competition was part of an effort by progressive middle-class coloured people to defend the public carnival against official repression and upper-class appropriation. The *Argos* editors and the coloured middle-class businessmen that supported the *Argos* competition cast themselves as champions of the "people's carnival." In addition to constraining performance, therefore, some early carnival competitions were also intended to defend and legitimize certain communities and their expressions.

PROMOTION THROUGH IMPROVEMENT

The *Argos* sponsors' efforts represent an early-twentieth-century trend of middle-class identification with lower-class performing arts, in opposition to the colonial elites and the hegemony of European culture, that became increasingly important to the development of Trinidad carnival. The *Argos* competition presents a clear example of modernist reform, in that its purpose was to simultaneously promote lower-class expressive forms and improve them, and sponsors hoped to attract middle-class patronage for calypso performances by insisting upon decency and refinement. Such a strategy of promotion through improvement, which facilitated a rapprochement between the elite private carnival and the people's public carnival, first expressed itself as a response to cultural friction between French creoles and English in the late nineteenth century.

At the time that England wrested the island of Trinidad from Spanish control in 1797, the white upper class in the island consisted mainly of French creoles. These French planters had come from other Caribbean islands, such as Martinique, Guadeloupe, and Haiti, responding to the 1783 Cedula of Population issued by the Spanish King Charles III, which offered land to Catholic settlers in Trinidad. Though the influx of French planters did not produce Spain's desired result of warding off the English and Dutch navies, it did create a powerful French cultural influence in Trinidad. This was expressed not only in the widespread use of French patois until the early twentieth century, but also in the general population's enthusiasm for the Catholic tradition of carnival.[5] Following emancipation in 1838, public carnival celebrations came to be dominated by bands of lower-class blacks, and the upper-class French creoles largely withdrew to the safety of private venues for their fêtes. Lower-class carnival bands frequently assumed the identities of rival European courts or armies and clashed with one another in

---

[5] Carnival is a festival that precedes the fasting period of Lent. The word comes from the Latin *carne vale*, meaning a farewell to meat. Although the festival is not sanctioned by the Catholic Church, it is pegged to the Christian calendar and is associated mainly with Catholic societies.

singing duels between chantwels or even in bloody stickfights accompanied by drumming and song. Interband aggression could also be redirected against the colonial authorities. The most famous example of this was the 1881 Canboulay riot, which erupted when a police captain named Baker tried to break up the torchlight procession known as *cannes brulées*, or canboulay (chap. 2). In response, stickfighters from different neighborhood bands joined ranks in a pitched battle with police. The Canboulay riot was a pivotal event in the history of Trinidad carnival for several reasons: it provoked legal restrictions on music and masquerade; it became a symbol of carnival's revolutionary potential; and it drew a sharply divided reaction from the social elite, an analysis of which can help us to see more clearly how later carnival competitions assumed functions of both control *and* resistance.

Some French creoles viewed Captain Baker's efforts to repress the lower-class black carnival as an attack on their own culture. To appease this upper-class constituency, the British governor reprimanded the police the day after the canboulay riots and confined them to their barracks. The governor's gesture failed, however, to prevent a cultural alliance that developed between French creoles and the lower-class *jamettes*. This was to some extent an alliance of convenience against British authority, but it was sometimes portrayed as an aesthetic affinity as well. In an 1883 letter to the *Port of Spain Gazette*, for example, the author distinguishes between the musical sensibilities of French creoles and more recently arrived Europeans (by which readers might understand him to mean British), taking as an example the Belair drum dance brought by slaves from Martinique and other French islands:

> To European ears the tambour and chac-chac produce nothing but the most
> discordant sounds; to Creoles, even of the higher classes, whose organs have
> been accustomed from their birth to this peculiar music, there is a cadence
> and rough harmony in their accompaniment of native songs which is far
> from disagreeable; and on the lower classes their effect is magical. We have
> only to look at a round of Belair and note the peculiar undulating motions
> of all present, as they follow with their heads, their hands, their whole bodies
> the peculiar cadence of the music, to be convinced that, to their ears, there is
> more, in the sound produced, than the discordant noise which alone strikes
> the European. (Cowley 1996: 96)

This perception of an expressive empathy between lower-class blacks and elite French creoles can be read as self-serving, but it is not entirely specious. Elite efforts to promote lower-class arts have played an important role in the development of Trinidad carnival at many points in history and have been motivated, at least in part, by genuine enthusiasms, even as they have steered carnival performances in new directions.

At the turn of the century, with British authorities continuing to inveigh against violence and obscenity in carnival, some carnival enthusiasts in Port of Spain responded by sponsoring competitions that would show the carnival arts to good advantage. Beginning in the 1890s, French creole, Spanish, and coloured businessmen such as Ignacio "Papa" Bodu offered prizes for masquerade:

> City fathers like Bodu and his colleagues from among the French Creole merchant class, Singuineau, Boissiere and Attale, were remembered for their donations of silver trophies and cash to the best costumed bands in the reformed post 1884 Carnival.[6] Business houses had already begun to make sizeable profits at Carnival time, and businessmen joined those whose main concern was the preservation of old French Creole customs and traditions, in defending the Carnival whenever its extinction was threatened. Their patronage was to change the style of the festival. (Rohlehr 1990: 26)

The focus on masquerade in these early competitions reflected the merchants' interest in selling costume materials, but music was an important part of the masquerade bands' presentations. By 1911, prizes for music were also awarded separately from masquerade (Cowley 1996: 179). Ann Lee writes that "one important effect of these competitions was to minimize aggression while retaining some of the excitement of rivalry" (1991: 426). While the merchants and French creoles who sponsored these competitions sought to establish certain kinds of control over lower-class performers, that is, they also sought to preserve some of carnival's creative and unpredictable impulses, and to protect the carnival arts against English efforts to abolish the festival altogether.

Born from both class conflict and friction between English and French elites, the early-twentieth-century carnival competitions established a precedent that was later followed by other groups who sought to promote or defend their aesthetic values and social positions. In the 1940s, cultural nationalism added urgency to the agenda of "improving" carnival, and competitions continued to be an important means to this end. A Carnival Improvement Committee was formed in 1939 to "lift the calypso," among other things (Rohlehr 1990: 328). This was a model for the later Carnival Development Committee, established in 1956 when nationalist politicians gained new power through a greatly expanded elected legislature. The committee (which continues to function today as the National Carnival Commission)

---

[6] In 1884, the Peace Preservation Ordinance was passed to prevent a recurrence of the 1881 riots by restricting certain kinds of carnival performance, such as drumming and canboulay (Cowley 1996: 99–101).

took charge of the Calypso King competition (formerly sponsored by the *Guardian* newspaper) in 1958 and also established the Panorama steelband competition in 1963, immediately after independence. Along with the Best Band competition for masquerade, these music competitions are center-pieces of what has come to be regarded as Trinidad and Tobago's national festival.

STAGING STREET MUSIC

Through staging and formal adjudication, the Best Band, Calypso Monarch, and Panorama competitions have transformed the very communal tradi-tions that they purport to celebrate, and any serious analysis of their role in Trinidadian nationalism must acknowledge that they are in many ways "in-vented traditions," newly constructed rituals that are portrayed as old and that "seek to inculcate certain values and norms of behaviour by repetition" (Hobsbawm and Ranger 1983: 1). Yet one must also be careful not to over-estimate the transformative power of such cosmopolitan or middle-class framing, as Zoila Mendoza has cautioned in relation to Peruvian *danzas*:

> Although public and private *instituciones culturales* have attempted to estab-lish boundaries around the forms and meanings of highland music and dance by classifying them as folkloric and modeling them after "invented traditions," these expressive forms have constantly surpassed these bound-aries even in the context of contests and other staged presentations.
> (2000: 82)

The case of carnival competitions is particularly complicated, compared to some other cosmopolitan framings of folklore, by the fact that *competition* per se is not an exclusively cosmopolitan mode of performance. Many con-ventions of competition that were common to the participatory perfor-mances of the jamette carnival persist in today's staged competitions. Such incursions of participatory folk practice make the formally adjudicated competitions of carnival a terrain in which diverse priorities and values contest with one another.

The song form called calypso, for example, developed mainly in the ca-lypso tents, where singers perform for a seated audience, and this mode of performance is reinforced by competitions as Calypso Monarch. Early ca-lypsonians, however, also performed in the older tradition of the chantwel, a kalinda song leader who was often a stickfighter as well (Elder 1966: 198). One of the roles of the chantwel was to take the lead in confrontations with other neighborhood bands. Opposing chantwels traded boasts and insults in song, contests which sometimes escalated into physical battles. This kind of verbal rivalry, referred to in Trinidad as *picong*, continued even when chantwels began to sing on stage before seated audiences in the 1910s. Calypso tents in the 1910s through the 1930s commonly featured "picong wars" between individual singers or opposing groups (Rohlehr 1990: 60–62 and passim). Even today calypsonians often compose songs that attack another calypsonian, initiating a battle that is waged over different venues and several carnival seasons, each year's songs responding to the previous year's. This kind of rivalry is exemplified by the exchange of insults between Lord Melody and the Mighty Sparrow in the late 1950s.[7]

Calypsonians are also expected to make incisive social and political commentaries (Rohlehr 1990; Regis 1999), which are often delivered in a combative tone. Even in the absence of a rival singer, the audience in the tent responds to the calypsonian's insults, criticisms, and jokes. They greet a particularly good lyric with gesticulations, bursts of laughter, or shouts of "kaiso!" to express their approval. By the same token, picong may develop between the calypsonian on stage and a member of the audience who is bold enough to taunt the performer. These kinds of behaviors are not compatible with a cosmopolitan presentational mode of performance, yet they strongly condition the style of calypso performance in the tents, a style that is largely reproduced in formal competitions. Participatory behaviors are thus influential and valued both in the tradition of the chantwel and in the modern tradition of adjudicated competitions for calypso.

In the case of the steelband, it could be argued that formally adjudicated competition has had a more transformative effect on performance. For one thing, calypsonians have since the 1910s (when tent performances began) popularized a style of stage performance that is relatively independent of formally adjudicated competitions. Though steelbands also performed in staged concerts for many years before Panorama, their supporters were generally more enthusiastic and numerous at fêtes or on the road, where they could dance to the music. At the same time, steelband musicians are distinguished from calypsonians by the ambition many of them have to explore beyond such participatory modes of performance. They may enjoy playing for dancers, but they also aspire to master a cosmopolitan repertoire, and they pride themselves on the kinds of discipline, uniformity, and formal complexity that are associated more with concert stage performances of the classics than dance parties. The Panorama competition has encouraged such aspirations to presentational standards of performance, affecting both the structure of the music and the manner of rehearsal and performance.

---

[7] Some great examples of the repartee between Sparrow and Melody can be heard on the Smithsonian Folkways compilation CD titled *Calypso Awakening* (2000).

Nonetheless, the intensity of competition in Panorama links its presentational mode to more participatory carnival performances. The shared expectations of players and supporters impose considerations of communal festivity (chap. 8) that make Panorama music very different from a symphony or other cosmopolitan stage performance. Even in the choosing of a winner, the crowd's response is sometimes said to be as important as the judges' evaluations. This was certainly the case before the era of Panorama, when informal competitions between bands were equally intense, and public opinion was the arbiter of success. Neville Jules remembers that, even when the Bomb began to be judged formally, the judges' decisions might not be as important to the bands as the popular consensus:

> Let's say if you might go to a competition where they judging the Bomb, you might have two, three, four, five people judging. So even though they say that band "A" is the best band, the people who around in the entire city, hearing all the bands, they giving their opinions too. So it would come like, you know, people's choice. Even though a band gets first for playing a Bomb, but if the people say they found that band "B" was better, that is good enough for the bands and them. It was good enough for us. (phone conversation, 1999)

To the extent that musicians value and respond to public opinion, then, the judges' preferences may have limited relevance to performance style.

Trinidadian musicologist Pat Bishop asserts that Panorama judges ultimately depend on crowd reaction to tell them which band is best (personal conversation, 1993). Criteria by which judges ostensibly calculate the winner have included, in various years, "arrangement," "interpretation," "tone," "rhythm," "phrasing," and "balance." But because judges tend to be formally trained musicians with little or no experience playing in a steelband, it is hard for them to be indifferent to the reactions of the fans. Those fans do everything they can to boost the excitement when a favorite band is performing, defying the efforts of security personnel to prevent them from dancing, jumping, and gesticulating on or near the stage. They roar with enthusiasm at the exciting moments of an arrangement, and howl in rage if, at the end of the night, they think the judges have cheated their band. Many Trinidadians would agree with Bishop about the crowd's influence. This opinion may be expressed as an accusation, as a way of complaining the competition is distorted by crowd pressure (see Harold Headley's comments quoted in chap. 8); in other contexts the crowd's influence may be viewed positively, as an assertion of the people's choice. In either perspective, neither the manner of performance nor the outcome of the competition can be predicted by official judging criteria alone.

Measured by its predictability, therefore, the Panorama competition is not a particularly efficient tool for controlling the musical expression of steelbands. Few people could have predicted, at the outset of the competition in 1963, what the music would be like today. Those who thought the North Stars' early Panorama success heralded a new era of refinement and sobriety were proved wrong when the Cavaliers decimated the opposition in 1965 with power, speed, and excitement. Cultural nationalists who intended that Panorama's calypso-only policy would encourage steelbands to play "local" music, rather than subscribe to colonial values of musical excellence, might have been surprised to find steelband arrangers employing theme and variation form, contrapuntal part writing, and Beethovenesque cadences in their calypso arrangements. Calypsonians who had hoped Panorama would compel the steelbands to promote their music were outraged when Ray Holman began composing his own tunes for Panorama in 1972, an innovation that later caught on with many other arrangers (chap. 10). All of these things are evidence of a creative energy that adapts communal patterns of festivity to new circumstances and that generates entirely new patterns as well.

Thus, compared to Turino's model of middle-class control through modernist reform (see chap. 1), it is less easy to say exactly whose interests are served by Trinidad carnival competitions such as Panorama. The dynamics of Panorama are driven by the interests of several distinct groups. The priorities of some cultural nationalists and calypsonians are expressed in the stipulation that steelbands play calypso only; British colonial values are represented in the attitudes of formally trained judges; businesses seek prestige and advertising opportunities through steelband sponsorship; musicians strive to please and impress; and a crowd of thousands voices *its* preferences. While it is easy to see how competitions like Panorama constrain performance, then, it is less clear that these constraints amount to an effective tool of control by any one group.

COMPETITION AS OPPORTUNITY

The constraints of formally adjudicated competitions are challenged not only through the incursion of participatory performance modes, but also through the staging of alternative competitions. A competition's validating power depends its ability to draw a crowd, and so the hegemonic influence of an established competition can be mitigated by the creation of an alternative that draws the participation of artists and their public. For example, despite the *Argos* competition's exclusion of tamboo bamboo in 1919, the practice continued to be popular in carnival, and Stuempfle reports that there was a competition as late as 1939 for "best bamboo band" (1995: 34).

The lineages of many carnival competitions show a similar pattern of new breakaway competitions challenging old orthodoxies. Thus the organization of alternative competitions has been a consistent response in Trinidad carnival to the perceived inequities of institutional competitions, providing one example of how competition enforces an "egalitarian code" in carnival (DaMatta 1991: 112; quoted above at length).

One of the most famous examples of this was the calypsonians' boycott of the *Guardian*'s carnival competition in 1957 (Rohlehr 1990: 451; Stuempfle 1995: 120–22; Ottley n.d.: 22). The boycott was led by Mighty Sparrow, who was unhappy about the exalted status of the Carnival Queen category, essentially a beauty pageant for light-skinned middle-class girls. Sparrow participated in and won an alternative calypso competition at the Globe theater with "Carnival Boycott," a song that proclaimed his disdain for competitions and attacked the *Guardian* for giving a motor car to the Carnival Queen, while other champions received only "two case of beer." (Sparrow had received a paltry $25 prize as Calypso King the previous year.) The boycott, the alternative competition, and Sparrow's biting commentary succeeded in bringing the Carnival Queen down a notch the following year, when the Carnival Development Committee took over from the *Guardian* as sponsors and raised prizes for calypsonians and masquerade bands.

More recently, the problems of Panorama have also been addressed through alternative competitions. A separate judging category was established in the 1970s,[8] for example, for small bands that could not compete in sheer volume with the large steelbands that dominate Panorama. Also beginning in the 1970s, a competition was dedicated to single pan or "pan around the neck" bands that use old-style pans suspended from the neck by straps and played while walking[9] (as opposed to the larger sets of modern steel pans that are mounted on racks). One of the most innovative alternative steelband competitions is Pan Ramajay, which features improvisation in ensembles of ten players or fewer. Pan Ramajay was founded as a fund-raising event during the carnival off-season by Exodus steelband in 1990, and its continuing popularity is attributed by Exodus's manager, Ainsworth Mohammed, to the fact that it "levels the playing field" (personal conversation, 1993), taking away the advantage from the big-name steelbands and providing pannists a more genuine opportunity to be judged on their skills.

Competitions may be conceived to challenge musical hierarchies as well as social hierarchies, although the promotion of a given musical genre is

---

[8] I have not come across the date for the beginning of the small-band category, but I did find two letters to the editor in the Trinidad *Guardian* dated May 1, 1972, that advocated a boycott of Panorama by small bands if such a category was not created.

[9] This single pan style was first revived by Tripoli steelband as a novelty for the Panorama competition in 1973.

often linked to the interests of a particular social group or ideological position. An example of this is the Chutney Soca Monarch competition, founded in 1996. Chutney is a dance music popular among Trinidadians of East Indian descent, influenced by North Indian folk music and Hindi film songs, as well as Afro-Trinidadian calypso and soca.[10] The more recent "chutney soca" label, though, and the attachment of this genre to a carnival season competition, constitute a claim by East Indians for their place in a national culture that has been officially defined (largely through carnival competitions) in Afro-Trinidadian terms. The advent of the Chutney Soca Monarch competition also coincides closely with the 1995 electoral victory of the United National Congress, which gave Trinidad its first prime minister of East Indian descent.

Even within the field of Afro-Trinidadian music, the creation of new competitions for new genres and new constituencies has been an important strategy for challenging conservative orthodoxies. The Soca Monarch competition, for example, was founded in 1993 to give official recognition to a style of music that was overwhelmingly popular for carnival fêtes and masquerade but was not favored by the judges of the Calypso Monarch competition. Some Trinidadians regret this bifurcation of their carnival song tradition, whereas others welcome the recognition of aesthetic diversity that the soca/calypso distinction represents. The preference for soca is also associated to some extent with a younger generation, and youth constituencies are even more clearly associated with other new competitions. The Ragga Soca Monarch, for example, promotes a fusion of Trinidadian (soca) and Jamaican (ragga or dance-hall) styles. Gender inequalities have also been addressed by the National Calypso Queen competition, which challenges the unspoken but powerful gender bias in calypso judging. By calling attention to this issue, the Calypso Queen competition may have influenced the recent victories of Singing Sandra (1999) and Denyse Plummer (2001) in the Calypso Monarch competition.

A striking feature of these recent competitions is the diversity of their sponsorship. In 2000, for example, the Calypso Monarch competition was organized by the Trinbago Unified Calypsonian Organisation; the Soca Monarch competition was organized jointly by that organization and Caribbean Prestige Promotions International; Ragga Soca Monarch by National Cultural Promotions; Chutney Soca Monarch by Southex Promo-

---

[10] Soca is a modern variant of calypso, dating from the late 1970s, generally distinguished by its function as dance and party music, as opposed to calypso's function as listening music with narrative lyrics. The modern distinction between calypso and soca could be conceived as analogous to the older distinction between tent calypsoes (for performance before a seated audience in the calypso tent) and road marches (to accompany dancing and masquerade on carnival day); but the boundaries in both these pairings are rather indistinct (see Dudley 1996 for a more detailed comparison).

218 MUSIC FROM BEHIND THE BRIDGE

tions; Panorama by Pan Trinbago (a steelband organization with substantial government funding).[11] This mix of private and government sponsors contrasts with the near monopoly on sponsorship of major carnival events by the National Carnival Commission in the years following independence. The change complicates government's ability to control and define the "national" culture in the way that the PNM once did—as the political party that led Trinidad's transition from colony to independent nation, the PNM created a particularly monolithic and Afro-Trinidadian image of the nation's culture through the staging of competitions for masquerade, calypso, and steelband. If competition has served as a tool of cultural nationalism, therefore, it now seems also to be a means of challenging nationalist hegemony and creating opportunities for a more diverse array of performance traditions.

The increase in private sponsorship also suggests that advertising and commodification are important forces behind the creation of adjudicated competitions. Although commercialization in carnival is not an exclusively modern malady (as evidenced by the competitions sponsored by Papa Bodu around 1900 or by the *Argos* and the *Guardian* a little later), one genuinely new development in the latter twentieth century is the increasing importance of record sales and international touring for Trinidadian musicians. This has made the media's hegemony a major concern for some Trinidadians.

When I presented a colloquium on carnival and competition at the University of the West Indies in March of 2000, for example, students were mainly interested in talking about the power of the media. Many felt that radio station management in particular, whether through passive ignorance and lack of interest in carnival music or through active corruption and payola, pushed simplistic and formulaic soca songs for profit, stacking the deck against less commercially controlled musical forms. Given the historical and contemporary involvement of private businesses in sponsoring carnival competitions, one might have expected these students to apply a similarly cynical interpretation to the Soca Monarch or Ragga Soca Monarch competitions, linked as these competitions are to the interests of record and concert promoters. The students tended, however, to take the contrary view that formally adjudicated competitions represent an alternative to "commercialization" and provide opportunities for creative artists.

A particular example that many of these university students cited was the Pan Kaiso competition, founded in 1999 by Pan Trinbago to respond to the trend toward party-oriented soca music, "two-chord" jams that do not provide the kind of harmonic and melodic material needed for an effective

---

[11] The names of sponsors for the song competitions listed here are from a *Trinidad Express* article titled "Carnival Competitions . . . And the List Goes On" (March 9, 2000, p. 32). The National Carnival Commission is also involved with the staging of some of these events, including the Calypso Monarch and Panorama competitions.

steelband arrangement. To counter the commercial pressures that radio stations and DJs exert on calypsonians, the Pan Kaiso competition has created
a monetary and prestige incentive for calypsonians to compose for the steelband. In a sense, this reestablishes the relationship that thrived in the 1950s
and 1960s, when steelbands played a more important role than DJs in popu-
larizing carnival music, and calypsonians had to write at least one "pan
tune" each year if they wanted their music to be heard on the road. Rather
than favoring the musical style of that earlier era, however, the Pan Kaiso
competition rewards innovation and new possibilities for steelband music.
In contrast to some competitions whose emphasis is mainly preservationist
(such as the extempo calypso competition, featuring improvised verse, or
the "ole mas'" competitions for traditional carnival characters), Pan Kaiso is
thus conceived of as a vehicle for certain kinds of innovation and creativity
that the commercial media do not support.

Despite their complaints about the excess of competition in modern carnival, therefore, many Trinidadians view competition as a positive tool in
relation to specific problems. Organized competitions are thought to level
the playing field, to promote marginalized art forms and communities, to
challenge official definitions of the national culture, and to resist the formulaic pressures of the marketplace.

SUMMARY: NOSTALGIA AND CULTURAL STEWARDSHIP

An important question to consider here is how much contemporary complaints about Panorama (and carnival competitions generally) reflect
unique contemporary problems, and how much they reflect nostalgia.
Though formally adjudicated competition has become more pervasive since
independence, it is not a new phenomenon in Trinidad carnival. And despite the tendency of Trinidadians to disparage its influence, even formally
adjudicated competition represents a creative and unpredictable potential.
Competitions often provide recognition for marginalized constituencies,
and certain community-based values and modes of performance continue
to manifest themselves even in elite-sponsored competitions. Indeed, formally adjudicated competitions play roles that might be regarded as natural,
or at any rate time-honored, in performance traditions that were borne of
the tensions and shifting alliances of a colonial society. For example, they
create opportunity, they articulate group identity and solidarity through rivalry, and they provide the simple thrill of play.

On the other hand, Panorama's almost monopolistic hold on the time
and energy of Trinidad steelbands amplifies the problems of formal adjudication. In contrast to the "pundits of pan" whose opinions were important

to Ray Holman, or the crowds on the street that Neville Jules and All Stars tried to impress, most (though not all) of the judges for Panorama are people who neither play in steelbands nor belong to the neighborhoods and communities that the steelbands represent.[12] The formal music education of Panorama judges contrasts markedly with the oral tradition of the pan-yards,[13] even though their differentiation by social class and education has become less stark with increased middle-class participation in steelbands. As in the competitions sponsored by Papa Bodu or the *Argos*, judges for more recent calypso and masquerade contests tend to represent an aesthetic that is more cosmopolitan than the aesthetic of the lower-class communi-ties in which these art forms developed historically. This fact is consistent with complaints that formally adjudicated competitions have distorted au-thentic "people's music" to serve the interests of modernist reform or tourism. One could argue furthermore that the judges' need to justify their decisions by explicit and "objective" criteria favors quantitative over qualita-tive judgments, rules over affective impact, superficial forms over vital artis-tic substance. People who feel a sense of responsibility for their culture are justifiably concerned about such problems.

If formally adjudicated competitions are an enduring feature of Trinidad carnival, their prevalence and their particular expressions vary from one era to another, along with changing social and political formations. In the early twentieth century, for example, private sponsorship of carnival competi-tions was driven by both commercial interests and class/ethnic tensions. During the independence era this was replaced to some extent by political patronage, driven more by nationalist and modernist reformist agendas. Now, at the beginning of the twenty-first century, tourism and the global commodification of culture are exerting new pressures on the carnival arts, to which formally adjudicated competitions respond in various ways. The social and ideological divisions to which carnival competitions respond have also shifted and changed, different kinds of divisions capturing the na-tional imagination in different eras: French creole versus English in the late nineteenth century; upper class versus lower class in the early nineteenth century (reflected in the *Argos*'s competition promotion); nationalist versus

---

[12] This is a matter not only of elite control but also of neutrality. Most steelband musicians would not trust a judge who was thought to have loyalty to a particular band. The resulting imperative to choose judges who are outsiders to the tradition is not unique to the steelbands. It is illustrated in a particular humorous way in the Jeremy Marre film, *Rhythm of Resistance* (1979), which docu-ments a competition between South African *isicathamiya* choral groups in a Durban factory hos-tel in South Africa. For a judge, the participants recruit a white man they encounter outside on the street, and he turns out to be a criminal just released from prison.

[13] The formal education of judges is expressed in judging criteria such as "reharmonization," "tone colour," "balance," as well as references in their written comments to "recapitulation," "coda," and "development" (Dudley 1997: 245–51).

colonialist in the 1940s and 1950s; African versus Indian following independence and the black power movement; cultural versus commercial in the late twentieth and early twenty-first centuries. Finally, modern carnival has been influenced by forces that operate quite independently of formally adjudicated competitions. Trinidadians have become wealthier; women have asserted a more prominent role in carnival, as in the workplace; cultural tourism, world music, and the growing importance of carnivals in the Caribbean diaspora (e.g., Brooklyn, Toronto, Miami, and London) require Trinidadian artists to respond to international as well as local tastes.

When Trinidadians express nostalgia for carnivals of the past, therefore, they are reacting to very real changes in the festival's character. Like the riots of the 1880s, the establishment of calypso tents in the 1910s, or the advent of the steelband in the 1940s, the burgeoning of formally adjudicated competitions in the late twentieth century will likely be seen as a watershed of change in the history of Trinidad carnival. The post-independence period may one day be seen as a time of declining vitality in carnival, or as a time of unprecedented spectacle and display; as a momentary aberration of decolonization, or as a transition to a dynamic new cultural era. It is even possible that, from that future vantage point, new performance rituals like Panorama will themselves be viewed nostalgically, as ingenious and appropriate responses to the issues of their time. Two important factors in determining this legacy are individual innovation and communal participation, forces that combine to resist the stifling constraints of Panorama's formal structure and adjudication. In the next chapter, therefore, I will explore the creative potential of Panorama through a more focused analysis of arranging strategy and its relationship to audience participation.

10

Writing Their Own Tunes

I don't like the idea of going to the Panorama with your own tune. I like to go to Panorama with something that belongs to the calypsonians because that is carnival. . . . The whole thing—masqueraders, calypsonians, the panmen, brass people, the bats[1]—everybody. It should be a golden link going through everybody for the carnival, you know? Let we just live so, even if it's just for two days; because the rest of the year we only eating up one another and bad-talking one another.

Clive Bradley (1977)

Beginning in the 1970s, Ray Holman and Boogsie Sharpe shook up Pano-rama by composing their own music, or "own tunes," for the competition. The controversy this provoked drew attention to the newly elevated status of steelband arrangers, and also to the cultural agenda of Panorama's organiz-ers. Critics of Holman and Sharpe argued that individual ambition and glory ran contrary to the spirit of carnival and accused them of being selfish and unresponsive to the people's fondness for calypso. Though such argu-ments appeared on the surface to affirm the value of community participa-tion, they also supported the government's longstanding efforts to impose its own priorities on carnival. Panorama was promoted over the Bomb competition, for example, despite the fact that steelband musicians and their communities enjoyed the Bomb (chap. 5). Indeed the nationalist ideal of an integrated carnival—a harmonious display of Trinidad's diverse ex-

---

[1] The bats are one of the traditional masquerades referred to as "old mas'" that are associated with the lower-class carnival, predating the "fancy" masquerade bands of the middle class that began to dominate carnival in the 1950s.

pressive arts and communities—has always depended on *discouraging* certain kinds of community participation in favor of others, obscuring the historical reality of a carnival in which diverse communities compete for space and attention with their public displays. In this perspective, the own tune threatened government and middle-class control over carnival more than it threatened community participation.

Though the growth of the own tune's popularity in the 1980s and 1990s points to the arranger's unique position of influence, a close analysis of the arranger's strategic choices also brings institutional constraints into relief and highlights the reciprocity between composition and public reception. In offering such an analysis here, my goal is to underscore the interdependence of individual innovation and community participation—a dynamic relationship, full of tensions and contradictions, which defies the institutional stagnation that sometimes seems to threaten Panorama.

THE OWN TUNE CONTROVERSY

Despite the increasingly specific expectations of audiences and judges that constrained Panorama after its first decade, arrangers' enthusiasm for new possibilities was undiminished, and they sought to continue innovating. Ray Holman, in particular, tested the boundaries of Panorama's new conformity by writing his own song for Starlift in 1972, titled "Pan on the Move." This was a challenge, of course, to one of Panorama's institutional priorities, and it was predictable that those intellectuals and government officials who sought to reinforce the connection between calypso and steelband would take a stand against Holman's efforts.

Some Panorama enthusiasts opposed the own tune on less ideological grounds, however. They had come to enjoy the way arrangers accentuated or commented on the meanings of calypsoes (the Panorama aesthetic that I referred to in chap. 8 as "song interpretation"), and they wanted to hear steelbands play familiar songs. To accommodate this expectation, Holman wrote "Pan on the Move" as a song with lyrics before he arranged it for steelband. He made both a recording and a sheet music version to distribute to the Panorama judges. The fact that his song was not composed and performed by a calypsonian was still of concern to some; but more important, since the recording got virtually no radio play and no exposure in the calypso tents, the lyrics and melody of "Pan on the Move" were unfamiliar to Panorama audiences. Holman's own tune therefore ran counter both to the nationalist ideology of integrating the carnival arts, and to the Panorama aesthetic of song interpretation, exposing him to accusations of selfishness and of detracting from the "carnival spirit."

Journalist John Babb's criticism of Holman's 1973 own tune "Pan on the Run," for example, reflects both the nationalist notion of suitable repertoire (appropriate "time and place") and the importance of audience familiarity (difficulty of relating to "a strange tune"):

> First and foremost of the recommended changes is CIBC Starlift,[2] which played its leader's own composition—Ray Holman's "Pan on the Run." Starlift did not click as their many supporters hoped they would have done. Starlift must learn that they start at a disadvantage playing a strange tune. This has its bad psychological effects. There is a time and a place for everything. And this should not be taken as a criticism of Holman. He deserves high praise. But I say Festival time—yes; Carnival time—no. (1973)

Another important constituency heard from were the calypsonians. This is how Mighty Sparrow, for example, was paraphrased in an interview published after the 1972 carnival:

> [Sparrow] said this effort by Ray [Holman] was "too exclusive." "Carnival is not an exclusive thing," he said, pointing out that it was like a singer coming with a "brand new Calypso" for the finals, which on the surface, appeared an achievement, but which was unfair to the spirit of Carnival[,] which is to "generate feelings of involvement" (*Trinidad Guardian*, May 3)

Sparrow had a professional stake in the matter, since steelbands helped to popularize his songs. So although his appeal to the carnival spirit mirrored that of John Babb, Sparrow's idealism was dismissed by many steelband musicians as a transparent disguise for professional self-interest. In Ray Holman's view, "Kitchener and Sparrow and these people used to kind of instigate these things" (personal conversation, 1993), and opposition from calypsonians only hardened his determination to play his own music.

Holman's decision to play his own tune was more than an act of defiance, however; it also allowed him to arrange music that suited his own taste and vision for the steelband. The creative fulfillment he sought was hampered at the time by an exceedingly narrow choice of repertoire. Not only did steelband arrangers have to play calypsoes for Panorama, but their choices were effectively limited to the songs of just two extremely popular calypsonians, the Lord Kitchener and the Mighty Sparrow. Between 1963 and 1979, only one other singer (Lord Melody in 1965) succeeded in penning a Panorama winner. In 1969, Starlift won Panorama with Holman's arrangement of Kitchener's "The Bull," and the band repeated in 1971 with Sparrow's

---

[2] CIBC (Canadian Imperial Bank of Commerce) is a bank that sponsored Starlift.

"Queen of the Bands." By this time, however, Holman had had enough of arranging other people's music. Feeling that "it was too much to make something out of that song ["Queen of the Bands"]" (personal conversation, 1999), Holman decided that he had achieved sufficient levels of both confidence and frustration to try his hand at composing.

CALYPSO MUSIC AND STEELBAND MUSIC

The own tune, when it finally became a widespread practice almost twenty years after Holman's innovation, brought steelband arrangers a new kind of recognition as composers. Most arguments about whether the own tune was a positive development proceeded from an assumption that this was a new role for steelband musicians, and so the own tune was portrayed either as a step forward for the steelband movement or an unwelcome break with carnival tradition. This way of evaluating the own tune obscured the fact, however, that panmen had composed for the steelband from early on. The most recognized opportunity for steelband "composers" before Panorama was the Music Festival. Some of the early steelband compositions for the Festival were created not by panmen, strictly speaking, but by trained musicians who worked with the steelbands (Lennox Pierre, Anthony Prospect, and Umilta McShine, for example, wrote Music Festival test pieces at various times). But Junior Pouchet also composed original music played by Silver Stars at festivals in the 1960s, and Anthony Williams wrote a few original compositions for North Stars.

More significant, perhaps, is that the very first music played on pan was created exclusively for steelband performance. From the improvised cutting of the ping pongs to the four-note songs discussed in chapter 2, panmen and their supporters created music to suit the new instrument when it was still in its rudimentary stages. Even after pans acquired the melodic range to play other repertoires, many steelbands continued to play home-grown songs, as Anthony Williams remembers:

> At some time during the period 1945 to 1950, some steelbands composed their own tunes. Sun Valley had composed "Sun Valley Coming Down." That goes like this [sings]: "Sun Valley coming down / Invaders bound to run." Invaders composed "Invaders Want to Use You." . . . And another tune was "Mothers Keep Your Daughters Inside" [sings]: "Mothers keep your daughters inside / Mothers keep your daughters inside / Mothers keep your daughters inside / because Invaders sailors offside." Casablanca also composed a piece, and that goes like this: "Invaders too bad / we go beat them outta they yard." Invaders also played a calypso "Tell Them Tell Them We Eh Fraid Nobody." (interview with Stephen Stuempfle, 1988)

The fact that these songs are not associated with individual composers is simply evidence that the culture of early steelbands and their communities did not elevate composition over performance in the same way European culture does. This changed as steelband musicians strove to master classical music and other repertoires, so that the own tune appealed to steelband "arrangers" who welcomed a new opportunity to identify themselves with the prestige of being a "composer." In terms of musical strategy, however, the own tune was consistent with the steelband musicians' long-standing impulse to create music that suited their instruments and their sense of style. It was this impulse as much as anything else that motivated Ray Holman and other own tune composers, just as it governed the adaptation of mambos, classics, and other songs that comprised the repertoire of the Bomb in the late 1950s and 1960s (see chap. 5).

Indeed, although Bomb tunes are often described as classics arranged in calypso rhythm, it would be more accurate to describe them as classics arranged in steelband style; or even more specifically as classics arranged in All Stars style, Invaders style, and so on. Although Panorama has naturalized the notion that calypso is the source for steelband repertoire and style, the steelbands did not really get their music from calypso any more than calypso got its music from pan. Rather, they are two distinct performance traditions, related through common origins and through continued borrowings back and forth. Both calypso and steelband have roots in the nineteenth century carnival bands that featured chantwels accompanied by a chorus with percussion accompaniment. Calypso first branched off from this tradition in the 1890s, when some chantwels began to preview their new songs each season in the weeks leading up to carnival, performing for audiences in temporary structures, or "tents." Songs for the tent, where the audience generally does not dance or sing along, developed more elaborate narrative texts and strophic forms to suit this type of presentation. On the road, meanwhile, lower-class carnival revelers continued to sing participatory call and response lavways with tamboo bamboo accompaniment.

When the panmen took over the carnival streets in the 1940s, their primary point of musical reference was tamboo bamboo, even though they were intrigued by the string band instruments heard in the calypso tents (as evidenced in their use of the terms "strumming" and the naming of the "cuatro" and "guitar" pans). They played calypsoes early on, but they also played other kinds of music, and not just "foreign" tunes. They created their own songs and drew upon a variety of indigenous musical forms. The importance of African drumming has already been discussed (chap. 2). There were also distinctive styles of music associated with the different carnival masquerade traditions, ranging from the music of Venezuelan-style string bands popular among the elite at the turn of the century to the music of

228 MUSIC FROM BEHIND THE BRIDGE

mobile brass bands to the distinctive rhythm that blue devils still beat on kerosene tins today. Indo-Trinidadian music was another musical resource for steelband musicians, particularly in the ethnically mixed neighborhood of St. James, where creoles participated in the exciting tassa drumming during the annual Hossay festival.

To appreciate the impact of these musics on steelband musicians, it is important to remember that calypso did not have the kind of media dissemination in the 1940s and 1950s that it has today. It is all too easy to infer from today's abundant commercial recordings, as well as scholarship and journalism, that calypso was the predominant popular music of Trinidad in the 1940s and 1950s and that all Trinidadians listened to it. In fact, however, lower-class panmen sometimes had few opportunities to hear calypso as it was performed in the tents and disseminated on records in the 1940s and 1950s. Many of them were more likely to hear calypsonians who performed solo on the street, to popularize their calypsoes outside the tents. Neville Jules, for example, remembers Tanti's tea shop, at the corner of George and Duke Streets, as a place where Lord Kitchener and other calypsonians brought their guitars to sing for tips and to sell printed copies of their lyrics (interview with Kim Johnson, 1996). But their more elaborate performances with full band accompaniment could only be heard in the tents, where the audience was largely middle class. Anthony Williams recalled in interviews with Kim Johnson that he could not afford the 25-cent ticket for a calypso tent show when he was starting out in pan and was more influenced by the music he heard in movie theaters (1996; 2004).

Another important source of repertoire for the steelbands was the radio, which in the 1940s and 1950s broadcast mostly foreign programming that included classical music, jazz, and mambo, but little calypso.[3] In the 1930s, when calypso was attaining significant popularity and radio play in the United States, Trinidad had only the Rediffusion cable service that transmitted programming recorded in England. Broadcast radio began in Trinidad with the U.S. Army base station during World War II and continued with the establishment of Radio Trinidad in 1947, which was still dominated by British programming. In 1957, a second broadcast station, Radio Guardian, introduced a format more weighted toward popular music, but it favored North American hits. Veteran radio programmer and executive Hamilton Clement remembers that Radio Guardian mostly played records that were sent to it free of charge by U.S. record companies, supplemented with a few records purchased from Trinidad retailers. Calypsoes could be heard at this

[3] My primary sources for the history of radio in Trinidad are personal interviews with Holly Betaudier, who began a career in radio and television when he got a job at the U.S. Army base radio station in the 1940s, and Hamilton Clement whose long career in radio began with Radio Guardian in the 1950s.

Table 10.1.   The Radio 610 Top 10
List from 1963

1. Stan Kenton
2. Dutchy Brothers
3. Clarence Curven Orchestra
4. Elvis Presley
5. Lord Creator
6. Mighty Sparrow
7. Nat King Cole
8. Gene Pitney
9. Cook All Stars Orchestra
10. Pan Am North Stars

Source: Trinidad Guardian, Jan. 13, 1963, p. 9.

time during carnival season, but they constituted a small portion of the radio programming even then, and they were carefully censored so that some controversial songs (especially those thought to be obscene) were not played on the radio at all.

Following independence in 1962, Radio Guardian made the bold decision to broadcast calypso during the Lenten season, challenging conservative views of calypso as a vulgar music. The top ten play list from Radio 610 (the national broadcasting system) during the carnival seasons of 1963 shows, however, that calypso was still heavily outweighed by other repertoires (table 10.1), competing with foreign artists, local brass band dance music (the Dutchy Brothers and Clarence Curven), and even steelband recordings.[4]

With recorded calypso still playing a minor role in carnival and with steelband violence on the wane, the early 1960s were the time of the steelbands' greatest popularity, and calypsonians wanted steelbands to play their music. Although calypsonians could achieve popularity in the tents and the Calypso Monarch competition, they also enhanced their reputations by writing "road marches" enjoyed by dancers on the road at carnival time[5]—

[4] Steelband music has never had much life in recorded or broadcast media, but radio stations played an important role in promoting the steelband in the 1950s through 1970s. Veteran radio executive Hamilton Clement told me that many of the steelband recordings published during this time were recorded by Radio Guardian technicians at the Strand Cinema on Tragarete Road and sold to record labels like Telco and ROC for distribution. After the 1970s, steelband recordings diminished in number, but they resumed in the late 1980s with the work of Simeon Sandiford who mainly has recorded Panorama music on his SANCH label, some of which is distributed on Delos.

[5] A road march can also be popular for performance in the tent and win the Calypso Monarch competition, Mighty Sparrow's 1956 song, "Jean and Dinah," being the most famous example. But in

and a road march could not be a hit if it wasn't played by steelbands. Calypsonians visited panyards and tried to personally persuade steelbands to arrange their songs, but they also became more attentive to the way their music could be arranged by steelbands.

In this regard, the leading innovator among calypsonians was Lord Kitchener, who initiated his role as a composer of road marches about and for the steelband with his 1944 calypso, "The Beat of the Steelband." The steelband subsequently became a favorite subject of Kitchener's lyrics,[6] and the catchy melodies and rhythmic hooks of his songs lent themselves to steelband arrangement. From 1948 to 1963, Kitchener lived and performed in England, but he never lost his ear for the steelband, and he added to his harmonic vocabulary through working with other musicians abroad. He returned to Trinidad in time for the first Panorama competition in 1963, and in 1964 North Stars won Panorama with an arrangement of Kitchener's song "Mama Dis Is Mas'." In the late 1960s and 1970s Kitchener's tunes had a near monopoly on the Panorama crown, and by the time of his death in 2000, arrangements of his songs had won eighteen of the first thirty-six Panorama competitions.[7] In the Calypso Monarch competition, by contrast, Kitchener won the crown only once (with the song "Winston Spree Simon" in 1975). The musical flare that so appealed to steelbands and carnival dancers, and which made Lord Kitchener the undisputed king of the road march, did not count as much in calypso tents and competitions, where audiences and judges placed a premium on wordplay and topical commentary. Though Kitchener penned dozens of classic tunes whose harmonies, melodies, and riffs helped to define steelband musical style, he was exceptional among calypsonians in this regard.

Apart from Kitchener, there were few calypsonians, especially in the 1940s and 1950s, whose music had significant appeal for the steelbands, so the panmen drew their repertoire from a much broader range of musical sources, as Neville Jules recalled in an interview with Kim Johnson:

---

general, there have always been important differences between calypso for the road and calypso for the tent. (For a more detailed discussion, see Dudley 2004, chap. 3.) Also, even before the steelbands, many road marches were not calypsoes, but "foreign" tunes. Rohlehr notes the popularity of the Jamaican song, "Sly Mongoose" in 1923, for example, and suggests that such foreign tunes may have been the norm rather than the exception for the road march; this is because the Trinidadian carnival bands all had their own songs, composed by their chantwels, and the only tunes that could be widely sung (and have a chance to become the most popular road march) were the ones that didn't belong to anyone locally (1990: 117–18).

[6] I made a note that Kitchener actually published a collection of his early song lyrics titled "Lord Kitchener and his Steelband Boys," but I cannot find the source or the date.

[7] For those who are checking the math: there was no Panorama in 1979 because of a boycott, and Kitchener died before the 2000 Panorama, so I am not counting either of those years.

At one time, the steelbands was separate from calypsonians, because at that time songs that were being made by the then-calypsonians was really no good. We had to depend on Kitchener from England. Whenever he made his records we would play those calypsoes. He would make like ". . . Gulf of Paria," "Trouble in Arima"; so we had was to play other songs, too. That's the reason why we used to play the mambos, the this and the that. (1996)

Jules's opinion that calypso was "no good" for steelband is consistent with a tendency to view calypso as a genre that recycles stock melodies and chord progressions and is relatively predictable in its music (as opposed to lyrics). This criticism of calypso might seem curious on the face of it, since it is common for other song genres, including European ballads or African American blues, to use a limited variety of musical patterns as a vehicle for text. In Trinidad, however, the concern over calypso's musical variety and worth became urgent precisely because the steelbands outstripped calypso musically, resulting in calls for calypsonians to keep pace, as in this *Trinidad Guardian* editorial from 1966:

The steelband has reached the most extra-ordinary level. Today calypsonians have to compose with the steelband in mind, for a tune is not a tune unless a panside carries it to the public. The public does not recognize a calypso un-less it is conveyed by a steelband. In short, the steelband is way ahead of the calypso as an "art form" and calypsonians who aspire to fame locally should bear this in mind. (Quashie 1966)

A trend toward increased formal and harmonic complexity in calypsoes during the 1950s and 1960s (Rohlehr 1999: 30) is evidence that calypsonians paid heed to such advice.

In the late 1970s, however, the steelbands' dominance on the road was challenged by DJ trucks, flatbeds carrying massive speakers that play re-corded music at earthshaking volume. As the new purveyors of the road march, the DJ trucks exerted a different musical influence on calypso, and especially on a new type of music called soca that diverged from calypso (Dudley 1996; 2004). Not only did soca songs avoid the long narrative texts of calypso (as had many road marches even before soca), they also stressed rhythm and studio sound effects over harmonic complexity, and used catchy call-and-response choruses that invited carnival revelers to partici-pate. On the one hand this emphasis on rhythm and participatory singing and dancing harkened back to much older carnival music traditions. On the other hand, however, soca provided little harmonic and melodic material for steelbands to work with, and its overpowering bass sounds, as experienced through DJ truck speakers, were an attraction that steelbands could not hope to match. The advent of DJ trucks and soca music thus disrupted the musical connection that had developed between steelbands and calypsonians, and created an incentive for steelband arrangers to write their own tunes for Panorama.

RISE OF THE OWN TUNE

Although Ray Holman's aesthetic vision enabled him to persist in arranging original compositions for Panorama, many members of his band, Starlift, soured on the own tune because it appeared to hurt their chances of winning the competition. Holman therefore left Starlift after 1974, and went on to arrange for a new band, Pandemonium, where he continued to write his own tunes, and later for Exodus, Tokyo, Hummingbird Pan Groove, and other steelbands. Although he did not succeed again in winning Panorama, Holman established a reputation for artistic integrity and beautiful music, eventually receiving the Humming Bird Silver Medal (a prestigious government award) in 1988 for his lifetime achievements. Holman's example also inspired other steelband arrangers, the most influential of whom was Len "Boogsie" Sharpe, a prodigiously talented pannist who played under Ray Holman in Starlift.

Born in St. James in 1953, Sharpe began beating a pan even before he was tall enough to reach it, standing on a box to play in the yard of Crossfire behind his house. By the age of eight, he was playing on the road with Crossfire, and in the mid-1960s he joined Starlift, where Selwyn Tarradath remembers seeing him play long complicated arrangements after just one listening:

> One night after a football game I came to play in the band and there was this little boy playing the bass pans. The next day there was this little boy again playing the tenor pans. Someone said, "Why are we still learning the tunes, and he is already playing the tenors?" I told them he was a pan jumbie, he is going to learn the tune on the tenors too. The next time I see him playing the seconds, and I said, "You really like pans!" I thought he was learning the tunes, but later I found he could play any pan by ear. . . .
>
> [One year] before carnival Starlift played Fatima College. The second pan player didn't come, so one of Boogsie's big brothers said Boogsie could play second pan. An older guy was watching him and showing him the chords. Then the session ended and they started playing the panorama tune from [the year before]. While they were playing, this guy was telegraphing to

Fig. 10.1. Len "Boogsie" Sharpe directing rehearsal of Phase II Pan Groove in 1994.

Boogsie the chords, but he was missing his chords while Boogsie was playing all the right chords! Boogsie played the whole tune right. Afterwards the guy asked Boogsie if he knew the tune and where did he learn it. Boogsie said he heard it on the radio. And he could play all Ray's [Holman's] chords better than the other player was playing them! (personal conversation, 2000)

If ever the pan jumbie has taken human form to make music, it is through Boogsie Sharpe. I have seen him demonstrating complex parts on every instrument in the band, sometimes playing them backward as he stands across the pan from the person he is teaching. Band mates have told me stories of their switching the arrangement of a set of pans to throw Boogsie off, then watching him play his part flawlessly after just a momentary reassessment. He cannot read a note of musical notation, yet he can memorize a ten-minute arrangement in one hearing, and he can take a pan with a completely unfamiliar pattern[8] and by "taking a picture of it" in his mind, as he explained to me, learn to play it in a few minutes. More than a technical wizard, he is a creative genius, breathtaking for his deep musicality as much as his speed and power as a performer.

Sharpe was among a small group of Starlift players who began an experimental group in 1971, rehearsing in Selwyn Tarradath's yard and calling themselves Phase II Pan Groove. When Ray Holman left Starlift in 1973, Phase II grew in size and Sharpe soon emerged as its musical leader. In 1975, he began to write his own tunes for Panorama, just like Holman. "From that time, we used to get a lot of pressure," Sharpe recalls. "A lot of people say, 'This own tune thing, what he trying to do?' . . . When we going down in the Savannah, people saying, 'What all you coming here with that for, why you goin' with that Chinee music[9] and that stupidness you playin'?!'" (personal conversation, 1993). Despite such detractors, a following of progressive-minded people soon galvanized behind Sharpe's unconventional and exciting arrangements, which featured daring harmonies and dissonances, creative sound effects like chromatic glissandi, and a "roughness" and funky rhythmic groove. Phase II had early success, winning the North Zone regional competition in 1977, but it took thirteen years of persistence and patience to win in the national finals of Panorama. In 1987 Phase II became the first band to take the crown with an own tune, "This Feelin' Nice," and in 1988 they repeated with "Woman Is Boss."[10]

Following these Panorama victories by Phase II, the own tune became commonplace in the 1990s, reaching a peak of popularity in 1993, when seven of the twelve steelbands in the finals played original compositions.

---

[8] Despite some recent standardization of tuning patterns (see appendix I), there are many different ones still, dating from the time that each band's tuner made pans his own way, and also due to new innovations. An experienced player will be familiar with quite a few different patterns, having grown up playing different pans and perhaps in different bands, but she or he will probably be most comfortable with one or two, and completely at a loss with some.

[9] This is a common way of saying that music sounds strange, and it doesn't necessarily mean that it sounds specifically Chinese.

[10] A videotape of Phase II playing "Woman Is Boss" is included in the *JVC/Smithsonian Video Anthology of Music and Dance of the Americas* (1995), Vol. 4: *The Caribbean*.

Other bands have since won Panorama with own tunes: Desperadoes, with arranger Robert Greenidge's own tunes in 1991 and 1994, as well as Exodus, with Pelham Goddard's own tunes in 1992 and 2001; and Phase II won again with Sharpe's own tunes in 2005 and 2006. It is far from clear, however, that the own tune will supplant arrangements of popular calypsoes. By the time I returned for carnival in 2000, the number of own tunes had declined somewhat, and the talk was of how many good pan tunes the calypsonians had put out. This was in part because of a Pan Kaiso (pan calypso) competition staged by Pan Trinbago, and also a compilation CD of pan calypsoes produced by Alvin Daniell.[11] This promotion of pan calypsoes is itself evidence of the own tune's influence, however. It shows that calypsonians, unhappy to lose their place in Panorama, have resorted to new strategies precisely because steelband arrangers have refused to content themselves with the prevailing fare of carnival road marches.

Although the number of steelbands playing own tunes has diminished somewhat in recent years, the viability of the own tune in Panorama is no longer in question. On the other hand, steelband own tunes have become increasingly hard to distinguish from other calypso and soca songs, since steelband arrangers often have them recorded by popular singers such as Super Blue, Denise Plummer, David Rudder, or even Mighty Sparrow. So if the own tune is still an arrangement of a calypso (albeit one composed by a steelband arranger), what new possibilities does it really offer? Through a comparison of three arrangements from the 1993 Panorama I will make the case that Boogsie Sharpe's own tunes, at least, have facilitated an arranging strategy that challenges the Panorama formula—and the ideologies and aesthetics to which it corresponds—in significant ways.

A BATTLE OF FORMS

In the 1993 Panorama finals, Phase II lost by a mere half point (out of 500 possible) to the Renegades. Renegades played Kitchener's "Mystery Band," arranged by Jit Samaroo, who, as the most dominant Panorama arranger of the 1980s and 1990s, was perhaps the closest thing to a "normative" Panorama arranger. The stark differences between Samaroo's "Mystery Band" and Sharpe's "Birthday Party" therefore represent a conflict not just between

---

[11] This promotion of pan calypsoes as a marketing category increasingly blurs the distinction between own tunes and calypsoes. Pelham Goddard's 2001 own tune for Exodus, for example, has lyrics written by Alvin Daniell and is available on Daniell's CD collection of pan calypsoes that also includes other own tunes as well as songs composed by calypsonians. As is the case with calypsoes, listeners may tend to identify such a song more by the singer than by the composer.

rival steelbands, but between rival musical paradigms. A comparison with respect to form, in particular, raises intriguing questions about the own tune's potential for innovation. I will argue here that Boogsie Sharpe's "Birthday Party" was composed in such a way that he could effectively disrupt the theme and variation formal convention of Panorama by expanding his cyclical jams.

I have chosen to focus on "Birthday Party" because it is one of my favorite Panorama arrangements[12] and also because it was a radical experiment with form; the fact that Phase II almost won Panorama with such an arrangement in 1993 (the year of the own tune's greatest popularity) raised the possibility of an exciting new approach to Panorama arranging.[13] Unfortunately, Boogsie Sharpe was absent from Panorama in the following two years[14] and was unable to capitalize on this momentum. So although it would make my argument more impressive to say that "Birthday Party" precipitated a new trend in arranging, I can make no such claim. Even considered as an isolated event, though, the success of "Birthday Party" demonstrates the power of individual musical strategies to promote innovation.

Figure 10.2 is a representation of Sharpe's and Samaroo's formal procedures, as well as the formal approach of another arranger, Godwin Bowen. This diagram is designed to show two things: first, the distinction between newly composed material ('N') and material from the original calypso (A,B,C . . .) or its variations (a,b,c. . .); and second, a contrast between two different experiences of musical time, linear and cyclical. The triangles and diamonds represent linear time—parts of the arrangement, that is, in which the listener is oriented toward what is coming, anticipating the next in a sequence of sections or variations. The perception of a linear advance "forward" in time is represented by the stringing together of these sections in the *vertical* dimension of this diagram. Circles, on the other hand, represent cyclical time—parts of the arrangement that are characterized by recurring patterns and simple repeating harmonies. The extension of these circles into *horizontal* ovals represents the extension into a different dimension of time experience, where the listener is oriented less toward what is coming next and more toward what is happening now.

---

[12] In addition to attending four Panoramas (1989, 1993, 1994, and 2000), I have listened to and analyzed recordings of the winning arrangements for almost every year since 1963, as well as many other Panorama recordings. I have also played with half a dozen bands in Trinidad for Panorama (four in 1993 alone), including Phase II when they did "Birthday Party," and have played a few other Panorama arrangements from written scores with steelbands in the United States.

[13] It should be noted that I am assuming for the present argument that winning Panorama is above all an index of the arranger's success, even though steelband competitions may also be won or lost on the strength of the players' execution.

[14] Sharpe was assigned to a drug treatment program in New York, which prevented him from traveling to Trinidad for two years.

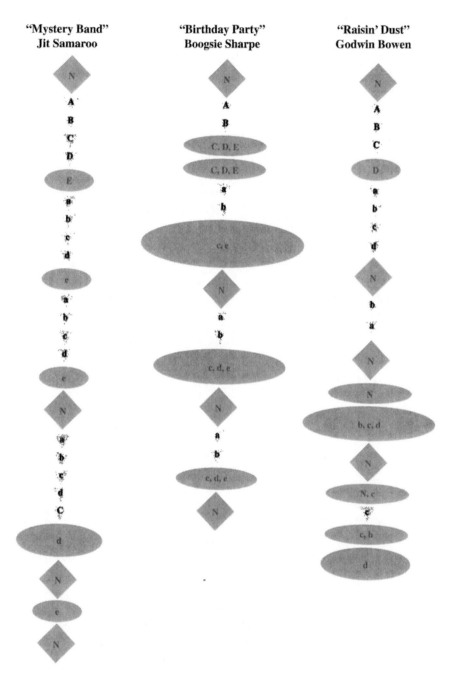

Fig. 10.2. Linear versus cyclical time.

The practice of theme and variation in Panorama tends to produce arrangements that are dominated by the linear experience of time. Jit Samaroo's "Mystery Band" is an example of a Panorama arrangement that keeps the original constantly in sight through a regular series of variations. The regular recurrence of the song's sections in sequence (a,b,c,d,e) constantly reward the listener's expectations of what will come next, a predictability that is balanced by inventive melodic variations, breaks, changes of key and mode, and various other devices. Variations on the verse and chorus are gratifying to the audience, who are attentive to the arranger's interpretation of the song's lyrics and sentiment. They also satisfy the judges, whose comments sometimes fault arrangers for "straying" too far from the original (Dudley 1997: 308–9).

I have heard more than one arranger complain about this requirement and express a desire for a freer hand to compose new material in their steelband arrangements. Calypso judge and media commentator Alvin Daniell expresses the hope that the own tune may help bring this about:

> Eventually I think it may be possible, especially with the own tune kind
> of approach now, for a guy to come and say, "I have created 10 minutes of
> music, this is what I'm going to present for Panorama 1993. I don't have to
> give you a verse and chorus. This is my offering for 1993. I have ten minutes
> of music that I have created." (personal conversation, 1993)

Godwin Bowen, whose 1993 own tune "Raising Dust," performed by Pamberi, is also represented in figure 10.2, may be the arranger who has come closest to this approach. After one set of variations on the original four sections of the melody, Bowen basically abandons the sequential repetition of those sections and creates long jams that use motives from the B and C sections of the song. Despite praise from progressive quarters, though, Bowen has never come close to winning in the Panorama finals, which suggests that his strategy has not successfully addressed the expectations of Panorama audiences and judges. The lesson one might take from the relative success of Jit Samaroo and Godwin Bowen is that theme and variation form win out over a more through-composed approach to Panorama arranging.

Sharpe's arrangement of "Birthday Party," however, represents a more successful alternative to Samaroo's theme and variation strategy. Like Bowen, Sharpe disrupts the pattern of sequential variations for much longer stretches than Samaroo. An important difference, though, is in the structure of the original song and the way Sharpe's jams relate to it. Sharpe explained to me that he designed the melody of "Birthday Party" to provide him with flexibility in his steelband arrangement: "I try and make it more simple, like

I leave a lot of space. . . . You're telling a story but you give a person a chance for it to soak into his head, to hear what he saying. Even with the arrangement, now, I tried a different type, you know? I could do plenty stuff and different ideas" (Sharpe 1993). The relative simplicity of "Birthday Party's" harmony and melody, then, give Sharpe more room for development.

In particular, the extensive use of call and response in the original complicates the perception of "variation" in his steelband arrangement. Of the five sections in "Birthday Party," three have call-and-response structures— short, regularly repeated choral refrains, interspersed with vocal or instrumental answering phrases that tend to sound spontaneous and varied. A simple repeated chord sequence accompanies the cycling of the refrain and answer. Variations on something like this, whose character seems rather unfixed even in its initial statement (one might describe them as "variations on variations"), do not evoke a sense of "the original" so strongly as do variations on more harmonically and melodically distinctive sections. Sharpe exploits the ambiguous identity of his call/response melodies to draw the listener's focus away from the music's linear progress, slipping seamlessly into long cyclical jams that seem naturally related to the original song and yet unconcerned with its sectional structure. He thus makes his challenge to the formal conventions of Panorama by invoking an African aesthetic of time that is pervasive in Trinidadian carnival music and dance—from the first steelbands that accompanied call-and-response *lavways* to modern road marches that blare from the massive speakers of DJ trucks. The use of cyclical call-and-response structures in all this music encourages listeners to join in a rhythmic and melodic conversation, inviting a greater level of both physical and verbal participation from the audience that is especially appropriate to carnival.

While challenging the linear model of form, Sharpe still manages to accommodate the Panorama aesthetic of interpretation or variation by building his jams on distinctive motives from the song's original melody. For example, the melody of the E section, with the lyrics "Birthday Party!" becomes a bass line in the longest jam of the steelband arrangement (fig. 10.3). As a bass line, functioning harmonically, it creates a new effect but still evokes the song's signature phrase, anchoring the listener in something familiar, perhaps at a subconscious level. In chapter 1 I described a similar device in Clive Bradley's 1989 arrangement of "Somebody." Like Sharpe, Bradley wrote a bass line for the jam to which the audience could sing the words of the original song: "Somebody to love up." The difference, however, is crucial. Bradley invented a *new* melody that matched the words and also served as a bass line; Sharpe, however, wrote the *original* melody in such a way that it would also serve as a bass line, making the link between bass line and lyrics more obvious to the audience.

Song

Birth-day par-ty! Birth-day par-ty! Birth-day par-ty! Birth - day par-ty!

Steelband jam (bass line)

Fig. 10.3. "Birthday Party" motive. A melody that was sung in the recording serves as a bass line (in a different key) in Boogsie Sharpe's steelband arrangement.

Most of Sharpe's own tune, in fact, is composed in short phrases or motives which, in the steelband arrangement, are manipulated to create a sense of connection and variation without reproducing entire chord progressions or melodies. These motivic hooks, along with the extensive use of call and response, are compositional techniques in the original song that facilitate Sharpe's steelband arranging strategy—and contrast starkly with the abundant variety of melody and harmony in a more conventional "pan" calypso, such as Kitchener's "Mystery Band." The case of "Birthday Party" thus demonstrates how Sharpe's ability to write his own tune facilitates his arranging innovations.

SUMMARY: INNOVATION AND TRADITION

My reading of Boogsie Sharpe's 1993 arrangement of "Birthday Party" speaks to the broader questions of how institutionalization has affected the steelband, and whether steelband musicians can play a significant role in the development of an art form that is shaped by so many forces beyond their control. Since 1962, steelband music has been shaped, for example, by the expectation that steelbands should play calypso at carnival, by financial incentives to concentrate on Panorama, and by competition from DJ sound systems that has squeezed steelbands out of other entertainment roles. These conditions have produced many musical changes, such as the elimination of improvisation and reduced danceability, that are not likely to be reversed within the framework of Panorama. Nonetheless, my analysis of Sharpe's compositional strategy suggests that Panorama still offers scope for other kinds of innovation.

The innovations discussed here—motivic development and the extensive integration of cyclical time—represent strategies by which Sharpe has successfully put forth his creative vision, while at the same time competing with other steelbands for reputation, and meeting the expectations of audiences and judges. Moreover, as they embrace this music, Trinidadians also embrace much broader ideas about their culture and society. In celebrating Phase II's music, specifically, musicians and audiences acknowledge their comfort with a more African way of experiencing musical time (a significant change particularly for middle- and upper-class Trinidadians),[15] moving farther away from the symphonic formal models that inspired early Panorama innovators like Tony Williams. Sharpe's and Holman's hard-won identities as *composers* (rather than arrangers of other people's compositions) also challenge the nationalist ideology of carnival arts integration that Panorama originally served, and further confirm the status of steelband musicians as artists.

One can argue, of course, that these are changes whose time has come. Just as Tony Williams's "classical" approach struck a chord in 1963 with a newly independent and culturally insecure nation, Sharpe's style appeals to audiences who have become accustomed since the 1980s to rhythmically conceived two-chord soca road marches. It is all too easy in hindsight, though, to explain musical developments as the product of their times. Williams's model of arranging was influential, in part, simply because he was the first to really conceive of Panorama as an opportunity for something new. Had Bobby Mohammed been ready with his exciting style in 1963, or had Ray Holman been a little older and more well-established, a significantly different kind of music could have become the "obvious" model for the new competition. To take a more recent example, the innovations of "Birthday Party" might have taken deeper root after 1993 if Boogsie Sharpe had returned to build on his success in the following year.

The work of individual artists therefore may matter as much as the social and political climate of a given era. And though some of the consequences of the own tune are political (its challenge to colonial models of musical form, for example, or to the nationalist integration of calypso and steelband), the struggles of Sharpe, Holman, and other Panorama innovators have been largely motivated by artistic concerns. Their genius lies not just in their vision of new musical possibilities for the steelband, but also their abil-

---

[15] African musical traditions have a long and unbroken history in Trinidad carnival. However, they have also been stigmatized, and middle- and upper-class Trinidadians who enjoyed the street music of the "people's" carnival have historically been seen as transgressors: for example, the middle-class "jacket men" who participated in stickfighting in the late nineteenth and early twentieth centuries; "college boys" from respectable families who got involved with steelbands in the 1950s; or the ritual of carnival J'ouvert morning generally, in which people from all walks of life cover themselves in mud and oil and "get on bad." The approbation of African musical aesthetics in a formal institutional setting like Panorama, though, removes them from the category of transgression.

ity to put new ideas across to a public that holds them to standards of tradition. If they are able to defy convention, it is because they provide alternatives that inspire and delight that public. Panorama's life energy flows from this relationship between individual innovation and community participation. Questions about Panorama's continuing vitality are best approached, therefore, through an understanding of the changing ambitions of steelband musicians as well as audience expectations.

11

From Panman to Pannist

So you could call me a dread man,
But not a one-tune panman,
It's time you start seeing me as a musician.
From the chorus of "One Tune Pan Man," by Black Stalin (Leroy Caliste), 1994

Black Stalin's lyrics reflect the steelband movement's long-standing mission to convince skeptics that, despite their rough ("dread") reputation, panmen take their music seriously. The song also points to a more recent problem that has little to do with rough behavior, and which steelband musicians may have created for themselves. As the steelband approached middle age in the 1980s, it was diagnosed with a malady called the "Panorama mentality" or "Panorama syndrome,"[1] which manifested as an unhealthy and exclusive obsession with adjudicated competition. Steelband supporters not only mourned the disappearance of pan on the road and in fêtes, and complained of formulaic arrangements; they also lamented that Panorama's technical demands were creating legions of "one-tune panmen" whose musical activity was largely restricted to the task of memorizing a ten-minute arrangement once a year. Such a musical dead end would of course be antithetical to the steelband movement's spirit of progress and to the ambitions of a new generation of pannists who want to be seen as trained and versatile musicians. Having made a case for Panorama's continuing relevance and

---

[1] The "Panorama mentality" is a term that Jeff Thomas reports hearing often during his research in the early 1980s (1986: 104); the term "Panorama syndrome" was coined, as far as I know, by Pan Trinbago education officer Selwyn Tarradath in an informational pamphlet in 1989.

creativity, therefore, I must also acknowledge some signs of its decline, or at least fundamental changes in its cultural role, and discuss alternative models of musicianship that complement or compete with Panorama.

A CHANGING PANORAMA

Questions about the changing nature and purpose of Panorama became a topic of public debate in 2002 and 2003 when changes to the competition's format provoked strong reactions. The first innovation that Pan Trinbago introduced was to hold the preliminary round of judging in the panyards, shuttling judges from one band to the next in a minivan instead of trucking thousands of people and instruments from all over the island to the Queen's Park Savannah. From an economic perspective, this saved the government a couple of million dollars in transportation costs and reduced the organizational burden on Pan Trinbago (Joseph 2002a). From an entertainment perspective, it meant that visitors to the Savannah, including tourists, would no longer have to endure mediocre performances by less well known bands while they waited for the heavy hitters; the Savannah would be reserved for concentrated displays of talent in the zone finals, semifinals, and finals. From a cultural perspective, however, the new preliminaries were a radical departure from a format that many regarded with all the reverence and conservatism of tradition.

Prior to 2002, Panorama preliminaries, held two weeks before carnival, had come to signal the beginning of the carnival season's major performance events. Even casual steelband fans looked forward to the chance to lime with friends against the exciting backdrop of dozens of steelbands playing in labored succession on a single stage, over the course of twelve hours or more. Indeed, for many fans, "Panorama" (as in, "will you be at Panorama this year?") meant the preliminary round in the Queen's Park Savannah. Players also looked forward to their moment of glory at the "Savannah Party," showing off their skills in the national limelight before a crowd of thousands. The switch to panyard judging for the preliminaries, however, meant that players in less competitive bands would almost certainly not make it to the big stage. Optimists hailed the new format's potential to bring in community supporters who might not travel to Port of Spain for the competition and to generate income through food and beverage sales in the yard; but some steelbands saw their numbers of players slip, compared with the previous year's preliminaries.

In response to criticisms and concerns about the new preliminary format, Pan Trinbago president Patrick Arnold tried to reassure audiences, at least, that the excitement of the prelims would not be lost in the zone final/national semifinal event, which was now scheduled for the same Sunday when preliminaries had formerly been held, two weeks prior to carnival. Arnold argued that it was essentially the same event as the old Panorama preliminaries, only more selective.

> The "bring your cooler," dancing with your rhythm section in the North
> Stand and several other staple aspects of the day as we knew it have been
> retained. . . . What is going to add value to the event is our plan to reduce
> delays caused by the changing of bands onstage, rigid enforcement of the
> seating arrangements in the special reserve areas and of course, bringing
> only top quality bands to the arena. We expect to deliver a show that begins
> punctually and runs through the evening smoothly and this is not just pro-
> motional chat. We have put a number of systems in place to enhance the
> value of the Panorama product and will be monitoring them for effective-
> ness as the event proceeds. (Joseph 2002b)

In a separate interview, Arnold added, "We are faced with dwindling audiences at our most viable event, and that signalled disaster down the road if we continued to stretch the tolerance of our audiences" (Joseph 2002a).

Not all of Panorama's diverse audiences were happy, however, about Arnold's vision of an enhanced "Panorama product." This became especially clear the following year, 2003, when Pan Trinbago decided to reroute the steelbands as they approached the stage, bringing them through a fenced-off staging ground to the west of the stage where only ticket holders were allowed to enter. The change in approach eliminated the whole musical and social scene of the "track" on the east side of the stage (fig. 1.2) where steelbands rehearsed their tunes, vendors sold food and drink, and spectators came and went freely and listened to the music and met with friends—a virtual extension of the street carnival within the Savannah grounds. From a business perspective, the creation of a new staging area was necessary to pressure "freeloaders" to pay to watch the steelbands perform. In the view of many longtime Panorama supporters, however, it eliminated the last vestige of Panorama's unmediated connection to the public carnival and deprived them of the chance to listen to steelband music in the way they liked best. Not surprisingly, many members of the community were outraged at this violation of what they saw as their rightful tradition, and the intense public backlash (compounded by protests from vendors who had paid for spots along the deserted track) forced Pan Trinbago to restore the traditional approach in subsequent rounds of the competition.

Panorama reforms and the attendant controversies in 2002 and 2003 thus brought into sharp relief the question of *which* audience the event should cater to. Patrick Arnold's assurances of punctuality, reserved seating, and consistent musical quality probably reflected the concerns of tourists, as well as those Trinidadians who pay good money for their seats and want to enjoy the staged spectacle from a privileged vantage point. For many other people in the audience, however, the "problems" Arnold sought to eliminate were part of Panorama's charm. Flexibility in seating, for example, permits people to move about and spend time with friends in different places. Delays between bands are an opportunity to socialize, go out for food and drink, and enjoy the recorded music that blares constantly during breaks. Consistent musical quality on stage is not critical as long as these other kinds of diversion are available. Indeed, mediocre performances and periods of waiting may enhance the excitement when one of the eagerly anticipated steelbands finally does arrive. Fans who are connoisseurs of steelband music can pick and choose the bands they want to pay close attention to, enjoying the lime in between. This participatory "street" aesthetic corresponds to an event that does not impose a rigid order of schedule or behavior on the participants, and which can be experienced in many different ways. It is largely incompatible with the presentational "stage" aesthetic implied in Arnold's vision of an enhanced "Panorama product," which values predictability, order, and control.[2]

Pan Trinbago's promotion of the stage aesthetic at the expense of the street aesthetic is difficult to reconcile with its usual stance of solidarity with roots communities. Patrick Arnold's business-minded pronouncements, in particular, seem to be at odds with his role as a community leader (Arnold is a tuner and the founder and leader of Our Boys steelband in Tobago, as well as a former member of parliament). What is important to remember, however, is that Pan Trinbago's first responsibility is to steelband musicians; Arnold and his colleagues conceived these Panorama reforms as a way to protect the steelbands' financial interests. Steelbands have come to depend on the income from Panorama appearance fees, prizes, and sponsorship, and steelband leaders expect Pan Trinbago to maintain such financial support. Legislators, on the other hand, complain about excessive spending on Panorama, and government agencies delay disbursements of funds. Pan Trinbago's efforts to court paying customers and keep Panorama financially

---

[2] In a similar vein, Turino writes, "Within middle-class ethics, the lack of control, organization, pre-planning, variety . . . make indigenous participatory style objectionable" (2000: 138). On the other hand, Scher cites the example of an international Carnival King competition staged in Trinidad during the off-season which was a miserable failure precisely because it did not include the spontaneity and participation of carnival. He suggests that audience participation provides the context in which commodified cultural products become appealing, so that "it is not in resistance to objectification that agency emerges, but in the implementation of those objectified and commodified cultural forms. There must be an audience" (2003: 149). Carnival, more than the staged folklore that Turino is mainly concerned with, requires that the participatory mode be integrated with the presentational to some degree.

solvent respond to both these concerns, even though they sometimes alienate the communities in which most steelbands are based. This dilemma is not new, for although the rhetoric of the steelband movement implies a convergence of interests between the steelbands and their socially disadvantaged communities, steelband musicians have always had professional aspirations that link them to more affluent communities and to tourism. Tensions over community ownership of Panorama were inevitable, therefore, as the competition cash cow became more bountiful.

The problems of Panorama are not exclusively financial, though; they are also musical. A 2004 letter to the *Express* editor, titled "Concert Music Killing Panorama," begins by noting "a significant drop in audience interest and participation in the Panorama performances" and invokes some of the concerns about formulaic arrangements, art music pretensions, narrowed repertoire, and other problems of adjudicated competition that I discussed in chapters 7 through 10:

> Panorama used to have more of a "party" atmosphere years ago, with audiences finding it easy to respond to the music being performed on stage. . . .
> I am of the opinion that the continuous rewarding of first place to bands that play musically correct, but uninteresting music is having a negative effect on the overall competition from the audience's standpoint. By their results, judges are encouraging the arrangers to take a more classical, "Queen's Hall" approach to arranging. The result is that the music being played now is largely boring, uninteresting and dull to the average listener. As a result, attending Panorama has lost its appeal. . . .
>
> Pan Trinbago and the judges that are chosen to judge Panorama need to review the signals that they are sending to the top and up-and-coming arrangers. Do they want bands to produce musically correct, but boring music, or do they want bands to make people get up and dance as pan music in Carnival was originally intended to do? (February 24)

While the judges may indeed share the blame for these problems, it is not entirely fair to put the onus on them. Steelbands also respond to the audience, and if they play differently today than they did in the 1960s and 1970s, it is partly because the audience at Panorama has changed.

In the early 1970s, when Panorama clearly came into its own as an event and as a musical style, recorded music was only just beginning to compete with live steelband music on the road during carnival, and many people who bought seats to cheer their favorite steelband at Panorama later jumped up with that same steelband on the road. That generation is now thinning, and fewer people in the audience at Panorama today can remember the excitement of following a steelband through the streets during carnival, so the relation between what they see on the Panorama stage and what they enjoy during carnival is less direct. As these generational and aesthetic distances widen, it becomes harder and harder for steelbands to "make people get up and dance as pan music in Carnival was originally intended to do." Because the relationship between musicians and audiences is increasingly shaped by stage performances, most steelband arrangers today have a less compelling sense of connection to their audiences than they would have had in the 1950s or 1960s, when adoring supporters danced and sang alongside them on the road. Ray Holman's description of audience response in his early days arranging for Starlift, for example, makes clear why a young man might pay more attention to the audience than to the judges:

> "I Feel Pretty" was the start of my misery in life with women. See, our street, Hunter Street, you couldn't pass in that street. That street was—imagine 1963, Trinidad didn't have so many cars at that time—that street used to be jam packed. One tune would cause that. Right? . . . We were like celebrities. Because I was nineteen, you know; a nineteen-year-old boy did that, move a whole country. (personal conversation, 1999)

Meeting women is still a good reason for a young man to play in a steelband, but only because half the players in the steelband are likely to be women. For both social and musical reasons, young people continue to participate in steelbands in large numbers, even while the audience at Panorama seems to be aging, but the kind of celebrity Holman describes is reserved today for the soca singers whose music blares from DJ trucks on the road at carnival, and who pump up crowds of sweating dancers at fêtes. The community status that steelband musicians enjoyed in the 1950s and 1960s, the excitement of being at the epicenter of carnival's festive energy, is not part of the experience of young pannists today.

Panorama has acquired a musical dynamic of its own, influenced by but no longer bound to the steelband's carnival origins, and Panorama arrangers no longer live or die by the pleasure of the dancers. Steelband musicians also take encouragement from the enthusiasm of their fellow players, from the praise and criticism of musicians, journalists, and radio commentators, and, not least, from success with the judges. The pan jumbie is still at large in Trinidad, and young people continue to dedicate themselves to the instrument and the art form. But as Panorama loses some of its grip on the collective imagination, young pan players increasingly explore other venues and other models of musicianship. Although many still take pride in the social identity of "panman" that is ritually enacted through the rivalry and display of Panorama, more and more of them are looking for other ways to express their musical identity of "pannist."

DOMESTICATION OF PAN

Although the danger and violence associated with the term "panman" have sometimes been rationalized, or even touted, as natural consequences of social disadvantage and rebellion, it is also true that steelband leaders made common cause early on with middle-class activists and politicians to restrain violence, to channel the energies of disadvantaged young men into music, and to make space for the less sociologically charged identity of "pannist." The steelband movement continues to be identified with the grievances of disadvantaged Afro-Trinidadian communities, but the transition from panman to pannist represents a certain domestication of the steelband during the latter half of the twentieth century, in the sense that participation in steelbands has become relatively safe and open to people of different classes, races, and genders, and steelband music making has moved from vacant lots and streets into the institutional settings of schools and concert halls. The participation of women, in particular, has been a significant factor in this domestication.

While some jamette women were known in the steelband's early days as active fighters or as instigators of steelband violence, the first female steelbands scrupulously distanced themselves from the pattern of neighborhood rivalry and violence. With the exception of the White Stars, who were associated with a reform school, the early female steelbands tended to be middle class, and their members had the benefit of formal musical training, often on piano or violin (chap. 4). In addition to the standard of musicality and seriousness they set, and their roles as advisors and arrangers for the predominantly male steelbands, some of these female pannists became pioneers of steelband instruction in a variety of institutional formats. Umilta McShine, for example, who taught folk dance at Tranquility Girls School in the 1940s, later became principal and promoted steel pan instruction at Tranquility as well (Nagahama 2000: 30). In the 1960s, Merle Albino de Coteau was appointed by the Ministry of Education and Culture to teach a musical literacy course for pannists, a program that benefited not just schoolchildren but members of conventional steelbands (Nagahama 2000: 30). Ester Kafiluddi Batson (whose daughter Dawn is discussed below) provided steel pan instruction at Arima Government Secondary and other schools in the 1960s. Although my information on the role of women in steelband education in the 1950s and 1960s is incomplete, it is clear that the collective activity of these pioneering women paved the way for the establishment of school steelbands in the 1970s.

One of the earliest formal school steelbands was established in 1974 at St. Francois Girls College in Belmont. St. Francois also took the bold step of forging ties with a community steelband, inviting McDonald Redhead of

Power Stars to provide instruction (Stuempfle 1995: 180). Other school steel-bands quickly sprouted up, and many of them also forged relationships with conventional steelbands.[3] By 1976, there were enough schools with steel-bands that the Carnival Development Commission inaugurated a Junior Panorama, which was won in its first year by Belmont Fifth Dimension. The list of winners in following years gives evidence of a burgeoning number of school steelband programs in the late 1970s and '80s: Petit Valley Royal Col-lege (winners in 1977), Woodbrook Secondary (1978), St. Francois Girls' College (1980), Mucurapo Junior Secondary (1982), Mucurapo Senior Com-prehensive (1983), South East Port of Spain Secondary (1984), and so on to the present day (Maxime n.d.).[4] Beginning in 1981, a Schools Steelband Music Festival was also added to the calendar.

Since the 1970s, steel pan training in the schools, combined with formal ties between school and community bands, has resulted in an infusion of young, educated pannists into the established steelbands in Trinidad. An early precedent for this was Birdsong steelband in St. Augustine, whose founding in 1973 was spurred by the cultural idealism of the Black Power movement, and which integrated community members with students from the University of the West Indies. More commonly today, however, students first learn to play in their school steelbands and then join established com-munity bands, often making this transition while they are still in school. When I first went to Trinidad in 1989, many of my companions in Pande-monium steelband had played in their schools. Also, Invaders, which had languished in relative obscurity since the departures of Ellie Mannette and Ray Holman in the 1960s, was enjoying something of a renaissance at that time because of the infusion of a large number of schoolchildren. Participa-tion by schoolchildren has transformed the culture of many panyards. Hummingbird Pan Groove in St. James, for example, with whom I played in 1993, so depended on schoolchildren that they enforced strict bans on smoking, drinking, and swearing in the panyard and tried to finish rehearsal by 11 o'clock at night. Other steelbands, of course, have made no such con-cessions, and so the degree of participation by schoolchildren varies signifi-cantly from one community band to the next. In general, however, the ranks of community steelbands in Trinidad are increasingly filled by young people, many of them women, who were introduced to steel pan in their schools.

In addition to the spread of school steelband programs, another impor-

---

[3] I have few data on this phenomenon, but when I first went to Trinidad in 1989 several members of the Belmont-based Pandemonium steelband, with whom I played that year, made regular visits to schools to teach in their steelband programs. Nagahama also notes that Renegades steelband has shared instruments and provided instruction for Belmont Secondary School and South East Port of Spain Secondary School.

[4] No Junior Panorama competition was held in 1979 or 1981.

tant factor in pan's domestication has been its international spread. Just as
TASPO's enthusiastic reception in London in the 1950s gave the steelband a
new status in Port of Spain, pan's international spread, especially its inclusion in institutions of higher education abroad, has helped to legitimize the
steelband in Trinidad and has added urgency to calls for institutional representation and support at home. I have already noted Ellie Mannette's role in
the establishment of school steelbands in the United States (see chap. 3).
The migrations of other Trinidadian pannists have seeded significant steelband movements in other places as well. This includes not only major centers of Caribbean population such as London and Toronto, but also countries where pan has been taken up by non-Trinidadians. Rudy Smith moved
to Sweden in the 1970s, for example, where he teamed with ethnomusicologist Krister Malm to promote the steelband movement in Scandinavia
(Smith now lives in Copenhagen, Denmark). And a 1976 performance by
Sterling Betancourt at a hotel in Switzerland inspired a group of Swiss to
begin their own steelband, called *Tropefieber* (Tropical Fever). In addition to
Betancourt, Swiss pan enthusiasts got help with tuning and instruction
from Trini pannist Ralph Richardson, who took up residence in Switzerland
and helped to spread the steelband there. Today there are more than 150
steelbands in Switzerland alone.[5] Steelbands have become popular on the
other side of the globe as well, in places like Japan and Taiwan.

In the United States, the steel pan's institutional status was boosted in
1985 when Dr. Alan O'Connor invited Trinidadian steel pan tuner Cliff
Alexis to join the music faculty at Northern Illinois University in DeKalb.
O'Connor and Alexis established an undergraduate steel pan degree in 1987
and recruited Trinidadian students, with the help of scholarships provided
by the Trinidad and Tobago government. The NIU program soon fed back
to Trinidad, particularly through the work of veteran pannist Harold
Headley, who completed his bachelor's and master's degrees in music at
NIU. Headley subsequently joined the faculty of the newly founded Centre
for the Creative Arts at the University of the West Indies at St. Augustine. In
1992, the centre established a certificate course in steel pan that provides formal training in musicianship and arranging for ambitious pannists; and in
1997, it established a bachelor's degree in musical arts, the first higher education music degree to be offered in Trinidad and Tobago, which includes a
significant steel pan component and is overseen by Dr. Anne Osborne.

Another leader in the development of steelband degree programs is
Dawn Batson, daughter of Ester Kafiluddi Batson. Trained on violin from a

---

[5] I am indebted to Monika Nicoletti for my information on Swiss steelbands (personal conversation,
2006); she also provided this Web site, which lists all the steelbands in Switzerland: www.pan-
jumbie.com/linksCH.htm.

Fig. 11.1. Cliff Alexis (left) with his apprentice in 1985.

young age, Dawn also got the chance to learn pan in her Barataria home because her mother taught steelband in the schools. As a youth, Dawn did not
play with a community band, although she toured internationally with Desperadoes playing violin with the Barataria Best Village[6] performing group in
1977. After receiving a B.S. in music education from Hofstra University on
Long Island, she returned to Trinidad in 1982 and took a job at Trinity College, where she directed the school steelband. She also joined Invaders, and
arranged and conducted for a variety of community bands, including Pamberi, Nutones, and Renegades. In the 1990s, Dawn returned to the United
States to complete a master's in music business and a Ph.D. in International
Affairs and Music at the University of Miami. She was subsequently hired at
Florida Memorial College, where she helped create a steel pan major and recruited Trinidadian students. Today Batson is the chair of Florida Memorial's Visual and Performing Arts program. While employed in the United

---

[6] Best Village competitions were introduced by the PNM around the time of independence (I
haven't found the exact date) to encourage cultural development at the local level. They include a
great variety of crafts and performing arts.

Fig. 11.2. Dr. Dawn Batson, steelband educator (photo courtesy of Dawn Batson).

States, she continues to work to expand opportunities for steelband musicians in Trinidad and Tobago. Appointed as chair of the board of directors for Trinidad and Tobago's National Steel Orchestra in 2000, Batson helped create an associate degree in performing arts for its members and other pannists. Batson's energetic promotion of steel pan education reflects both the steelband movement's urge for progress and the patriotism of many middle-class Trinidadians who have worked to legitimize the steelband as a cultural form in which all Trinidadians can take pride.

MARKETING CULTURE

Though the educators and steel pan advocates listed above are motivated in various degrees by social and cultural ideals, their work also serves the larger goal of converting Trinidad and Tobago's cultural capital to financial profit. In setting standards of formal training for the National Steel Orchestra, for example, Dawn Batson's intention was to prepare members and other interested pannists for professional opportunities outside of carnival, and even outside of Trinidad and Tobago:

> This really is for me the bottom line because that was my dissertation, using the steelband as an economic force. So many people are involved in the world of the steelband and in turn don't gain anything. They are very, very poor, and they don't know how to make money from it. That has been my focus, that is why I have been focused on getting a number of students from there to go that step further. (phone conversation, 2001)

This economic perspective links the steelband movement's concern for the betterment of disadvantaged panmen to a vision of carnival's economic potential that is embraced at many levels of Trinidadian society.

The notion of carnival as an export industry has its roots in tourism, which provided the earliest impetus to package Trinidad's expressive culture for the entertainment of foreigners, beginning in the 1920s and accelerating after World War II. The first exportable "products" of this industry were calypso records, which sold significantly in the United States in the 1930s and 1940s (D. Hill 1998). Beginning especially in the 1960s, after U.S. immigration restrictions were relaxed, the growth of organized carnival celebrations in Caribbean diaspora centers made carnival itself a product and fueled a new demand for the services of Trinidadian artists, as West Indian immigrants sought to re-create the culture of their home. By the 1990s, a series of international events, scheduled so as not to conflict with the Trinidad carnival or with each other, constituted an international professional circuit traveled by Trinidadian mas' men, calypso and soca singers, and pannists. These events include, to name only the largest and most famous, Caribana in Toronto (July), Notting Hill Carnival in London (August), West Indian American Day in Brooklyn (September), and Miami Carnival (October). Some carnival artisans have parlayed their festival exposure into other kinds of artistic success, an example being the work of Trinidadian mas' man Peter Minshall in designing shows for major international events, including the opening ceremonies for the Olympics at Barcelona in 1992 and Atlanta in 1996. Overseas opportunities for steelband musicians are generally more mundane but are also more numerous. They include sponsored tours for established steelbands, cruise ship and theme park jobs for smaller sides, and individual opportunities to arrange for Panorama competitions in Brooklyn and elsewhere, or to conduct workshops and performances at schools and universities. All of this increasingly shapes the ambitions of young pannists and puts pressure on the Trinidad and Tobago government to enact policies that will help them.

A 1999 plan for development of the steelband drafted by the Pan Trinbago Foundation Board, for example, begins with this observation:

> Pan is a unique product invented in Trinidad and Tobago [which] has tremendous export potential constrained only by limited international

awareness due to insufficient marketing and domestic cultural bias. . . . In spite of the competitive threat arising from the upsurge of T&T style Carnivals around the world, there has been no strategic plan until now to keep Pan and T&T Carnival preeminent.

An especially common complaint leveled at the government is that it has failed to provide steel pan tuners with the engineering and marketing resources needed to capitalize on the international demand for instruments, and to secure Trinidad and Tobago's position as the source of the steel pan. In this regard, a patent granted in 2002 to two Americans for a hydraulic press that sinks and shapes steel pans generated a lot of anxiety in Trinidad. Letters to the editor expressed outrage over the prospect of Trinidad's national instrument being "stolen" by foreigners, and in an article titled "Pan Shocker: Americans Patent Pan Plan," journalist Terry Joseph detailed the Trinidad government's failure to secure a national patent for the instrument (2002b).

Such concerns about appropriation of the steel pan by foreigners are almost as old as the instrument itself, dating at least to the early 1950s when Antigua's Brute Force steelband made some of the earliest steelband recordings. A 1985 calypso titled "Pan in Danger," by Merchant (Dennis Franklin), lamented the lack of recognition and reward for the panmen's struggle, and struck a sensitive nerve with Trinis, who still invoke its warning today:

Save pan, well let that be more than just a slogan
Give it your utmost attention
Or, as Black Stalin say,
We might wake up one day
And hear that steelband come from
In the United Kingdom
Sweden done start already
Setting a pan factory
To manufacture we own culture
(Franklin 1995)

Control and ownership of the steel pan has become a matter of increasing concern in recent years, as demand for instruments has sent prices soaring. In 1986, when I bought my first double seconds from Cliff Alexis in St. Paul, Minnesota, I paid $250 U.S. (which was more than I would have paid had I bought them in Trinidad). In 1997, when I ordered instruments from Alexis for the University of Washington, he was charging almost $1,000 per set. And at the time of this writing, in 2006, prices advertised by leading makers in the United States, such as Mannette Instruments Ltd. and Panyard Inc., range from $2,300 to $9,000 per set, depending on type and quality.

While Trinidadian tuners maneuver to get a piece of this action, players and arrangers also respond to the rising demand for repertoire and training, positioning themselves as clinicians, and publishing written arrangements of music that for most of the steelband's history has been taught aurally. Simeon Sandiford's SANCH company, which has for years published recordings of steelband music on the Delos label, has recently launched a new series of steelband recordings and scores called "Pan in Education." The company's Web site proclaims that "the financial future of Trinidad and Tobago, and by extension the entire Caribbean, lies in harnessing, promoting and marketing its culture, of which the main economic source is music." For the Pan in Education product, specifically, "The global marketing thrust will be aimed principally at educational institutions. This should provide job opportunities outside of Trinidad and Tobago for participating steel orchestras and others involved in the local music industry" (http://www.sanch .com/pan-in-education.htm). Like SANCH's publishing project, the concern for formal music training and the creation of degree programs for pannists also responds to the reality that the rising demand for steelband instruments and expertise worldwide is fueled by school and university steelbands. Pan has thus found a unique niche in the global marketplace, and Trinidadian tuners, players and entrepreneurs are in some ways retooling, adapting their skills and products to take advantage of this.

Despite its unique market potential, however, the steel pan is also promoted as part of a larger export package of "traditional" carnival arts that includes mas', calypso, and soca. Indeed, the proliferation of T&T-style carnivals in North America and Europe is not seen simply as a "competitive threat," as stated in the Pan Trinbago Foundation Board report cited above, but it is also exploited as a marketing opportunity. Trinidadian government agencies concerned with tourism and export, including the National Carnival Commission and the Tourist and Industrial Development Corporation, promote the kinds of performance events that they think will most effectively bolster Trinidad and Tobago's status as the "Mecca" of carnival (Scher 2003: 148, and passim). To the extent that they succeed in this effort, they create a demand abroad for Trinidadian mas' designers, calypso and soca singers, and steelband tuners and arrangers. These artists and artisans are sought after in the carnivals of Brooklyn, Toronto, London, and other cities not only for their skills but also, because of their association with the Mecca of carnival, for the "authenticity" that they confer on those festivals and on the West Indian expatriate communities that generate them. In turn, government sponsors and carnival organizers in Trinidad must insure that the Trinidad carnival is compelling not just for local audiences but for carnival enthusiasts from abroad.

Carnival in Trinidad is thus constrained not only by the expectations of foreign tourists, but also by the many Trinidadian emigrants who return for the occasion to affirm their cultural roots and who become, in a sense, "tourists of themselves" (Scher 2003: 151). This puts a premium on nostalgia, favoring "traditional" forms over new ones and favoring cultural commodities—reproducible forms and spectacles like Panorama—over the less easily exportable spirit of the carnival. Like the cultural nationalism of the 1960s, therefore, the increasingly systematic efforts of the Trinidadian government to market carnival put pressure on steelbands to conform to a presentational mode of performance and to collaborate in the creation of a brand-name spectacle that can represent Trinidad in the global community.

COMMUNITY OR CAREER

Panorama continues for the time being to attract enthusiastic participation and crowds, but Pan Trinbago's reforms reflect a growing tension between the imperative to maintain a cherished tradition and the reality of cultural and economic change in Trinidad and Tobago. Consider this recent statement by Pan Trinbago President Patrick Arnold:

> No matter how good a saxophonist or keyboard player you might be, you just can't walk into Roy Cape & the Kaiso All Stars or Traffik or one of those brass bands and expect to be supplied with expensive instruments and then borrow them to practice at home. On the other hand, a steelband is expected to supply the instruments—tenor pans cost about $4,000 [TT] each—then provide uniforms for the players, teach and drill them and then turn around and pay them for playing. . . . The strain on the band is tremendous and several of them are finding difficulty in continuing to supply and maintain the instruments, so the solution has to be that players bring their own as happens in any other type of band. (Joseph 2006)

This suggestion is radical for the way it frames pan as an individual enterprise. When steelbands began in the 1940s, most tuners worked exclusively for their own bands and kept their tuning techniques secret for the advantage and prestige of their neighborhoods. Even after it became acceptable for tuners to sell their work to multiple bands, the instruments were almost invariably made available as a community resource. When I played in Trinidad steelbands in the 1990s, I was impressed by the ease with which other players switched between pans that were slightly different in their note placement, and it struck me that this was because, unlike me, none of them owned their own instrument and yet all could play the ones that belonged to the band. A switch to personal ownership of instruments would therefore not only favor people who have the means to purchase an expensive musical instrument (what an ironic thing to say about an art form that grew out of junk metal!), it would also erode the fundamental conception of the steelband as a community enterprise.

By comparing steelband musicians to professional brass band musicians, Arnold affirms the steel pan's hard-won status as a legitimate musical instrument; yet by the same token he points out that the art form cannot continue to rely on exceptional treatment—that the steel pan cannot have its cake and eat it, too. This is not what everyone in the steelband movement wants to hear, but Arnold's pragmatism may be what is best for the movement at this time. Though his efforts to make Panorama profitable do accommodate the interests of tourism and cultural commodification, he has also taken positions that conflict with the priorities of the carnival establishment. In 2005, for example, Pan Trinbago changed the rules of Panorama to allow arrangements of past years' calypsoes. By freeing steelbands from the obligation to tout the *current* season's calypsoes, this change went against the forced integration of carnival arts that Panorama was originally intended to promote (chaps. 5 and 10). Such steps to free the steelband from the burden of its cultural symbolism, something steelband musicians have always wanted and yet not wanted, can encourage innovation and nurture the potential of pannists to operate as music professionals. The specific form that innovation will take, of course, is largely up to the musicians.

The first people one might look to for innovative ideas, especially for alternatives to the large ensemble conception of the steelband, are the handful of successful steel pan soloists. From the earliest days, individuals like Zigilee were famous for their soloing ability, following in the tradition of master drummers in Orisha worship and other African music. In the 1950s and 1960s, players like Emmanuel "Corbeau Jack" Riley (Invaders), or Belgrade Bonaparte (Southern Symphony) thrilled panyard audiences with virtuosic improvisations played over full steelband accompaniment. By the 1980s some talented soloists began to pursue individual career opportunities, often outside Trinidad. These include Othello Molineaux, who made groundbreaking Caribbean and fusion recordings with Jamaican pianist Monty Alexander and American bassist Jaco Pastorius in the 1980s; Earl Rodney, whose tasteful steel pan work graces calypso recordings by Lord Kitchener and others from the 1970s and 1980s; Rudy Smith, who has performed extensively in Scandinavia since the 1970s and made a number of jazz steel pan recordings; Robert Greenidge, who played the pan solo on the extended version of Grover Washington Jr.'s "Just the Two of Us" in 1980, and who has played regularly with faux-island pop singer Jimmy Buffett since then; Ken "Professor" Philmore, who does frequent performances and workshops abroad; Ray Holman, who taught at the University of Washington as visiting artist in the late 1990s, does numerous school and university workshops, and recorded his own solo CD (Holman 2003) (by "solo," I mean steel pan in a small combo setting with other instruments); Ron Reid, who teaches at the Berklee School of Music in Boston, and has recorded two excellent solo steel pan CDs that blend Caribbean and Latin styles (Reid n.d.); and the most prodigiously gifted pan soloist, Len "Boogsie" Sharpe, who performs abroad extensively but who, to my knowledge, has yet to make a solo recording that is worthy of his talent.[7] Credit is also due to U.S. pannist Andy Narrel, whose innovative recordings from the 1970s onward blended Caribbean styles with jazz and helped create a niche for pan on radio and in the international recording industry. But the window is closing for this generation to propose new directions for the steel pan, and younger musicians must step in to expand the possibilities their elders have opened up, or to propose entirely new visions.

There is no shortage of young pannists who would like to blaze new trails. This is clear from the enrollment in UWI's pan certificate program and other educational opportunities. It can also be seen in the formation of small pan sides that seek to cultivate an audience through broad repertoires and improvisational skills. In Trinidad, the only professionally viable band of this kind to date is the Samaroo Jets. Others are trying, though, particularly since the 1990 implementation of the Pan Ramajay competition, which encourages small bands and improvisation. One of the most influential groups to come out of this movement is the Panazz Players, a side of about a dozen musicians that performs extensively in Trinidad and abroad and has released several CDs. Many pannists also find work as sidemen and soloists, particularly on cruise ships and in U.S. theme parks. More dignified opportunities for soloists may present themselves at home in studios and calypso tents—Jimi Phillip played pan for Lord Kitchener's Review in the late 1980s and 1990s, for example, and Panazz's only female member, Natasha Joseph, was the house pannist for Kaiso House when I attended in 2000. Surprisingly, however, integration of the steel pan into calypso and soca in Trinidad has not happened on a significant scale.

I would argue that the failure of the steel pan to integrate into calypso, or other musical idioms, is partly due to a habit of spectacle and rivalry that makes it difficult for Trinidadian pannists to operate in the supportive and interactive roles expected of instrumentalists in calypso, jazz, and other styles. At a Pan Jazz concert that I attended in 1993, for example, Boogsie Sharpe, Robert Greenidge, and Ken "Professor" Philmore performed with

[7] In addition to their individual projects, many of the soloists mentioned here, along with a few others, collaborated on a series of "Pan Assembly" recordings during the 1980s. For more citations of recordings by these musicians, see Jeffrey Thomas's discography of steelband music, *Forty Years of Steel* (1992), published by Greenwood Press.

Puerto Rican pianist Hilton Ruiz. When it came time to feature the steel pan soloists, Ruiz laid down a twelve-bar blues progression. The Professor played first, diving into his tenor pan with elbows flying (as though he were trying to rip the metal with his bare hands, I thought!) and firing off a barrage of rapid scales and arpeggios. Next came Robbie, who played with a disciplined and smooth touch on the double seconds, but his solo was more notable for its daunting speed and complexity than for its musical interest. Finally it was Boogsie's turn, also on double seconds, and to my relief he began with gentle, lyrical improvisations that left space to hear the other musicians in the band. Hilton Ruiz at the piano smiled and cocked his head, sensing for the first time that someone was playing *with* him. Then Boogsie began to fill the spaces between his notes. His lyrical melody still sounded, but it was constructed now from the peaks and valleys of rushing chromatic scales. It was an extraordinary technical feat, and my friend George, seated next to me, jumped to his feet and shouted, "Boogsie now start!" The crowd was on its feet, and Hilton Ruiz went back to accompanying a spectacular pan solo.

The expectation of virtuosic performances like these is linked to Panorama, which has ritualized steelband rivalry by framing it as a staged spectacle in which the most tantalizing question is, Who will win? In recognition of Panorama's limitations, various efforts have been made to promote alternative venues, but the fascination with winning and losing is hard to overcome. At the Pan Ramajay competition in the 1990s, for example, which was conceived to provide opportunities for improvisation and spontaneity, small pan sides performed on a stage underneath a banner that featured a glittering pair of crossed pistols and the words "OK Corral." The metaphor of the shoot-out is evoked in many other solo pan performances as well. This belligerent conception of performance, which was fundamental to the neighborhood rivalries of early steelbands, is perpetuated and glorified today in Panorama. In this sense, the continuing popularity of Panorama (and competitions generally) and its entrenched position as a primary carnival "product," inhibits the development of skills and musical sensibilities that are required in other idioms. That is one of the reasons innovative young pannists look for opportunities abroad, even while they may keep one foot planted back in Trinidad.

A case in point is Liam Teague, born in San Fernando in 1974. Attracted at an early age to the classical music his parents loved, Teague first learned recorder in school, then picked up the steel pan and the violin. At the age of 15, he did a Panorama arrangement for his community steelband, Hillside Symphony, but was dissatisfied with the experience, and continued to concentrate on the steel pan's possibilities as a solo instrument. In 1992, he shared the soloist title with Chantal Esdelle at the Pan Is Beautiful festival,

Fig. 11.3. Tenor pan virtuoso Liam Teague (photo courtesy of Liam Teague).

and in 1993 he was admitted into Northern Illinois University's steel pan degree program, where he went on to complete his master's degree in music. He was eventually hired by that university, in 2005, as an assistant professor of music, a first for a Trinidadian pannist. In addition to his academic accomplishments, Teague has performed at numerous college venues in the United States, debuted a steel pan concerto with the Chicago Sinfonietta, and played with many other municipal symphonies in the United States and abroad.[8] He has recorded six CDs whose eclectic repertoire, ranging from calypso to classics, mirrors the omnivorous musical appetites of Trinidad steelbands. He also credits some of his extraordinary speed and dexterity to the competitive ethos of the steelband in Trinidad. Teague has recently returned to the Panorama stage as an arranger for Skiffle Bunch and enjoys composing for top players, with or without support from the judges. "Where better to show your wares," he asked me, "than at Panorama?" (telephone interview, 2006).

[8] Teague performed Jan Bach's "Concerto for Steelpan and Orchestra" with the Chicago Sinfonietta in 1995 at Orchestra Hall, Chicago. Other symphonies he has performed with include the Czech National Symphony, Panama National Symphony, Saint Louis Symphony, Buffalo Symphony, Sinfonia Da Camera, Rockford Symphony, Dartmouth Wind Ensemble, North Shore Concert Band, and University of Wisconsin–Madison Marching Band.

The pull of Panorama is still strong, therefore, even for young pannists who seek to transcend some of its constraints. Some, such as Sean Thomas, the arranger for Moods steelband in Curepe and a promising young soloist, have become disillusioned with pan altogether because it seems so inescapably tied to the narrow possibilities of Panorama (personal conversation, 2000). But others, such as Glenford Sobers, whom I met in 2005 when he performed at a function with Moyenne Caribbean jazz ensemble,[9] feel a positive spiritual connection to Panorama. Glenford told me that he still likes to play with a big steelband because "you couldn't get that feeling of unity anywhere else." In addition to playing with Moyenne, Glenford was at the time directing his own single pan side, and I have often wondered whether the next great innovation in steelband might come from some neighborhood pan-around-the-neck band—a band that, like my favorite little band from Belmont in 1989, is unburdened by the aspiration to "win" anything. The community-building spirit of pan seems also to be expressing itself today in the proliferation of "riddim sections," ensembles of irons, scrapers, and miscellaneous drums that seem almost to reenact the resourceful and defiant innovations of the early steelband, and which have become a significant presence on the road on carnival j'ouvert morning. Does this portend something about the future of pan? Or might the next compelling new vision for the steel pan soon come from outside carnival, even from outside Trinidad, through the creative work of young pannists from London, or Brooklyn, or DeKalb, Illinois?

SUMMARY: YOUTH AND INNOVATION

It is hard to predict where the steel pan will go from here. At least I hope so. Because it was only by the enthusiasm of youth, unburdened by notions of what is likely or realistic, that teenagers like Zigilee, Ellie Mannette, Neville Jules, and Spree Simon were able to draw sweet music out of junk metal. In the generations of steelband youth that followed them came college boys who defied their parents and teachers to play a forbidden instrument, bold young women who integrated a male-dominated culture, and impossibly ambitious arrangers who invented a new style of music for Panorama. Today's Trinidadian youth are exhorted to preserve those achievements, but they will also need to address the style and sentiment of their own time. Their most important contributions to pan will be the ones that provide that thrill every teenager relishes, of being part of something exciting and *new*.

[9] Moyenne features Chantal Esdelle on keyboards, and Donald Noel Jr. on percussion, and has recorded at least one CD (*New Hope, 2000*).

12

Popular Culture and Nationalism

Can't beat me drum
In my own, my native land.
Can't have we Carnival
In my own, my native land,
In my own, native land.

In me own native land,
Moen pasca dancer, come moen vile
(I cannot dance as I wish).

Hollis Liverpool (2001: 331) cites this stickfighter's song as evidence that lower-class black people in the 1880s already identified themselves as Trinidadians rather than Africans, a sentiment that suggests an early precedent for nationalist thinking, and which appears to parallel the creole identity of French-descended Trinidadians. Indeed the cultural alliance between blacks and French creoles in the late nineteenth century helped to keep carnival alive and to propel it into the new era of formal competitions and modernist reform (chap. 9). Despite this history of lower-class participation, however, it is usually the educated elite, including black and coloured people of middle-class status, that are credited or blamed for modernist reform in the arts and for the nationalist movement generally. This parallels the tendency of scholars to treat nationalism as an elite ideology. The case of the steelband in Trinidad suggests, however, that "the masses" should share more credit for nationalism's successes and failures than most academic theories would admit. As an epilogue to this study, therefore, I would like to consider the implications of such "popular nationalism" for Trinidad and for the study of culture generally.

POPULAR NATIONALISM

The most well defined use of the term "popular nationalism" that I have seen comes from Benedict Anderson (1991), who contrasts it with the "official nationalism" of hereditary rulers such as the Russian czars or the kings of Siam, who justified and consolidated their power through the modern ideology of the nation-state. Anderson's popular nationalism is generated, in contrast, by intellectuals and administrators who have no stake in the old order, and it is a progressive force in relation to the monarchies and empires they sought to replace. Although Anderson's discussion of popular nationalism does not include anything quite so plebeian as the steelband movement, it nonetheless opens a way to imagining a popular nationalism that takes shape in and through popular culture—a nationalism that is generated by interactions between diverse individuals and groups, and that is not easily controlled by a single constituency.

Such a usage would contradict the very definition of nationalism that some scholars hold to. Turino, for example, holds that the term "nationalism" should be reserved for projects of state-building, and defines musical nationalism, in particular, as "the conscious use of any preexisting or newly created music in the service of a political nationalist movement" (2000: 190). He insists that a distinction must be drawn between "explicit political nationalism [and] nationalist sentiment (vaguer feelings of belonging to a nation)" (2000: 262). Though this is a useful distinction for some analytical purposes, it tends to privilege the agency of politicians. The fact is that political nationalism invariably depends on nationalist sentiment, and so nationalist sentiment—whether or not it is congruent with politicians' interests—contributes to the character and the course of nationalism.

One theorist who has tried to explain the role of sentiment in nationalism is John Hutchinson, who finds it useful to distinguish between cultural nationalism and political nationalism. Hutchinson notes that cultural nationalists (especially artists) often promote national sentiments that are incompatible with the project of political nationalists.[1] With their focus on

---

[1] Hutchinson cites Irish artists' promotion of Celtic language and culture, which alienated the English-educated intelligentsia. Similarly, the steelband's association with Black Pride movements and African culture presented a problem at the time of independence for Trinidad politicians who didn't want to alienate the Indian community.

moral regeneration, rather than political organizing, cultural nationalists are also less troubled by the paradoxes of nationalism, Hutchinson argues: "As an integrative movement, [cultural nationalism] repudiates both traditionalism and modernism as degenerations from a national vision that combines the virtues of each: the sense of unique identity given by the former with the idea of the community, embraced by the latter, as an active and equal participator in human progress" (1987: 33). Though Hutchinson is mainly concerned with writers, painters, or composers whom one might associate with an elite position, he opens up the possibility of a nationalism that is not limited to or constrained by considerations of elite control. His description of the artist's untroubled integration of tradition and modernity, for example, rings true for lower-class steelband musicians in Trinidad, whose impulse to rearrange the classics for carnival were antithetical to the elite ideology of promoting "local" culture.

Indeed, the case of the steelband challenges us to think beyond definitions of nationalism that portray it as an exclusively political *or* exclusively elite phenomenon; and the steelband is not unique in this regard. Scholarship on popular music during the last few decades raises questions about the ability of any elite to control people's definitions of or feelings about their nation. Marisol Berríos-Miranda's work (2003) on *salsa* music, for example, demonstrates the consolidation of Puerto Rican national sentiment through popular music, in what she calls a process of "expressive liberation" that defies Puerto Rico's colonial subjugation and makes common cause with urban Latinos all over the Americas. The meanings attached to *salsa* music, furthermore, are generated not only by producers of the music, but also through the active participation of listeners and dancers. Frances Aparicio's ethnographic study of working-class Puerto Rican women in Michigan provides examples of "how listeners reinterpret specific [salsa] lyrics, transforming them and literally rewriting them to be able to identify and seek pleasure and reaffirmation in their life situation" (1998: 235). Though such people may not expect their "rewritings" to carry political weight, their ideas and sentiments always have the potential to motivate larger political actions.

Kelly Askew points out that in the case of Tanzanian *taraab* music, for example, "some of the least privileged citizens of one emergent African nation hijacked and reconfigured the process of nationalism" (2002: 12). In Askew's examples, the participation of thousands of people at festive events both promotes and complicates the state's efforts to define expressive forms and meanings, as audience response (especially in the form of tipping) validates some singers and not others. Collective performances thus become a medium for the exchange and critique of ideas—a medium that Askew correctly observes has been overlooked in most theories of nationalism because of "the literate bias subsumed within the Eurocentric bias" (2002: 10) of Western scholars. Askew's critique is directed especially at Anderson's influential theory that print and print capitalism is a fundamental impetus to "imagining community" at the abstract level of a nation. What Askew calls the "national imaginary" encompasses even more diverse media and more diverse points of view than Anderson's "imagined community."

Popular culture also differs from print capitalism in the way community is experienced. Festive gatherings such as *taraab* performances create a community that is not merely imagined but tangible—seen, felt, smelled, and heard—and forge compelling bonds of affect and style. In Trinidad, carnival festivities may bring a significant proportion of the national community together in the same time and place, so one might argue that the role of festival in nationalism is especially significant in such small nation-states. Television, radio, Internet, and other modern media, however, also act as surrogates for the festive experience of community, creating the possibility of affective bonding in much larger national and transnational populations. As Arjun Appadurai points out:

> The revolution of print capitalism, and the cultural affinities and dialogues unleashed by it, were only modest precursors to the world we live in now. For in the last century, there has been a technological explosion, largely in the domain of transportation and information, which makes the interactions of a print-dominated world seem as hard-won and as easily erased as the print revolution made earlier forms of cultural traffic appear. (1990: 2)

This revolution in the flow of people and ideas has made individuals more preoccupied than ever with the work of defining their identities and their sense of community in an unstable world. In this context, "culture becomes ... an arena for conscious choice, justification and representation" (Appadurai 1990: 18). Such active choice complicates state control, or indeed any unified control, over national sentiment, and also creates the possibility for transnational identities that defy the typology of nation-states.

The idea of the nation-state continues to appeal, it seems, to our human need for community, and yet state efforts to define national culture are clearly complicated by the variety of choices and the diverse avenues of communication that modern technologies make possible. Ulf Hannerz (1987) proposes that popular culture in Nigeria, for example, seems to have accomplished what the government could not, as radio, television, and cinema have begun to give real meaning to "the nation of Nigeria"—an idea that, in the absence of these shared idioms, was abstract and arbitrary. While acknowledging the importance of nation, Hannerz proposes the term "creolization" (instead of "modernization") to describe the development of

Nigeria's national culture, challenging the dominance of European thought and values.

Earlier uses of this term in Caribbean cultural discourse were similarly intended to accentuate non-European contributions to these new societies, and to question the dominance of the upper classes in shaping society and culture (e.g., E. Brathwaite 1974; Craig 1974). This antihierarchical dimension of creolization is clearly significant in the Caribbean, where everyone is a newcomer (native cultures and people having been largely lost). Yet even in the Caribbean the cruel hierarchy of plantation society constitutes an established order that resists change, and that depends on distinctions of high and low culture to justify privilege. One cannot simply assume that the promotion of "people's culture" challenges this hierarchy, because new cultural forms may be appropriated to justify the privilege of elites. An aspiring creole elite promoted calypso and steelband, for example, as authentic expressions of the Trinidadian people, but some of them also tried (not necessarily successfully) to abstract these art forms from their traditional contexts, to make them comparable to the *chanson* and the symphony of the old European elite. Creolization, on the other hand, is generally thought of as a social and cultural force that challenges hierarchy and privilege, that takes place not merely through the promotion of new and hybrid forms, but through the input of diverse communities. Thus creolization challenges the ideological separation between elite culture and popular culture that justifies hierarchy and resists diversity. I will turn now to a consideration of this separation.

POPULAR CULTURE AND MODERNIST REFORM

The idea that the middle and upper classes' cosmopolitan education and values are incompatible with authentic lower-class expressive traditions pervades the literature on nationalism. Ernst Gellner writes, for example, that "the basic deception and self-deception practised by nationalism is this: nationalism is, essentially, the general imposition of a high culture on society, where previously low cultures had taken up the lives of the majority" (1994: 65). This deception involves the incorporation of popular culture icons into a format that is more congruent with elite aesthetics—folk tales compiled in books by the brothers Grimm, for example, or folk dances staged by the Ballet Folklorico de Mexico. The common people's arts are thereby "elevated" to a new status, but in such a way that the common people themselves do not need to be involved.

Trinidadian intellectuals have identified this problem in their own nationalist movement. Barbara Powrie, for example, writing about the emerging sense of cultural nationalism among the Trinidadian middle class around 1950, described a group of people who were "pre-occupied with the cultivation of negative personal character" (1951: 225), as a result of a long habit of trying to distance themselves from their African heritage. She suggests that their attitudes were beginning to change, but in rather superficial ways:

> The middle class are at last inclined to take pride in something which is Trinidadian. In doing so they are developing a sense of nationality, or rather, expressing the emergence of this sense. But behind this new attitude there still lurks the old attitude to national unity. White is still the colour to respect and bow to, black is still the colour to despise. The coloured people have not yet grasped the fact that it is the craftsmanship, artistry, and inventiveness of the lower class which has given Carnival its wider appeal as a special attraction of Trinidad. (1951: 231)

A decade later, C. L. R. James similarly observed that the middle-class politicians who took the reins of the newly independent nation of Trinidad and Tobago still held to the "unshakeable principle that they [were] in status, education, morals and manners, separate and distinct from the masses of the people" (1962: 86–88).

This social and cultural gap between the elite and the masses has caused some Trinidadians to mistrust the government's stewardship of culture, and has generated a discourse of authenticity that valorizes the lower-class carnival arts while denouncing cultural reforms perceived as elitist. A letter to the *Guardian* newspaper from Father Terrence Julien in 1973, for example, expresses anguish over the way even steelband music was becoming "colonized":

> On Friday night I went to the Queen's Park Savannah to hear the finals of the Steelband Festival. I left halfway through, sick in my stomach at the most pathetic sight I have had to endure for years—the colonisation of the calypso and the steel pan. There before our very eyes were groups of performing Trinidadians, like so many classes, sitting a musical G.C.E. [General Certificate of Education],[2] under the expert ears of examiner in chief—Professor Tom Manoff, of the Manhattan School of Music.
>
>   It is the most painful experience to have grown up during the movement for "political independence" and "massa day done"[3] and to have to face the

---

[2] General Certificate of Education exams in a variety of subjects were designed and corrected at Cambridge and London universities and administered as a diploma exam in high schools throughout the British Empire.

[3] "Massa Day Done" (Master's Day Is Done) was the title of a famous speech given by Trinidad's first prime minister, Eric Williams, in which he proclaimed the end of colonial authority and influence.

sickening fact that the movement in our society is not towards independence through creativity but towards total enslavement through meticulous aping.

I don't know which was more pathetic! The "conductors" or the "orchestras" trying to achieve the correct frenzy and mannerisms of Toscanini, agonisingly wringing out from their classes the correct answers to the European Test Piece. Or the bloodless abortion of the calypso-road-march as "symphonised" by these steel orchestras. (Dec. 13)

A corollary to this polemic—which accuses panmen of betraying their culture by "aping" the concert stage behavior of symphony musicians—is that middle-class participation in street carnival is similarly inauthentic. In his novel *The Dragon Can't Dance,* Earl Lovelace ridicules the pretense that carnival brings all classes together, portraying the participation of light-skinned sponsors in steelbands as a tragic negation of behind the bridge community solidarity:

For Desperadoes was the baddest band in the island, the band where the people was one. When they appeared on the road with new pans and emblem and waving a new flag: Sampoco Oil Company Gay Desperadoes, well, [Fisheye] nearly went out his head. Gay? *Gay* Desperadoes. That was the end. And instead of the little fellars pushing the pans, you had the sponsors: the sponsor's wife and the sponsor's daughter and the sponsor's friends, a whole section of them, their faces reddened by the excitement and the sun, smiling and jumping out of time, singing, All Ah We Is One. (1979: 68)

The polemical habit of valorizing lower-class culture while portraying middle-class influences in carnival as a detriment has become something of an orthodoxy in Trinidad; but like all orthodoxies, it has its enemies. Trinidadian journalist and radio host Morgan Job, in particular, has made a career of challenging the politically correct view that lower-class culture should be the model for national culture.

It is mischievous to tell a nation, composed as Trinidad and Tobago is, that Best Village[4] (Afrocentric), calypso and Panorama is our culture. This is dangerous nonsense good to keep illiterates happy in their favourite dreamland immune from the wasteland of the spirit in which they exist, while worshipping at the shrine of false and fallen heroes, their minds numbed and intoxicated with ignorance. (1994)

Job advocates Culture with a capital C, urging Trinidadians to "[enlarge their] experience through contact with powerful individual minds and the

---

[4] Best Village is a competition showcasing the arts and crafts of villages all over Trinidad.

inheritance of our European, Indian and Chinese ancestors." He cites the music of Beethoven and "Naavada and his raaginis of Locanakavi and Saaran agadeva" as worthy musical icons. Such statements may recall an earlier generation of Trinidadian intellectuals and artists (including C. L. R. James and Beryl McBurnie) who unapologetically embraced "high" culture paradigms in their efforts to develop and uplift Caribbean culture. The tables have turned since their time, however, and Job now finds it necessary to focus on the defense of high culture instead of the improvement of folk culture.

Whether one reads Lovelace or Job, however, the rhetorical tendency to separate the concepts of local and foreign, elite and popular, high and low obscures an important reality: the musical experiences of real people do not respect those boundaries. The diverse range of experiences that motivates any particular musician, for example, cannot be completely accounted for by broadly defined class or ethnic attitudes. What musical preferences might one expect from a man who came from a poor family, went to an elite school, listened to classical records at his friend's house and on the radio, and learned to play music in a panyard from laborers and illiterates? We could assume that one of these experiences represents his "true" class position, and the others merely influence this position, and there might be some merit in such an interpretation. As Pierre Bourdieu notes, however, "an act of classification depends on the practical function it fulfills" (1987: 510). It might be more useful, therefore, to think of such a musician's preferences and opinions as interpretive stances he takes in regard to particular questions, and to acknowledge that the same person may take a lower-class stance in one context and a middle-class stance in another. For example, the interpretive stances taken at different times by journalist Pete Simon (chap. 5) suggest permeability and overlap between different class identities. He identified with the pride that lower-class panmen took in rendering the works of Mozart and Beethoven faithfully; but with regard to carnival celebrations, he sided with middle-class cultural nationalists in denouncing the steelbands' penchant for playing "foreign" music. While any given opinion on the steelband, carnival, or another cultural question may reinforce binary oppositions like local and foreign, the collective opinions of one individual, expressed in a variety of contexts, are likely to show a more complex understanding of the interactions and middle ground between these categories.

In regard to this complexity of individual views on culture, Morgan Job's popularity is instructive. Although Job himself takes unrealistically extreme positions, I would not dismiss his impatience with populism and political correctness as an exclusively elitist point of view. Indeed, I have heard many working-class Trinidadians express appreciation for Job. Though that may be due in part to their carnivalesque enjoyment of contrariness (Job is a sort of intellectual "shock jock"), I am sure that Job's concern for refinement and upliftment are shared by people from different walks of life, many of whom may *also* support Best Village, calypso, and Panorama. And if these performance events differ from earlier community-based models, it is partly because people from lower-class communities were interested in making changes and played creative roles in shaping them.

Thus, though the Panorama competition in some ways exemplifies the cosmopolitan values of presentation and control, it also partakes of the participatory and unpredictable nature of festive performance and of popular culture generally. This pattern of shared control has also been observed in other Caribbean examples of modernist reform. Kate Ramsey shows, for example, how difficult it was for officials of the Haitian Bureau d'Ethnologie in the 1940s to enforce in their dance shows "a conservative fixing of identity—one which the performance of folklore, in any context, would always exceed" (1997). And Katherine Hagedorn, observing that representations of sacred Santería music and dance by Cuba's Conjunto Folklorico continue to be meaningful to traditional religious practitioners, explains that "offense [to the religious community] is avoided precisely because the religious practitioners themselves have taken part and continue to take part in the process of borrowing and reshaping the religious material; that is, the rendering is impelled both by the community of religious practitioners and by the secular, state-run institution" (2001: 66). Hagedorn also stresses the audience's role in "the negotiation and perpetuation of meaning" (58), which requires her to consider the influence not only of performers and government officials, but also of religious believers, tourists, and hustlers.

These examples suggest that modernist reformism need not be starkly opposed to community tradition, that it is not an exclusively elite concern but the product of dialogue and contention between politicians, intellectuals, artists, and audiences, none of whom has a definitive say in its outcome. It is of course important to recognize the hegemonic function of modernist reform, and to consider that it *is* likely to privilege middle-class cosmopolitan values over lower-class values *to the extent that*: (1) it is pitched to a middle-class, cosmopolitan, or tourist audience; (2) it substitutes professional or folklore-oriented performers for community-oriented performers; (3) it substitutes a presentational mode of performance for a participatory mode. If Panorama has lost some of its former vitality, then, that might be attributed to a changing audience (more tourists, more expatriates, fewer youth and working-class adults) and decreased community participation in steelband performance generally. Community representation in Panorama is still strong, however, especially among performers, and participatory impulses have proven remarkably persistent. Despite concerns about Panorama's role in the "concertization" of the steelband, the aesthetics of Panorama performances cannot be simply equated with those of the concert hall or opposed to those of the carnival parade. The case of the steelband also underscores the folly of assuming that a concert/presentational mode is for the elite while a street/presentational mode is for the masses. Laborers have delighted in the refinement of the North Stars rendering Strauss on stage; business executives have reveled in the festive communion of Desperadoes going down the road; and Panorama performances draw on both of these experiences to create something new.

SUMMARY: TAKING PLAY SERIOUSLY

Those who mistrust popular culture may ignore its impulses toward refinement and order, whereas those who celebrate popular culture often draw attention to its defiant and transgressive impulses. Either way, we (academics, critics, and others) tend to reinforce a distinction between the playfulness of popular culture and the serious business of running an institution or a state. Where popular culture is valued, it is often precisely for its separation from or opposition to the establishment. Johannes Fabian argues, for example, that the discursive distinction between "popular culture" and "culture" implies an awareness of alternatives to a dominant norm, a belief in "the existence of spaces of freedom and creativity in situations of oppression and supposedly passive mass consumption" (1998: 2). The question then becomes whether these spaces of freedom can effect significant changes. Much of the literature on carnival, in particular, is devoted to an inconclusive debate about whether its seasonal outpouring of playful energy has a lasting social impact or is merely a psychological "safety valve" that protects the status quo. David Kertzer, for example, cites historical examples of carnivals in Europe that developed into full-scale peasant revolts; but he also notes that European rulers and elites recognized "the safety valve effect of rites of rebellion ... long before it was first formulated by anthropologists" (1988: 144). Neither safety valve nor peasant massacre, however, is a very reassuring metaphor for the role of play in social organization. In either case, play appears to lack the element of responsibility and hence seriousness.

Huizinga, however, points out the problem with opposing play to seriousness:

> To our way of thinking, play is the direct opposite of seriousness. . . . Examined more closely, however, the contrast between play and seriousness proves to be neither conclusive nor fixed. We can say: play is non-seriousness. But apart from the fact that this proposition tells us nothing about the positive qualities of play, it is extraordinarily easy to refute. As soon as we proceed

from "play is non-seriousness" to "play is not serious," the contrast leaves us in the lurch—for some play can be very serious indeed. (1950: 5)

Any theory of popular culture's role in nationalism must address the seriousness of play. Consider the way college boys in Trinidad in the 1950s risked expulsion from school (a very serious risk for a middle-class teenage boy) to beat pan. Their playful engagement opened a floodgate of middle-class participation in the street carnival and helped the steel pan to achieve a new legitimacy. This illustrates not only the serious attraction of play, but also the shifting boundaries between "serious" and "frivolous" play. It is not so much that people do not regard play as serious, that is, but rather that people make ideological distinctions between those forms of play that are to be regarded as serious and those that are not. What is the difference between the president's review of the troops on Independence Day accompanied by a military band, and the stylized posing of the stickfighter accompanied by drumming and singing? What is the difference between an English impresario wooing Franz Joseph Haydn to London to compose and perform new works, and Rudolph Charles wooing Corbeaux Jack up the Hill to tune steel pans for Desperadoes? The notion of "popular nationalism" exhorts us to consider that people at all levels of society, not just the rich and powerful, have a stake in building community, and that they engage this project in a variety of creative, performative, and competitive ways.

One way in which the play of political leaders sometimes differs from the play of common people, however, is in its predictability. Roberto DaMatta's observation that competition is "incompatible with hierarchized social systems" (see chap. 9) helps to explain why play in general is so exciting: because its outcome is contested, unpredictable, and charged with the thrill of new possibilities. Governments sometimes engage in such unpredictable contests, as in the case of war (Huizinga 1950: 89–104). But powerful people also try to stack the odds in their favor, which can render play less satisfying. Some of Panorama's tensions and controversies, in particular, are rooted in the inherent contradiction of attempting to control play, of harnessing its unpredictable energy to a specific political agenda. Who wants to play if the outcome is decided ahead of time? Panorama's ideological force depends on popular participation, but that same participation generates new and unexpected ideas that politicians seek to contain. The unpredictability of play is thus both necessary and problematic for those who wield power.

The steelband began as an expression of people who did not wield power in the political sense—people who were located literally or figuratively "behind the bridge," on the margins of society, and for whom the play of carnival presented more opportunities than risks. Thanks to the creativity of young musicians, the support of their communities, and the work of well-connected people who were receptive to its possibilities, the steelband movement in Trinidad and Tobago became an arena for the coming together of high and low, local and foreign, presentation and participation. In this way it created space in the national dialogue for people who did not presume to control their world but who engaged life with a spirit of striving and play. As the steelband movement today assumes broader responsibilities, its challenge is to hold onto that spirit.

APPENDIX I

Steel Pan Instruments

This appendix complements the narrative of early steel pan tuning in chapter 3, which is more complete in many respects. The development of the various steelband instruments took place through an extraordinary variety of competing innovations, in the course of which new ideas and models that originated with one person or one band were selectively copied or adapted by others. The account provided here is imperfect, but I have done my best to identify widely used instrument types and names, and to give a rough sense of their chronological development. For information on early pans I have relied especially on interviews with Neville Jules, Ellie Mannette, and Anthony Williams (conducted by me or by Kim Johnson or Stephen Stuempfle, who graciously shared their transcripts). Descriptions of modern pans are based on my own observations, and on the excellent and much more extensive tuning diagrams of Jeff Thomas (1990) and Felix Blake (1995).

MATERIALS

Steel pans have been constructed over the years from a variety of containers. The **Bermudez biscuit drum** was the most popular for the deeper sounding "booms" and "kittles" in the first steel bands. The **caustic soda drum** was widely used for tuned basses in the late 1940s and early 1950s because of its light weight and good sound. Ping pongs and other smaller pans were constructed from a variety of containers, including paint cans and garbage cans. The **55-gallon oil drum**, made from 18-gauge steel, originally was found to be too heavy to carry while walking; but with the development of stage instruments around 1950 and the advent of mobile pan racks in 1956, the 55-gallon drum became the container of choice for all steel pans.

Fig. A.1. Containers used to make pans, from left: Bermudez biscuit drum, caustic soda drum, miscellaneous containers, 55-gallon drum (illustration created by David Dudley).

THE STEELBAND IN 1945

Many of the steelbands that first made a public impact at Victory in Europe and Victory in Japan celebrations in 1945 used an instrumentation similar to what is illustrated below, which mainly played rhythmic accompaniment to call-and-response singing.

Fig. A.2. Early pans being played, from left: Cuff boom, tenor kittle, ping pong (illustration created by David Dudley).

Ping pong—an onomatopoetic name given to the highest pitched pan that "cut" rhythmic improvisations above the steady patterns of the other percussion. The first ping pongs had their faces pounded out in a convex dome and had only two or three "notes," not necessarily well defined in pitch. The ping pong was held in one hand, sometimes with a loop of wire around the wrist or waist, and played with a stick held in the other hand.

Tenor kittle—this pan played an accompanying pattern for singers or for the ping pong and may have been the first to acquire a well-defined pattern of pitches. Like the ping pong, it was convex and suspended by a wire around the wrist or shoulder. Some played with two sticks like a side drum, and others played with one. Several contemporary observers sang for me the following tenor kittle pattern, with individual variations:

Fig. A.3. Early tenor kittle melody.

Boom—named after its bamboo counterpart, this was a low-pitched pan made from a biscuit drum. It was also called by various versions of the name "kittle" (e.g., **bass kittle**, **kittle boom**), which was the word Trinidadians used for the conventional bass drum played in brass bands. The boom was held by a neck strap and played either with the bare hand (which made it a **cuff boom**), or with sticks, sometimes striking the side as well as the face. The **dudup** was tuned with two pitches, playing bass lines like the following:

Fig. A.4. Dudup rhythm.

STEELBAND ADDITIONS IN THE LATE 1940S

Competition between bands led to a rapidly increasing number of notes on the ping pongs, leading first to diatonic scales, then fully chromatic ping pongs by 1950. The ping pong sketched below, dating from the late 1940s, was tuned with the notes of a major scale. In contrast to the early ping pong illustrated above, this one was sunk in a concave shape, with grooves separating the notes, an innovation that is credited to Ellie Mannette.

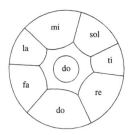

Fig. A.5. Diatonic ping pong (adapted from photo in Blake 1995: 42, also featured in Coming of Age museum exhibit, Port of Spain, 1993).

Strumming pans—a variety of pans were developed to play an accompanying role to the ping pong (as the tenor kittle originally did). The **second pan** was one of the earliest of these, which Neville Jules remembers first seeing in the Sun Valley steelband, tuned by Sonny Roach. The invention of the second pan has also been credited to Selwyn Gomes of Tropitones (James 1980). Neville Jules tuned a **cuatro pan**, inspired by the Venezuelan instrument by the same name that strums chords in a string band, and the **guitar pan** was another variation on this idea. Several other names were given to low-pitched strumming or accompanying pans, including the **bélé** (a name taken from a folk drum and dance style), the **grundig** (named for a make of German radio), and the **grumbler.**

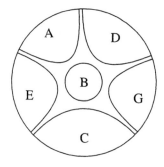

Fig. A.6. Early strumming pan, perhaps cuatro or guitar (based on pan featured in Coming of Age museum exhibit, Port of Spain, 1993).

Bass—Neville Jules is credited with first tuning notes on a boom to defined pitches (as opposed to the indistinct pitches of the early dudup). This resulted in the **tune boom,** a four-note pan made from a biscuit drum, commonly tuned to *do, re, fa,* and *sol.* Jules modeled this pan on the "bass box," a poor man's bass played throughout the Caribbean (also called *marimbula* in Spanish), which is a lamellophone on which low bass sounds are produced by plucking metal prongs fastened to a box resonator. A year or two later, Jules came out with his **bass pan,** made from a caustic soda drum that was lighter in weight and more powerful sounding than the biscuit drum, though its metal cracked easily. With only four notes to choose from, bass players sometimes had to play "wrong" notes that could deceive the ear when combined with the more distinct pitches of higher pans. A tonic triad of C-E-G, for example, might be played C-F-G because there was no E on the bass pan.

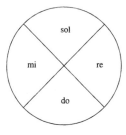

Fig. A.7. Four-note bass, first tuned by Neville Jules from a caustic soda drum.

MODERN PANS

The formation of the Trinidad All Steel Percussion Orchestra (TASPO) in 1950 facilitated a sharing and exploration of tuning ideas that resulted in a range of fully chromatic stage instruments tuned from 55-gallon oil drums. On the road, lightweight caustic soda drums continued to be used for bass pans during the early 1950s, while other portable single pans were tuned from 55-gallon drums. Of these, only the high-pitched ping pongs were chromatic, since only their notes were small enough to fit twelve or more in one pan. The picture below illustrates a "pan-around-the neck" or "single pan" group.

Fig. A.8. Single pans, as played in the early 1950s. All were tuned from 55-gallon drums, except the bass, made from the more lightweight caustic soda drum (illustration created by David Dudley).

After Anthony Williams devised wheeled racks for North Stars' bass pans in 1956, steelbands quickly abandoned the single pan style and used mobile racks for the road that permitted them to play the more musically versatile multiple sets of pans already in use for stage performances. (The single pan style has regained popularity, however, since it was revived in 1973 by Tripoli steelband as a nostalgic throwback.)

> **Tenors**—in the 1950s, the ping pong was renamed the "tenor," but tuners continued to make this highest pitched melody pan with a variety of patterns. The first widely influential chromatic pattern was Ellie Mannette's low tenor, commonly referred to today as the **Invader tenor** (or Invader lead). Note that the pitches of the C-major scale (shaded) are arranged in basically the same pattern as the earlier diatonic tenor sketched above. The Invader pattern thus exemplifies the somewhat haphazard, incremental process by which new notes were added to pans as they became known or necessary. A related pattern that continues to be popular among some bands and tenor players is the **thirds and fourths tenor**, whose outside notes are similar to the Invader—with the F# moved to the rim, and the higher octaves removed—but whose inside notes are aligned with their matching octaves.

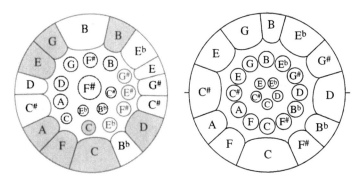

Fig. A.9. Ellie Mannette's Invader tenor (left), and the thirds and fourths tenor (right). Shaded notes in Invader tenor show its relation to the early diatonic ping pong above.

Inspired by the idea of "balance" and musical logic (see chap. 3), Anthony Williams invented the **spider web tenor** in the early 1950s, which had a symmetrical arrangement of notes based on the circle of fifths. It did not catch on at first, but it became the model for the **fourths and fifths tenor** that is by far the most common pattern in use today.

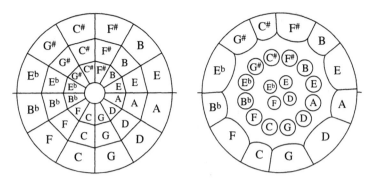

Fig. A.10. Anthony Williams's spider web tenor (left) and the modern fifths tenor.

Multiple sets—the advent of mobile pan racks not only made it possible to tune all pans from the heavy 55-gallon drum, it also made it possible for multiple sets of pans to be played both on the road and on the stage. Multiple sets are necessary to make the lower pans fully chromatic, since lower pitched notes must be larger. Though the list here is by no means exhaustive, the basic patterns illustrated are commonly known and used by many tuners today, with variations in register and note placement.

The increasing standardization of tuning patterns, as represented in these examples, illustrates a trend toward the kind of balance and musical logic that Anthony Williams introduced with his spider web pan. The double seconds, for example, divide the chromatic scale into two whole tone scales; the triple cellos divide it into three diminished chords; the quadrophonics divide it into four augmented chords; and the six-bass divides it into six pairs of fifths. Such musical logic does not necessarily correspond to the kinetic logic of the player, however, or to the tuner's logic of which notes sound best next to one another. This is perhaps one reason that alternative tuning patterns have not gone out of use.

Double second—one of the most widely standardized pans, the double second is used in a steelband to double or harmonize the melody, or sometimes to strum. The distinctive feature of this pan as it is tuned today is its complementary whole tone scales, one in each drum, which makes it possible to play a chromatic scale by a simple alternation of right and left hand strokes. Ellie Mannette is commonly credited with inventing this design in the early 1950s. The **double guitar** pan is also based on this whole-tone pattern, but tuned in a lower register with a longer skirt and used almost exclusively for strumming.

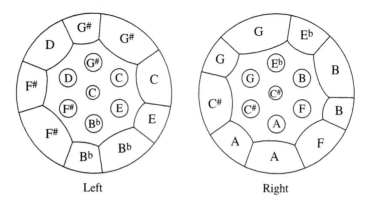

Fig. A.11. Double seconds, tuned from low F# (some also begin at low E).

Double tenor—Invented by Bertie Marshall in the early 1960s, this pan has a register similar to that of the double second, but is used almost exclusively to double or harmonize the melody. When they were first introduced, Marshall's double tenors impressed panmen with their bright sound, which he achieved by tuning of the harmonics (chap. 3), and by note placement and double grooving. The distribution of notes has a less obvious musical logic, however, compared to the double seconds, and perhaps for that reason the double tenor is used less today.

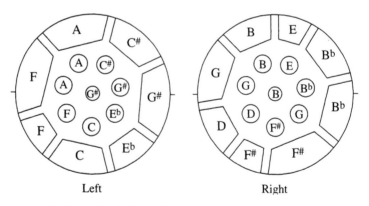

Fig. A.12. Bertie Marshall's double tenors.

Cello—This pan, sometimes called **triple guitar** when its skirt is cut shorter, was invented by Ellie Mannette in the late 1950s. It is tuned in a pattern of three complementary diminished chords, one in each drum.

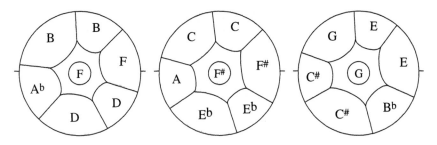

Fig. A.13. Triple cellos.

Another pattern that has been used for several distinct pans is based on complementary augmented chords. Ellie Mannette used this for his **tenor bass** in the late 1950s, but it was later adapted by Rudolph Charles, who added more notes and tipped two of the pans up vertically to make the **quadrophonic**, used for melodic lines across a wide register. The same basic pattern is used for the **four-pan**, which has all four pans hanging flat, with longer skirts like those of guitar pans.

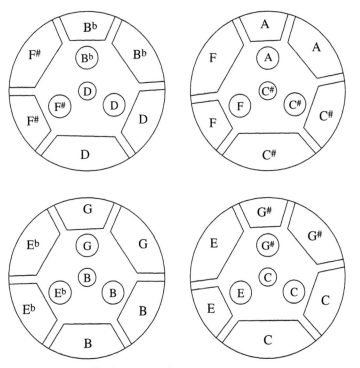

Fig. A.14. Quadrophonics (see fig. 3.6).

Bass—Featuring the largest and lowest notes of all pans, basses are tuned in sets of six to twelve, each a full-size 55-gallon drum. The most common configuration is the **six-bass**, which does not require the complicated horizontal suspension of drums that the **nine-bass** and **twelve-bass** have (see fig. 3.5). The player stands in the middle of this configuration, and the energetic movement required to get around on all pans creates an engaging visual spectacle.

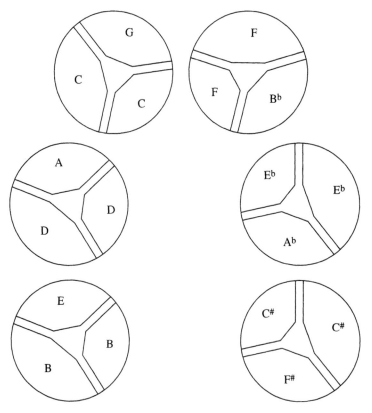

Fig. A.15. Six-bass.

THE TUNING PROCESS

Some pans today are being made from rolled steel welded to hoops of custom diameters.[1] The majority of tuners, however, continue to build pans from 55-gallon drums, which are approximately two feet in diameter. The typical stages in this process include sinking, shaping, grooving, burning, and tuning.

[1] Panyard Inc., based in Akron, Ohio, pioneered this process, which it calls "solid hoop." You can read more about it at www.panyard.com.

The bottom of a 55-gallon drum is first sunk into a concave form with a modified sledge hammer, to a depth ranging from as much as nine inches (for a tenor) to two or three inches (for a bass). Next the tuner scribes the notes using patterns of the size and shape that he knows work best for him. When the notes have been marked he sinks further down between them, using a smaller hammer, to bring the notes into convex relief. Next he uses a nail set with its head ground flat to hammer out a groove around each note, which will help prevent its vibrations from getting mixed up with the sounds of adjacent notes.

When the pan has been sunk, shaped, and grooved, its skirt (side) is cut to the appropriate length: a short skirt for a tenor, and successively longer skirts for deeper sounding pans, up to a full-length skirt (i.e., a full-size oil barrel) for a bass. The pan is then burned over a fire to clean it and normalize the metal. The last stage is the most complex, as the tuner beats each note with a hammer, tightening and loosening its surface, and striking control points that change the pitches of the fundamental and the harmonics to bring them into tune with one another at the desired frequency, and with the desired timbre. Frontline pans (tenors, double tenors, and double seconds) are commonly chromed before the final tuning touches. (For a more detailed explanation of steel pan tuning, see Kronman 1991.)

APPENDIX II

Repertoire

(All the steelband tunes mentioned in this book, not including calypso)

Title	Composer	Original Context	Cited (Page #s)
Acceleration Waltz	Johann Strauss	Waltz	132
Anniversary Waltz	Dubin and Franklin	Best-selling record by Bing Crosby, 1941	116
Another Night Like This	Ernesto Lecuona	Bolero, featured in the film *Carnival in Costa Rica* (1947)	115
Ave Maria	Schubert	German lied, heard in religious settings with Latin text substituted	31, 40, 57, 116
Bartered Bride	Smetana	Opera, 19th century	99
Bells of St. Mary's	Adams and Furbur	Film: *Bells of St. Mary's* (1945), starring Bing Crosby	122
Capriccio Español	Rimsky Korsakov	Symphony	99
Carmen	Bizet	Opera: *Carmen* (probably the Habanera or Toreador aria)	131
Cradle Song (*Wiegenlied*)	Brahms	German lied	97
Dance of the Hours	Ponchielli	Opera: *La Gioconda*	116
Drink to Me Only		Old English air	97
Eine kleine Nachtmusik	Mozart	Serenade for strings	99

(*continued*)

Title	Composer	Original Context	Cited (Page #s)
Elizabethan Serenade	Ronald Binge	Light classical, popularized esp. by the Mantovani orchestra	122
Enjoy Yourself	Magidson and Sigman	Samba, best-selling record in 1950 by Guy Lombardo and his Royal Canadians	97
Estudiantina	Ernesto Lecuona	Waltz, 1936	122
God Save the King	Thomas Arne	British national anthem	31, 40
Golden Earrings	Victor Young	From film of same name starring Marlene Dietrich; 1948 best-selling recording by Peggy Lee	97
Hallelujah Chorus	Handel	Oratorio: *The Messiah*	116, 132, 133
I Feel Pretty	Leonard Bernstein	Broadway musical: *West Side Story*	142, 248
In a Monastery Garden	Albert W. Ketelbay	Light classical	106
Indian Love Call	Friml, Harbach, and Hammerstein	1924 operetta: *Rose-Marie*; 1951 best-selling record by Slim Whitman	105
Jupiter	Holst	Symphony	99
Just the Two of Us	Grover Washington	1980 recording, #2 on U.S. charts	258
Liebestraum	Liszt	Piano etude	132, 133
Mambo Jambo (Que Rico el Mambo)	Perez Prado	Mambo, 1950 recording	97
Mango Walk		Jamaican mento (labeled in TASPO program as "rumba"), recorded by Lord Messam	97
Mary Had a Little Lamb		Nursery rhyme	40, 51
Messiah	Handel	Oratorio	116, 126, 132, 133
Minuet in G	Beethoven	Piano minuet	115–17, 130
Musetta's Waltz	Pucini	Opera: *La Bohème*	116
The Night Has a Thousand Eyes	Victor Young	1948 film by the same name starring Edward G. Robinson	

Title	Composer	Original Context	Cited (Page #s)
Parang		Rumba (as listed in TASPO program; more likely parang)	97
Puerto Rico Mambo	Perez Prado	Mambo	71
Return of the Allies	Lt. Joseph Griffith	March composed for TASPO, 1951	97
Roses from the South	Johann Strauss	Waltz	122
Salut d'Amor	Edward Elgar	Violin sonata, 1888	101
Serenata	Enrico Toscelli	Serenade for violin and piano	97
Skokian	August Msarurgwa	South African recording by Bulawayo Sweet Rhythms Band; 1954 best-selling recording by The Four Lads and by Ralph Marterie	114
Somewhere over the Rainbow	Harold Arlen	1939 film: *The Wizard of Oz*	105
Sonny Boy	Al Jolson, De Sylva, Brown, and Henderson	Films: *The Singing Fool* (1928); *Jolson Sings Again* (1949) (steel-band version labeled in TASPO program as fox trot)	97
Tannhäuser Overture	Richard Wagner	Opera, 19th century	99
Tennessee Waltz	Redd Stewart and Pee Wee King	1950 hit record by Patti Page	96, 97
Voices of Spring	Strauss	Waltz	122
Waltzing Matilda	Traditional/also attributed to A. B. "The Banjo" Patterson	Popularized as theme song of the Australian Army during World War II	101
William Tell Overture	Rossini	Opera, 19th century	99
A Whiter Shade of Pale	Procol Harum	Progressive rock, 1967 recording	13

APPENDIX III

Panorama Winners, 1963–2007

1963   North Stars: "Dan Is the Man in the Van" (Mighty Sparrow), arr. Anthony Williams.

1964   North Stars: "Mama This Is Mas'" (Lord Kitchener), arr. Anthony Williams.

1965   Cavaliers: "Melody Mas'" (Lord Melody), arr. Lennox "Bobby" Mohammed.

1966   Desperadoes: "Obeah Wedding (Melda)" (Sparrow), arr. Beverly Griffith.

1967   Cavaliers: "67" (Kitchener), arr. Lennox "Bobby" Mohammed.

1968   Harmonites: "Wrecker" (Kitchener), arr. Earl Rodney.

1969   Starlift: "The Bull" (Kitchener), arr. Ray Holman.

1970   Desperadoes: "Margie" (Kitchener), arr. Clive Bradley.

1971   (tie) Starlift: "Queen of the Bands" (Sparrow), arr. Ray Holman.

1971   (tie) Harmonites: "Play Mas'" (Kitchener), arr. Earl Rodney.

1972   Harmonites: "St. Thomas Girl" (Kitchener), arr. Earl Rodney.

1973   Trinidad All Stars: "Rain-O-Rama" (Kitchener), arr. Rudolph Wells.

1974   Harmonites: "Jerico" (Kitchener), arr. Earl Rodney.

1975   Hatters: "Tribute to Spree Simon" (Kitchener), arr. Steve Achaiba.

1976   Desperadoes: "Pan in Harmony" (Kitchener), arr. Clive Bradley.

1977   Desperadoes: "Haseley Crawford" (Kitchener), arr. Clive Bradley.

1978   Starlift: "Du Du Yemi" (Sparrow), arr. Hershell Pukerin.

1979   (Boycott).

1980   All Stars: "Woman on the Bass" (Scrunter), arr. Leon "Smooth" Edwards.

1981   Trinidad All Stars: "Unknown Band" (Blue Boy), arr. Leon "Smooth" Edwards.

1982   Renegades: "Pan Explosion" (Kitchener), arr. Jit Samaroo.

1983   Desperadoes: "Rebecca" (Blue Boy), arr. Clive Bradley.

1984   Renegades: "Sweet Pan" (Kitchener), arr. Jit Samaroo.

1985   (tie) Renegades: "Pan Night and Day" (Kitchener), arr. Jit Samaroo.

1985   (tie) Desperados: "Pan Night and Day" (Kitchener).

1986   Trinidad All Stars: "The Hammer" (David Rudder), arr. Leon "Smooth" Edwards.

1987 Phase II Pan Groove: "This Feelin Nice," composed and arr. by Len "Boogsie" Sharpe.

1988 Phase II Pan Groove: "Woman Is Boss," composed and arr. by Len "Boogsie" Sharpe.

1989 Renegades: "Somebody" (Winsford Devine), arr. Jit Samaroo.

1990 Renegades: "Iron Man" (Kitchener), arr. Jit Samaroo.

1991 Desperadoes: "Musical Volcano," composed and arr. by Robert Greenidge.

1992 Exodus: "Savannah Party" (Rudder/Goddard), arr. Pelham Goddard.

1993 Renegades: "Mystery Band" (Kitchener), arr. Jit Samaroo.

1994 Desperados: "Fire Coming Down," composed and arr. by Robert Greenidge.

1995 Renegades: "Four Lara Four" (Winston Scarborough, "The Original DeFosto Himself"), arr. Jit Samaroo.

1996 Renegades: "Pan in a Rage" (DeFosto), arr. Jit Samaroo.

1997 Renegades: "Guitar Pan" (Kitchener), arr. Jit Samaroo.

1998 Arima Nutones: "High Mas'" (D. Rudder), arr. Clive Bradley.

1999 Desperadoes: "In My House" (Oba), arr. Clive Bradley.

2000 Desperadoes: "Picture on my Wall (Oba), arr. Clive Bradley.

2001 Exodus: "A Happy Song," composed and arr. by Pelham Goddard.

2002 All Stars: "Fire Storm" (DeFosto), arr. Leon "Smooth" Edwards.

2003 Exodus: "Pandora" (DeFosto), arr. Pelham Goddard.

2004 Exodus: "War 2004" (DeFosto), arr. Pelham Goddard.

2005 Phase II: "Trini Gone Wild," composed and arr. by Len "Boogsie" Sharpe.

2006 Phase II: "This One's For You, Bradley," composed and arr. by Len "Boogsie" Sharpe.

2007 All Stars: "Pan Lamentation" (DeFosto), arr. Leon "Smooth" Edwards.

BIBLIOGRAPHY

Agawu, Kofi. 1995a. *African Rhythm: A Northern Ewe Perspective*. Cambridge: Cambridge University Press.

———. 1995b. "The Invention of African Rhythm." *JAMS* 48(3): 380–95.

Aho, William. 1987. "Steelband Music in Trinidad and Tobago." *Latin American Music Review* 8(1): 26–58.

Ahye, Molly. 1983. *Cradle of Caribbean Dance: Beryl McBurnie and the Little Carib Theatre*. Port of Spain, Trinidad: Heritage Cultures.

Allen, Matthew. 1997. "Rewriting the Script for South Indian Dance." *The Drama Review* 41(3): 63–100.

Alonso, Ana Maria. 1990. "Men in 'Rags' and the Devil on the Throne: A Study of Protest and Inversion in the Carnival of Post-Emancipation Trinidad." *Plantation Society in the Americas* 3(1): 73–120.

Anderson, Benedict. 1991. *Imagined Communities: Reflections on the Origin and Spread of Nationalism*. 2nd ed. London: Verso.

Aparicio, Frances. 1998. *Listening to Salsa: Gender, Latin Popular Music, and Puerto Rican Cultures*. Hanover, N.H.: Wesleyan University Press.

Appadurai, Arjun. 1990. "Disjuncture and Difference in the Global Cultural Economy." *Public Culture* 2(2): 1–24.

Askew, Kelly. 2002. *Performing the Nation: Swahili Music and Cultural Politics in Tanzania.* Chicago: University of Chicago Press.

Austerlitz, Paul. 1997. *Merengue: Dominican Music and Dominican Identity.* Philadelphia: Temple University Press.

Averill, Gage. 1997. *A Day for the Hunter, A Day for the Prey: Popular Music and Power in Haiti.* Chicago: University of Chicago Press.

Avorgbedor, Daniel. 2001. "Competition and Conflict as a Framework for Understanding Performance Culture among the Urban Anlo-Ewe." *Ethnomusicology* 45(2): 260–82.

Babb, John. 1973. "When Pan Made Crowd Eat Grass." *Trinidad Guardian,* Feb. 25, p. 4.

Babcock, Barbara. 1978. *The Reversible World: Symbolic Inversion in Art and Society.* Ithaca, N.Y.: Cornell University Press.

Bakhtin, Mikhail. 1984. *Rabelais and His World.* Bloomington: Indiana University Press.

Barber, Karin, and Christopher Waterman. 1995. "Traversing the Global and the Local: *Fuji* Music and Praise Poetry in the Production of Contemporary Yoruba Popular Culture." In Daniel Miller, ed., *Worlds Apart: Modernity through the Prism of the Local.* London: Routledge, pp. 240–62.

Batson, Dawn. 1995. *Pan into the Twenty-First Century: The Steelband as an Economic Force in Trinidad and Tobago.* Ph.D. diss., University of Miami.

Belmosa, Trevor. 1989. *The Soul of Pan.* Trinidad: Servol Print.

Berliner, Paul. 1978. *The Soul of Mbira: Music and Traditions of the Shona People of Zimbabwe.* Berkeley: University of California Press.

Berríos-Miranda, Marisol. 2004. "Salsa Music as Expressive Liberation." *Journal of the Center for Puerto Rican Studies* 16(2): 158–73.

Blacking, John. 1995. *Music, Culture, and Experience.* Chicago: University of Chicago Press.

Blake, Felix I. R. 1995. *The Trinidad and Tobago Steel Pan: History and Evolution.* Port of Spain, Trinidad: Self-published.

Bourdieu, Pierre. 1987. "What Makes a Social Class? On the Theoretical and Practical Existence of Groups." *Berkeley Journal of Sociology* 32: 1–18.

Bradley, Clive. 1977. "Interview, Tapes #238 and 239." *Government Broadcasting Unit, Trinidad and Tobago.*

Braithwaite, Lloyd. 1975. *Social Stratification in Trinidad: A Preliminary Analysis.* Mona, Jamaica: Institute of Social and Economic Research, University of the West Indies.

Brathwaite, Edward. 1974. *Contradictory Omens: Cultural Diversity and Cultural Integration in the Caribbean.* Mona, Jamaica: Savacou.

Brereton, Bridget. 1975. "Trinidad Carnival 1870–1900." *Savacou* 11(12): 46–110.

———. 1989 (1981). *A History of Modern Trinidad, 1783–1962.* Portsmouth, N.H.: Heinemann.

Carr, Andrew. 1956. "Pierrot Grenade." *Caribbean Quarterly* 4(3–4): 281–314.

Chatterjee, Partha. 1986. *Nationalist Thought and the Colonial World: A Derivative Discourse?* Minneapolis: University of Minnesota Press.

————. 1990. "The Nationalist Resolution of the Women's Question." In Kumkum Sangari and Sudesh Vaid, eds., *Recasting Women: Essays in Indian Colonial History.* New Brunswick, N.J.: Rutgers University Press, pp. 233–53.

Cowley, John. 1996. *Carnival, Canboulay, and Calypso: Traditions in the Making.* Cambridge: Cambridge University Press.

Craig, Susan E. 1974. "Sociological Theorizing in the English-Speaking Caribbean: A Review." In *Contemporary Caribbean: A Sociological Reader.* St. Augustine, Trinidad: self-published, pp. 143–80.

DaMatta, Roberto. 1991. *Carnivals, Rogues, and Heroes: An Interpretation of the Brazilian Dilemma.* London: University of Notre Dame Press.

Daniell, Alvin, producer. 1993. *The Birth of Pan.* Trinidad and Tobago Television.

Diehl, Keila Mackie. 1992. *Tempered Steel: The Steel Drum as a Site for Social, Political, and Aesthetic Negotiation in Trinidad.* Master's thesis, University of Texas, Austin.

Diethrich, Gregory. 2004. *Living in Both Sides of the World: Music, Diaspora, and Nation in Trinidad.* Ph.D. diss., University of Illinois.

Dudley, Shannon. 1996. "Judging by the Beat: Calypso versus Soca." *Ethnomusicology* 40(2): 269–98.

————. 1997. *Making Music for the Nation: Competing Identities and Esthetics in Trinidad and Tobago's Panorama Steelband Competition.* Ph.D. diss., University of California, Berkeley.

————. 2001. "Ray Holman and the Changing Role of the Steelband, 1957–72." *Latin American Music Review* 22(2): 183–98.

————. 2002a. "Dropping the Bomb: Steelband Performance and Meaning in 1960s Trinidad." *Ethnomusicology* 46(1): 135–64.

————. 2002b. "The Steelband "Own Tune": Nationalism, Festivity, and Musical Strategies in Trinidad's Panorama Competition." *Black Music Research Journal* 22(1): 13–36.

————. 2002c. "Tradition and Modernity in Trinidad Steelband Performance." In Frances Aparicio and Candida Jaquez, eds., *Musical Migrations.* New York: Palgrave Macmillan, pp. 147–60.

————. 2003. "Creativity and Constraint in Trinidad Carnival Competitions." *World of Music.* 45(1): 11–34.

————. 2004. *Carnival Music in Trinidad.* Oxford: Oxford University Press.

Eagleton, Terry. 1990. *The Ideology of the Aesthetic.* Oxford: Basil Blackwell.

Elder, Jacob D. 1966. "Kalinda—Song of the Battling Troubadours of Trinidad." *Journal of the Folklore Institute* (Bloomington) 3(2): 192–203.

————. 1969. *From Congo Drum to Steelband: A Socio-Historical Account of the Emergence and Evolution of the Trinidad Steel Orchestra.* St. Augustine, Trinidad: University of the West Indies Press.

Eldridge, Michael. 2002. "There Goes the Transnational Neighborhood: Calypso Buys a Bungalow." *Callaloo* 25(2): 620–38.

Engel, Carl. 1866. *An Introduction to the Study of National Music.* London: Longmans, Green, Reader, and Dyer.

Epstein, Dena. 1977. *Sinful Tunes and Spirituals: Black Folk Music to the Civil War*. Urbana: University of Illinois Press.

Erlmann, Veit. 1992. "'The Past Is Far and the Future Is Far': Power and Performance among Zulu Migrant Workers." *American Ethnologist* 19(4): 688–709.

———. 1996. *Nightsong: Performance, Power, and Practice in South Africa*. Chicago: University of Chicago Press.

Espinet, Charles S., and Harry Pitts. 1944. *Land of the Calypso: The Origin and Development of Trinidad's Folk Song*. Port of Spain: Guardian Commercial Printery.

Fabian, Johannes. 1998. *Moments of Freedom: Anthropology and Popular Culture*. Charlottesville: University Press of Virginia.

Feld, Steven. 1984/1994. "Communication, Music, and Speech about Music." In *Music Grooves*. Chicago: University of Chicago Press, pp. 77–95.

Fernandez, James. 1986. "The Argument of Images and the Experience of Returning to the Whole." In Victor Turner and Edward Bruner, eds., *The Anthropology of Experience*. Urbana: University of Illinois Press, pp. 159–187.

Floyd, Samuel. 1995. *The Power of Black Music*. New York: Oxford University Press.

Ganase, Pat. 1993. "Return of the Savage." *Trinidad Guardian Magazine*, April 25, p. 3.

Geertz, Clifford. 1971/1973. "After the Revolution: The Fate of Nationalism in the New States." In *The Interpretation of Cultures*. New York: Basic Books, pp. 234–54.

Gellner, Ernst. 1994. "Nationalism and Modernization." In John Hutchinson and Anthony Smith, eds., *Nationalism*. Oxford: Oxford University Press, pp. 55–62.

Gibbons, Rawle. n.d. "The Second Coming: The Orisha Factor in the Emergence of the Steelband in Trinidad and Tobago." St. Augustine, Trinidad: Unpublished manuscript.

Gilroy, Paul. 1991. "Sounds Authentic: Black Music, Ethnicity, and the Challenge of a "Changing" Same." *Black Music Research Journal* 11(2): 111–36.

———. 1993. *The Black Atlantic: Modernity and Double Consciousness*. Cambridge, Mass.: Harvard University Press.

Goddard, George. 1980. "Goddard: I Am the Only Man Qualified to Write on Our Panorama. Why? I Started It." *Trinidad Guardian*, Feb. 10, p. 8.

———. 1991. *Forty Years in the Steelbands: 1939–1979*. Edited by Roy D. Thomas. London: Karia Press.

Guilbault, Jocelyne. 1987. "The La Rose and La Marguerite Organizations in St. Lucia: Oral and Literate Strategies in Performance." *Yearbook for Traditional Music* 19: 97–115.

———. 1993. *Zouk: World Music in the West Indies*. Chicago: University of Chicago Press.

Gunderson, Frank, and Gregory Barz, eds. 2000. *Mashindano! Competitive Music Performance in East Africa*. Dar es Salaam: Mkuki na Nyota Publishers.

Guss, David. 2002. *The Festive State: Race, Ethnicity, and Nationalism as Cultural Performance*. Berkeley: University of California Press.

Hackett, Jeff. 1984. "A Pannist at Seven." *Trinidad Guardian*, Feb. 23, p. 18.

Hagedorn, Katherine. 2001. *Divine Utterances: The Performance of Afro-Cuban Santeria*. Washington, D.C.: Smithsonian Institution Press.

Hall, Stuart. 1998. "What Is This 'Black' in Black Popular Culture?" In *Black Popular Culture.* New York: New Press, pp. 21–33.

Handler, Jerome S., and Charlotte J. Frisbie. 1972. "Aspects of Slave Life in Barbados: Music and Its Cultural Context." *Caribbean Studies (Puerto Rico)* 11(2): 5–46.

Handler, Richard, and Jocelyn Linnekin. 1984. "Tradition, Genuine or Spurious." *Journal of American Folklore* 97(385): 273–90.

Hannerz, Ulf. 1987. "The World in Creolization." *Africa* 57(4): 546–59.

Harris, John. 1975. *The PNM Government and the Steelband Movement from 1956 to the Present.* Caribbean Studies Project, University of the West Indies.

Helmlinger, Aurelie. 2001. "Geste individuel, mémoire collective: Le jeu du pan dans les steelbands de Trinidad and Tobago." *Cahiers de Musiques Traditionnelles* 14: 181–202.

Herskovits, Melville. 1941. *The Myth of the Negro Past.* New York: Harper Brothers.

Hewitt, Khalick. 2006. "The Last Panorama, Master Clive Bradley, and the Steelband Library." *Pan Jumbie,* http://www.pan-jumbie.com/tishof/rendezvous7.htm.

Hill, Donald. 1993. *Calypso Calaloo: Early Carnival Music in Trinidad.* Gainesville: University Press of Florida.

———. 1998. "'I am happy just to be in this sweet land of liberty': The New York City Calypso Craze of the 1930s and 1940s." In Ray Allen and Lois Wilcken, eds., *Island Sounds in the Global City.* New York: Institute for Studies in American Music and the New York Folklore Society, pp. 74–92.

Hill, Errol. 1971. "Calypso." *Jamaica Journal* 5(1): 23–27.

———. 1972/1997. *The Trinidad Carnival: Mandate for a National Theater.* London: New Beacon Books.

Hobsbawm, Eric, and Terrence Ranger, eds. 1983. *The Invention of Tradition.* Cambridge: Cambridge University Press.

Huizinga, Johann. 1950. *Homo Ludens: A Study of the Play Element in Culture.* Boston: Beacon Press.

Hutchinson, John. 1987. *The Dynamics of Cultural Nationalism: The Gaelic Revival and the Creation of the Irish Nation State.* London, Allen & Unwin.

James, C. L. R. 1962. "The Middle Classes." In *Consequences of Class and Color.* New York: Anchor Books, pp. 78–92.

———. 1959/1977. "The Artist in the Caribbean." In *The Future in the Present.* London: Alison and Busby, pp. 183–90.

Job, Morgan. 1994. "Panorama Worship." *Express,* Feb. 1, p. 8.

Johnson, Kim. 1996. "Tin Pan Alley, Part 1: The Soul in Iron: Considerations in Steelband Historiography." *Pan Lime* (Akron, Ohio) 3(11–12).

Johnson, Kim, Hélène Bellour, Jeffrey Chock, and Milla Riggio. 2002. *Renegades: The History of the Renegades Steel Orchestra of Trinidad and Tobago.* Oxford: Macmillan Education.

Jones, LeRoi. 1963. *Blues People.* New York: Morrow Quill Paperbacks.

Joseph, Terry. 2001. "Panorama Prize Leaps to $320,000." *Trinidad Express,* Feb. 2.

———. 2002a. "New Style Panorama Kicks Off Tonight." *Trinidad Express,* Jan. 27.

————. 2002b. "Pan Shocker: Americans Patent Pan Plan." *Trinidad Express,* April 16.

————. 2002c. "Savannah Party." *Trinidad Express,* Jan. 26.

————. 2006. "Coming Soon: Walk with Your Pan." *Trinidad Guardian,* Jan. 15.

Keil, Charles. 1993. *My Music.* Hanover, N.H.: University Press of New England.

————. 1994. "Motion and Feeling through Music." In *Music Grooves.* Chicago: University of Chicago Press, pp. 53–76. Originally published in 1966 in *Journal of Aesthetics and Art Criticism* 24(3): 337–49.

————. 1995. "The Theory of Participatory Discrepancies: A Progress Report." *Ethnomusicology* 39(1): 1–20.

Keil, Charles, and Angeliki V. Keil. 1992. *Polka Happiness.* Philadelphia: Temple University Press.

Kertzer, David. 1988. "Conflict and Crisis." In *Ritual, Politics, and Power.* New Haven, Conn.: Yale University Press, pp. 125–50.

Kirshenblatt-Gimblett, Barbara. 2002. "Sounds of Sensibility." In *American Klezmer: Its Roots and Offshoots.* Berkeley: University of California Press, pp. 129–73.

Koetting, James. 1970. "Analysis and Notation of West African Drum Ensemble Music." *Selected Reports in Ethnomusicology* 1(3): 115–36.

Kronman, Ulf. 1991. *Steel Pan Tuning: A Handbook for Steelpan Making and Tuning.* Stockholm: Musikmuseet.

Lee, Ann. 1991. "Class, Race, Colour, and Carnival." In Selwyn Ryan, ed., *Social and Occupational Stratification in Contemporary Trinidad and Tobago.* St. Augustine, Trinidad: Institute of Social and Economic Research, University of the West Indies, pp. 417–33.

————. 1997. "The Steelband Movement and Community Politics in Laventille." In Selwyn Ryan, ed., *Behind the Bridge.* St. Augustine, Trinidad: Institute of Social and Economic Research, University of the West Indies, pp. 69–90.

Lee, Simon. 1993. "Pan in We Head." *Trinidad Guardian, Carnival Magazine,* Feb. 24, p. 42.

Levine, Lawrence. 1988. *High Brow Low Brow.* Cambridge, Mass.: Harvard University Press.

Liverpool, Hollis. 1993. *Rituals of Power and Rebellion: The Carnival Tradition in Trinidad and Tobago (Vols. 1 and 2).* Ph.D. diss., University of Michigan.

————. 1994. "Researching Steelband and Calypso Music in the British Caribbean and the U.S. Virgin Islands." *Black Music Research Journal* 14(2): 179–201.

————. 2001. *Rituals of Power and Rebellion: The Carnival Tradition in Trinidad and Tobago, 1763–1962.* Chicago: Research Associates School Times Publications.

Lovelace, Earl. 1979. *The Dragon Can't Dance.* Harlow, England: Longman.

————. 1998. "The Emancipation-Jouvay Tradition and the Almost Loss of Pan." *The Drama Review* 42(3): 54–60.

Mahabir, Noorkumar. 1987. *The Influence of the Tassa on the Making of the Steelband: The East Indian Contribution to the Trinidad Carnival.* Carapichaima, Trinidad: Caribbean Institute of Indian Studies and Research.

Marre, Jeremy, producer. 1979. *Rhythm of Resistance: The Black Music of South Africa.* Film distributed by Shanachie.

Maultsby, Portia K. 1979. "Influences and Retentions of West African Musical Concepts in U.S. Black Music." *Western Journal of Black Studies* 3(3): 197–215.

Maxime, Gideon. n.d. *41 Years of Pan.* Port of Spain, Trinidad: Self-published.

McClary, Susan. 2000. *Conventional Wisdom: The Content of Musical Form.* Berkeley: University of California Press.

Mendoza, Zoila. 2000. *Shaping Society through Dance: Mestizo Ritual Performance in the Peruvian Andes.* Chicago: University of Chicago Press.

Meyer, Leonard. 1956. *Emotion and Meaning in Music.* Chicago: University of Chicago Press.

Miller, Daniel. 1991. "Absolute Freedom in Trinidad." *Man* 26: 323–41.

Moore, Robin. 1997. *Nationalizing Blackness: Afrocubanismo and Artistic Revolution in Havana, 1920–1940.* Pittsburgh: University of Pittsburgh Press.

Murray, Albert. 1982. *Stomping the Blues.* New York: Vintage Books.

Myers, Helen. 1998. *Music of Hindu Trinidad: Songs from the India Diaspora.* Chicago: University of Chicago Press.

Nagahama, Eiko. 2000. *Women in the Steelband Movement: History of Women's Participation in the Steelband Movement of Trinidad and Tobago.* Senior thesis, University of Washington.

Naipaul, V. S. 1962. *The Middle Passage.* New York: Vintage Books.

Najera-Ramirez, Olga. 1997. *La Fiesta de los Tastoanes: Critical Encounters in Mexican Festival Performance.* Albuquerque: University of New Mexico Press.

Nettl, Bruno. 1983. *The Study of Ethnomusicology.* Urbana: University of Illinois Press.

———. 1985. *The Western Impact on World Music: Change, Adaptation, and Survival.* New York. Schirmer.

Odingi, Eddie. 1992. "Pan Jumbie editorial column." *Trinidad Express,* Feb. 21.

Ortner, Sherry. 1984. "Theory in Anthropology since the 1960s." *Contemporary Studies in Society and History* 26(1): 126–66.

Ottley, Rudolph. n.d. *Calypsonians from Then to Now, Part II.* Port of Spain: Self-published.

Oxaal, Ivar. 1971. *Race and Revolutionary Consciousness: A Documentary Interpretation of the 1970 Black Power Revolt in Trinidad.* Cambridge, Mass.: Schenkman.

Pacini-Hernandez, Deborah. 1995. *Bachata: A Social History of a Dominican Popular Music.* Philadelphia: Temple University Press.

Pan Trinbago Foundation Board. 1999. *Pan: Strategic Plan for Sustainable Development.* (Draft for public comment.)

Pearse, Andrew. 1956. "Mitto Sampson on Calypso Legends of the Nineteenth Century." *Caribbean Quarterly* 4: 250–62.

———. 1971. "Carnival in Nineteenth-Century Trinidad." In Michael M. Horowitz, ed., *Peoples and Cultures of the Caribbean: An Anthropological Reader.* New York: Natural History Press for the Museum of Natural History, pp. 528–52.

Pierre, Lennox. 1962. "From Dustbins to Classics." *Trinidad Guardian, Independence Supplement,* August 26, pp. 107–10.

Powrie, Barbara E. 1951. "The Changing Attitude of the Coloured Middle Class towards Carnival." *Caribbean Quarterly* 4(3–4): 224–32.

Quashie. 1966. "The Versatile Archie." *Trinidad Guardian*, Feb. 20, p. 8.

Quintero Rivera, Angel. 1998. *Salsa, Sabor y Control: Sociologia de la Musica Tropical.* Mexico City: Siglo Veintiuno Editores.

Ramsey, Kate. 1997. "Vodou and Nationalism: The Staging of Folklore in Mid-Twentieth Century Haiti." In Jane Desmond, ed., *Meaning in Motion: New Cultural Studies of Dance.* Durham, N.C.: Duke University Press, pp. 345–78.

Ranger, Terence. 1975. *Dance and Society in Eastern Africa, 1890–1970.* Berkeley: University of California Press.

Regis, Louis. 1999. *The Political Calypso: True Opposition in Trinidad and Tobago, 1962–87.* Gainesville: University Press of Florida.

Rice, Timothy. 1987. "Toward the Remodeling of Ethnomusicology." *Ethnomusicology* 31(3): 469–88 (plus responses through p. 516).

———. 1994. *May It Fill Your Soul.* Chicago: University of Chicago Press.

Rohlehr, Gordon. 1990. *Calypso and Society in Pre-Independence Trinidad.* St. Augustine, Trinidad: Self-published.

———. 1999. "The State of Calypso Today." In Ralph Premdas, ed., *Identity, Ethnicity, and Culture in the Caribbean.* St. Augustine, Trinidad: University of the West Indies Press, pp. 29–46.

Rouse, Ewart. 1966. "The Steelband: Classics versus Folk." *Trinidad Guardian,* Nov. 23, p. 18.

Ryan, Selwyn. 1972. *Race and Nationalism in Trinidad and Tobago.* Toronto: University of Toronto Press.

———. 1991. *Social and Occupational Stratification in Contemporary Trinidad and Tobago.* St. Augustine, Trinidad: Institute for Social and Economic Research, University of the West Indies.

———. 1997. *Behind the Bridge: Poverty, Politics and Patronage in Laventille, Trinidad.* St. Augustine, Trinidad: Institute for Social and Economic Research, University of the West Indies.

Said, Edward. 1979. *Orientalism.* New York: Vintage Books.

———. 1993. *Culture and Imperialism.* New York: Alfred Knopf.

Saldhena, Robert. 1984. *The Innovations of Anthony Williams and How They Revolutionized the Steelband, Steelband Music, and Carnival.* Caribbean Studies Project, University of the West Indies, St. Augustine, Trinidad.

Samaroo, Jit. 1993. *Mystery Band, Score Transcribed by Stever Popernack.* Akron, Ohio: Panyard.

Scher, Philip. 2003. *Carnival and the Formation of a Caribbean Transnation.* Gainesville: University Press of Florida.

Sharpe, Len "Boogsie." 1993. *Birthday Party.* Score Transcribed by Mark O'Brien, Shelly Irvine, and Ron Kerns. Akron, Ohio: Panyard.

Shelemay, Kay. 1987. "Response to Timothy Rice." *Ethnomusicology* 31(3): 489–90.

Simmonds, Austin. 1964. "Calypsoes versus Classics." *Trinidad Guardian,* Feb. 9, p. 9.

Simon, Pete. 1969. "Is the 'Bomb' Destroying the Spirit of Carnival?" *Trinidad Guardian,* Jan. 19, p. 9.

———. 1970. "Pete Simon Replies to Chalkdust." *Trinidad Guardian,* Feb. 1, p. 5.

———. 1974. "Trinidad's Privy Council of Pan." *Trinidad Guardian,* Jan. 27, and Feb. 3, p. 4.

Small, Christopher. 1998. *Musicking: The Meaning of Performance and Listening.* Hanover, N.H.: University Press of New England.

Stewart, John. 1986. "Patronage and Control in the Trinidad Carnival." In Victor M. Turner and Edward M. Bruner, eds., *The Anthropology of Experience.* Urbana: University of Illinois Press, pp. 289–315.

Stolzoff, Norman. 2000. *Wake the Town and Tell the People: Dancehall Culture in Jamaica.* Durham, N.C.: Duke University Press.

Stuempfle, Steve. 1990. *The Steelband Movement in Trinidad and Tobago: Music, Politics, and National Identity in a New World Society.* Ph.D. diss., University of Pennsylvania.

———. 1995. *The Steelband Movement: The Forging of a National Art in Trinidad and Tobago.* Philadelphia: University of Pennsylvania Press.

Taitt, Anthony. 1972. *The Effect of Sponsorship on the Steelband Movement.* Caribbean Studies Project, University of the West Indies, St. Augustine, Trinidad.

Tarradath, Selwyn. 1991. "Race, Class, Politics, and Gender in the Steelband Movement." In Selwyn Ryan, ed., *Social and Occupational Stratification in Contemporary Trinidad and Tobago.* St. Augustine, Trinidad: Institute of Social and Economic Research, University of the West Indies, pp. 377–84.

Thomas, Jeffrey. 1985. *A History of Pan and the Evolution of the Steelband in Trinidad and Tobago.* Master's thesis, Northwestern University. Self-published as a book in 1990.

———. 1986. "The Changing Role of the Steel Band in Trinidad and Tobago: Panorama and the Carnival Tradition." *Studies in Popular Culture* 9(2): 96–108.

———. 1992. *Forty Years of Steel: An Annotated Discography of Steel Band and Pan Recordings, 1951–1991.* Westport, Conn.: Greenwood Press.

Turino, Thomas. 1993. *Moving away from Silence.* Chicago: University of Chicago Press.

———. 2000. *Nationalists, Cosmopolitans, and Popular Music in Zimbabwe.* Chicago: University of Chicago Press.

Turner, Victor. 1969. *The Ritual Process: Structure and Anti-Structure.* Ithaca, N.Y.: Cornell University Press.

———, ed. 1982. *Celebration: Studies in Festivity and Ritual.* Washington D.C.: Smithsonian Institution Press.

———. 1987. "Carnival, Ritual, and Play in Rio de Janeiro." In Alessandro Falassi, ed., *Time out of Time: Essays on the Festival.* Albuquerque: University of New Mexico Press, pp. 74–90.

Van Gennep, Arnold. 1960. *The Rites of Passage.* Chicago: University of Chicago Press.

Washburne, Chris. 1998. "Play It *con filin!*: The Swing and Expression of Salsa." *Latin American Music Review* 19(2): 160–85.

Waterman, Chris. 1991. "Juju History: Toward a Theory of Sociomusical Practice." In

Ethnomusicology and Modern Music History. Urbana: University of Illinois Press, pp. 121–38.

Williams, Eric. 1949. "West Indian Culture Upheld by 'Nobility' of 'Little Carib.'" *Trinidad Guardian*, Sept. 24, p. 8.

Williams, Raymond. 1977. *Marxism and Literature.* Oxford: Oxford University Press.

Williams, Ronald. 1980. "Panorama a CDC Brainchild." *Trinidad Guardian*, Feb. 14, p. 12.

Wilson, Olly. 1974. "The Significance of the Relationship between Afro-American Music and West African Music." *Black Perspective in Music* 2(1): 3–22.

———. 1992. "The Heterogeneous Sound Ideal in African-American Music." In Josephine Wright and Samuel A. Floyd Jr., eds., *New Perspectives on Music: Essays in Honor of Eileen Southern.* Warren, Mich.: Harmonie Park Press, pp. 327–38.

Wilson, William. 1973. "Herder, Folklore, and Romantic Nationalism." *Journal of Popular Culture* 6: 819–35.

Wood, Donald. 1968. *Trinidad in Transition: The Years after Slavery.* London: Oxford University Press.

Yelvington, Kevin, ed. 1993. *Trinidad Ethnicity.* London: Macmillan Caribbean.

DISCOGRAPHY

Cook, Emory, producer. 1956/1994. *Jump Up Carnival in Trinidad.* Smithsonian Institution, Cook Cassette Series: CK1072.

Franklin, Dennis "Merchant." 1995. *Merchant: The Early Years.* JW Productions JW1016-CD.

Francisco, Slinger (The Mighty Sparrow). 1964. *The Outcast.* National NLP 4199.

Holman, Ray. 2003. *In Touch.* Ramajay Records RR 70009-2.

Moyenne. 2000. *New Hope.* The Ethnic Jazz Co. Ltd. EJC 001.

Phase II Pan Groove. 1986. *Pan Rising.* SANCH 8601.

Reid, Ron, and Sunsteel. n.d. *Calypsoldier.* Mud Hut Records.

Reid, Ron, Orville Wright, and David "Happy" Williams. n.d. *Reid, Wright, and Be Happy.* SANCH.

Smithsonian Folkways. 2000. *Calypso Awakening.* Smithsonian Folkways SFW CD 40453.

Spice. 1989. *In de Congaline.* Freedom Records SP 013.

Spottswood, Dick, and Donald Hill, producers. 1989. *Calypso Pioneers.* Rounder 1039.

Trinidad All Stars. 1958. *Minuet in G.* RCA 7-9017.

INDEX

CPSIA information can be obtained at www.ICGtesting.com
Printed in the USA
BVOW02s1920290915

420242BV00001B/5/P